MOZART
AND THE
ENLIGHTENMENT

Truth, Virtue and Beauty
in Mozart's Operas

MOZART
AND THE
ENLIGHTENMENT

Truth, Virtue and Beauty
in Mozart's Operas

NICHOLAS TILL

W·W·NORTON & COMPANY
New York   London

Library of Congress Cataloging-in-Publication Data
Till, Nicholas, 1955–
Mozart and the Enlightenment : truth, virtue and beauty in
Mozart's operas / Nicholas Till.—1st American ed.
p.   cm.
Includes bibliographical references and index.
1. Mozart, Wolfgang Amadeus, 1756–1791. Operas.
2. Opera—Austria—18th century.   3. Enlightenment—
Austria.   I. Title.
ML410.M9T64   1993
782.1'092—dc20   93–711

ISBN 0-393-03495-X

W. W. Norton & Company, Inc.
500 Fifth Avenue, New York, N. Y. 10110
W. W. Norton & Company Ltd.
10 Coptic Street, London WC1A 1PU

1 2 3 4 5 6 7 8 9 0

Contents

===

CONTENTS

Illustrations

All photographs copyright of the Österreichische Nationalbibliothek, Vienna, unless otherwise stated

1. i   Ludovico Muratori (1672–1750)
1. ii Christian Fürchtegott Gellert (1715–69)
1. iii Baron Friedrich Melchior Grimm (1723–1807)
1. iv Christoph Martin Wieland (1733–1813)

2.   Joseph II and his brother, Leopold of Tuscany.
       Courtesy of the Kunsthistorischen Museum,
       Vienna.

3. i   Karl Anton Martini (1726–1800)
3. ii Tobias von Gebler (1726–86)
3. iii Gottfried Van Swieten (1734–1803)
3. iv Joseph von Sonnenfels (1733–1817)

4.   Count Franz Joseph Thun (1734–1800)

5. i   Countess Maria Wilhelmine Thun (1744–1800)
5. ii Franz Sales von Greiner (1730–98)
5. iii Prince Karl Lichnowsky (1756–1814)

6. i   Franz von Heufeld (1731–95)
6. ii Friedrich Ludwig Schröder (1744–1816)
6. iii Gottlieb Stephanie the Younger (1741–1800)
6. iv Karl Friedrich Hensler (1759–1825)

7. i   Ignaz von Born (1742–91)
7. ii Aloys Blumauer (1755–98)
7. iii Karl Leonhard Reinhold (1758–1823)
7. iv Johann Baptiste Alxinger (1755–97)

8.   Frontispiece to *Faustin*, by Johann Pezzl, 1785.
       Copyright the British Library.

9. i   Otto von Gemmingen (1755–1836)
9. ii Leopold Aloys Hoffmann (1748–1806)
9. iii Marc Anton Wittola (d. 1797)

10. i Wolfgang Heribert von Dalberg (1749–1806)

Preface

During the preparation and rehearsals of a play or opera for production one constantly comes across interpretive puzzles. Thus, when staging *Le nozze di Figaro*, one faces the problem of the chorus of peasants who trip in and out of the noble château of Aguasfrescas with such curious insouciance, even penetrating the domestic apartments adjoining the Countess's bedroom. Who are these peasants? They are an unlikely and troublesome presence, no trace of whom can be found in any contemporary description or depiction of an eighteenth-century aristocratic household; indeed, it is difficult to find any historical parallel for the curious etiquette which prevails at Aguasfrescas – now strangely casual, now (as in the Third Act betrothal festivities) improbably formal.

The chorus of peasants, as it appears in *Le nozze di Figaro*, reflects no obvious reality of late eighteenth-century society. Peasants did not wander in and out of the private apartments of grandees, Spanish or otherwise. But they have to be made sense of in a production of the opera. We can decide that they are intended to be purely comic, and thence play them up with muddy boots, hayseed hair and ungainly manners (wiping their feet on the Aubusson and their noses on the Gobelins?) But if we take this option, it may be difficult to persuade the audience of the emotional credibility of the main characters, or of the social reality of their confrontations. Alternatively, we could deliberately decide to strip the opera of all social references; to present it as a Watteauesque dream of illusion and nostalgia, in which the chorus of peasants appear like Meissen figurines in a pastoral *bergerie* such as those which so delighted poor Marie-Antoinette at Rambouillet. Or we may conclude instead that the peasants are menacing – threatening riff-raff who offer a prescient warning of the revolutionary hordes who but a few years later were to sweep so violently through the real châteaux of France.

Interpretive problems such as this abound in all of Mozart's operas: apparent contradictions between content and style, ambiguities of tone, uncertainties of emphasis. In the rehearsal room these are often in fact the key to entry into a dramatic work; meaning often reveals itself most tellingly in the inevitable pressures and dislocations that occur when multiple discourses jostle for space in the over-determined work of art.

It is here that the creative interpreter learns to prospect for meaning, examining the surface patterns and flaws, divining those 'absences' (spoken with a French accent to get the full flavour) so beloved of the structuralist critic. It is here that parallel narratives emerge in which it may become evident that the 'plot' is not the real 'story'.

Frequently one has to search outside the confines of the play or opera itself for elucidation of its apparent contradictions. 'In poetry there are no contradictions', Goethe once said; 'These exist only in the real world . . . what the poet creates must be accepted as he created it'.[1] For the critical interpreter this demands that rather than ignoring or glossing over the contradictions which present themselves in any work of art, we must understand the contradictions in the 'real world' (historical, biographical, intellectual) which give rise to them. Having done so, the great work of art invariably reveals its profounder truths. It is the history of the Emperor Joseph II's reforms in Austria in the mid-1780s, and the response of people like Mozart to those reforms, which enable us to understand the role of the troublesome peasants in *Figaro*.

The study that follows arose out of my work on Mozart's operas in the theatre, and my desire to answer, more satisfactorily than is allowed under the customary pressure of the rehearsal room, some of the dramatic and interpretative puzzles that I had so often come across. It started out as a project of practical curiosity rather than systematic enquiry, arising from the irrepressible feeling when preparing certain works that 'something is going on here' beyond immediate dramaturgical explanation. Its originating impulses will be readily apparent. Much as I admire some of Mozart's early operas, they do not seize me with that mysterious impulse, on first reading a play or listening to an operatic score, to rush out and reveal a work to the world. Similarly, I cannot summon up the same creative enthusiasm for *La clemenza di Tito* (an opera I would be reluctant to tackle in the theatre) as for *Die Zauberflöte*; whether the relative shortness of my discussion of the former confirms my dramaturgical instinct, or merely reflects a lack of insight, the reader will decide.

On the other hand, I have long been fascinated, even before the rediscovery of the missing sections of the work in the 1970s, by the early opera *La finta giardiniera*, written by Mozart in 1774–5. In 1986 I was able to persuade the Camden Festival to mount the first production of the complete opera in Britain which I hope vindicated my enthusiasm for the work. Closer examination of the opera seems to confirm its importance in Mozart's own *œuvre*. *La finta giardiniera* is, I believe, the first work in which Mozart is revealed (in the words of one of his contemporaries, who was more percipient than most subsequent critics) as a 'thinking artist' (*denkenden Künstler*).[2] Through his operas, this book traces the development of Mozart's thought from that crucial moment.

I did not set out to write a biography of Mozart but a critical study of his operas in relation to the Enlightenment. However, as I came to understand the Enlightenment, and to see how intimately Mozart's operas were wedded to its history, a great many hitherto overlooked biographical clues stood out, and a biography of sorts inevitably emerged – the biography of a man whose creative life closely reflected his own search for personal and artistic identity; who possessed one of the most penetrating intellects of his age, and who was undoubtedly one of the great religious artists of Western culture. It is, of course, a very selective biography, which cannot do full justice to those parts of Mozart's creative life which were not dedicated to opera. But since I have no doubt that opera lay at the core of Mozart's life as a thinking artist, I make no apology.

When I started my work on this study it was six years since I had undertaken any academic work – and that only as an undergraduate. The speed – and, often, the superficiality – of preparation for most theatre productions had allowed me to forget the horribly meticulous procedures of scholarship. I am therefore hugely grateful to Professor Derek Beales of Cambridge University, who devoted considerable time to discussing some of my early work on the book with me, gave me invaluable advice, and above all, boosted my confidence by taking my academic efforts seriously. With Professor Peter Branscombe of St Andrews University, Patrick Carnegy, Dramaturg of the Royal Opera House, and Michael Graubart of Morley College, he also kindly supported my applications for financial assistance for the book. I would also like to thank: Helen Sprott of Faber and Faber, who has displayed unwavering faith in the project; my stepmother Antonia Till, who took one look at my first muddled efforts and instantly pointed me in the right direction, and who, with my father, has provided me with enormous moral support and encouragement throughout the writing of this book; Alison Truefitt, who nursed me supportively but firmly through several gruelling rewrites, inspiring me with devoted confidence in her instinct and judgement; and Ingrid Grimes, who has wrestled my text into its final shape and repeatedly saved me from myself. Any errors and lapses which remain are entirely due to my own obstinacy.

I also acknowledge with grateful thanks financial support for research on the book from the David Cohen Family Charitable Trust, the Authors' Foundation (administered by the Society of Authors), and the Music and Letters Trust.

July 1991

Introduction: Enlightenment and the eighteenth century

The eighteenth century has often been portrayed as an era of extra-ordinary tranquillity and grace flanked by two violent and turbulent centuries, an age in which social order and political stability allowed the development of an amiable civilization that combined moderation and manners with critical enquiry and a rational programme of social reform which was conducted with passion tempered by wit. This vision of culture and progress stretched with an apparent unity of purpose from late seventeenth-century England to late eighteenth-century Germany, and was known as the Enlightenment, or, in German, the *Aufklärung*. That this chimerical vision should have collapsed so brutally into the bloodshed of the French Revolution and the chaos of the wars that subsequently swept Europe has, of course, led historians to question the foundations upon which the apparent stability of eighteenth-century culture was based, and to unearth tensions lurking beneath the surface calm.

Famines and riots, wars and political coups were no strangers to the eighteenth century, and the Enlightenment's decision to ignore so many of the realities of the age betrays an anxiety that counters the facile image of the eighteenth century as the 'age of optimism'. The *philosophes* and *Aufklärer* were certainly believers in progress; but while one eye of the Enlightenment was always focused gladly on the bright future, the other eye was trained uneasily on the recent past. For the Enlightenment had been born in the shadow of the disintegration of social order which had occurred throughout Europe in the seventeenth century, following what had seemed like an almost total collapse of political and religious authority. Civil war on a scale hitherto unknown had riven nations and overthrown established political powers; religious doubt had come to assail those not possessed and consumed by the new fanaticisms; status and property no longer offered security and certainty.

The unrest of the mid-seventeenth century forced a fundamental reappraisal of the principles of social order, which led people to ask whether the traditional bonds could ever again be adequate. The brutal spectre of anarchy so pitilessly portrayed in Hobbes's *Leviathan* haunts eighteenth-century Europe as surely as the spectre of Communism, raised by Marx and Engels, haunts the nineteenth century. Alexander Pope's lines from the *The Dunciad*, written in 1728, conjures up its image with the vividness of true fear:

> She comes! she comes! The sable throne behold
> Of Night primeval and of Chaos old! . . .
> Philosophy that lean'd on Heaven before,
> Shrinks to her second cause and is no more.
> Religion blushing veils her sacred fires
> And unawares morality expires . . .
> Lo thy dread Empire, CHAOS! is restor'd;
> Light dies before thy uncreating word:
> Thy hand great Anarch! lets the curtain fall;
> And Universal Darkness buries All.[1]

The Queen of Night 'primeval and of Chaos old' still lurks in the underground vaults ('in unterirdischen Gewölben') of the Enlightenment's psyche in Mozart's *Die Zauberflöte* of 1791. And only a few years later, when events had overtaken the age's worst nightmares, Goya's painting *The Colossus* (*c.* 1810) presented another horrifying incarnation of chaos: a giant who stalks the earth shaking his fists at puny mankind, bringing in his wake revolution, war and destruction. It was such scenes that prompted Goethe to the unwilling declaration that even injustice was preferable to chaos.[2]

The Enlightenment itself was in no doubt about where the spectre of chaos lurked. It came from the past: from the Middle Ages, when murderous obscurantism and lawless might was supposed to have ruled the earth. The Enlightenment loved to paint this past in gory colours, and frequently projected its image upon the modern-day remnant of the Middle Ages, the aristocrat, who was often depicted in Enlightenment art as a lascivious, brawling lout. The Enlightenment could not, of course, acknowledge that the real causes of social instability lay in its own times: in the very forces of progress and freedom it espoused with such passionate righteousness. In truth the despised medieval world had been based upon the more certain and permanent structures of social order which the Enlightenment itself longed for. Most people had been born into a predetermined social position that defined them throughout their life, and placed them within a network of hierarchies and institutions understood to be part of the divine, unchanging order: a person was inseparable from his or her role in society; he or she was a peasant, an artisan, a knight, and not an individual who happened to have this or that occupation; and the medieval person's role carried with it a number of pre-ordained obligations such

2

as those of kinship or feudal duty. Binding this multiplicity of institutions and hierarchies together was the authority and power of the Church, ever intent upon extending its influence over all aspects of people's lives, and guiding them to the certainty of ultimate bliss in heaven.

The stability of medieval society was undermined from within by the dynamics of economic growth: the opening-up of markets, the widening circulation of commodities, the accumulation of wealth by a new class that derived its power from money rather than status. This in turn forced into being another class without status obligations, which sold its labour in exchange for a wage. Thus the demands of economic activity gave rise to some of the basic ideals of the Enlightenment itself: individual freedom, legal equality, religious toleration.

The requirements of the exchange market led to the basic demand for the freedom and autonomy of the individual, who must be free of all feudal ties and obligations in order to engage in economic transactions, and to dispose freely of his or her property or labour. With this went the demand for equality (as defined in bourgeois terms): the rational standardization of the law, and the abolition of the exclusive rights and privileges of feudal society that had prevented people entering into social and commercial transactions on an equal basis. Even the demand for religious toleration, one of the most distinctive tenets of Enlightenment thought, is the result of an *economic* requirement that religious differences should not hinder trade and economic growth. 'Where there is not liberty of conscience, there is seldom liberty of trade',[3] claimed Voltaire, the era's most persuasive advocate of religious toleration. When he and Montesquieu visited England in the 1720s they were presented with striking evidence of the relationship between social, political and religious freedoms, and economic growth. 'Go into the London Stock Exchange,' Voltaire urged the reader of his *Lettres philosophiques*, 'a more respectable place than many a court . . . Here Jew, Mohammedan and Christian deal with each other as though they were all of the same faith.'[4]

But capitalism, and the demands for individualism and freedom it brought in its wake, were, as the political chaos of the seventeenth century had so clearly demonstrated, inimical to social order. In order to survive and flourish, a successful capitalist society needed to establish alternative sources of social authority which would guarantee stability without threatening the liberties upon which it depended. Around this essential dilemma turns much of modern history, and it was the Enlightenment which first found itself forced to confront the problem of how to ensure that the progress it espoused did not outrun the social cohesion it longed for.

The immediate solution to the restoration of order after the chaos of the seventeenth century was the Hobbesian one of absolutism: the creation of strong monarchies backed up by the resources of the modern centralized state, dedicated to wiping out the pluralism of rights and allegiances that typified the medieval world, and to replacing them with the sole, un-mediated obligation of the subject to the state and to the law. Absolutism was therefore far from inimical to capitalism, since it created the conditions of security and the rationalization and uniformity of law necessary for economic progress, and it undermined the traditional feudal powers of the aristocracy which did so much to hinder that progress. Louis XIV domesticating the French nobility in the exacting routines of Versailles; Gustavus III effecting a *coup d'état* against the aristocratic oligarchy which ruled Sweden; Frederick the Great transforming the Prussian Junkers into superior civil-servants; Joseph II stripping the Austrian aristocracy of their privileges and sending them out to sweep the streets for petty criminal transgressions: in each case a monarch was advancing the aims of the capitalist bourgeoisie.

For this reason, absolutism was often welcomed by the bourgeoisie and its spokespeople. Voltaire liked to contrast the reign of Louis XIV (accused by his aristocratic detractors of having ruled in favour of the bourgeoisie) with the Middle Ages: 'During nine hundred years the French genius was almost always cramped by a gothic government and by civil war and dissension. There were no fixed laws and customs; the language was changed every other century, but remained uncouth; the nobility was without discipline, knowing only war and idleness; the clergy lived in disorder and ignorance and the people without industry and sunk in misery.'[5] (That is, until the advent of the all-powerful Sun King, whose modernizing vision had provided the wealth and security to allow progress and civilization to flourish in France.)

But having summoned the leviathan of the absolutist state to its service, the bourgeoisie found it had invoked a monster that threatened to turn and devour it. And thus there emerged in eighteenth-century Europe a triangular confrontation of three social forces: the old aristocratic feudal order, statist absolutism, and the emerging bourgeois order. The confrontation between bourgeois individualism and the absolutist state first took place in England, where by the seventeenth century the Tudor monarchy had effectively destroyed feudalism and undertaken the structural trans-formation of the country required for free economic growth. But the subsequent attempts by the Stuart monarchs to extend their power started to encroach upon the self-interest of the new economic and social order that they had brought into being, and the presumptuous dynasty was ousted. In London in the 1720s Voltaire encountered a confident bourgeoisie which, having got rid of James II, 'congratulate themselves upon having made a very good bargain with King William of Orange'. Under the first William, the Conquerer, one of Voltaire's informants tells him, they were 'cattle'; since then 'we have changed into men, but we've kept the horns, and we use them to strike anyone who wants to make us work for him, and not for ourselves'.[6]

In England, crucible of the Enlightenment, the new power-alliance of progressive aristocracy and mercantile bourgeoisie, whose creed was freedom and progress, had attained the strength to dispense with the services of the monarchy. But having done so it urgently sought to rein in the revolution it had unleashed. The history of eighteenth-century England, and of the bourgeois Enlightenment in general, is of a society learning how to gauge the fine balance between individual freedom and the requirements of social cohesion, between the pursuit of pleasure and happiness and the demands of social duty. In France, where the Enlightenment found its most eloquent and influential advocates, a monarchy weakened during the declining years of Louis XIV and the subsequent Regency merely basked in the reflected glitter of absolutism, and found itself unable to move fast enough to satisfy the demands of the economically progressive elements of society. The French Enlightenment established itself in clear opposition to the monarchy, and elaborated powerful arguments for the conventionally liberal ideals of freedom, autonomy, equality and toleration. But it hedged its bets. Strident in its attacks upon the Church, feudalism and despotism, it was prudently assiduous in mapping the alternative constructions for non-coercive forms of social cohesion upon which the success of its project would depend.

But it was the late eighteenth-century Habsburg Empire, in which Mozart lived and worked during his maturity, that most clearly and painfully embodied the contradictions underlying the Enlightenment's espousal of the opposing prerogatives of economic freedom and social cohesion. During the reigns of Maria Theresa and her son Joseph II between 1740 and 1790, the Habsburg Empire, backward and impoverished, was dragged breathlessly and traumatically from the medieval into the modern age, a process that had taken place over three centuries in England (and over two centuries in France). These two monarchs launched a sustained assault against the power of the feudal nobility and the influence of the Church, and introduced a dramatic series of rationalizing reforms – all of which met the fundamental demands of the Enlightenment itself, and earned Joseph II the soubriquet of the *'Philosophe* on the throne'.[7]

As a result of the Habsburg reforms the Austrian economy began to flourish, bringing into being a liberal, capitalist bourgeoisie with its own expectations and demands. Confrontation was inevitable. As the pace of change accelerated under the impetuous Joseph II (who ruled from 1780 to 1790) the destruction of the traditional institutions of social cohesion led to an economic and social individualism – even libertarianism – that threatened to undermine the authority and security of the state itself and forced Joseph to rescind many of his reforms. It was during these ten years, when Mozart lived and worked in Vienna, that the Enlightenment was to be impaled most cruelly upon its own contradictions. The enlightened bourgeoisie of Mozart's Austria found itself torn between those who had placed all their faith in the dynamic, rationalizing powers of the absolute monarchy, and those who recognized that this modern absolutism threatened individual freedoms far more effectively than had the Church and feudal order from which they had recently escaped. It was also riven between the desire to maintain its liberties and its fear of the inevitable social outcome of liberty.

The rift split Mozart's immediate society – the coterie of statesmen, intellectuals, freemasons and artists who constituted the Viennese *Aufklärung*, whose ideals of social and material progress were to collapse into disillusion, retreat and reaction by the end of the decade. The greatest chronicler of that history and – to the extent that it encapsulated the whole history of the Enlightenment – of the Enlightenment itself was Mozart, the only member of the Viennese *Aufklärung* able to see beyond the Enlightenment's limiting polarities to a more profound understanding of the spiritual as well as the social needs of humanity.

People living in societies undergoing the fundamental transition from closed, customary and religious patterns of organization to more open, individualistic, relativistic and secular systems experience with special intensity humankind's otherwise universal (since all human beings must abandon infancy) sense of a lost past in which order, wholeness and certainty prevailed. It is in these periods that the characteristic modern experiences of deracination, alienation and doubt arise, and in which people seek the new certainties of truth, virtue and beauty. No artist has been more acutely aware of the deeply unsettling nature of that transition than Mozart; his operas are not only passionately engaged with the immediate social and intellectual problems of their era, but also (like the plays of Shakespeare, with which they share many common themes and preoccupations) reflect upon the lasting spiritual condition of modern man. And no art has met modern humanity's longing for wholeness and reconciliation as has Mozart's music.

PART ONE
SALZBURG AND THE YEARS OF TRAVEL
1756–1781

I

The education of a bourgeois artist

The Salzburg into which Mozart was born in 1756 was a small independent state sandwiched uncomfortably between Austria and Bavaria, ruled by a prince-archbishop. Under four notably progressive archbishops during the eighteenth century Salzburg had enjoyed a reputation as the most liberal state in Catholic Germany. Its famous university was run by Benedictines, more tolerant than the Jesuits who controlled education in Austria and Bavaria, and Salzburg University was an important centre for the introduction to southern Germany of the rationalism of Leibniz and his disciple Christian Wolff, and for the study of natural law.[1]

Salzburg was also a centre for the propagation of the teachings of the Italian church reformer Ludovico Muratori (1672–1750). A court librarian in Milan and Modena, and a literary scholar and historian, Muratori produced a number of influential books outlining a programme of Catholic devotion dedicated to practical 'good works' and charity, and a rejection of superstitious customs and what he called in his most widely read book, *The Science of Rational Devotion*, 'abuses of piety'.[2] Attacked by the Roman Church, Muratori was protected in Vienna, and established close contact with Archbishop Firmian of Salzburg, where a Muratori circle was established in the 1740s. Salzburg's reputation as a progressive religious centre was maintained by Archbishop Colloredo, a keen social and religious reformer, who ruled from 1772. Colloredo was an austere man, educated at the Jansenist Collegium Germanicum in Rome, and ruled his small state as a model enlightened despot. On the walls of his study hung portraits of Voltaire and Rousseau. His famous *Pastoral Letter* of 1782 is to this day considered the best résumé of the aims of the reformed Catholicism espoused by Joseph II himself (and was sourly adjudged by Mozart to have been written to curry favour with the emperor).[3] His agenda included a clergy dedicated to pastoral duties, the abolition of medieval customs and superstitious rites, and the use of German rather than Latin in church.

Leopold Mozart, born in Augsburg, had arrived in Salzburg in the early 1740s to study at the university, where, intending to enter the Church, he had read philosophy and law. His religious beliefs, which he transmitted to his son with considerable success, were typical of the educated bourgeois of his day. He was contemptuous of the superstitious customs which the Roman Church allowed to flourish in countries like Italy, boldly describing the practices he saw in Naples as 'heresy',[4] and both his letters and those of his son are peppered with anti-clerical comments. His own faith combined a devout belief in the providential will of God, naturally revealed (in the literal, theological sense) by the gift of genius to his son, with a sentimental piety and a dedication to humanitarian charity. He owned works by both Muratori and Christian Gellert (with whom he also corresponded). The poet and playwright Gellert was the literary doyen of German sentimental devotionalism and natural religion (the belief that God's beneficence was revealed in nature), and his much-used *Geistliche Öden und Lieder* ('Spiritual Odes and Songs' – hymn-like devotional poems in praise of the creation, somewhat similar to those of Joseph Addison in England) were presented to Wolfgang in 1764.[5]

Although Leopold subsequently became a musician rather than entering the Church, he remained a man of broad and lively interests, and was well read in both classical and modern literature. He believed it important that musicians be soundly schooled in the classical educational disciplines such as grammar and rhetoric, and was constantly reminding his son of the importance of maintaining his education and reading. 'Good morals and knowledge [*Wissenschaften*], a good enlightened reason, and a skill' were his educational priorities.[6] Mozart's sister Nannerl was to recall in 1792 that, apart from his music, her brother Wolfgang had often occupied himself as a boy with 'anderen Wissenschaften' (other sciences/disciplines).[7] Leopold himself, like so many of his age, conducted amateur scientific experiments, and possessed a collection of fine microscopes.

Our picture of Mozart's daily life on his travels, and in particular subsequently in Vienna, does not readily allow for Mozart the reader. Living often in small apartments, surrounded by his wife and children, managing his career, organizing concerts and subscriptions, traipsing across Vienna to give lessons, making frequent visits to the theatre, indulging what was clearly an intensely gregarious nature, and producing a prodigious amount of music: all of these discount much leisure for studious reading. He was of course an ardent playgoer, and a cursory examination of the plays he could have seen in the repertory of the touring companies of Emmanuel Schikaneder and Johann Böhm which visited Salzburg in the 1770s (for both of whom Mozart undertook work), the National Theatre in Mannheim, and the theatres in Vienna, shows few gaps: Shakespeare (Schikaneder was a noted Hamlet), Corneille, Molière,

Vanbrugh, Farquhar, Voltaire, Marivaux, Lessing, Sheridan, Goethe; adaptations of novels by Fielding, Rousseau and Fanny Burney. He also read voraciously in search of opera librettos, telling his father in 1783 that he had read over a hundred librettos to find a suitable subject.[8]

There are hints that he may have read more widely while still living in Salzburg, and a letter to his father from Mannheim in December 1777 gives us an interesting glimpse of Mozart's reading habits at that period: 'At six I go to Cannabich's and give Mlle Rosa her lesson. I stay there for supper, after which we talk or occasionally someone plays. If it is the latter, I always take a book out of my pocket and read – as I used to in Salzburg.'[9] At first it appears a curious lapse of manners on Mozart's part, taking a book with him to read at a social gathering. But it does have a certain logic. Conversation might engage his attention (as indeed, we know, did Mlle Rosa);[10] but second-rate music-making surely could not. However, it presumably also prevented him from composing his own music (much of which we know to have been done in his head, and only subsequently written down). What better opportunity could there be for catching up on some reading?

Curiously enough, the letter describing his reading habits had crossed with one from Leopold which had exhorted Mozart not to waste any opportunities for dipping into 'useful branches of knowledge and training your reason by reading good books in several languages'.[11] What Leopold meant by 'good books' we may infer when five years later he wrote to Wolfgang's patroness Baroness von Waldstätten that both she and he enjoyed 'good books and music', and cited Wieland's early prose work *Sympathien* as an example of the former.[12] Indeed, it would seem that, under the guidance of Leopold, the Mozart family was well acquainted with the works of Wieland, whose philosophical parable *Diogenes von Sinope* and verse epic *Oberon* were both in Mozart's library. Wieland, the most amiable German writer of the second half of the eighteenth century, was a poet and novelist whose graceful, fluent style (sometimes dubbed rococo) and gentle irony did much to loosen the formality and pomposity of contemporary German prose and verse (often mocked and parodied by Mozart). In almost all his works he portrayed the bourgeois vision of a well-regulated life steering a balanced path between the extremes of stoic self-denial or conformist obedience, and excessive licence, pursuing 'the search for an ideal of humanity combining morality and sensuous enjoyment'.[13] *Sympathien* itself is a neo-platonic vision of souls who once knew spiritual harmony in heaven reunited in human sympathy and love on earth.

Leopold was proud of his son's education ('in all branches of knowledge you have always grasped everything with the greatest of ease')[14] for he considered an independent mind and intellectual curiosity to be a fundamental precondition for the autonomy and dignity he sought for himself and his family. 'Our greatest wealth is in our head and cannot be taken away from us,' he wrote in 1778.[15] Leopold's travels with the young Mozart were therefore undertaken with two purposes in mind: to display the child to the world (which Leopold conceived as a God-given responsibility) and to give Wolfgang the broadest education possible. Aware of his son's extraordinary facility for imitation and absorption of musical styles, Leopold ensured that Wolfgang came into contact with as many of the best masters of the day as was feasible, and was determined that, in an age of cultural cosmopolitanism, Wolfgang should master every possible form and style. In Paris he was introduced to the expressive sentimental style of composers like Schobart; in London he absorbed the *galant* language of its master J. C. Bach; in Italy he learned how to write Italian opera, and studied the *stile antico* (necessary for the composer of church music) with the greatest guardian of the tradition, Padre Martini, in Bologna.

Leopold did not, however, confine himself to the boy's musical education. He was an assiduous sightseer, and with the dogged curiosity of the autodidact he sought out the liveliest intellectual company wherever he went. When in Paris, this, of course, meant the circle of *philosophes* and *encyclopédistes* who constituted the French Enlightenment, a circle that included some of the most radical thinkers of the age.

Upon their first visit to Paris in 1763 the Mozart family had been taken up by the Baron Melchior Grimm, who, like so many of the materialist *philosophes* at this date, was fascinated by the phenomenon of the boy Mozart's genius. German by birth (probably another reason for his adoption of the Mozarts), Grimm was a close associate of Diderot, and is prominent as a poisonous conspirator against Rousseau in page after page of Rousseau's *Confessions*.[16] His true importance (recognized many years later by Goethe) was as one of the most influential propagandists of the French Enlightenment to Germany through his editorship of the *Correspondance littéraire* during the 1750s and 1760s. The *Correspondance*, a periodical circulated in manuscript, was produced for the rulers of a number of German states to enable them to keep abreast of the latest social, intellectual and cultural developments in Paris, and in theory was only available to crowned heads. 'I made it a rule some time ago to give this correspondence to Princes only',[17] Grimm was to declare in 1766 (the *philosophes* rarely aimed lower than the top), and he allowed few exceptions to his rule (Catherine the Great of Russia, Leopold of Tuscany and the Queen of Sweden, to whom the *Correspondance* was also circulated, were all originally of German birth).

The subscription lists for the years 1763–6 accordingly contain few uncrowned names: M. and Mme Necker (Necker was a fellow Alsatian, and subsequently to be the king of France's Minister); Grimm's colleagues Helvétius and Diderot (who as an occasional contributor got his copies free); Horace Walpole; the Marquis of Tavistock (who was probably a good deal more powerful, and certainly richer, than many petty German princes). Among these eminent names one finds that of 'Mozart, maître de chapelle'. Although not even dignified with the 'M.' given to the other commoners, and although his account was only for a few livres, the presence of Kapellmeister Leopold Mozart's name on this list is remarkable. It indicates that Leopold must have received a certain degree of acceptance within the advanced circle of the *philosophes* in Paris, an indication that was to be borne out on Wolfgang's later visit to Paris in 1777.[18]

Leopold's intellectual independence was a token of his jealousy of his dignity as a professional artist and a free man, a dignity that was often compromised in Salzburg, where his status as a court musician was little better than that of a lackey. Like so many of his age, he had an idealized vision of England as a land of freedom where the ordinary man was accorded respect and could earn a decent living through hard work and a virtuous life; where the king himself did not consider it demeaning to doff his hat to the Mozart family as they strolled in St James's Park.[19] It was an ideal his son retained all his life. Significantly, though, for Wolfgang's own future attitudes, Leopold declined to stay in London with his children in 1765, when tempting offers were made for him to do so, because of his dislike of the licentiousness and irreligion he found there: 'I will not bring up my children in such a dangerous place'.[20] Liberty manifestly had its costs.

Leopold transmitted his profound sense of his own dignity and honour to his son. Not surprisingly, both Leopold's and Wolfgang's notions of honour were often based upon the essentially bourgeois relationship between honour and financial reward ('the value or Worth of a man is his Price,' says Hobbes, the first philosopher of capitalism. 'To Value a man at a high rate is to Honour him; at a low rate is to Dishonour him.')[21] Leopold often had to remind Wolfgang that he should not price himself 'too cheaply',[22] and one of the attractions of London was that one earned a fair reward for one's labours there. As Wolfgang himself came to recognize his own value in Vienna he demonstrated that Leopold's lesson had sunk in. He could have many more pupils, he tells Leopold, 'if I chose to lower my terms, but by doing so I should lose my repute'.[23] More belligerently, he holds out for a proper price from the emperor himself. 'The Emperor is a niggard. If he wants me, he must pay for me, for the honour alone of serving him is not enough.'[24]

But Leopold's notion of honour was also based upon the more fundamental insistence that his son be accorded the social respect that was due to his genius. Demonstrating a marked lack of deference himself, he never ceased to remind Wolfgang that he should present himself and his genius to the very greatest without false social modesty; enlightened monarchs and rulers, Leopold knew, often displayed fewer affectations of status and grandeur than their subjects. The theme of social honour runs through Mozart's letters to the point of obsession: 'My honour is more precious to me than anything else, and I know that it is to you also.'[25] 'My honour was insulted . . . But my honour – *that* I prize, and you must prize it, above everything.'[26] Mozart was so distressed at the demeaning insults ('knave, scoundrel, rascal, dissolute fellow') shouted at him by the furious Archbishop Colloredo after their final confrontation in 1781 that he suffered a violent physical attack of feverish trembling which forced him to leave an opera performance early and take to his bed.[27]

Throughout his life Mozart retained a tinderbox touchiness about his dignity, and was always quick to sense an insult, in particular when it came from those who had, as Beaumarchais's Figaro says, done nothing more to earn their place in society than bother to be born. Visiting his father's home city in 1777 Mozart wore his insignia as a papal knight and received humiliating mockery from a loutish young group of the nobility who ruled the city.[28] Mozart's resolve from that moment 'to let the whole company of patricians lick my arse'[29] never left him. From his visit to Paris later in 1777 he frequently complained to his father about not being treated with due respect by the nobility, and in 1781, after being kicked down the stairs by Count Arco (we can only wince at the provocation Mozart must have offered to arouse Arco, who had been trying to mediate between Mozart and the Archbishop, to such behaviour), he expressed a furious desire to visit some form of retribution upon the hapless count in order to restore his own self-esteem.

In his wish to gain financial independence and social respect for his son, Leopold Mozart instilled in Wolfgang the hatred of Salzburg and of its autocratic Archbishop Colloredo (who had succeeded the more genial Schrattenbach in 1772) that so preoccupied Wolfgang's youth. It was Leopold who taught his son the tortuous delaying tactics (last minute commitments, or faked illnesses) with which to put off the moment of return to the hated place of confinement; and it was Leopold, knowing that his own confinement was inescapable, who taught Wolfgang the intemperate language of that hatred: 'You have long since forgotten the Salzburg Cross on which I am still hanging', he writes, almost blasphemously, in February 1778.[30]

Wolfgang's imprecations against his home town are notorious: 'you are well aware how I detest Salzburg . . . Salzburg is no place for my talent'.[31] 'What disgusts me about Salzburg is the impossibility of mixing freely with people, and the low estimation in which musicians are held there.'[32] 'In Salzburg . . . when I play or when any of my compositions are performed, it is as if the audience were all tables and chairs. If only there were a tolerably good theatre in Salzburg.'[33] (It is not even certain that the one opera Mozart wrote in Salzburg during his early maturity, *Il re pastore* of 1775, was actually staged.) Archbishop Colloredo showed a patrician aloofness towards his employees, and treated his musicians like valets (which was precisely how their job descriptions defined them; Haydn, we recall, wore the livery of a servant for most of his life). Upon his accession in 1772, Colloredo instantly cut back on the displays of religious and secular pomp which absolutist rulers of an earlier age had considered essential to their station. It was a cruel irony that the very attributes of power which the Mozarts, as good independent bourgeois, so despised had also provided the conditions of the family's creative livelihood.

By 1773 Leopold considered that his son's education was complete. Now seventeen years old, Wolfgang had demonstrated in his opera *Lucio Silla*, written for Milan the previous year, a mastery quite equal to that of better known and more experienced composers. Already Leopold's thoughts were turning to more permanent opportunities for Wolfgang outside Salzburg. In August 1773, when the Archbishop was away from the city, Leopold took the chance to sneak away to Vienna with his son to see whether Wolfgang might be able to find employment there. True to form, Leopold insinuated himself and Wolfgang into the highest circles, and obtained a commission for him to write incidental music and some choruses for a play, *Thamos, König in Ägypten*, by one of the most prominent members of the Viennese Enlightenment, the Privy Councillor and Vice-Chancellor of the Bohemian Chancery, Tobias von Gebler. Gebler, the friend of Lessing and the Berlin *Aufklärer* Friedrich Nicolai, provided the main focus of contact between Vienna and the northern German Enlightenment in the 1760s and 1770s, and was also a prolific playwright accorded some respect by his contemporaries.[34] Despite Gebler's satisfaction with Mozart's efforts (which also received Wieland's approbation the following year) no more lasting offers came Mozart's way, a fact that confirmed in Leopold an old hostility to Vienna as a culturally backward city in which the staid court of Maria Theresa and her austere son had little to offer. Leopold and Wolfgang returned to penal servitude in Salzburg, where at last a more promising commission arose the following year, when Wolfgang was asked to write a comic opera for the Munich Carnival season of 1774–5.

II

La finta giardiniera

━━━━━━

La finta giardiniera was Mozart's ninth dramatic composition, and for Charles Rosen in *The Classical Style* it is the work that marks the emergence of his mature style.[1] Mozart had already put his extraordinary facility for musical assimilation to fluent use, combining it with a melodic flair and an instinctive command of dramatic expression that had been fully revealed (as far as was possible within the confines of *opera seria*) in *Lucio Silla*. While working on *La finta giardiniera* Mozart was also writing three symphonies (nos. 25, 28 and 29) which musicologists have often identified as his first truly original instrumental achievements. But *La finta giardiniera* is the earliest opera in which Mozart speaks not only as a miraculously precocious musician, but as an individual giving voice to his own experience, and engaging with the concerns of his generation and class in a language that was unequivocally his own.

AN OPERA REDISCOVERED

The true status of *La finta giardiniera* in Mozart's canon has not been recognized for a number of reasons. Firstly, because it is only in the past ten or so years that the complete opera has been known to scholars and performers, who had previously to make do with an incomplete text and bastard performing versions. The reason is that, although when the opera opened in the Redoutensaal in Munich on 13 January 1775, it was by all accounts (including Mozart's own to his mother) an enormous success, it was not, however, called for beyond the three scheduled performances in Munich. So Mozart packed up the score and took it back to Salzburg with him. There it sat in a drawer until 1779, when the travelling theatre company of Johann Böhm, on a visit to Salzburg, approached Mozart for a new German Singspiel, and obtained instead permission to perform a German version of *La finta giardiniera*, with spoken dialogue replacing the Italian sung recitatives. Mozart's hand in this version is unclear, and it makes a number of significant musical departures from the original Italian score.

For the next two hundred years this was the only performable edition of *La finta giardiniera*, for at some point the first act of the original Italian score was lost. So although the music for the instrumental numbers of the first act survived in the modified Singspiel version, and the full text of the recitatives was known from an earlier setting of the same libretto by Pasquale Anfossi, all performances of the full opera were based on this German version with its truncated dialogue which frequently made the plot difficult to follow. It was not until a copy of the missing score turned up in the mid-1970s in a library in Czechoslovakia that the complete opera could be performed as Mozart wrote it, and the work properly appraised.

The libretto for *La finta giardiniera* has been attributed at various times to several of the best known librettists of the period, including the author of Gluck's great reform operas *Orfeo* and *Alceste*, Calzabigi; but it is now thought, on circumstantial evidence, to be by Giuseppe Petrosellini.[2] His text has been dismissed by critics as a 'farrago of nonsense', and 'a confused and confusing potboiler'.[3] On the contrary, the libretto is carefully constructed, full of verbal wit, and shows evidence of some considered engagement with its chosen themes. Italian opera librettists of the second half of the eighteenth century were a sophisticated and widely read breed. They were often playwrights *manqué* in an age when, until the arrival of Alfieri in the 1780s, there was virtually no serious spoken Italian theatre, and would-be dramatists were forced to write opera librettos or nothing. They were quite capable of drawing upon distinguished literary antecedents and fashionable social and artistic preoccupations to ensure that opera remained topical and relevant. One of the most prolific, Pietro Coltellini (another writer to whom the text for *La finta giardiniera* used to be attributed), who served as court poet in Vienna after Metastasio, was also editor of the Italian edition of the *Encyclopédie*. And Giuseppe Petrosellini was, along with Carlo Goldoni, one of a handful of librettists who brought a new social and emotional realism to *opera buffa* in the mid-eighteenth century.

Underestimation of *La finta giardiniera* has been compounded by failure to recognize the opera's true generic form and its remarkable literary antecedents. If considered purely in terms of *opera buffa*, *La finta giardiniera* is indeed a baffling work. For sure, it contains many of the elements which we expect of Italian *opera buffa*: comic servants and an elderly suitor from *commedia dell'arte* (we are not actually told that the Podestà who so longs for the *finta giardiniera*, Sandrina, is elderly, but his name, Don Anchises – after Aeneas's decrepit father – indicates this). But the *dramatis personae* also lists two characters who are described as *parte serie*; and the plot itself, which includes characters who have travelled incognito far from home, surprising revelations of identity, and the strange journey into a dark forest which lies at the centre of the story, is positively

Shakespearean. It reminds us of the importance of the romance elements that entered later eighteenth-century *opera buffa* alongside the knockabout *commedia* traditions with which we are more familiar. The seriousness which Mozart alone is often said to have brought to comic opera is in fact inherent in the history of the form itself.

PAMELA SINGS

It becomes much easier to categorize *La finta giardiniera*, and to understand the development of *opera buffa* in the eighteenth century, however, if one recognizes that *La finta giardiniera* is a *Pamela* opera, a direct descendant of the most influential bourgeois novel of the eighteenth century.

Samuel Richardson's *Pamela*, published in 1740, tells the story of a virtuous young maidservant who is subjected to a series of increasingly cruel trials by her master in his attempts to seduce her, culminating in her abduction and imprisonment. For her stalwart resistance she is eventually rewarded with marriage. The novel is a perfect example of the eighteenth-century bourgeois desire to be reassured that the social demands of virtue were consistent with the pursuit of self-interest. 'There is nothing so likely to make a man's fortune as virtue,' wrote Benjamin Franklin in his autobiography;[4] and *Pamela*, subtitled 'Virtue Rewarded', set out to confirm this piety. This thesis was more easily demonstrated in art than life (which, as the Abbé Terrasson pointed out in his didactic novel *Sethos* provides all too many examples of 'a series of disappointed projects and crimes unpunished').[5] 'Virtue my soul shall embrace,/Goodness shall make me great', sings Jephtha, one of Handel's typically bourgeois biblical heroes, and the young Mozart himself firmly believed that God would reward him with earthly success (and cash) for steadfastness to his religion and loyalty to his friends.[6]

Pamela, spicing its reassuring moral message with enough sublimated sexual frissons to satisfy even the most jaded Georgian roué who might sneak a glance at his wife's or mistress's copy, was a phenomenal success, and the eponymous heroine made a triumphant progress throughout the whole of Europe. In the year 1742 alone, there were three dramatic versions of the novel on the London stage. By the following year Pamela had found her way to France, where she was adapted, imitated, dramatized, sequelized and parodied by numerous authors, including Voltaire, whose play *Nanine* is an acknowledged version.

From France, Pamela travelled to Italy, where Goldoni again turned the story into a play, a tense domestic drama that remained remarkably faithful to the novel although, unable to stomach the notion of a maidservant marrying her master, Goldoni allowed it to be revealed that his Pamela was, after all, of noble birth[7] – a change also introduced by Voltaire. Goldoni had to depart further from Richardson's novel when he came to adapt his play as an opera libretto, *La buona figliuola*, set by a number of composers, but most successfully by Niccolò Piccinni in 1760. Most of the action takes place in a garden, where Pamela (called La Cecchina) is now a *giardiniera*, or gardener's girl. She is pursued by her master, whose plan to marry her is foiled when his maidservant Sandrina, who has set her cap at him herself, informs his pedigree-conscious sister (the appalling Lady Danvers of Richardson's novel) of her brother's ignoble plans to marry a humble gardening-girl. The sister effects the arrest of La Cecchina, and she is submitted to various torments before the secret of her noble birth is finally revealed, making her eligible to marry her former master with impunity.

This, in essence, is the story of Mozart's *La finta giardiniera*. Much of the opera takes place in a garden, where Sandrina, the 'pretend *giardiniera*' of the title, works. She is in fact the Marchesa Violante in disguise, and she is being pursued by her new master, the Podestà (or local mayor), who wants to marry her. He in turn is being eyed by his jealous maid-servant Serpetta, who has designs upon him. The plot is set in motion when Count Belfiore, formerly betrothed to Violante, arrives to claim the hand of his new bride, the haughty Arminda, niece of the Podestà. Arminda is not best pleased at her uncle's intentions for the lowly Sand-rina, and is even more furious when she finds out that Belfiore has recovered his former love for Sandrina/Violante. Arminda has Sandrina abducted and carried off to a dark and deserted wilderness, where she is abandoned to her fate and wild beasts.

Such torments seem exotic and fanciful within the context of an *opera buffa*. But as soon as one recognizes that they really belong to the *Pamela* theme they cease to be out of place. Goldoni's and Piccinni's heroine, La Cecchina, wafts limply through her opera, from one pathetic aria (of which Piccinni was a master) to the next, the epithet 'poverina' never far from her lips: a born victim. Mozart's Sandrina is similarly presented as a virtuous maiden, ripe for all kinds of victimization. In her first aria, she bemoans the plight of 'noi donne poverine' ('we poor women') condemned from birth to misery and wretchedness, cursed by the torments of love, and suggests that it would be better to die, or never to have been born. The musical language of the aria, with its naïvely simple melody (as befits Sandrina's ostensible status as a servant), making brief forays into more turbulent minor keys, is in a mode that Mozart borrowed directly from Piccinni.

In Sandrina's second aria, her status as sentimental heroine is confirmed. On her own for the first time, Sandrina can express her true
feelings. With its wistfully muted melody over a triplet accompaniment
and plucked bass, the *cavatina* is an accomplished exercise in the sentimental style perfected by Piccinni (given a later, ironic airing in Barbarina's aria of loss in *Le nozze di Figaro*), in which Sandrina likens her
desolation to that of the lost turtle-dove who coos its grief to the world.
The note of sentimental appeal is reiterated in Sandrina's third aria, in
a scene which imitates the seduction scene in Goldoni's dramatic version
of *Pamela*. Sandrina is approached by her master the Podestà, and, when
she demurs, he threatens her, reminding her she is only a servant: 'what
is to stop me from ruining you now?' Sandrina's response is exactly that
of Goldoni's Pamela: although she is only a servant, she retorts, she still
has a mind, a heart and feelings. In the aria that follows, Sandrina appeals
directly to the pity of both the Podestà and the audience.

In the following scene Sandrina is put through the sentimental heroine's
final 'sadistic' test when she is abducted by her jealous rival Arminda and
abandoned in a deserted wilderness. Her *scena* of terror is worthy of the
contemporary Gothic mode in English fiction and French drama, and
places her close to the heroines of Mrs Radcliffe (who invariably find
themselves similarly afflicted) or the French Gothic playwright Bacaulard
d'Arnaud (whose own interest in the torments of virtuous maidens was
particularly salacious.)[8] Through-composed, leaping back and forth from
recitative to arioso and aria, the *scena* is full of jagged contrasts of mood,
emotion, key and tempo. It impressively employs all the devices of the
new, feverish *Sturm und Drang* musical style brought to perfection by C.
P. E. Bach (a master much admired by Mozart), intended to wring from
an audience violent extremes of emotional identification.

What lies behind this insidious theme of the virtuous maiden in distress
in so much mid-eighteenth-century art, a theme whose torrid presentation
so clearly undermines the eighteenth century's proud claims to be the
Age of Reason?

SENSIBILITY: THE AESTHETICS OF THE HEART

The maiden in distress was the most characteristic representative of the
attempt by the eighteenth-century bourgeoisie to base its autonomy upon
the foundation of a system of universal morality by which society might
be regulated without recourse to the authority of the Church or state.
'Morality is a subject that interests us above all others,' wrote David
Hume. 'We imagine the peace of society to be at stake in every decision
concerning it.'[9]

For the seventeenth century the most powerful weapon against the obdurate authority of tradition and custom, or of religious dogma, had been reason. 'Every individual dogma is false when refuted by the clear and distinct perceptions of natural reason,'[10] claimed the Cartesian Pierre Bayle, arguing against much traditional religious belief. 'Nature we know, Reason we know, but who are you? You, Custom, are . . . an Invader of Nature, and a Usurper of the Throne of Reason,'[11] wrote Defoe. In place of the traditional precepts of custom and dogma the rationalists elevated the universal laws of nature, founded upon reason, as the new basis of law and social morality.

But to the eighteenth-century bourgeoisie, the abstract and supposedly universal imperatives of reason, its tendency to become embodied in immovable rules and precepts, and to give undesired authority to the new laws of the absolutist state, threatened the very individualism it had originally served. Accordingly, the bourgeoisie relocated its ethical authority where it could not be reached by others: within the inalienable feelings and instincts of the human body. 'The things I know every man can know,' proclaimed Goethe's young bourgeois hero Werther, the icon of later eighteenth-century individualism, 'but Oh, my heart is mine alone!'[12]

The bourgeois Enlightenment rejected the great systems spun by seventeenth-century philosophers like Spinoza and Leibniz out of webs of deductive logic, and demoted reason to the safer status of common sense, allowing it a limited, critical application. In its place arose empiricism, the philosophy of the bourgeoisie, which promoted the claims of the individual's experience of the here-and-now gained through the senses to provide the more certain basis of knowledge. When Leopold Mozart wrote in his *Violinschule* that 'All our perceptions originate in the external senses',[13] he was doing no more than reiterating the basic premise of John Locke's empiricism, the very foundation of the bourgeois freedom to which he aspired.

Nature was no longer an abstract norm (like the ideal nature of the classical artist), but was rooted in human nature. And the logic of empiricism was that if all areas of human knowledge are attributable to experience gained through the senses, then the senses must also be the source of moral knowledge. In *An Enquiry Concerning the Principles of Morals* Hume asserted that the basic ethical question was whether moral principles 'be derived from REASON or SENTIMENT; whether we attain the knowledge of them by a chain of argument and induction, or by an immediate feeling and finer internal sense'.[14] His resounding answer was that 'Morality is more properly felt than judged of'.[15] The *Encyclopédie* suggests that physical 'sensibility . . . gives one a kind of wisdom concerning matters of virtue and is far more penetrating than the intellect acting alone'.[16] The eighteenth-century bourgeois Enlightenment might more truly be called the Age of Feeling rather than the Age of Reason.

Pamela and her numerous victimized progeny were the artistic offspring of this new bourgeois morality of feeling. According to Hume and the moral sense theorists, social morality arose out of feelings and sentiments that were innate to humankind, and prompted men and women to behave in an acceptably social manner without coercion, and to temper their more antisocial passions (although, as we shall see, the Enlightenment acknowledged very few of these). Pity, argued Rousseau, is 'a natural sentiment which, by moderating in each individual the activity of self-love, contributes to the mutual preservation of the whole species'.[17] And moral sentiments like pity were, Hume maintained, dependably contagious. ''Tis also evident, that the ideas of the affections of others are converted into the very impressions they represent, and that the passions arise in conformity to the images we form of them,' he wrote in *A Treatise of Human Nature*:[18] 'As in strings equally wound up the motion of one communicates itself to the rest; so all the affections readily pass from one person to another, and beget correspondent movements in every human creature.'[19] (Thus, incidentally, furnishing musicians like Leopold Mozart with splendid grounds for affirming the moral power of music.)

To maintain these sociable moral sentiments such as compassion in a constant state of arousal became one of the prerequisites of the mid-eighteenth-century art of Sensibility. The widespread cult of Sensibility which swept Europe, with its lachrimose dramas, its torrid tableaux of familial emotion by painters like Greuze, and its willing expenditure of public tears (Fanny Burney claimed to have wept some twenty times on the day when she heard the news of George III's recovery from madness; Burke and Fox sobbed in the House of Commons after a public row)[20] may be at odds with an Age of Reason. But it was the expression of a bourgeois society that had placed its faith in a pleasurable ethics of the heart, and was determined to display its workings.

In the aesthetics of Sensibility the purpose of art was, as Lessing argued, 'to extend our capacity for feeling pity. The compassionate man is the best man . . . and he who makes us compassionate makes us better and more virtuous.'[21] 'No appeal to the soul of man by impressions of pity and compassion can be too strong', the French sentimental playwright Mercier wrote,[22] and the cult of Sensibility soon discovered that the most efficient method of triggering compassion was to represent, in ever more excessive forms, what Diderot readily identified as 'the misfortunes of virtue'.[23] Richardson, who declared that 'the man is to be honour'd who can weep for the distresses of others'[24] was the first virtuoso of this manipulative scenario; hence the popularity of Pamela, who was duly put through her paces wherever the ethics of sentiment alighted to quicken feeling hearts.

In *La finta giardiniera* Lessing's appeal for an art that arouses compassion is satisfied in Sandrina's third aria, in which she pleads pathetically not only to her master, but directly to the audience:

> Maidens who hear me,
> If you feel pity for me,
> An unfortunate unhappy,
> Deserted girl, oh come and console me.

Eighteenth-century audiences, we are often told, responded to such heart-breaking pleas with torrents of all-too-ready emotion. When Paisiello's *Nina*, one of the most successful of the operatic 'virtue in distress' genre, was performed in Naples in 1790 the audience rose from their seats with cries of sympathy to reassure the opera's heroine that everything would turn out for the best after her pathetic aria 'Il mio ben'.

Mozart's youthful *Pamela* opera is one of the finest examples of operatic sensibility. As such, it places its young composer at the centre of a mid-eighteenth-century European bourgeois culture largely influenced by English models. The ethics of feeling freed the bourgeoisie from recourse to authority, legitimizing and strengthening the undeniable natural social instincts. Not everyone might be equally endowed with the powers of reason, but human beings enjoyed a natural equality of feeling. And Mozart, like Goldoni's Pamela and his own Sandrina, was quick to lay claim to the independent authority and dignity of his feelings. Writing shortly after his dismissal from Archbishop Colloredo's employ in 1781, Mozart issued a moral justification for his behaviour: 'I have but to consult my own feelings and judgement and therefore do not need the advice of a person of rank to help me to do what is right and fitting ... It is the heart that ennobles a man; and though I am no count, yet I have probably more honour in me than many a count.'[25]

In addition to Sensibility, *La finta giardiniera* draws upon a second, more drastic strain in mid-eighteenth century culture: that of Rousseauism – or to be more exact, of what should be called 'popular' Rousseauism.

POPULAR ROUSSEAUISM

In 1749 Jean-Jacques Rousseau was walking from Paris to Vincennes to pay a prison visit to his friend Diderot (being a *philosophe* carried risks) when he experienced a revelation that shattered both him and the Enlightenment.[26] He realized that modern society, the only divinity which Diderot himself was prepared to worship,[27] had corrupted humankind, turning it away from the path to true human progress and fulfilment.

The social philosophers of the bourgeois Enlightenment, terrified of the destructive effects of individualism, had insisted that society was the condition of human happiness. 'A Creature void of natural Affection, and wholly destitute of communicative and social Principle . . . feels but small Enjoyment in Life, and finds little Satisfaction in the more sensual Pleasures which remain with him after the Loss of social Enjoyment; and all that can be called Humanity or Good Nature,' wrote Locke's pupil, the Earl of Shaftesbury;[28] and Diderot insisted that 'Only the evil man lives alone'.[29] The bourgeois Enlightenment persuaded itself that within society the aggressive pursuit of naked self-interest might be tempered in a pleasurable fashion, without need for self-denial or submissive conformity to externally imposed laws. The march of civilization itself, and all its agreeable appurtenances, would ameliorate the interrelation of individuals in society; numerous *philosophes* produced convenient arguments for the civilizing benefits of luxury. Shaftesbury, who brought some of the grace of his aristocratic pedigree to bear upon the rougher edges of the Whigs' bourgeois partners (and who was widely read by German writers such as Wieland, Herder and Goethe), considered that his task as a moral philosopher was 'to recommend morals on the same foot with what in a lower sense is called manners, and to advance philosophy (as harsh a subject as it may appear) on the very foundation of what is called agreeable and polite'.[30] For Edmund Burke at the end of the century the position was quite clear: 'Manners are of more importance than laws.'[31]

Rousseau's Pauline conversion on the road to Vincennes occurred as he was pondering a question put for a prize essay by the Dijon Academy upon this very question: 'Has the restoration of the arts and sciences had a purifying effect upon morals?' In the essay that emerged, entitled *Discours sur les sciences et les arts* (but usually referred to as the *First Discourse*), Rousseau argued that those things identified as the blessings of contemporary civilization – its arts, its sciences, its cultivated manners – serve simply to mask its evils. Modern society is not natural; the much-lauded values of civilization are artifice, breeding deception, dishonesty and insincerity rather than real human virtue and happiness: 'Jealousy, suspicion, fear, coldness, reserve, hate and fraud lie constantly concealed under that uniform and deceitful veil of politeness; that boasted candour and urbanity, for which we are indebted to the enlightened spirit of this age.'[32] Manners, and all that go with civilized behaviour besides, are not, as Shaftesbury and his followers had tried to argue, the same as morals.

In his *Second Discourse* Rousseau set out to discover how humanity had allowed itself to become so enslaved in modern society. He set about his mission with biblical seriousness, burying himself deep in the Forest of Saint-Germain to contemplate his vision of primitive times. What might men and women have been like before society corrupted them? His conclusion was that in their natural state (envisaged by Hobbes and Locke as one of anarchy and brutality, from which humanity had been rescued by the discipline of government) people must have enjoyed equality, and must have been both happy and good, only subsequently enslaving themselves to the rich and powerful few.

From his former colleagues amongst the *encyclopédistes*, Rousseau's conversion was seen as dangerous apostasy. For Rousseau had exposed some of the basic contradictions of modern bourgeois society – contradictions that the Enlightenment as a whole chose to ignore or to sidestep. (Among the French *philosophes*, the only other thinker willing to confront such contradictions was Rousseau's former ally Diderot. But Diderot saw contradictions as paradoxes and delighted in them. Rousseau could only see contradictions as tragic gulfs which alienated man from his true self.) Rousseau's insight was to recognize the reality of individualism in a society that had refused to acknowledge the real implications of that individualism. Rousseau forced his age to consider that there may be no natural, pre-ordained identity between the (barely acknowledged) spiritual needs of the individual and the demands of society. And in forcing this perception, he articulated for the first time one of the most insistent themes of all modern discourse, planting in people's minds the idea that man is doubly alienated: once from his original natural estate in which he lived in harmony with nature, his fellow men and himself, and then again, as an individual, from the society in which he finds himself, and which seeks to destroy his sense of personal identity. Modern Man may be free, but his freedom brings dislocation and doubt.

Rousseau later recalled his feelings upon having brought his speculations in the forest to a successful conclusion. 'Exalted by these sublime meditations, my soul soared towards the Divinity; and from that height, I looked down on my fellow men pursuing the blind path of their prejudices, of their errors, of their misfortunes and their crimes. Then I cried to them in a feeble voice which they could not hear, "Madmen who ceaselessly complain of Nature, learn that all your misfortunes arise from yourselves." '[33] Rousseau's messianic tone was not unjustified; the extraordinary resonance that his writings struck in the collective psyche of the mid-eighteenth century brought Rousseau to a wider public than any of his erstwhile colleagues. His mastery of a rhetorical style that infused classical clarity with intense emotional sensibility (Kant longed to be able to emulate the lucidity of Rousseau's prose), struck a far richer chord than the journalistic flurries and literary ironies of a Voltaire, or the teasing paradoxes of a Diderot ever could. But more significant was the romantic myth of his far from romantic life. Tortured by his own sense of alienation from society, and his knowledge of the impossibility of maintaining moral integrity within society, Rousseau sought solitude and the solace of nature in a succession of rural retreats. On his return to Paris, where he was forced to earn his living at the drudgery of copying music, he adopted the dress and manners of a social dissident, and insisted on subjecting himself to public self-inquisition in pursuit of an honesty that he felt he had failed to achieve in his life. To his followers, Rousseau was a secular saint and martyr; after his death, squads of people paid what can only be described as pilgrimages to his tomb on the island of Ermonville. So directly did Rousseau speak to his age that throughout Europe his readers referred to him intimately as 'Jean-Jacques', or often even 'ami Jean-Jacques'.

Rousseau's cult swept Europe. His great epic of romantic love *La nouvelle Héloïse*[34] went into an astonishing seventy-two editions during the eighteenth century. The composer Piccinni was himself so ardent an admirer of the novel that he christened his daughters Giulia and Chiarella after Rousseau's heroines.[35] Rousseau's most enthusiastic following was among the disaffected lesser bourgeoisie, excluded from the social and political rewards they felt were their due. 'Yes!' cried his readers. 'We too always sensed that modern city life was degenerate and corrupt, a hotbed of deceit, frivolity and vice; yes, we always felt better and more virtuous in the country; and we always suspected that it was a good idea to keep oneself to oneself.' And thus the cult of popular Rousseauism grew up. People started to behave in a fashion which they believed to be more 'natural'; Rousseau's own recommendation for maternal breast-feeding was eagerly adopted throughout Europe, and more informal modes of dress, hairstyling, and manners were affected as evidence of moral integrity.

Popular Rousseauism attracted its most widespread following in Germany, where a rising generation of young bourgeois artists and intellectuals, alienated from a predominately aristocratic culture, and with no access to more conventional means of political or cultural expression, gave vent to their frustration in the movement of the 1770s known (after the title of a representative play of the movement) as *Sturm und Drang* ('Storm and Stress').

Sturm und Drang was short-lived, a brief whirlwind of adolescent revolt

27

against the conventions of a static and restrictive society. The most important and influential work to arise from it was *The Sorrows of Young Werther*. Written by the twenty-five-year-old Goethe in 1774 (the same year as *La finta giardiniera*), *Werther* is a short book of raw-nerved intensity. It tells the story of a young man who is an outsider, alienated from both the philistine mundanity of small-town bourgeois life, and the more sophisticated, but essentially frivolous aristocratic circles in which he is employed but not socially accepted (and where he is eventually humiliated). Werther turns away from society and communes with nature, but eventually his sense of alienation, and his despair at being unable to fulfil his love for the virtuous Charlotte, leads him to shoot himself.

MOZART'S *STURM UND DRANG* OPERA

Before the action of *La finta giardiniera* we are told that the Count Belfiore has stabbed his mistress Violante in a lovers' quarrel. It is a curiously melodramatic incident for an *opera buffa*, and one for which he should surely be punished. Belfiore is forgiven, however, by Violante/Sandrina, and saved from the arrest and imprisonment with which he is threatened, for as in many *Sturm und Drang* works an apparently criminal deed is seen as evidence of the possession of sincere emotion – the sign of a potentially great soul – rather than of felony (in Schiller's play *Die Räuber*, the last important work of the *Sturm und Drang*, the hero is a Robin Hood bandit, a criminal who sets out to redress the injustices of society).

It is not fanciful to see *La finta giardiniera* as Mozart's own essay in the popular Rousseauism of *Sturm und Drang*. For Mozart, like Werther, was a young man chafing at the petty humiliations meted out to those of his age and class by the aristocratic society to which he was forced to sue for work, and frustrated at the small-minded, cosy bourgeois philistinism of his home town (captured for ever in the mind-numbing banality of Nannerl Mozart's journal). Wieland's satire on provincialism, *Die Abderiten*, published in 1774, was a favourite of the Mozart family and was cited by Leopold on the occasion of Wolfgang's far from petty humiliation at the hands of the loutish Augsburg patriciate in 1777.

In the opera's opening scene we are at once confronted with a bold statement of the Rousseauist dichotomy between the role-playing requirements of society and the individual's desire for personal integrity. The first ensemble, in which five of the opera's seven characters are presented, runs straight on from the overture without a break, and constitutes the expected third section of the conventional fast-slow-fast operatic overture. In conforming musically to this device, the characters present us with a direct analogy of society's demands on the individual to conform to the outward expectations of social etiquette. 'Che lieto giorno!' ('What a happy day!') the five characters sing jauntily together; collectively and publicly, they tell of the happiness and bliss of love. But as soon as they are allowed to voice their own individual sentiments, privately and separately, and to their own music, they sing of the inward misery, torments or confusions of love. Rousseau's contention that society forces dissimulation on its members is placed firmly on the agenda from the start of the opera.[36]

For Rousseau, all social intercourse entailed dissimulation of some sort, and forced people to adopt some form of disguise. The earlier eighteenth century had relished disguise, and in particular the masquerade, as one of the central symbols of the new openness (Rousseau's 'boasted candour') of eighteenth-century urban society. The masquerade was a place where people could with impunity escape from their accustomed positions in society and take up new roles; whores could pass for nuns, servants for duchesses, and duchesses for whores if they so desired. But for Rousseau, the masquerade, and more especially the theatre, became an emblem of the fundamental hypocrisy and deceit of social intercourse itself. The theatre was institutionalized deception, and in his *Lettre à d'Alembert*, written in furious response to the great *encyclopédiste's* suggestion that a theatre would be beneficial to Calvinistic Genevan society, Rousseau expressed his contempt for the theatre, and in particular, for actors: 'What is the talent of the actor? It is the art of counterfeiting himself, of putting on another character than his own, of appearing different than he is . . .'[37] It was Fielding who had pointed out before him that the Greek word hypocrite originally referred to both the actor and the dissembler.[38]

Rousseau's scorn for the art of the actor quite clearly reflects his perception of the workings of society as a whole, and his understanding of the way in which modern society, far from being natural and self-regulating, depends upon complex conventions, codes and patterns of signification. In such a society, people as actors must learn to play roles, which involves hiding true feelings. In his famous *Letters to his Son*, the English patrician Lord Chesterfield had warned the youth against displaying too much candour in public, and of giving away his emotions. Beware of frankness; master one's passions so that no one may discover 'by words, actions or even looks' what one is really feeling, he advised the aspirant to society.[39]

Rousseau would surely have agreed with Dr Johnson's famous quip that Chesterfield's book taught the 'morals of a whore and the manners of a dancing master'.[40] The demand that one conform to conventional codes of behaviour – in effect, that everyone in society become an actor – ensures that there is no way that people's true worth may be assessed from their behaviour. For Rousseau and Johnson this was a moral problem; for the rebels without a cause of *Sturm und Drang* the problem was how the individual could maintain his personal integrity in a society that exerted all its powers to dispossess him of it.

Mozart was well aware of these confusions. His father had often warned him of the importance of maintaining his integrity while being able to see through the disguises of others. 'The greatest art of all is to know oneself, and then, my dear son . . . to endeavour to get to know others through and through,' he told his son.[41] In the preface to his much-admired *Violinschule*, a work conceived as a programme of humanist as well as technical instruction for the instrumentalist, he advised the sincere musician who wished to be true to himself and his art of the importance of not being deceived by social appearances ('Attire, wealth, status . . . wigs').[42] In turn, Mozart himself often had to remind his father that he too should not judge his son's behaviour by 'appearances' (largely, the reports Leopold received of Wolfgang from others). But he had also to acknowledge that sometimes one had no choice but to gauge one's behaviour according to the appearance it gave.[43] For as Leopold, like Lord Chesterfield, had advised his son, it was often necessary also to maintain one's reserve in society and not reveal oneself too openly.[44]

La finta giardiniera addresses these problems in its very title. Having established the gap between social manners and true individual integrity at the outset, the disjunction is sustained as the opera progresses. In a series of arias the *buffo* characters all express attitudes to love that are in some way shallow, limited or affected. The Podestà sings an aria of his love for Sandrina; but when he tells how in his rapture he hears the sounds of flutes and oboes which fill him with joy, then of violas which turn him to melancholy, and finally of trumpets and drums which drive him wild, we know that his love has far more to do with the clichés of second-rate art than the reality of true feeling. (Mozart, of course, takes every opportunity to display suitable musical illustrations to the text; art, as Rousseau always said, willingly serves the cause of deception). Next comes Violante/Sandrina's manservant Nardo, who is in pursuit of Serpetta, and who employs the over-elaborate (and for a *buffo* character, inappropriate) metaphors of Baroque opera to rage against the fickleness of womankind as angrily as his later *buffo* counterparts Figaro and Guglielmo, but with even less justification for his attitude. Only a little earlier he had himself suggested to his mistress Sandrina that she should adopt the general fashion of society and pretend to encourage the Podestà's attentions, a counsel of insincerity which, of course, the sentimental heroine refuses to follow.

Serpetta, the Podestà's maidservant, on the other hand, is portrayed with just the realism that the virtuous maiden lacks. A forerunner of Despina in *Così fan tutte*, she is cynical and opportunistic; a sorry illustration of the calculated deceit which is prompted by society. Serpetta's aria is a brazen display of sexual coquetry in which Mozart allows her to reveal how effectively the conventions of amorous gallantry may be manipulated by the unscrupulous; the music turns to beguiling sweetness as she mimics the advances of a lovelorn swain, before turning mockingly on her heels to leave him bereft. This is followed by Sandrina's guileless turtle-dove aria, her true and honest emotions unmediated by the expected transitional recitative; the simple juxtaposition tells all.

In contrast to the *buffo* characters, the aristocratic Belfiore and Arminda are presented as caricatures of affectation, illustrating all that is wrong in those for whom social display has overtaken the expression of true feelings. Their love-language is an absurd parody of Tasso and Ariosto, and apes the empty, high-flown rhetoric of *opera seria*. Belfiore, actually in the presence of his bride to be, apostrophizes not her but her portrait in an irrelevantly flowery conceit:

> Proud and beautiful,
> Lovely forehead, lovely eyes, lovely cheeks
> Lovely nose, lovely little mouth;
> Ah my dear, you are a jasmine.

The pair then swap ever more nonsensical banalities; socialized language employed like this loses all real meaning. 'As soon as I was in a position to observe men, I watched what they did and listened to what they said,' reported Rousseau in a letter; 'then seeing that their actions bore no resemblance to their speech, I sought the reasons for this dissembling, and discovered that existence and appearance were for them two things as different as deeds and speech.'[45]

Later in the opera Belfiore, tormented and confused by Sandrina's equivocation in admitting whether she is really Violante, goes mad and declines into what is clearly regarded as the *reductio ad absurdum* of his earlier behaviour. Having wooed Arminda with flowery epithets, and then attempted to gain Sandrina/Violante's forgiveness by flattering her as Venus, in his madness Belfiore believes himself to be in a classical dreamland constructed entirely of the inflatedly poetic language of *opera seria*. Social artifice is exposed as its own sort of madness, destroying the personal integrity of the individual as cruelly as insanity.

'Is he faithful?' Arminda asks on first meeting Belfiore. The audience already knows of Belfiore's fickleness, but the Podestà duly inspects his prospective relative: 'Let me observe him: from his face he seems . . . if I'm not mistaken . . . niece, he is a faithful man!' Of course, as we have already been warned, we cannot possibly know in modern society whether someone is honest or faithful simply by looking at them. 'Before art had moulded our behaviour, and taught our passions to speak an artificial language, our morals were rude but natural, and the different ways in which we behaved proclaimed at the first glance the difference of our dispositions,' wrote Rousseau. 'Human nature was not at bottom better than now; but men found their security in the ease with which they could see through one another, and this advantage, of which we no longer feel the value, prevented their having many vices.'[46] Late eighteenth-century literature is full of plausible charmers with immaculate manners like Don Giovanni, Laclos's Valmont or Jane Austen's Mr Willoughby in *Sense and Sensibility*, who display the essential outward traits of virtue all the better to dupe and seduce innocents like Laclos's pious Mme de Tourvel or Austen's impressionable Marianne.

Mr Willoughby presents himself to Marianne's mother Mrs Dashwood as a man of 'honour and sensibility'.[47] Had Mrs Dashwood known that these were just the attributes upon which Casanova prided himself then perhaps she would have found them less of a recommendation. Montesquieu had considered that in most modern societies, aristocratic pride and honour, the jealous preservation of lineage and reputation, might serve as a fall-back where the rigours of social virtue failed. But in the *Lettre à d'Alembert*, Rousseau was to write of 'the big city, where *mœurs* and honour are nothing because each, easily hiding his conduct from the public eye, shows himself only by his reputation'.[48] The outward tokens of birth and ancestral inheritance become the aristocratic substitutes for virtue. To support his claims to be worthy of Arminda's hand Belfiore can offer no more than pedigree, and regales the Podestà in an absurdly pompous aria (a catalogue aria, always a favourite in *opera buffa*) with a list of his implausible aristocratic forbears from Marcus Aurelius to Cato.

Only the *opera seria* character of Ramiro, the abandoned lover of Arminda, retains his integrity. He is a beacon of steadfastness amidst the general chaos; his three noble arias of love, warmly coloured (often with the divided violas which Mozart frequently employed at this period), heartfelt but never sentimental, provide a constant point of reference. In the Act II Finale, Ramiro is the only character who does not enter the entanglement of mistaken identities in the dark, but instead quite literally brings torches to cast light upon the confusion (to music that clearly anticipates the arrival of Anna and Ottavio with torches in the Act II 'sextet of confusion' in *Don Giovanni*).

Into the complex webs of social and self-deception in which the other characters are caught, truth and reality suddenly intrude in the Act I Finale. The music indicates quite clearly the moment of confrontation and recognition between the estranged lovers by plunging into a stabbing minor key that conveys Belfiore's shock and recalls the moment before the opera began when Belfiore did in truth stab Sandrina. This is followed by the equally real and heartfelt pathos of Sandrina's response as she arises from her swoon (announced by a poignant phrase on the oboe), and greets her cruel and faithless lover, quite unable to conceal, as prudence would dictate, her true love for him. For a moment, all the characters are forced to drop their game-playing and to acknowledge real emotional truth.

THE ENLIGHTENMENT'S GARDEN

The full attainment of truth promises to be brought about by a Rousseau-ist return to nature when all of the characters in the opera leave the safe confines of the garden and follow the abducted Sandrina into the wilderness. Only nature, it seems, can correct the maladministrations of society and return the characters to the truth of their emotions, restoring them to their 'natural' partners. It is, of course, an old theme: the *selva d'amore* of renaissance literature, most familiar to us from *A Midsummer Night's Dream*. Except that in *La finta giardiniera* the forest does *not* return the characters to health, or society to harmony. Sandrina and Belfiore fall into madness, and instead of restoring the remaining characters to their rightful partners, as happens in *A Midsummer Night's Dream*, the intricate Finale to the act merely compounds the confusion by thrusting the Podestà into the arms of his niece Arminda, and Belfiore into the rapacious clutches of Serpetta.

'I believe that were Rousseau alive,' wrote Edmund Burke, 'and in one of his lucid intervals, he would be shocked at the practical phrensy of his scholars.'[49] The 'phrensy' of Rousseau's scholars has still not been dispelled, for just as Marx paradoxically denied that he was a Marxist, so Rousseau was never a Rousseauist. The headstrong disciples of popular Rousseauism had run off to the woods without waiting to hear Rousseau's own mature solution to the problems he had identified. 'What then must be done?' Rousseau had asked in the *Second Discourse*, having painted his lurid picture of modern society. 'Must we destroy societies, abolish mine and thine, and return to live in the forests with the bears?'[50] Of course not. 'But remember', Rousseau would later write in his educational treatise *Emile*, 'in the first place, that when I want to train a natural man I do not want to make him a savage and to send him back to the woods'.[51] Bourgeois society cannot afford to endow its members with the natural rights that substantiate its claims against feudal or despotic authority, nor allow the individual's natural inclinations full rein, lest society itself disintegrate. 'He who would preserve the supremacy of natural feelings in social life knows not what he asks,' warned Rousseau; 'Ever at war with himself, hesitating between his wishes and his duties, he will be neither a man nor a citizen.'[52]

This was clearly understood by Rousseau's more percipient readers. For brute nature is far from gentle, and has little consideration for man in his naked state. When he is at peace with himself and with society, Werther discovers the pathetic fallacy that the beauty of nature confirms his feelings; but when he attempts to flee the society which rejects him and to find consolation in nature, he finds that she has become 'an eternally devouring monster'.[53] Men and women cannot live outside society, however uncongenial society may have become. The forest simply leads Sandrina and Belfiore into its equivalent state within human nature – madness. In *Sense and Sensibility*, the efforts of Marianne to preserve her integrity in the face of society, and her refusal to perpetrate the polite lies which her sister Elinor knows are necessary lead to her hysterical breakdown and ultimately, to her far more conformist submission to social expectations than that of Elinor.[54]

As Rousseau recognized, the real return to health cannot take place in the forest. Nature – natural rights, natural desires – must be maintained *within* society, which must subdue and tame them without suppressing them altogether. The garden provided the Enlightenment with a potent metaphor for the ideal integration of nature and culture in bourgeois society. Traditionally, the garden was a symbol of nature sweetly tamed and ordered. But it is an ambiguous symbol, for nature tamed and ordered may be nature suppressed and subjugated to the instrumental power of man. The great classical French gardens of the seventeenth century are laid out in strict geometrical patterns which numb any natural feeling but awe. They impose art and reason upon nature with an authoritarian fist which, at Versailles, presses right to the visible horizon, banishing untidiness altogether.

By the early eighteenth century, Le Nôtre's gardens were frequently being criticized for their ruthlessly totalitarian artifice, and were seen by English writers as a fitting emblem of the absolutist tyranny of Louis XIV, the king for whom they were designed. The English response to the despotism of Versailles was to develop a style of gardening considered more suitable to a land of liberty in which man was able to enjoy his natural rights. The English gardener acknowledged rather than suppressed nature, and in creating his garden, consulted, in Pope's famous phrase, 'the genius of the place', perceiving the essential order of nature beneath her surface blemishes. In the landscaped parks of designers like Capability Brown, civilized Man set out to forge an even more natural relationship with nature. Rather than banishing nature from view as at Versailles, there was instead to be a seamless gradation between house and country. The invention of the ha-ha, the hidden ditch separating the garden from the park, ensured that the English country gentleman was able to live in apparent proximity to nature without allowing pastoral reality to impinge too strongly on his ordered lifestyle.

The ideals of the English garden spread widely throughout Europe during the course of the eighteenth century. When Montesquieu returned home to France from his famous visit to England in 1729, he promptly remodelled his garden at La Brede in the style of a *jardin anglais* before embarking upon his famous polemic in support of English liberties in *L'esprit des lois*. One of the English garden's most important theorists, William Shenstone, advised Rousseau's patron the Marquis de Girardin on the planning of his *jardin à l'anglaise* at Ermonville, where Rousseau was himself able to die in the tidy lap of nature in 1774.

The image of the landscape garden plays a central part in Rousseau's novel *La nouvelle Héloïse*, a story of natural love alienated by social convention turning into a tragedy of unnatural repression. *La finta giardiniera*, as befits a comedy, moves from unnatural repression to natural love restored within society. At the beginning of the opera the garden in which the action takes place is a symbol of artifice, of rational civilization's tendency to suppress man's truer instincts. Here truth cannot be spoken, and the Marchesa Violante's disguise as the gardener's girl Sandrina is not a gesture of liberation from social constraint but an unsatisfactory attempt to run away from emotional reality.

But the eighteenth-century garden may also be the place where nature and civilization achieve harmony, and where society re-admits the natural impulses which it has hitherto unnaturally banished. It is recognized that those who seek selfish gratification of individual desires risk destroying social order, but also that a society which attempts to suppress the natural needs of the individual altogether courts disaster. 'Thrust nature back with a pitchfork, it will return,' says Richardson's libertine Lovelace.[55] The barriers of rational authority or social convention with which over-civilized society tries to hedge itself about are always inadequate. In Jane Austen's *Mansfield Park* just such a society is depicted, founded upon a benign but repressive authority, an authority disguised by a brittle veneer of social manners. The fickle Henry Crawford and the over-repressed Maria Betram escape from a garden (which had seemed to the more balanced characters to offer 'air and liberty' from a stuffy house) by slipping round the edge of an iron gate into an unenclosed park beyond.[56]

The repressed individual may often find a gap through which to slip – even if escape leads, as in La finta giardiniera, to madness. Indeed, if society is too effective in its efforts to contain the instincts, then it may become necessary for people to venture through the gate. The garden creates only the narrowest safety-zone between the outposts of civilization (represented by the house) and the wilderness beyond. At one point during Act II of La finta giardiniera we are within the Podestà's palace, and being treated to a lecture by Serpetta on the fine art of flirtatious deception; the next moment, without even time for a conventional scene change, we are plunged into the dark and dangerous terrain in which Sandrina has been abandoned to wild beasts. There is no musical pause, or even a musical transition to smooth the change. One can only imagine that in the original productions the flimsy walls of the palace must literally have flown out of sight, exposing to sudden view the ravenous forces which lurk outside.

In the final act of the opera the garden regains its proper function as the place where nature and society may be re-integrated. The garden to which Belfiore and Sandrina return from the forest, and in which they awaken to sanity 'to the sound of sweet music' is now a place of natural rather than unnatural order. (Both music and nature were commonly considered the best cures for madness in the eighteenth century; Mozart's music, unmistakeably drawn from the rustling breezes of Gluck's Elysium, has itself been restored to nature.) The benign workings of nature (implanted in man and the world, after all, by God) reveal their friendliness, reassuring the bourgeoisie that 'self-love and social' are indeed, as Pope claimed, the same, or that 'private vices' may be enlisted as 'public virtues' (as Bernard de Mandeville insisted). 'I have often tried to decide which government was most in conformity with reason,' wrote Montesquieu. 'I have come to think that the most perfect is the one which attains its purpose with the least trouble, so that the one which controls men in the manner best adapted to their inclinations and desires is the most perfect.'[57]

MOZART IN AN ENGLISH GARDEN

Mozart arrived in Munich for the performances of La finta giardiniera some years too early to have visited one of the finest examples of the

English-style garden on the Continent of Europe, the Englischer Garten in Munich, upon which work started in 1789. But in one of his letters Mozart could not resist a delighted exclamation upon a visit to the country estate outside Vienna of an aristocratic patron, Count Coblenzl, in the August of 1781. Although Mozart was apparently uninterested in nature itself – his letters convey little response to the weather or to the landscapes he passed through on his travels – he was enchanted to find in the forest surrounding the house 'a grotto which looks just as if Nature herself had fashioned it!'[58] In the simple topography of Mozart's account the eighteenth century's ideal of nature in harmony with civilization, the individual and society mediated by the garden, is perfectly encapsulated. 'Here Art serves like a servant', wrote Mozart's colleague Aloys Blumauer in a poem about Coblenzl's garden, 'and gives Nature her sway; it allows her every charm which the Creator gave her.'[59] *La finta giardiniera* is itself one of the Enlightenment's most charming expressions of this idyll.

III

Opera and the Enlightenment

Recognition of the novelistic antecedents of *La finta giardiniera*, and of its expression of the bourgeois aesthetics of emotional truth and sensibility, provides an important clue to our understanding of the development of opera in the eighteenth century. 'In the presence of the novel all other genres somehow have a different resonance,' wrote the Russian critic Bakhtin; 'A lengthy battle for the novelization of the other genres began, a battle to drag them into the zone of contact with reality.'[1] With hindsight we know that the novel carved out the most important and distinctive arena for social and moral discourse in eighteenth-century art. Its persuasively empirical and factual observation of life ensured that the novel was a powerful vehicle for the promotion of the myths of the new bourgeois order, which could be presented in the guise of 'nature' or 'reality'. The novel was also uniquely able to convey the relationship between the new consciousness of the individual (especially through the first-person narratives of Defoe or the introspective epistles of Richardson) and the bustling complexities of society at large with which the individual must negotiate in making moral decisions, and through which the writer explores those perennial ethical problems: how do we behave, how should we behave, how might we behave?

But during the eighteenth century the novel was generally held in low critical esteem, and it was not until 1774 (in Germany) that a comprehensive attempt was made to establish a basis for critical consideration of the novel as an autonomous art form.[2] Throughout most of the century drama was considered the most important of the arts, largely because it was believed that the theatre exerted a powerful moral influence upon society. This belief in the moral purpose of art was essential to eighteenth-century aesthetics, for it provided the bourgeois artist who had liberated his art from the service of religion or court with an answer to the troubling question of what his art was *for*.

THE THEATRE AS A MORAL INSTITUTION

The idea that theatre has a moral function derives from the Aristotelian notion, revived in renaissance and classical dramaturgy, that the theatre served as an important constituent of a well-ordered *polis*. It was a forum for the expression of communal identity and a purgator of anti-social tendencies. The revival of classical poetics in the seventeenth century coincided with the crisis of political and religious authority. Greek theatre, with its clearly defined moral function, was seen to have eased the transition in Athenian culture from a religious to a more secular society; although old religious prejudices against the antics of theatre folk were to survive well into the eighteenth century, neo-classical poetics became one of the cornerstones of seventeenth-century absolutism, espoused by those determined to enforce not only the centralized control of all artistic discourse, but also to ensure that the moral behaviour of citizens was directed by the state and not the Church.

Typically, English classicists insisted that rules should be 'founded upon good sense, and sound reason, rather than on authority' (as Dryden put it).[3] But in post-revolutionary England the theatre served an even more important role as a disseminator of the new bourgeois moral consensus. The arbiters of public opinion in England, Addison and Steele, launched a sustained campaign against the cynicism and immorality of the Restoration stage, promoting in its place a new moral theatre. By the end of the century Edmund Burke, fulminating against those radical divines who preached in favour of the French Revolution from their pulpits, could argue that 'Indeed the theatre is a better school of moral sentiments than churches'.[4]

Addison's own play *Cato*, on the elevated theme of civic virtue, was imitated by Johann Christian Gottsched, the first important reformer of the German theatre and a tireless promoter of the idea that the regeneration of German culture and society depended upon that reform. For all the opprobrium poured upon him for his pedantic, rule-bound authoritarianism by later generations of German writers, Gottsched's inspiration led eventually to the foundation of the three National Theatres of eighteenth-century Germany in Hamburg, Mannheim and Vienna. Behind the Hamburg project was Lessing, who as *Dramaturg* at the Hamburg Theatre elaborated his programme for a moral German theatre in the influential *Hamburgische Dramaturgie* of 1767–8. For the National Theatre in Mannheim Mozart's friend, colleague and later masonic lodge-master Otto von Gemmingen wrote his *Mannheimer Dramaturgie* of 1779, in which he urged that the theatre be taken seriously as a 'moral institution';[5] and in 1784, also in Mannheim, Schiller offered his views on the moral role of the theatre in society: *Was kann ein gut stehendes Schaubühne eigentlich werken?* ('What can an Upstanding Theatre really achieve?')[6]

In this address Schiller presents the familiar bourgeois argument that the strength of the theatre as a moral institution derives from its necessary divorce from the political sphere, and its freedom to act as a moral tribunal that promotes 'a living flame of desire for virtue, and a burning hatred of vice'.[7] For Schiller, 'The jurisdiction of the stage begins at the point where the sphere of civil law ends'. The theatre 'punishes a thousand vices which [civil justice] tolerates with impunity, while a thousand virtues kept secret by the latter are acclaimed by the stage'.[8] In brief, Schiller's theatre had assumed the function once assigned to God.

It is perhaps not immediately obvious how opera fitted into Schiller's programme of moral education. Indeed, it was an art form which had been treated at the beginning of the century with the greatest suspicion. To the seventeenth-century classicists, Aristotelian rule-book in hand, opera was, as Dr Johnson later quipped, 'an exotic and irrational entertainment'.[9] For the prosaic Gottsched, opera was to be equated with all things anti-classical (and therefore reprehensible): Gothic architecture, Chinese theatre and even (God forbid) harlequinades.[10] For the early eighteenth-century bourgeoisie, on the other hand, opera was irredeemably associated with monarchical and aristocratic culture; in the *Tatler* in the 1700s Richard Steele assumed the tones of a Tory squire up from the country to attack the insidious new fashion for Italian opera in London.[11]

'Love, that dangerous and tyrannical passion, love alone is the soul of opera and its sole subject,'[12] exclaimed Gottsched in alarm. It was a dangerous subject for an age in which Racine could congratulate himself that in *Phèdre*, 'The weaknesses of love are truly shown as weaknesses; the passions are only presented to the eyes to show all the disorder of which they are the cause'.[13] Boileau, the absolute monarch of French classicism, was concerned enough to issue a stern word of advice to a young man about the dangers of taking his sweetheart to hear the lascivious operas of Lully.[14] For music, as Plato had warned, had a particularly insidious power to arouse undesirable passions, and in 1693 the Sorbonne itself decreed that 'opera is all the more dangerous since through music . . . the soul is much more susceptible to passion'.[15]

'I have among men of parts and business . . . seldom heard any one commended or esteemed for having an excellency in Music', wrote Locke.[16] The response of composers and musicians to such attitudes was to attempt to force music into line with the prevailing rational aesthetics. Rameau made heroic efforts to demonstrate that the mathematical laws of musical harmony met the requirement of Fontenelle (the other great despot of classicism) that the Cartesian rules of geometry should be applied to the arts (earning Rameau's system praise as 'le Newtonisme de la musique').[17] Bach is believed to have applied the principles of

Leibnizian logic to his music,[18] and Handel's friend, the Hamburg composer Johann Mattheson (translator of Richardson into German) attempted a Cartesian taxonomy of the musical passions (somewhat like that of Le Brun in the visual arts) to enable the composer scientifically 'to represent virtue and vice with his music . . . For it is the true purpose of music to be above all else a moral lesson.'[19]

Most immediately effective of all the endeavours to justify opera in an age of reason were the efforts of reformers like Apostelo Zeno and Pietro Metastasio to bring opera closer to the conventions of neo-Aristotelian drama. According to Metastasio, who succeeded him as Caesarean Poet at the imperial court in Vienna, Zeno had proved that opera was not incompatible with reason.[20] Metastasian *opera seria* was intended to expunge the worst excesses of Italian (and particularly Venetian) seventeenth-century opera: its Shakespearean confusion of comic and serious elements; its presentation of the lascivious and frivolous antics of the gods; its delight in exoticism and magic; its conspicuous lack of moral edification (eighteenth-century rational moralists would never have allowed Monteverdi's Nero and Poppea to get away with their crimes). In place of this, Metastasio drew upon the dramas of Corneille and Racine, with their formal clarity and espousal of rational virtue, and supplied opera composers all over Europe with a stream of suitable texts which served well into the nineteenth century. For his drama *La clemenza di Tito*, set by Mozart in 1791, Metastasio earned from Voltaire the praise that it was worthy of Racine himself.[21]

In the end, however, the reinstatement of opera came about not through the attempts of classicists to align opera with the rationalism of the early eighteenth century, but as the result of the bourgeois shift to the ethics and aesthetics of feeling. The fundamental purpose of classicizing drama had been to teach moral lessons through rational argument and demonstration. 'The poet first chooses a moral thesis which he wants to impress on his audience in a concrete manner,' wrote Gottsched; 'Then he invents a general story to illustrate the truth of his thesis. Next he searches in history for famous people to whom something similar has happened, and borrows their names for the characters of his story to lend it dignity', an artistic procedure that strikes a chill in the heart.[22] By the middle of the eighteenth century, with the ascendancy of the moral aesthetics of the heart, this kind of didacticism – the idea of the theatre as a sort of animated homily – had been rejected. In France, Diderot and Grimm launched a campaign against both traditional classical drama (which had become conventional, rule-bound, and – greatest sin of all – unnatural) and the newer *tragédie philosophique*, dedicated to the promulgation of enlightened ideals, and to extolling the virtues of such mundane activities as trade and industry. Although devoted to ends of which they approved, Grimm and Diderot considered the means of *tragédie philosophique* wrong. The purpose of drama was not to edify, complained Grimm, but 'nous rendre plus sensible' – make us more capable of feeling.[23] Influenced by his reading of Diderot, Lessing suggested that the purpose of Aristotelian catharsis was not to purge the passions (as the classicists had interpreted Aristotle) but to effect 'the transformation of the passions into virtuous capabilities'.[24]

If the power to arouse the emotions was intrinsic to the moral purpose of art, and music was, as the eighteenth century believed, the art which above all others possessed that power, it was perhaps inevitable that Enlightenment critics would turn with renewed attention to opera. The *philosophes* were notably hostile to abstract, instrumental music, for which they could see no purpose. 'Sonate, que me veux-tu?' ('Sonata, what do you want of me?') Rousseau recalled, with approval, Fontenelle had demanded.[25] The mathematical justification of music was ridiculous, argued d'Alembert, speaking as a true geometer who knew his business. Music must no longer be considered inferior to the other arts because it could not literally imitate nature, for it was capable of actually expressing nature – or natural feelings – directly.[26] The aesthetician Dubos claimed that music was closer to nature than was language, since it was not dependent upon the arbitrary signs and conventions of language,[27] and Rousseau suggested that the origin of language itself lay in music and song. Music was not a sophisticated elaboration of a basic language, but was that basic language itself; language was prone to social misinterpretation and abuse, but music spoke directly from and to the heart.[28]

In his *Dictionnaire de musique* Rousseau identified the source of music's moral power in melody: 'Now the pleasure in harmony is a pleasure of the senses pure and simple, and the pleasure of the senses is always brief; saturation and boredom follow it quickly. But the pleasure in melody and song is a pleasure of interest and feeling which speaks to the heart'.[29] The belief that the emotional, and therefore the moral, power of music lay in melody, is what lies behind the passionate engagement of the French *encyclopédistes* in the *Guerre des bouffons*, mid-eighteenth century battles between the partisans of the French opera and the supporters of the new Italian *opera buffa*, and in the later conflict of the 1770s between the Piccinnists and the Gluckists (of which Mozart was advisedly warned to steer clear). For it was the simple vocal lyricism of Italian opera, introduced to France through *opera buffa*, which was considered to carry the greatest potential for sentimental arousal. Mozart was to find his own music criticized in Paris for appealing to the mind with counterpoint 'without ever touching the heart' with melody.[30]

This profound shift in the aesthetics of music extended throughout Europe. In mid-eighteenth-century Germany, Christian Gottfried Krause inspired a group of poets and composers known as the first Berlin *Liederschule*, who were devoted to the exploration and re-creation of the folk origins of German song. As early as 1752 Krause wrote in his work *Von der musikalischen Poesie*: 'The gentle feelings of charming sounds make the morals finer . . . Their impression arouses readiness, love, beneficence and compassion.'[31] That this belief in the moral capabilities of music entered into the general thought of the period is evident from the ideas of Mozart's friend and patron Gottfried van Swieten in his capacity as Joseph II's minister of education. Van Swieten argued that moral education in schools should take place through the heart rather than through rational precept, and stressed the role of music in school education. He believed that 'through the stirring language of music, understanding of religion in the soul of the sensitive youth would be instilled without compulsion and with the most pleasant sensations.'[32] Mozart himself was especially keen that his small son Karl should be educated by the Piarists, an order which placed particular emphasis upon the use of music in their teaching methods.

OPERA AS A BOURGEOIS ART

It is with these aesthetics in mind that we must approach the operatic reform movement of the mid-eighteenth century, and in particular the operas of Gluck. The aesthetic principles of Gluck's reform opera have often been associated with the neo-classical theories of the contemporary German art historian Winckelmann, whose rediscovery and rhapsodic interpretation of Greek sculpture was so influential in the development of eighteenth-century European neo-classicism. The equation is tempting; the phrase by which Winckelmann defined the essential features of Greek art, praising 'eine edle Einfalt und eine stille Grösse' ('a noble simplicity and still power')[33] seems to resonate through the text of the manifesto of Gluckian reform opera, the dedicatory letter to *Alceste* of 1769 (probably written by the opera's librettist Calzabigi). The text is full of painterly metaphors: 'telling colours', 'correct and well-ordered drawing', 'assorted contrasts of light and shade'. In the best-known passage its authors talk about seeking 'a beautiful simplicity', and later propose that 'simplicity, truth and naturalness are the great principles of beauty in all artistic manifestations'.[34]

But as Lessing was to argue in his critical essay *Laokoon*, Winckelmann was wrong in attributing the calm beauty of Greek sculpture to an essential serenity of the Greek soul, as if the Greeks were somehow exempted from mortal pain and suffering. A glance at their literature dispelled this notion, and Lessing cited the 'complaints, outcry and wild curses' of Sophocles's Philoctetes, or the screams and shrieks of Homer's Mars and Venus.[35] As with Diderot, who had reproached French dramatists for avoiding the great emotional effects of Aeschylus and Sophocles, and suggested that Richardson's novel *Clarissa* was truer to the spirit of Greek drama than most so-called classical dramas, it was the very passion of Greek art that had attracted Lessing to it.[36] Earlier rationalist-classical critics had not warmed to Homer and the Greek dramatists, whom they considered to be but semi-barbarian, and whose heroes and heroines were most certainly not fit for the polite corridors of Versailles and salons of Paris. Voltaire believed that even Euripides would have been a better playwright had he been born in a more enlightened age.[37]

The real impetus behind Gluckian neo-classicism was not the frigid and attenuated visual style that we associate with lesser neo-classical artists, but emotionalism that acted as both a moral and aesthetic spur to virtually all mid-eighteenth-century artists and critics. Gluck's famous simplicity is designed to ensure directness and immediacy of expression so that the music will affect the heart more quickly. Look more closely at the *Alceste* dedication, and we find that the virtue of Calzabigi as librettist of the opera is that he has 'substituted heartfelt language and strong passions for florid descriptions, unnatural paragons and sententious, cold morality' (the attributes of Metastasian opera).[38] Gluck himself confirmed these aims in *Alceste* when in 1780 he wrote to the poet Klopstock about performing the opera, 'As regards the songs, it is easy for a person who has feeling; all that is needed is to follow the dictates of the heart.'[39] (Herder found Gluck's music admirably in accord with the aesthetic principles of folksong, and claimed that 'most of the arias in his opera *Orpheus* are as plain and simple as those of the English ballads'.)[40]

There could be no clearer description of the purposes of neo-classicism. The truth of the matter is that lurking behind the apparent severity and purity of much great neo-classical art is a strongly sentimentalist aesthetic. David, that paragon of anti-rococo austerity, and apparent iconographer of the sternest civic virtue, broke off work on his painting of the *Death of Socrates* to renew his inspiration in a quite different sort of death-scene – the extravagantly tearful departure of Clarissa.[41] His description of the grimmest of all his paintings, *Brutus*, was not in the language of any didactic programme of civic heroism such as we might expect, nor that of formal aesthetic purism, but in terms of the emotional effect he hoped it would arouse in the viewer. 'Feeling and composition, these are the real masters for learning how to stir the brush', was his avowed secret.[42]

With Gluck, *opera seria* came of age in a bourgeois era. The genre that had once served as the ideological vehicle for the absolutist order, promoting the rationalist ideals of personal sacrifice and duty to the state was transformed to embody the ideals of a new ascendency. In the spoken theatre the status of the bourgeois order could be elevated by clothing classical subjects in modern bourgeois attire; Lessing's domestic tragedies *Miss Sara Sampson* (1755) and *Emilia Galotti* (1772) were, typically, modern reworkings of classical stories (respectively Medea, and the Roman story of Virginia).[43] In Gluckian opera, on the other hand, the universality of bourgeois moral values was confirmed by draping them in timeless mythological dress, in order to assure audiences that the new values they espoused had always existed. When *Alceste* was first performed in Vienna, its admirable bourgeois morality caused the arbiter of Viennese opinion and taste, Joseph von Sonnenfels, to dedicate pages of delighted praise to the opera in his weekly journal *Der Mann ohne Vorurtheil*.[44]

Gluck's reform operas all skilfully propagate the universal values of bourgeois society. Conjugal love is celebrated in *Orfeo*, and is combined with sentimental loyalty to the monarch in *Alceste; Iphigénie en Aulide* tells the story of a cruel father who sacrifices his daughter for dynastic reasons (as in *Clarissa*). In *Iphigénie en Tauride*, the power of the family is affirmed when brother and sister are reunited in foreign climes, and the sentimental friendship of Orestes and Pylades is celebrated in a fashion that recalls the homilies of Mozart's own family and friends on the values of bourgeois friendship.[45]

THE NOVELIZATION OF OPERA

'The names of nobles and heroes can give pomp and majesty to a play; but they do not move. The misfortune of those whose station is nearest ours will naturally strike deepest into our souls', wrote Lessing in the *Hamburgische Dramaturgie*.[46] To have put heroic subjects in modern dress would have confounded the ideological purpose of Gluckian *opera seria*. But conversely, in the development of a modern realist drama, Diderot argued that if tragedy could be made domestic, then comedy could be made more serious.[47] Somewhere in the middle the *comédie larmoyante* and the *drame bourgeois* (essayed by Diderot himself) would meet to create a drama of realism capable of handling all of the complexities of modern life.

Much the same happened in opera. Rising to meet the sentimental *opere serie* of Gluck was the sentimental comic opera of composers like Piccinni. 'Comedy, which is an imitation of nature, ought not to reject virtuous and pathetic sentiment, if the essential object be observed of enlivening it with those comic and prominent traits which constitute the very foundations of its existence,'[48] Goldoni had declared. And in introducing the shameless sentimentality of bourgeois art into his comic opera librettos, Goldoni was able to pull *opera buffa* closer to the social realities of the age, even drawing, as we have seen, from the novel itself for sharper social comment and more naturalistic characterization.

In its quest for more natural expression and characterization sentimental *opera buffa* was able to bend the stylistic rules of an earlier generation. These had assigned appropriate musical idioms to the status of characters, to ensure that if aristocratic characters appeared in comic opera they sang in the language of *opera seria*, and did not join in ensembles with *buffa* characters. Sentimental opera, and the designation of *parte semiseria* (or *mezza carattere*) allowed characters with *buffa* social status to aspire to serious emotions, and *seria* characters to relinquish their hierarchical straitjackets (an ambiguity of social and musical status which is clearly evident in Mozart's Violante/Sandrina, an aristocrat disguised as a servant, and designated a *parte semiseria*). This is what lies behind Mozart's comment that a good *opera buffa* librettist 'ought to introduce *two equally good female parts*, one of these to be *seria*, the other *mezza carattere*, but both parts equal in *importance and excellence*. The third female character, however, may be entirely buffa.'[49] Starting with *La finta giardiniera* Mozart's *opere buffe* all follow this prescription to the letter, enabling Mozart when he came to write *Le nozze di Figaro* to present a complex social world in which different classes interact through an integrated musical language.

By the mid-eighteenth century *opera buffa* had been liberated from its origins in entr'acte parody of *opera seria* to join *opera seria* and assume the moral role, and hence the social justification, once reserved for the spoken theatre alone. In 1794 some citizens of Turin were so struck by a performance of Paisiello's sentimental opera *Nina* that they wrote to the composer claiming that they no longer opposed the virtuous marital desires of their children, that they loved nature more, and that if all operas were like *Nina*, composers should be generally honoured as 'extirpators of vice, producers of virtue, and correctors of customs'.[50] 'Opera itself can serve to reform morals and destroy superstition' in 'a heretic country', wrote Frederick the Great to his opera-reforming friend Algarotti;[51] and Joseph II, whose passionate belief in the moral power of the theatre led him to promote the Viennese theatre as one of the cornerstones of his reforming programme, was as keen on opera as on spoken drama (and much keener on *opera buffa* than *opera seria*, of which there were no new examples in Vienna during his reign).

The new status of opera in the later eighteenth century can only have confirmed the young Mozart's desire to make his contributions to the genre, and hence to fulfil his role as an independent artist and musician in society. But Italian opera, the universal genre of the age, was not what Mozart, who was becoming increasingly conscious of his cultural identity, was primarily interested in. More than anything in the second half of the 1770s he wanted to write German opera.

IV

The German artist

'I thank God that I am a good honest German', wrote Mozart in a letter written during his disastrous trip to Paris in 1778.[1] More fervently, in another letter from Paris, he proclaimed his wish to 'do honour to the whole German nation',[2] and the year before had expressed his desire to 'help forward the German national theatre'.[3] Yet, for all his longing to take part in the great movement for a German national theatre, at various other moments in his career he was to express categorical desires to write now only French opera, or now only Italian *opera buffa*. And in 1785, protesting his German patriotism all the while, he turned down the possibility of an important commission for a German opera from Mannheim, at that time one of the most important theatrical centres in all Germany. Why, then, was Mozart so anxious to assert his identity as a 'German' artist?

In the eighteenth century, national boundaries and identities were often fluid and uncertain, nowhere more so than in Germany, a country fragmented into hundreds of tiny states and principalities, free cities and ecclesiastical domains, further separated by the split between the Protestant north and the Catholic south, and held together by no more than a common tongue and nominal allegiance to the Holy Roman Emperor in Vienna. These divisions made it particularly difficult for the German artist to identify with a coherent culture and a clearly defined audience for his work. 'From the people as such we get little nourishment,' Goethe was still complaining in 1827, 'and all the talents and brains among us are scattered all over Germany: one in Vienna, one in Berlin, another in Königsberg, another in Bonn or Düsseldorf, all hundreds of miles apart, so that any personal contact and personal exchange of ideas is a rare thing.'[4]

Furthermore, German economic and cultural life had been devastated by the Thirty Years War in the seventeenth century, and the subsequent slowness of economic growth in the eighteenth century. The insularity of the small German states had prevented the development of an economically and culturally progressive bourgeoisie such as had emerged in England and France. In marked contrast to England, where Oxford and Cambridge were at the nadir of their intellectual influence during the eighteenth century, the most energetic centres of intellectual activity in Germany throughout the century were its universities. The scattered provincialism of cultural life in Germany, and the prosaic and inexpressive state of the German language, drove early eighteenth-century German writers and artists to try and restore German culture by bringing it into line with what were considered to be the universal principles of classical art. In effect what this meant in literature was the adoption and imitation of the rules of the dominant French classicism, a project undertaken by Gottsched, who in the 1730s proposed to modernize the German theatre strictly according to the principles of French drama. In music it entailed the systematic introduction of Italian opera. But in practice, the adoption of French and Italian classical models often became no more than a convenient excuse for the profligate princes and aristocracy of petty German states to ape the culture of Louis XIV's Versailles, a culture that German visual artists and musicians might hope to imitate but from which German writers were automatically excluded.

It is ironic that the man who more than anyone laid down the roots of German political nationalism, Frederick the Great of Prussia, was obsessed with the superiority of French culture. He attempted to import it wholesale to Prussia, declining to speak or write in German, dismissing German literature as provincial and bourgeois, and refusing to employ German writers, scholars and intellectuals in Berlin. As late as 1780 he wrote a book entitled *De la littérature allemande*, outlining his (by then) bizarrely outdated theory that the revival of German letters could only take place within the rules laid down by the classical French writers and critics of a previous absolutist régime a hundred years earlier.

The only German writer whom Frederick would acknowledge was the Viennese soldier–playwright Cornelius Ayrenhoff, prolific author of neo-classical dramas modelled on the French example, and vehement opponent of the Shakespeareanization of German theatre taking place in those areas of northern Germany beyond the reach of Frederick.[5] The promotion of French theatre was a conscious part of the political pro-gramme of Maria Theresa and her Chancellor Kaunitz, and throughout the 1760s a French troupe held sway in Vienna with the latest imports from Paris (Maria Theresa herself would only visit plays in French). When Joseph II succeeded in expelling the French company in 1772, French repertory in German translation continued to dominate the Vien-nese stage.

The predominance of French classicism meant that German writers (and increasingly also those German musicians dedicated to promoting a German opera) found themselves alienated from the very culture in which they lived and worked. Lessing, disappointed by the collapse of numerous projects and plans for a national theatre in Germany, came to the embittered conclusion that there would never be a German theatre or culture until there existed first a German nation.[6] Instead, a whole generation of German writers and artists of the 1770s, seeking to overcome the regionalism and aristocratic dominance of culture in Germany, deliberately promoted the bourgeois liberal cosmopolitanism exemplified in masonic works such as Lessing's *Ernst und Falk* and Wieland's *Das Geheimnisse des Kosmopolitenordens*, or in the neo-Hellenism of Winckelmann. Similarly, Gluck sought to transcend the pigeonholing of cultural styles (French *tragédie lyrique* was of a very different order from Italian *opera seria*; *opera buffa* quite unlike German Singspiel) to which the successful composer was supposed to conform by pursuing a universalizing classicism that would 'wipe out the ridiculous differences in national music'. Instead, he set out to write 'a strong music that speaks to the heart', and that would 'appeal to all peoples'.[7]

In 1773 the young Goethe, in sympathy with the prevailing cosmopolitanism of the age, had written an attack on the *Love of the Fatherland*, an essay by the most prominent figure in the Austrian Enlightenment, Joseph von Sonnenfels. Goethe argued strongly against 'the vain striving for a feeling which we cannot and indeed do not desire to entertain, which is the result of special circumstances in certain peoples and at certain times';[8] but as he matured he came to be increasingly preoccupied by the importance of the relationship between an artist and a national culture. In particular, he recognized the problems of the bourgeois artist who had thrown off the shackles of servitude to prince or church, but who lacked in their place a close and living contact with a community capable of providing him with his subject matter and his audience. This was what the classical artist of the past had enjoyed.

'When and where does a classical national author appear?' asked Goethe. 'When he finds in the history of his nation a harmonious and meaningful unity of great events and their effects; when he does not search in vain for greatness in the spirit of his countrymen, profundity in their sentiments, strength and value in their deeds; when he himself, filled with the spirit of the nation, feels capable of sympathizing, through an indwelling genius, both with the past and the present; when he finds his nation at a high level of culture so that his own education becomes easier; when he sees before him many collected materials, the perfect or only imperfect efforts of his predecessors, and encounters so many external and internal situations that he need not pay a heavy price for experience; that he is able to conceive, order and execute a great work in a unified state of mind in the best years of his life.'[9]

The search for artistic identity, for a cultural environment in which he could 'conceive, order and execute a great work in a unified state of mind in the best years of his life' was quite clearly crucial to Mozart. For Haydn, born a generation earlier than Mozart, the close-knit community of the court of Eszterháza had provided the security and the musical conditions necessary to make his own slow evolution towards classical mastery. As he himself said, Eszterháza gave him the freedom to become original. In deliberately striving for a universalizing simplicity of style, Gluck's music occasionally lapses into blandness. But Haydn, unafraid to draw upon a rich variety of many different musical styles from the popular to the learned, discovered that his music had also come in the process to 'speak to all peoples'.[10] By 1790, when Haydn had become weary of his exile and was longing to break free of Eszterháza, he was able to do so when the opportunity arrived with the certainty that he and his music would have an audience wherever he went.

Mozart was quite different. He had a keener and less humble sense of his own genius than Haydn (a facet of his character that gave rise to his often-noted arrogance and to occasional carelessness in promoting his career), and resented his confinement as a musical lackey in a provincial court. When Mozart described himself as a 'German' artist he was conveying his need to belong to a community greater than that which could be characterized by the political entity of Salzburg, of which he was nominally a subject. He never called himself a 'Salzburger' artist, a concept that would have been meaningless to him even had it not been so distasteful. But in describing himself as German he was also rejecting the rootless cosmopolitanism which, for an artist of the 1770s, appeared to be the only alternative to stagnation in a cultural backwater like Salzburg.

The travels undertaken in Germany and France by Mozart and his mother (while she lived) between September 1777 and January 1779 were made with the purpose of trying to escape Salzburg to find a place where Mozart's genius would be properly recognized and rewarded. Mozart had a prodigious talent for musical mimicry, as he himself often acknowledged ('I can more or less adopt or imitate any kind of style of composition')[11] and it was upon this talent that Leopold had placed his hopes that Wolfgang would be able to secure employment outside Salzburg, frequently reminding his son of the need to compose music that would meet the expectations of his public – be it in Mannheim or Paris. But it is perfectly clear that, for all his desire to travel and experience different cultures to enrich his own art (one of the conditions he attempted to impose upon his remaining in his post at Salzburg) Mozart felt unable to adopt either the chameleon-cosmopolitanism which an earlier generation of composers had accepted as an inevitable accompaniment to a career in music, or the transcending simplicity of Gluck. He wished to be a German, not a European, artist, and 'to do honour to the whole German nation' (see above, p. 48) – a German nation which did not even, at that date, exist. The miserable failure of the expedition of 1777–9 was largely the result of his impossible desire to identify himself as a German artist.

Leopold's main concern was that Wolfgang should establish himself in a major centre, either a court like Munich (his first port of call) where Wolfgang might secure an appointment, or a city like Paris with a flourishing free market. In Paris, above all, he believed that 'The name and fame of a man of great talent resounds throughout the whole world. There the nobility treat men of genius with the greatest deference, esteem and courtesy.'[12] To tempt Wolfgang even more strongly to go on to Paris from Mannheim, where he was lingering unprofitably, Leopold sent him a list of the 'acquaintances we had in Paris' on their former visit. 'All, or at least most of them, are the leading people in that city.'[13] Leopold further provided Wolfgang with letters of introduction to 'Diderot, d'Alembert and the rest',[14] two distinguished editors of the crowning achievement of the French Enlightenment, the *Encyclopédie*. In another letter Leopold reminded his son that 'M. de Voltaire' was also now in Paris, having just made his triumphal return to the city.[15] Leopold was obviously convinced that Wolfgang would be seduced by the promise of mixing with the some of the greatest representatives of the Enlightenment.

As in 1764, Mozart's chief contact in Paris was to be Grimm, and Mozart lodged in Paris for six months with Grimm's mistress, the famous Madame d'Epinay. She was the hostess whose salon was one of the centres of the *Encyclopédiste* circle, the patroness of both Diderot and Rousseau, in whose *Confessions* she plays a prominent role at the hub of an imagined cabal (made up of Diderot, Grimm and herself) to destroy the persecuted Rousseau. Mozart was therefore residing at the very epicentre of the French Enlightenment. But the visit to Paris was an unmitigated disaster: Mozart failed to find employment; his mother died; Grimm wearied of his protégé's bloody-minded independence. Nonetheless, intellectually the Paris months must have contributed immeasurably to Mozart's education.

While he was in Paris Mozart started to feel culturally homesick, and began frequently to describe himself as 'German'. But it was a notion of Germanness which defined itself negatively, as a reaction against the hedonism and frivolity of the Parisian aristocracy among whom he was forced to seek patronage (and perhaps, too, of the Grimm circle among whom he lived). The notion was so vague that ultimately it could not provide an artist like Mozart with any adequate sense of cultural identity. At exactly the same moment this problem was also being explored by Goethe in the first version of his novel *Wilhelm Meister*, in which the young bourgeois Wilhelm's artistic ambitions are trapped between the provincial philistinism of his own class and background, and the shallowness and frivolity of the aristocratic society which appears to offer the only cultural alternative.

It was Mozart's desire to establish his identity as a German artist that had made him reluctant to leave Mannheim for Paris. In October 1777, writing from Munich, Wolfgang had hinted at his longing to write German opera, and even at the possibility of contributing to the reform of the German theatre itself.[16] German opera, still in its infancy, was largely modelled on the simple and popular styles of English ballad opera and the French *opéra comique*, a bourgeois art deliberately turning its back on the complexity and display of the Italian opera preferred by the aristocracy. Mozart clearly had ambitions (which were to stay with him until the composition of *Die Entführung aus dem Serail*) to make something more of the form. In late October he travelled to Mannheim, for Leopold had advised him that 'German operas are always being performed there'.[17] Wolfgang spent five months there, between October 1777 and March 1778, returning in November/December of 1778 on his way home from Paris.

It was a moment when Mannheim was enjoying an explosion of artistic activity under its Elector Karl Theodor that was to push the city into a prominence to rival that of Weimar. Music and opera in the city were already long famous, and in September 1778 Karl Theodor gave instructions for a German national theatre to be founded in Mannheim – a consolation to the Palatinate capital for the fact that he was about to remove the renowned Mannheim orchestra and opera with him to his new seat in Munich.[18] (The reason for the astonishing richness and virtuosity of the orchestral writing in *Idomeneo* was that Mozart was effectively writing for the Mannheim orchestra.)

The National Theatre was properly constituted the following year. It was run by a team of young German literary patriots, its manager Baron Wolfgang Heribert Dalberg, and its *Dramaturg* Otto von Gemmingen. Under their leadership the theatre enjoyed considerable success, and came to evolve a distinctive 'Mannheim' theatre-style and tradition, outlined programmatically by Gemmingen's Lessing-influenced *Mannheimer Dramaturgie* of 1779, and characterized by the sentimental bourgeois dramas of Dalberg and the actor Iffland (and Gemmingen's own hugely popular *Der deutsche Hausvater* of 1780, modelled on Diderot). The Mannheim theatre was also to establish and maintain an important contact with Schiller, who delivered his paper on the revival of German theatre at a meeting of Gemmingen's Kurpfälzische deutsche Gesellschaft (Palatinate German Society). In 1782 Schiller's rousing *Sturm und Drang* play *Die Räuber* was given its first performance in Mannheim, and in 1784 *Kabale und Liebe* was performed in Mannheim only two days after its première in Frankfurt.

Sadly, Mozart's sojourns in Mannheim preceded the Schiller era. But if the National Theatre failed to attain the peak of its success until after Mozart had reluctantly returned to Salzburg, a glimpse at the list of plays performed in the season that started in October 1778, shortly before Mozart arrived for his second visit, gives an idea of the breadth and catholicity of the theatre's repertory that so excited him.[19] It includes plays by Corneille, Molière, Marivaux, Voltaire, Beaumarchais, Shakespeare, Sheridan, Goldsmith, Goldoni, Gozzi, Lessing and Goethe, all of which he would have undoubtedly seen. (During his bachelor days in Vienna he claimed to attend the theatre nightly.) Furthermore, he attended performances of a new opera, *Günther von Schwarzburg*, the first self-consciously patriotic German opera, whose librettist Anton von Klein had issued a rousing manifesto denouncing the 'slavish habit' of German writers in forever imitating foreigners, and had proudly served up an *echt* German hero, Günther von Schwarzburg, the first in German history to propose 'the salvation of Germany'.[20] The opera clearly highlights the problems Mozart faced in wishing to create a distinctively German opera, for formally, with its succession of exit arias, it is merely an old-fashioned Metastasian *opera seria* tricked out in medieval costume. Mozart disliked the pompous libretto, but must have been struck by its patriotic sentiments.

Mozart's desire to stay in Mannheim when his father was pressing him to go on to Paris gave rise to the greatest of all the rifts between father and son. And Mozart again defied his father after the Paris débâcle by returning to Mannheim rather than following the Elector to his new musical capital in Munich, even though Aloysia Weber, whom his father had previously blamed for his lingering in Mannheim, had also moved to Munich. 'Mannheim loves me as much as I love Mannheim,' he declared bullishly,[21] to the fury of Leopold.

On his return visit, after the Elector had given the go-ahead for Dalberg and Gemmingen to start recruiting for the new theatre, Mozart was soon on the doorstep pressing for employment, and clearly more interested in taking part in the revival of German theatre in Mannheim than in following the famous court orchestra to Munich. Within a short time he had been commissioned by Dalberg to work with Gemmingen on what he described as a *Duodrama* (what we would now call a melodrama – spoken text over music), *Semiramis* – an uncompleted (and subsequently lost) project by which he was so excited that he started work on it before being paid anything. That the project aborted was an ominous sign.

On his first stay in Mannheim Mozart had met Wieland, the literary hero of the Mozart household, whose new German opera *Rosemunde*, with music by Anton Schweitzer, was due to be performed there. But Mozart had been far from impressed with Schweitzer's previous 'dreary' German opera based on Wieland's *Alceste* (the first serious German opera to be composed by a German composer to a German text, performed in 1775).[22] The reception he accorded the opera did not bode well for his own future as a 'German' composer in Mannheim. For all its cultural fecundity, Mannheim was by 1778 no longer the seat of a court, and the main hindrance to the development of German opera had consistently been the fact that it was invariably seen as a second-best substitute where there were not the resources for mounting full-scale Italian opera. The composer of German opera had to put up with scrappy stage bands and actors untrained as operatic singers. For this reason Wieland in his *Versuch über das deutsche Singspiel*, published as the preface to *Alceste*, had deliberately argued for simplicity in German opera, and at Weimar Goethe had committed himself to writing and producing Singspiels for the small, semi-amateur court theatre that clearly reflect the naïvety and simplicity imposed upon the form in most places where it was deployed. Mozart himself had complained about the 'wretched singers' in the Mannheim Singspiels on his first trip.[23] Despite his unwillingness to return to Salzburg, he soon realized Mannheim had little to offer. In Paris he had felt the need to affirm his Germanness; it was, significantly, from Mannheim that he started to reiterate his desire to write French, or even better, Italian operas. His next completed opera, *Idomeneo*, was to achieve both aims in one work.

V

Zaide

Mozart returned to Salzburg early in 1779, all his projects for independence having failed. There he set to work on the composition of a major work, a German Singspiel, apparently without a commission and without guarantee of performance. The untitled opera, known after its heroine as *Zaide*, was never completed.

Early in 1778, while he was in Mannheim, Mozart had heard that Joseph II was planning to establish a German opera company in Vienna. An enquiry by Leopold to an old acquaintance, the dramatist Franz von Heufeld, drew the suggestion that Wolfgang should write an opera and submit it to the emperor for consideration. Though the suggestion had elicited a furious response from Mozart,[1] it is likely that he wrote the unfinished Singspiel with the specific intention of having something in hand with which to interest Joseph II and his new German opera, should the opportunity arise. Accordingly, he requested Leopold to send the score to him in Munich when he was working on *Idomeneo*, and again considered completing it for the German opera when he arrived in Vienna in 1781, eventually rejecting it as 'too serious' for the Viennese.[2]

The reason was that *Zaide* was Mozart's most personal, even autobiographical, work, and reveals his desperate state of mind in Salzburg during 1779 and 1780. He worked on the text of the opera with the Salzburg trumpeter and literary dilettante Johann Andreas Schachtner; but it was based upon an already extant Singspiel libretto with the somewhat unwieldy title *Das Serail, oder die unvermütete Zusammenkunft in der Sklaverey zwischen Vater, Tochter und Sohn* ('The Seraglio, or the Unexpected Encounter in Slavery between Father, Daughter and Son')[3] itself unmistakably derived from Voltaire's play *Zaïre*. Although Schachtner's spoken dialogue is lost, it is clear that both he and Mozart worked from *Das Serail*, which therefore provides us with the missing dialogue for most of Mozart's own opera.[4]

The opera is an oriental escape story somewhat like that of *Die Entführung aus dem Serail*. Its two opening numbers were added to the text of *Das Serail* by Mozart and Schachtner. The first is a chorus of slaves singing, to a grotesquely jaunty tune, the words:

> Brothers, let us be merry,
> And bear our burdens bravely . . .
> Let us sing, let us laugh,
> For man can do nothing else.
> World and misery are one and the same,
> No one is free from cares.

The theme which the slaves sing seems to have been associated in Mozart's mind with servitude; it is a motif of repeated fourths which recurs in the opening scene of *Don Giovanni* to accompany Leporello's grumbles at a servant's lot, and again in the penultimate scene of *Die Zauberflöte* as the Queen and her minions prowl impotently in the subterranean passages beneath Sarastro's sacred Temple.

Mozart's disdain for such servile acceptance of captivity is made clear in the following number, a *melodrama* for the opera's hero Gomatz, a Western captive among the slaves. Gomatz rails against his fate, speaking over some of Mozart's most urgently expressive *Sturm and Drang* music: restlessly syncopated rhythms; rising phrases of passionate, despairing longing tailing off into silence, or interrupted by violent, offbeat *sforzandi*:

> Inscrutable fate!
> You cast me among these hopeless criminals.
> Among those,
> Who through their own misdeeds have forged
> Their own deserved chains.
> Myself innocent among them!
> God!
> Why do you not give me too a heart like theirs?
> Hard as the stone which they wearily break.
> Terrible!
> Insensitive to the hardest labour,
> They cheerfully shout their nonsense.

Happiness has deserted Gomatz, and the enforced leisure of the night gives him no rest. All comforts are without effect upon his wounded soul. To a poignant oboe phrase he longs for death to free him from his misery, until at last exhaustion lulls him to fitful sleep.

As he sleeps a female figure appears: Zaide, the favourite of the Sultan's harem but also, like Gomatz, a captive European. She gazes tenderly at Gomatz, recognizes his origins as hers, then lays a portrait of herself beside him: 'I will not awaken him, but I'll sweeten his slavery with these gifts'. Hovering over Gomatz, like the vision of hope which sustains Beethoven's Florestan in his dungeon, she sings an exquisite lullaby, accompanied by gently plucked strings, and leaves. Gomatz wakes and recalls a beautiful dream. At first he dismisses it as another cruel deception, but then he spots the picture, and some precious jewels beside it. Taking both, and strengthened by the newfound hope offered by the portrait, he sings in defiance of fate: 'This picture makes all good,' he proclaims, to mounting joy.

Zaide returns, veiled, and reproaches Gomatz for stealing her trinkets. Protesting his native virtue and honour (but lamenting that an exile in chains is deprived of honour) Gomatz returns the treasures but insists on keeping the portrait. 'What would you do before its original, if you were to see her languishing for love of you, in a thousand sighing tears?' Zaide asks, unveiling herself to him. Blissfully they fall into each others' arms.

Mozart loved word-games and cryptic puzzles. I believe that Gomatz is Mozart: the name itself would certainly have been spotted by him as an anagram of G[ottlieb] Moza[r]t. (Though Mozart infrequently signed himself Gottlieb, preferring the French form of his name 'Amadè', it would have been appropriate for him to do so as he was brooding over his identity as a German artist; in one of his letters he had also signed himself 'Romatz').[5] Like Gomatz, he endures servitude ('Slavery in Salzburg' is how he described it to his father)[6], and feels deprived of his true honour. Zaide, the vision who appears to him in his despairing sleep, is his muse: opera, or more particularly, German opera, whose portrait keeps the flame of hope alive in his breast. 'See me here before you, dearest slave!' she exhorts, 'See the original of the picture for which you are willing to die! See the original of that picture who has already sent you so many thousand sighs, who tenderly and constantly loves you.' But German opera is unliberated too, an exile like Mozart, 'tearfully yearning for her fatherland' and for the saviour who will rescue her. United at last (they are really brother and sister, as the title of the libretto makes clear) together they will escape and conquer destiny.

The trinkets which Gomatz takes, and for which Zaide reproaches him, are the false lures of money which Mozart must resist if he is to serve his art without compromise. ('Yet, even assuming that you were willing to give me fifty louis d'or, I should still as an honest man most certainly dissuade you from the undertaking,' he had courageously written to Dalberg about an aborted project for an opera in Mannheim. 'An opera without male and female singers! What an extraordinary idea!')[7] But in the service of his art ('These jewels shall pave the way for us' says Gomatz of their intended escape) or as the reward earned from his true art ('It is I who placed these precious treasures before you' says Zaide) the material rewards of money carry no dishonour.

In the following scene the would-be elopers are apprehended by Allazim, the Captain of the Palace Guard who is a renegade, a Western captive who has converted to Islam. 'Sir, you are, just like me, a slave,' Gomatz appeals to him; 'Save that fortune has given you power over me. I have always perceived something exalted in your deeds, something virtuous, and much nobleness; you have always loved me, and made my fate more bearable in many ways.' As we have seen, Allazim is eventually revealed to be the father of both Gomatz and Zaide. Clearly, for Mozart, he represents his father Leopold. Like Wolfgang, Leopold is a slave, although one who has accepted his servitude and relinquished the dream of freedom. But he is a slave with authority over Wolfgang, and has the power to help his son to escape to fulfil his destiny, or to restrain him. 'You would not restrain our joy,' says Gomatz. 'You are too noble and too great for such a shameful deed. Help me to attain my freedom and the freedom of Zaide.'

Allazim agrees to help the lovers escape, staying behind to face the furious wrath of the Sultan (as Leopold was indeed to be left behind in Salzburg to deal with Archbishop Colloredo's anger when Mozart did finally abscond). Gomatz sings an aria of gratitude which reflects Mozart's own ambivalent feelings about his need to break free of his father: 'Let me embrace your knee, although I must soon leave you, for I burn with love.' The three then join in a radiant trio in which Gomatz and Zaide look forward to bliss as the reward for their constancy.

In the second half of the opera the escaping lovers are captured and brought before the tyrannous Sultan. Mozart's score concludes with a quartet in which the Sultan refuses the lovers' pleas for mercy, and they beg to be allowed to die together. The reason that Mozart could not complete the opera, of course, was that the outcome of his own story was as yet unknown.

VI

Idomeneo

The story of Idomeneo, the Cretan King who, returning home from Troy, sacrificed his own son to propitiate the god Poseidon warrants only brief mentions in classical literature. It plays an important part, though, in Fénelon's *Télémaque* (1699) which had been read by Mozart when a boy, and it was employed several times in eighteenth-century opera and drama. One version of the story, a play by a prolific French dramatist Lemierre, appeared in Paris in 1764, while the Mozart family were in Paris. The play was reviewed by Baron Grimm in the *Correspondance littéraire*, where it was identified as a *tragédie philosophique*. He described the play as 'cold and without interest', and proposed that ancient myth was not the right vehicle for modern philosophical debate more suited to a Paris salon than to ancient Crete, 'when the gods would have replied to the arguments of *philosophes* with thunder and pestilential plagues'.[1] Grimm proceeded to suggest, with some prescience, that the subject of Idomeneo would in fact be much better suited to an opera than a tragedy. In fact, Diderot had already suggested in the prefaces to his bourgeois dramas *Le fils naturel* and *Le père de famille* that stories from Greek classical myth were suitable only for opera. He longed for a revival of the genuine, archaic spirit of Greek classical drama and believed, as did many before and since, from the Florentine Camerata to Wagner, that it would take place through opera; he urged playwrights to leave the world of gods, tempests and supernatural revelation to the opera stage.

Idomeneo is a representative work of later Enlightenment neo-classicism; part of a calculated revolt against the conventions of Metastasian *opera seria* and rationalist *tragédie philosophique*, in which the rules of propriety and good taste were deliberately flouted in the quest for a drama of heightened expression and raw passions, rather than of logical argument. ('Make me weep, make me shudder,' Diderot had implored the modern dramatist.)[2] The fact that the libretto was drawn from a French *tragédie lyrique* of 1712, gave Mozart the opportunity to work on scenes of high drama unprecedented in conventional Italian opera (shipwrecks, storms, sea-monsters, oracular voices), and to depict a world that Man shared once again with the deities banished as 'fausses divinités' from French classical drama and Metastasian opera.

Idomeneo was written at a time when German writers like Herder and Wieland were urging that a revival of Greek drama through opera could be the vehicle for a wider reform of German culture, encouraging German composers in the task of creating 'a modern Euripidean drama'.[3] Mozart's festal choruses for the incidental music which he had written for Tobias von Gebler's play *Thamos, König in Ägypten* (originally performed in Vienna in 1774, but revised in 1779) had already earned the praise of one reviewer for bringing 'the choruses of the ancients into heroic tragedy'.[4] Now in *Idomeneo* Mozart made the chorus a crucial element in the drama, projecting a powerful sense of the communal identity which was so lacking in German cultural life at that date. But like Gluck, he also used his archaic world to replace the old absolutist, rational, submission to duty with a persuasive argument for the universality of modern bourgeois values.

EURIPIDES AND SACRIFICE DRAMA

At the heart of the opera is the story of Idomeneo's fateful vow, made to secure his safe passage home as a victorious conquerer from Troy, to sacrifice the first person he meets to the god Neptune. The theme of human sacrifice was one of the most insistent in Enlightenment art. The archetypal treatment of the theme in the story of Agamemnon's sacrifice of his daughter Iphigenia to ensure the passage of the Greek fleet, becalmed on the island of Aulis, to Troy, had been revived by Racine in the seventeenth century. Eighteenth-century dramatists and operatic composers returned repeatedly to the two Iphigenia stories, of which Gluck's operatic settings and Goethe's play are only the best known. The theme of human sacrifice also recurs in several settings of the biblical story of Jephthah (most notably in Handel's oratorio), and in four versions, two dramatic, two operatic, of the less familiar Idomeneo story.

Why such a number of works on this singularly abhorrent theme? 'On the surface,' writes Daniel Heartz 'human sacrifice, or even the threat of it, would seem to be as remote from the ideals of the Enlightenment as were religious miracles.'[5] Yes indeed! In the seventeenth century the English neo-classical critic Thomas Rymer had already raised the problem of the predominance of such themes from classical drama in more rational times: 'Some would laugh to find me mentioning Sacrifices, Oracles, and Goddesses: old Superstitions, say they, not practicable, but more than ridiculous on our Stage.'[6] In his preface to *Iphigénie* Racine had accordingly felt obliged to offer an apology for introducing such distressing subjects and Metastasio, for whom the purpose of tragedy was to arouse 'admiration of virtue under a thousand different aspects; as friendship, gratitude, patriotism, fortitude, generosity', had similarly inveighed against the 'tragical terrorism' of the Greeks, and considered that they were no better than 'semi-barbarous'.[7]

Euripides, the later eighteenth-century's favourite and most widely-read Greek dramatist, provides us with the clue to why Enlightenment writers and musicians kept returning to the sacrificial theme. To his eighteenth-century readers Euripides, whether the dramatist of the passions or Nietzsche's purveyor of 'bourgeois mediocrity',[8] was the poet of what has been called the 'Greek Enlightenment', who had lived in an age of intellectual enquiry and religious scepticism apparently like their own. He had often challenged the myths in his plays, questioning their truth and authority, and regarding blind belief in them as a shackle binding men to primitive traditions and customs. His King Thoas in *Iphigenia in Tauris* is a caricature of a man in the thrall of barbarian superstitions who clearly deserves to have his savage credulity turned against him by the escaping Greeks at the end of the play (quite unlike his honourable Enlightenment heirs in Goethe's play on the same story, and Mozart's Pasha in *Die Entführung*).[9]

Euripides also condemned those who encourage and, often as not, take advantage of people's credulity. In his *Helen* the prophecies and oracles which had brought about the Trojan war are revealed to be worthless, a fact that prompts the bitter comment that 'The art was invented as a bait for making money'.[10] We recognize instantly the familiar Enlightenment argument that organized religion is manipulated by priests to dupe and fleece the credulous. Voltaire, perhaps the Enlightenment's most persistent critic of the Church, restates the point in *Oedipe*, his first play, when his Jocasta rebels not (as had Sophocles' Jocasta) against belief in a divine plan to the universe, but more specifically against the influence of oracles and priestcraft.[11] Voltaire, however, for all his hostility to institutional religion, never lost his belief in God, a position that is again anticipated in Euripides, for whom scepticism about oracles does not mean that man should reject the gods themselves:

> We should sacrifice to the gods,
> Ask them for blessings, and let prophecy go.[12]

But it is not simply sacrifice to the gods that Euripides demands. In *Iphigenia in Tauris* Orestes, having dismissed the capacity of dreams and oracles to guide people's behaviour, insists that:

> The wisest men follow their own direction
> And listen to no prophets guiding them.
> None but the fools believe in oracles,

> Forsaking their own judgement. Those who know,
> Know that such men can only come to grief.[13]

The ways of the gods are unknowable. As instruments of fate or destiny, dreams and oracles may or may not be correct, but either way they do not absolve people from making their own moral decisions, or from accepting responsibility for their own actions, an issue that lies at the heart of the Enlightenment's own secular relocation of moral authority. 'Enlightenment is man's leaving his self-caused immaturity', is Kant's famous definition; 'Immaturity is the incapacity to use one's intelligence without the guidance of another.'[14] And for Kant it was 'primarily in matters of religion'[15] that people needed to free themselves.

Rightly or wrongly, the Enlightenment read Euripides as an honoured precursor. And it was above all in Euripides' *Iphigenia* dramas of human sacrifice that the Enlightenment found the theme it sought to promote its belief in the superiority of natural law to customary and religious law. For human sacrifice, as a sacramental deed, provides a religious sanction for a basic transgression against nature: murder. Hence Gluck's Iphigénie inveighs against the injunction of human sacrifice imposed upon her, cursing it as 'saintement barbare' – sanctified barbarity. Voltaire sought and found evidence for such organized crime in all religions, citing the biblical story of Jephthah and the myth of Iphigenia sacrificed on Aulis in support for his argument against priestcraft: 'From Calchas, who murdered the daughter of Agamemnon . . . sacerdotal power has been disastrous to the world'.[16]

And, of course, the murderous crimes of religion did not lie in the past alone. In 1762 a scandalous case had occurred which roused Voltaire to his greatest outpouring of polemical energies. A Protestant trader from Toulouse called Jean Calas, alleged to have murdered his son to prevent him abjuring his Protestant faith for Catholicism, was horribly tortured and executed. (In *Idomeneo* the Cretan Idamante is blamed by Idomeneo for having shown leniency to the enemy Trojan Princess Ilia, a comparable crime perhaps.) The evidence for Calas's having committed the deed, based upon an extorted confession, was palpably inadequate, and to Voltaire the case presented a Chinese box of indictments against religious law. 'Either way,' he wrote, 'whether Calas be guilty or innocent, human nature is dishonoured, and it is essential to discover the truth.'[17] The idea that a father might kill his son for his religious faith was in itself horrific, but just as appalling to Voltaire was the possibility that the combined paternal authority of Church and state had committed judicial

63

murder upon one of its sons. The case became the banner under which he conducted his campaign to 'Ecrasez l'infâme'.

Human sacrifice presented the starkest possible conflict between the eternal laws of nature and the commands of religion. Gluck's Iphigenie, discovering that it is her own brother she is commanded to sacrifice, cries out to the gods in anguish:

> Dieux! Etouffez en moi le cri de la nature!
> Si mon devoir est saint, hélas, qu'il est cruel.
>
> [Gods! Smother the cry of nature in me!
> If my duty is holy, alas it is cruel.]

In Schiller's *Don Carlos*, written only a few years after *Idomeneo*, the argument between religious and natural law is returned to the specific father–son relationship when in the famous scene between the king and the Grand Inquisitor, the old priest demands that the king destroy his subversive son Don Carlos. In response to the king's plea that this would be a sin against nature, the Grand Inquisitor declares that the voice of nature has no worth before the commands of faith.[18] In *Idomeneo* too, it is the granite-voiced High Priest who is most obdurate in his insistence that Idomeneo carry out his religious duty and sacrifice his victim.

THE JUST GOD

'Morality is one, it comes from God. Dogmas differ, they are ours,' wrote Voltaire.[19] To uphold its claim to be able to establish a natural moral law against the claims of Church and state, the Enlightenment needed to believe in a just and moral God, for as both Hobbes and Locke had asserted, anything called a law presupposed the existence of a legislator capable of administering punishment and reward. 'If there is a God, he must be just,' insisted Montesquieu.[20] But as the Enlightenment discovered, the attempt to construct an ethical and just deity always founders on the scandalous but immovable fact that the world is unjust; the wicked go unpunished and the virtuous unrewarded; disasters (such as the cataclysmic Lisbon earthquake of 1749) fall indiscriminately on deserving and undeserving alike.

Traditional theology had addressed this problem by arguing that earthly evil was the fault of every living being who had inherited the original sin of Adam, for which no earthly reparation could be made. But the Enlightenment vehemently rejected the Christian dogma of original sin, which ruled out all efforts at improvement of the individual or his world.[21] Instead, the Enlightenment engaged in the elaborate arguments of theodicy to justify the ways of God to man. Thus Leibniz argued that the universe was as perfect as it could be given that only God could be absolutely perfect. But the most influential of Enlightenment theodicies was Pope's *Essay on Man*, often read in prose translation as a philosophical treatise rather than the masterly example of Augustan poetic rhetoric for which it is enjoyed today. Man, according to Pope, cannot hope to know God or his intentions. His vision of justice is limited and partial:

> Remember, Man, 'the Universal Cause
> Acts not by partial, but by gen'ral laws;'[22]

Who but God can say who is truly virtuous and deserves reward? Everything that happens happens according to God's unknowable overall plan for the universe:

> All Nature is but Art unknown to thee;
> All Chance direction which thou cans't not see;
> All Discord Harmony not understood;
> All partial Evil universal Good.
> And spite of Pride, in erring Reason's spite,
> One truth is clear, 'Whatever is, is RIGHT.'[23]

Pope's famous words, often cited as an example of the Enlightenment's complacent optimism, were more often taken as a counsel of stoic resignation, as Handel's great choral setting of the words in the chorus 'How dark, O Lord, are Thy decrees' in *Jephtha* makes clear. Mozart himself was strongly imbued with tendencies to resignation of this kind, for Leopold had drummed into him that 'God orders all things for good, however strange they may seem'.[24] In his letters from Paris upon his mother's death there, the theme of Mozart's 'submission to God's will', of God's 'unsearchable, unfathomable and all-wide providence',[25] of Mozart's certainty that 'God orders all things for our good'[26] tolls its knell of dogged comfort. Occasionally Leopold even felt that he had to reproach his son for allowing such providentialism to lapse into the passive fatalism of believing that all human planning or striving was useless.[27]

There are very few true tragedies in Enlightenment art. However blind and confused mortals might be, the Enlightenment could never ultimately relinquish a belief in the justice and rightness of God. And if God's justice was not always apparent in the real world, it could be represented to be so in art. In the 1712 libretto by Danchet upon which Mozart and Varesco drew for their opera, the gods Neptune and Venus to whom Idomeneo falls victim are the cruel and vindictive supporters of vanquished Troy. They are Racine's 'fausses divinités', rationalized in classical drama as the embodiment of the passions that wreak such tragic havoc in men's lives.[28]

Mozart's and Varesco's Neptune is a quite different deity: the Enlightenment's moral legislator, 'He who ... is called Jehovah, or God or Brama', as the text of one of Mozart's masonic cantatas has it.[29] He is not the Cartesian watchmaker of the rationalist Deists, who having created his machinery for the universe, set it going and then withdrew into empyrian indifference, safely insulated from the moral muddles of his creation. Nor is he like Pascal's and Racine's terrifying *Deus Absconditus*, the Jansenist God who watches every moment of man's life, but who offers no token or indication of whether his predetermined grace has been granted or withdrawn. In *Idomeneo* Neptune becomes executor of his own inviolable natural law; he hovers close to the sphere of human action, letting his pleasure or anger be known through signs and tokens of nature, and eventually manifests himself to exercise his grace and to ensure that natural justice is upheld – and is seen to be upheld.

To Idamante, Ilia and the Cretans upon whom Neptune's wrath falls, and who have to suffer the scourge of monsters and plague, the universe is indeed inexplicable. The gods appear cruel and unjust, and their human victims ceaselessly rail against the 'dei tiranni'. But this is because they enjoy only Pope's 'partial' view of the situation, being ignorant of the real cause of events: Idomeneo's vow. Neptune may be a fierce god, but he is a just god. Like Aristotle, Enlightenment dramatists considered the punishment of a completely virtuous hero to be gratuitous, so to convey their vision of a just and ordered universe they invariably constructed carefully balanced dramas which neatly ensured that human guilt and blame were apportioned where they were due.

Accordingly, Idomeneo is presented as a flawed Aristotelian hero whose punishment matches his fault, and Idomeneo's *hamartia*, his tragic flaw, is programmed with almost pedantic precision by Varesco. At the beginning of Act II, Idomeneo recounts to his Minister Arbace the events which led to his making the fatal vow to Neptune, and describes how he left Troy a victorious warrior: 'Puffed up with my exploits, as I set to sea proud Neptune awaited me.' The point is neatly made. Poseidon (Neptune) along with Aphrodite and Hera, supported Troy in the wars; Idomeneo, swollen-headed with pride [*hubris*][30] has courted the anger of Neptune, and in attempting to escape the justified wrath, makes his fateful vow against the law of nature. There is, significantly, no discussion of the kind of moral struggle which might have helped to absolve Idomeneo; no anguished weighing-up of the choice between the lives of a boatload of battle-weary heroes against the life of a solitary, possibly inconsequential, unknown.

In the *Oresteia* Aeschylus implies that there is a rough justice in Artemis's demand that if Agamemnon is prepared to shed so much innocent blood in the war at Troy he must also be prepared to shed his own daughter's innocent blood. Varesco's and Mozart's Neptune upholds a similar justice for Idomeneo. In Lemierre's more didactically explicit handling of the story, the High Priest specifically defends the god against Idomeneo's complaint at the cruel injustice of his having set eyes upon his own son. Had Idomeneo met with a stranger, the High Priest points out, he would have plunged a completely innocent family into grief. The very fact that he met Idamante and that it is Idamante he must sacrifice in fulfilment of his promise, is evidence that the gods are, indeed, just.[31]

But Idomeneo's real crime is in the very promise he makes to Neptune, for in making that vow Idomeneo has contravened one of the Enlightenment's most basic injunctions – against making vows to gods.

VOWS AND CONTRACTS

Vows made to God troubled the *philosophes* greatly, and *Idomeneo* is only one amongst numerous Enlightenment stories that present the danger of making such promises. Voltaire's last *conte*, published in two parts in the *Correspondance littéraire* in 1773 and 1774, is a more than usually surreal tale called *Le taureau blanc*. Another parental sacrifice story, it tells of a king of Egypt who has sworn a vow that he will decapitate his daughter if she mentions the name of her lover Nabuchodonosor. (The reason for the vow remains obscure.) Inevitably, the princess Amaside transgresses the injunction and calls upon her lover, whereupon it looks as if her father is going to be forced to implement his vow. He apologizes somewhat lamely to his daughter, but there is nothing for it: 'When a king has sworn to cut his daughter's neck, he must fulfil his vow, otherwise he is thrown into hell for ever, and I do not wish so to condemn myself for love of my daughter.'[32]

Voltaire's story (which ends happily ever after) warns against making, and being tied by, vows to God which contravene the laws of nature and society. For one of the most important projects of the Enlightenment was to replace the old commitments to religion and custom with the secular social contract. The underlying pattern which marks the shift between medieval and modern social structures was described by the nineteenth-century German sociologist Ferdinand Tönnies as the transition from social relationships rooted in 'Gemeinschaft' (natural communities of interest, evolved by custom and tradition, and usually entered by birth) to those based upon 'Gesellschaft' (artificial organizations – economic, social, political – in which free and equal individuals unite on the basis of contractual agreements).[33] The Victorian legal historian Henry Sumner Maine traced the changes in legal thinking which accompanied this development in a famous definition which stated that 'The movement of the progressive societies has hitherto been a movement from Status to Contract'.[34]

The theory of social contract was the eighteenth century's most workable and lasting answer to the problem of how a society in which the traditional bonds have loosened may be saved from dissolution. And for the Enlightenment therefore the establishment of sound social and legal sanctions for contractual agreements obviously constituted one of the essential preconditions for social stability. From Hobbes to Kant the keeping of promises was agreed to be the fundamental precondition of any social organization. Both Hobbes and Locke, arguing that civil society itself had been brought into being by contractual agreements, suggested that the keeping of promises was a basic law of nature.[35] Their theories reflected their specific understanding of the new bourgeois economic order emerging in England. But recognition of the importance of contract permeates philosophical and legal discussion throughout eighteenth-century Europe. Even in the absolutist state (where the citizen was supposed to have handed over all his natural political rights to the sovereign ruler) it was recognized that there were areas of intermediate, contractual social exchange between citizens which needed to be codified. The great legal compendium, the *Lehrbegriff*, produced by the Austrian jurist Martini (Maria Theresa's Professor of Natural Law at Vienna University), contains a large section on contractual law, and surveys the crucial questions about what sort of contracts people could legitimately enter into.

When is a contract not a contract? Firstly, according to the Enlightenment, when it is really a vow. Diderot thought it so important to recognize the true nature of vows that he put an entry in the *Encyclopédie* on the subject, ensuring that a distinction was drawn between vows (*voeux*) and oaths (*serments*). Oaths are engagements made between two people who 'who take God as a mere witness to what is being undertaken'.[36] But vows, on the other hand, are more dangerous, since they are undertakings made directly with God himself, and as such, in modern legal terms, must be viewed as pseudo-contracts. And as Hobbes warns: 'To make Covenant with God, is impossible . . . for . . . we know not whether our Covenants be accepted, or not.'[37] To the Enlightenment lawyer, vows are, apart from anything else, badly drawn-up contracts.

In the article on *Contrat*, the *Encyclopédie* makes it a condition of the 'mutual and reciprocal' nature of contracts that the contracting parties should be free and equal.[38] In making vows with divinities that rule is contravened, for the partners are in no way equal, and therefore do not have reciprocal powers of enforcement or retribution if one party reneges on the contract. Nor is Idomeneo free when he makes his quasi-contractual vow. The partners to a contract must be under no obligation or duress when they enter into the agreement, and Idomeneo is on the point of drowning in a storm whipped up by Neptune himself when he makes his vow.

One of the Enlightenment's favourite stories was that of the woman forced against her will to take orders and become a nun. It was an obvious target for attacks upon the Catholic Church, and inspired Diderot to write his erotic quasi-novel *La religieuse* ('The Nun').

How binding are oaths taken under duress? Which is the greater fault – to make a vow (or by implication, a contract) that one doesn't believe in, or to break vows made against one's will? Traditional dogma had taught that the latter was the greater sin. When Aphra Behn asserted that 'Of all the sins, incident to human nature, there is none of which heaven has took so particular, visible, and frequent notice, and revenge, as on that of violated vows which never go unpunished',[39] she was writing as someone for whom such vows provided the stable foundation of society. Whether made to God, or made to a monarch, vows did not imply for Aphra Behn (as do contracts) any mutual obligation, and were unbreakable. But Enlightenment jurists knew that vows made under duress did more to undermine the status of the contractual relationship upon which social stability depended than the breaking of enforced vows. Religious commands are often arbitrary or irrational, as Kant noted of God's wilful command to Abraham to sacrifice Isaac.[40] In Gluck's *Orfeo* the baffling and unexplained agreement that Orpheus may take his wife Euridice if he does not look back at her on pain of losing her (a condition accepted by Orpheus) is interpreted as a typical religious injunction against the natural laws of conjugal affection.

In the parental sacrifice story, the father who agrees to kill his son contravenes a basic law forbidding murder. 'A promise of something illegal is invalid' argues Martini in the *Lehrbegriff*;[41] and more specifically, Hobbes stated that 'they that Vow anything contrary to any law of Nature, Vow in vain'.[42] Voltaire's king in *Le taureau blanc* is clearly prey to a basic moral confusion when he indicates that he is more frightened of going to hell for breaking his vow than for murdering his daughter. In Handel's *Jephtha* the Angel who stays the 'slaught'rous hand' of Jephtha is obviously invoking a new ethical deity, who will not accept illegal vows, when she declares that 'No vow can disannul the law of God'.

In Danchet's libretto, the old gods are ultimately unrelenting and Idamante has to die. It is at this point in the story that Mozart and Varesco made their most significant alteration to the text, for just as the sacrifice is about to be performed Ilia makes a dramatic entry to the scene, and offers herself as victim to Neptune instead of Idamante, in hope of appeasing the god. Her offer of redemptive self-sacrifice lies at the very heart of the Enlightenment's reappraisal of the moral commands of religion; 'The Gods are not tyrants; you are all mistaken in your interpretation of the divine will,' Ilia exclaims in her moment of enlightenment. As explained by Goethe's *Iphigenie* (conceived only a year before *Idomeneo*), Ilia has recognized that 'He who believes the gods to be bloodthirsty misunderstands them; he is only imputing to them his own fearsome desires.'[43] Men have projected their own crimes upon the gods.

In her certainty that the gods are just and that guilt must be apportioned on earth, Ilia none the less mistakes the true human culprit, believing that she herself must be the cause of Neptune's wrath. It is notable that Idomeneo spends much of the opera railing against the cruelty of the gods; but his real inadequacy, the fault for which Neptune continues to punish him, is that he will not admit his own responsibility for the events which are taking place. He even attempts to find blame in Idamante: perhaps Idamante is being punished for his love of the captive Trojan Princess Ilia? 'Too readily, Idamante, were you prepared to loose those chains . . . Here then is the misdeed for which Heaven is punishing you.' This self-justificatory explanation, sung by Idomeneo in the accompanied recitative which precedes his heroically despairing aria 'Fuor del mar', is set as the climax to the recitative, the wilful self-deception of the line given cruelly ironic force in Mozart's setting. When Idamante then slays the monster sent by Neptune as a sign of his anger that Idomeneo has not carried out his promise, the king persuades himself that Idamante's defiance must have provoked Neptune's further wrath and earned him additional cause for punishment. Even as Idomeneo stands over Idamante with the sacrificial knife he weakly protests to Idamante that he is the victim of 'barbarous, unjust fate'. But Ilia's leap of faith affirms the Enlightenment's belief that the moral law of nature is supported by a just God, and her faith is instantly upheld by Neptune's sudden incarnation and intervention to halt the sacrifice.

At the end of Gluck's and Guillard's *Iphigénie en Tauride*, the goddess Diana had appeared to confirm that her laws and altars had been sullied by human sacrifice; the opera, which had opened with a magnificent storm expressive of the turmoil of the ruptured laws of nature, ends with a prayer for peace to descend upon the waves. *Idomeneo* similarly opens with a terrible storm, reflecting Idomeneo's crime against nature, and at the end of Act II Elettra's wishful longing for gentle breezes to carry her and Idamante from stricken Crete to safety is brutally interrupted by another storm which prevents the departure, and tells us quite clearly that Elettra's jealous desires for Idamante are not blessed by nature.

Only Ilia, sheltered in a garden at the beginning of the following act, is vouchsafed the power over nature for which the others long. She is even able to command the very same breezes which had so cruelly defied Elettra, tenderly and confidingly bidding them carry her love to Idamante. For only Ilia is able to recognize the true beneficence and justice of the laws of nature. But the law which Ilia recognizes is not the abstract moral law of reason promoted by the natural lawyers of the seventeenth century, but rather, the sentimental law of love. Neptune confirms this when he calls a halt to the sacrifice: 'Ha vinto amore' – 'Love has triumphed . . . let innocence be rewarded' the dramatic sepulchral voice announces. It is a complete reversal of the primary theme of rationalist art: the elevation instead of the denigration of romantic love.

THE LAWS OF LOVE

Seventeenth-century rationalists had argued that men and women needed only to suppress their passions to allow reason to triumph and lead them to virtue. 'There is no passion so strong that it cannot be overcome by the free working of reason,'[44] Descartes had confidently asserted. In rationalist art, sexual love is invariably presented as a debilitating and destructive force, as witnessed in Racine's notorious preface to *Phèdre* (see p. 40). Corneille's plays are frequently founded upon the familiar conflict of characters caught between their desires and the demands of duty, and Milton portrayed the disastrous 'effeminacy' of characters like Adam and Samson who allow themselves to be tempted by women.[45] Similarly, the comic characters of Molière and Handel are driven by mad obsessions, and are even, in the case of Handel's lovesick Xerxes, capable of falling in love with trees. For the Abbé Prévost, a Jansenist like Racine, sexual passion was evidence of man's original sin, and the source of man's inherently tragic inability to rise above his fate and attain grace. In his *Manon Lescaut*, a realist novella with all the taut discipline and cumulative tension of a tragedy by Racine, the entrancing Manon is Eve or Delilah to Prévost's young hero Des Grieux, who is a tragic example of the 'perpetual conflict between good feelings and bad actions . . . a terrible example of the force of the passions'.[46]

The neo-stoic virtues of rational self-denial and delayed gratification of pleasure had served not only absolutism, but also the early phase of bourgeois capitalist endeavour. However, the expansion of capitalism demanded a more forcefully consumerist ethic, and as a new monied and leisured class emerged in the eighteenth century it also began to require an ethic that would absolve the pursuit of individual self-gratification and pleasure. To its shopping-list of essential human rights the Enlightenment added happiness, 'our being's end aim', as Pope said.[47] 'All of our institutions, our reflections, our knowledge, has for its only objective to procure for us that happiness towards which our own natures force us ceaselessly to tend,' insisted Holbach.[48]

The human sacrifice condemned in Enlightenment sacrifice dramas is not only the tyranny of religion. It is the self-sacrifice demanded by rational stoicism and by the dictates of public duty. To support its new claims the Enlightenment therefore created the image of a loving and beneficent God who would condone the pursuit of earthly happiness and the fulfilment of natural desires. Diderot's deity, Nature, tells men to reject the old tyrannical God of Christianity: 'In vain, O slaves of superstition, do you seek your happiness beyond the limits of the world in which I have placed you . . . Cast out the Gods who have usurped my power, and return to my laws.'[49] Ludovico Muratori insisted reassuringly that 'God commands us nothing, and we are not bound to anything with respect to Him, which is not after all really and substantially for our own Good and Happiness'.[50] 'I desire mercy and not sacrifice,' says the God of the propagandist for Joseph II's religious reforms, Joseph Eybel.[51] 'A God who demands sacrifice?' asked Mozart's friend and colleague Otto von Gemmingen. 'Perish the thought! Such a God would suppress all of man's truest social instincts.'[52] The unnatural horrors of the monastery and convent loomed ever large in Enlightenment art. And the central drama of Christianity, Christ's redemptive death on the cross, sacrificed by God his father, plays notably little part in the Enlightenment's religious iconography.

In his recognition of Ilia's love, Neptune proves himself to be a reformed deity of the new school, happy to accede to the bourgeois desire to indulge the passions. According to Holbach, 'To forbid men their passions is to forbid them to be men,'[53] for, as Diderot reminded, 'they are also the source of men's pleasures'.[54] Mozart was in clear agreement with these sentiments. 'We are created for man's pleasures. How can we help it if an accident befalls by which we become the opposite of them?' asks the subject of one of his 'Zoroastrian Riddles' of 1786. 'If he is lacking one of us, then he is – defective.' The answer to the riddle (not given by Mozart) must, of course, be 'the passions'.[55]

The passions had to be legitimized to ensure that there would no longer be a conflict between pleasure and duty. 'To make man happy through virtue: that is the great problem which ethics must undertake to resolve,' Holbach recognized.[56] Instead of suppressing the passions the Enlightenment attempted to sublimate them into the principle of social harmony, a process that is clearly evident in the alterations made by Varesco and Mozart to Danchet's libretto.

Danchet's *Idomenée* is an obviously rationalist work, posing a clear conflict between reason and the passions, presented in the progress of Ilia and Electra through the drama. The introduction of Electra into the Idomeneo story by Danchet has no legendary precedent. Primarily she exists to bring with her into the story all the associations of sacrifice and retribution which haunt the family of Agamemnon. *Idomenée* opens with a scene which deliberately recalls the opening of the *Oresteia*, with its announcement of the storm that has destroyed the victorious homecoming fleet from Troy, drowned those aboard, and deprived Argos/Crete of its ruler. Electra awaits the arrival of the fleet in both plays, and Ilia, the captive daughter of the vanquished Priam, is the exact counterpart of Cassandra, another daughter of Priam in the *Oresteia*.

The passage of the two women through the opera charts the alternation of reason and unreason. Both women start off determined upon vengeance – Elettra for her betrayal by Idamante, Ilia for her family and city. Ilia, as we shall see, transcends the conflict. But Elettra is unable to overcome her passions, and so is destroyed by them. In Danchet's text, she appeals to Venus to help her. To the rationalist, Venus the goddess of love personifies the most dangerous and debilitating passion of all. As Aphrodite in Euripides's *Hippolytus* and in Racine's *Phèdre* (and also from the story of *Psyche*) Venus is a dangerous goddess, jealous, wilful, unforgiving. 'Implacable Vénus, trop cruelle Déesse!'[57] is how Danchet's Electra advisedly addresses her, a designation which survives in Varesco's adaptation.

In Danchet's *Idomenée*, Vénus exacts her revenge on the victorious Idomeneo by creating a love triangle between Idomeneo, Idamante and Ilia, summoning Jalousie, her closest associate, to 'rend the sacred bonds of blood and nature and extinguish the murmur of reason and duty'. In Varesco's adaptation of the libretto for Mozart the personification of the passions, so popular in baroque works, is excised. Electra retains her jealous longings and her fearsome desire for vengeance, expressed in an aria of awesome fury; but it becomes evident that her behaviour is due to mental derangement, the Enlightenment's preferred rationalization of such excessively anti-social behaviour.

Ilia follows a different course. In her opening aria in Mozart's and Varesco's opera, she weighs the conflicting demands of vengeance for her family and love for her captor Idamante: 'Vengeance is due to him who gave me life, but gratitude to him who spared me.' It is a classic Corneillean conflict between love and duty, but one which the bourgeois Enlightenment wishes to deny by rejecting the neo-stoical suppression of feelings like love. Voltaire had mocked the classical portrayal of love as 'wild, barbaric, doomed, and followed by crimes and remorse',[58] and in *La religieuse* Diderot clearly indicated the dangers of attempting to deny natural sexuality.[59]

Pleasurable passions like love were instead to be moralized, and turned into 'virtuous capabilities'. Thus Norman Bryson describes the subject of Watteau's *Meeting in a Park* in which 'an attempt is being conducted, by a small group of highly civilized people, to take the greedy, raw material of eros and transform it into a principle of social harmony'.[60] Sexual love was now to be shown to be beneficent. 'Why should it not be possible to unite love and virtue?' asked Wieland in his widely read novel *Agathon* of 1766–7.[61] For Hume, the 'natural appetite between the sexes' was, like Freud's famous libido, 'the first and original principle of human society',[62] and for Rousseau's follower Bernardin de Saint-Pierre, love was quite simply 'le lien de tous'.[63] In *An Essay on Man* Pope draws a ravishing picture of a whole world held together by erotic attraction:

> Look round our World; behold the Chain of Love
> Combining all below and all above.
> See plastic Nature working to this end,
> The single atoms each to other tend,
> Attract, attracted to, the next in place,
> Form'd and impell'd its neighbour to embrace.[64]

It was the natural instinct of love, not the coercive power of external rules, or personal self-denial in the cause of duty, which held society together, the bourgeois Enlightenment claimed. And as Kierkegaard recognized, the power of the erotic lies at the core of Mozart's operas, present in almost every bar of his sensuous, and yes, sensual music.

There are few love duets in baroque opera, and one of the most telling alterations made to the text of *Idomeneo* by Mozart and Varesco was the addition of a love duet between Ilia and Idamante. It guides us to Ilia's true role in the story, adumbrated from the very outset of the opera when she is described as the agent of reconciliation: 'Helen armed Greece and

Asia, but now this new heroine, this most lovable and beautiful princess, disarms and reunites Greece and Troy.' The sundering of the known world, which had been caused by Helen's submission to an adulterous sexual passion, will be repaired through the moral, conjugal love of Ilia for Idamante.

LOVE AND MARRIAGE

Idomeneo concludes with a long ballet, a masque celebrating the marriage of Idamante and Ilia in which Amor, Hymen and Juno, the gods of love and marriage, are enjoined to descend from heaven to bless the couple. In the past the goddesses of love and marriage, Venus and Juno, had always been implacable enemies, their realms apparently mutually exclusive;[65] seventeenth-century moralists like Milton had invariably lauded the superior virtues of rational, companionate marriage rather than marriage based upon sexual love. But the Enlightenment was able to signal its moralization of love by enthroning a benign Amor (or Eros) in place of Venus as the new god of love. Eros is accordingly the presiding deity of eighteenth-century art, an apt externalization of the Enlightenment's pagan morality of feeling. Many of Mozart's heroes and heroines address their prayers to Love as a deity: Ramiro in *La finta giardiniera*, the Countess in *Le nozze di Figaro*, and Belmonte in *Die Entführung aus dem Serail* all pray to Love to aid and succour them:

> For ah, what works
> Have been brought about by you!
> What seems impossible to all the world
> Can still be achieved by love.

sings Belmonte in his tender tribute to Amor, bringing to the altar of Love his garlands of vocal fioritura.

In replacing Venus with Amor, the Enlightenment was able to reconcile love and marriage. And it was in marriage that any possible contradictions between erotic love and the needs of society could be overcome. Marriage became one of the central institutions of bourgeois society, capable of mediating the whole network of potentially conflicting demands of society: individual desire, family and property, religion and the state. Above all, marriage assumed the magical prowess of being able to unite 'virtue and happiness, innocence and pleasure'.[66]

In most European societies in the Middle Ages, marriage had been considered a private agreement in which the simple exchange of vows between two partners was the crucial condition; betrothal before witnesses was more binding than a church wedding, and was regarded even in ecclesiastical law as irrevocable.[67] The Church itself, with its idealization of celibacy, had long disdained to involve itself with matters sexual, even in marriage. But gradually the view that marriage should be regulated by the Church came to predominate, although marriage only became a sacrament in the fifteenth century, and it was not until the sixteenth century that the presence of a priest was required for a marriage to be valid.[68]

The Church's new interest in marriage was to be matched by that of the state, and by the eighteenth century Montesquieu could argue that 'as marriage is of all human actions that in which society is most interested, it becomes proper that this should be regulated by civil laws'.[69] In England, the Hardwicke Marriage Act of 1754 became the first piece of state legislation on marriage;[70] on the Continent, rationalizing monarchies with enlightened aims attempted to cut through the tangled accretions of local custom and feudal law surrounding marriage to establish uniform regulations that could be policed by the state. Joseph II's marriage decree, the *Ehepatent* of 1783, to effect just this was a crucial item in his reform programme.

As always, mythologization of the new values accompanied social and political reality. In Gluck's *Orfeo* Orpheus is rewarded for his conjugal devotion in rescuing Euridice, and in defying the unnatural injunction not to look at her, by Euridice's restoration to life by Amor, rather than being punished for his weakness ('conquered by his emotions') as in Monteverdi's earlier version of the story. The most popular of conjugal myths in the eighteenth century was that of Alcestis, the story of the wife of a much-beloved king who has been told that he is soon to die, and who offers herself to the gods in his place. Euripides's play *Alkestis*, from which all later versions derive, is primarily about the Greek laws of hospitality. But in its eighteenth-century variants, in particular by Wieland, and Gluck and Calzabigi, the story was taken to exemplify the strength of the new marital ideals, (as is also well recognized in a French operatic setting of the story in 1755, entitled not *Alceste* but *Le triomphe de l'amour conjugal*).[71]

The complete absorption of the Enlightenment's ethical ideal of marriage is nowhere more clearly articulated than in the letters of Mozart himself. In 1778 Mozart wrote to his father from the fleshpots of Paris to report on the successful performance there of a new symphony: the 'Paris' symphony. His account shows how completely he had absorbed the bourgeois Enlightenment's casual elision of pleasure, virtue and easy-going religious observance:

As soon as the symphony was over, I went off to the Palais Royal, where I had a large ice, said the Rosary as I had vowed to do – and went home – for I always am and always will be happiest there, or else in the company of some good, true, honest German who, if he is a bachelor, lives alone like a good Christian, or, if married, loves his wife and brings up his children properly.[72]

Mozart's picture of good German bourgeois morals holding out against the allure of French *ancien-régime* decadence was a clear expression of his own sense of dislocation in Paris. But although Mozart continued to be faithful to the ideal of the honest German throughout his life, he did not recommend the state of bachelordom for long: 'A bachelor, in my opinion', he told Leopold in 1781, 'is only half alive'.[73] Sexuality was natural and could not be artificially repressed, and Mozart was healthily frank about his sexual desires and needs, unabashedly telling his father that 'The voice of nature speaks as loud in me as in others, louder perhaps than in many a big strong lout of a fellow'.[74]

But a certain sexual fastidiousness, evident in the disgust he expresses elsewhere in recounting the advances of a fat and sweaty pupil, combined with his undoubted religious feelings and his sense of propriety and self-respect, prevented him from satisfying his sexual needs in the customary manner for young men at the time.

I simply cannot live as most young men do in these days. In the first place, I have too much religion; in the second place I have too high a feeling of honour to seduce an innocent girl; and in the third place, I have too much horror and disgust, too much dread and fear of diseases and too much care for my health to fool around with whores.[75]

This letter was written to prepare Leopold for the news of Mozart's impending engagement to Constanze Weber, and to explain why it was so important that he marry her. There is no reason to suppose that Mozart was simply mouthing pieties his father wanted to hear. Each of his sentiments is corroborated by what we know of him elsewhere: his religious beliefs; his rigid sense of sexual honour (conveyed in several letters reproaching Constanze for making too free with her favours); and above all his fear of venereal disease, which had been drummed into him by Leopold.[76] (Mozart must certainly have borne constantly in mind too the horrific fate of the composer Mysliwicek, his face eaten away by syphilis, whom he had visited in hospital in Munich.) Shortly after writing to his father about his sexual needs, Mozart announced his marriage to Constanze. That Mozart should have regarded marriage as the natural place in which to fulfil his sexual desires indicates how well the Enlightenment had done its job of persuasion, and how effectively marriage had become a means of licensing pleasure whilst invisibly restraining it.

THE FAMILY

The celebration of the moral power of love and marriage in *Idomeneo* to restore political harmony between Greece and Troy is supported by a second theme central to the bourgeois Enlightenment: the sentimental idealization of the family. For it is not only Ilia's love for Idamante that heals the wounds between Troy and Greece and between Idomeneo and his son, but also Ilia's deliberate transference of filial affection and loyalty from her dead father to Idomeneo. Two out of Ilia's three arias are declarations of filial love. In her troubled opening aria 'Padre, germani', Ilia laments the loss of her father and relatives, and contemplates avenging their deaths. But in her second aria, Ilia transfers her filial love to Idomeneo himself, adopting him as a new father:

> Since I have lost my father,
> My fatherland and peace,
> You shall be my father.

The rationalist conflict which Ilia had initially perceived between love and duty is overcome by recognizing an ideal superior to family vengeance: a duty to the present and future, rather than to the past.[77] The gentle benediction of her love briefly soothes Idomeneo's own torment, lingering on in the music that accompanies his recitative of defiance against fate.

Ilia's change of heart is telling. For the abandonment of customary systems of vengeance and retribution has always been one of the crucial indications of the transition from primitive forms of social organization to more developed social structures. If a rationalization of law is to take place, the ancient rules of tribal vendetta and familial revenge which dominate a warrior society (as medieval feudal society had largely been) must be abandoned. In *Idomeneo*, however, the obligation to revenge is transcended not by the state (as in the *Oresteia*), but by the sentimental power of the family.

In *Les lettres persanes*, Montesquieu noted the emergence of the new ideal of sentimental social harmony in early eighteenth-century England (an ideal that overturned Hobbes's contention that people only enter into social relations out of fear and the desire for mutual protection): 'According to them [the English], there is only one thing which can form a bond between men, and that is gratitude: husband and wife, father and daughter are united only by their love for each other or the benefits they confer on each other; and these different motives for gratitude lie at the origin of every kingdom and every society.'[78] In the sentimental vision of the Enlightenment, society may itself become one big family. 'By the exercise of brotherly love', wrote Lessing, in his masonic dialogues *Ernst und Falk*, 'we are taught to regard the whole human race as one family, the high and the low, the rich and the poor, created by one Almighty Being, and sent into the world for the aid, support and protection of each other.'[79] Brotherhood is, of course, the ideal relationship promoted by free-masonry, based upon the notion of an order whose familial ties transcend national, social and religious differences; *fraternité* is also one of the ideals of the bourgeois revolutionaries of the French Revolution.

The realities of power in society were thus to be masked by sentimental fictions designed to replace coercive obedience with familial loyalty, serv-ing, as Burke admitted with curious candour, to promote 'pleasing illusions, which made power gentle and obedience liberal.'[80] For Metasta-sio (who had evidently read Montesquieu on this matter), however desir-able the civic ideal of republican virtue might be, 'supreme paternal authority' was a more reliable and amenable basis for social submission.[81] The sentimental adulation of one of Metastasio's own patrons, Maria Theresa, was admiringly observed in 1777 by a visitor to Vienna: 'Nothing can more strongly prove the species of maternal power which the Empress exercises over her people, which sometimes assumes a religious, at other times a political, or moral character. They obey with a sort of filial submission, in which respect and attachment are blended.'[82] The com-poser Karl Dittersdorf related in his autobiography how – 'like Ilia' – he had appealed to his employer the Bishop of Pressburg to call him his son; the bishop agreed in the fullest sentimental spirit of the request: ' "Well", the Bishop said after a short pause, "granted if you really want it so badly. And if you want me to act like a father, then I must be permitted to consider you my son." At that he dried his tears which were running down his cheeks.'[83] 'To us, through feelings of caring love, he is both king and father,' sing the loyal chorus in Gebler's play *Thamos*, set to music by Mozart.

By the mid-century the monarch is no longer represented as the remote, quasi-divine figure of baroque art, but presides at the centre of his family. George III is portrayed in domestic informality by Zoffany; the Emperor Francis-Stephen and his wife Maria Theresa take tea, teapot, cups and saucers on the table beside them. The image of the bourgeois king and his family was carefully cultivated to confer moral authority upon the monarchy; a French diarist describes the libertine Louis XV greeting his children at Fontainebleau, noting how 'The king kissed them, first one, then the other, for a quarter of an hour, crying like a good Parisian bourgeois head of the family.'[84] In 1785 maternal images of Marie-Antoinette with her children were displayed at the Paris Salon in an effort to counter the queen's increasing unpopularity and the (quite unwarranted) rumours that she was wicked and wanton.

This adulation of the family skilfully blurred the distinctions between individual desires and public duty; in Gluck's *Alceste*, Alceste demonstrates that there need be no conflict: familial devotion and duty are shown to be one and same thing. 'Non, ce n'est point un sacrifice' she sings (in the final version of the opera) as she confirms her decision to die to save her husband. As Idomeneo laments the prospect of losing his son, Idamante reminds him that 'Your People are your sons'. When Idomeneo accepts the filial love of Ilia he is not simply accepting a replacement for the love of his doomed son; he is gaining a new subject: 'If you are seeking one in my place to obey and love you', Idamante says as he urges Idomeneo to fulfil the command to kill him '. . . then let me commend Ilia to you . . . if she is not to be my bride, then let her be your daughter.'

But the second purpose of the promotion of the family has always been to locate alternative sources of authority within bourgeois society itself, to provide a stabilizing counterweight to the anarchic effects of capitalist individualism. The bourgeois Enlightenment therefore enthroned the family as an unchanging institution of nature. 'The most ancient of all societies, and the only one that is natural, is the family,' writes Rousseau in *Du contrat social*.[85] Once naturalized and mythologized, it could be endowed with the supreme moral authority of society. Voltaire's 'natural law, independent of all human conventions' includes the command 'I must honour my father and my mother'.[86] And it was during the eighteenth century that the family first assumed the aura of quasi-religious sanctity which was to become so nauseating in the nineteenth century.[87]

We need be in no doubt of the authoritarian implications that lie behind the promotion of the family. Locke, while in exile in Holland from the would-be absolutism of James II in England, had argued in his *Treatises of Government* against the biblical principle of patriarchy as the basis of society. But for Addison, writing in a post-revolutionary society in 1711, the patriarchal family was brought firmly back to the centre as the foundation and guarantee of social order: 'The Obedience of Children to their parents is the basis for all Government,'[88] he asserted firmly. The quasi-anarchic vision of a society without princes and rulers imagined by Adam Weishaupt, founder of the late eighteenth-century masonic Illuminati (see p. 193) in the 1780s, is of a society like that of the tribes of Israel during the time of Abraham, in which every head of family is both 'priest and unlimited ruler' of his family.[89]

During the course of the eighteenth century, family virtues became sacrosanct. The 'filial piety' of Hercules' son Hylas inspired Handel to one of his finest choruses in the oratorio *Hercules*, and filial piety became one of the catchphrases of the age, the title of numerous sentimental dramas. (The quasi-religious term used – filial *piety* rather than filial love – is, of course, not fortuitous.) To complement the frequent portrayal of filial loyalty, the Enlightenment promoted numerous images of the good and loving father, such as Diderot's *Le père de famille*, and Gemmingen's Diderot-inspired *Der deutsche Hausvater*, written the same year as *Idomeneo*. In France Greuze's famous paintings of patriarchal families are matched by numerous literary works with titles such as *Le respect filial, Le pouvoir de l'amour paternel*, and *Le bon fils*.[90]

This elevation of the patriarchal family as a vehicle of alternative authority within an individualistic society creates enormous tensions and conflicts; tensions which are fully evident in *Idomeneo*. For of course, the father who sacrifices his son is in some ways merely enacting the reality of patriarchal authority in society; a bourgeois society needs strong fathers. But overly despotic, sacrificing fathers limit the freedom of their children and prevent the progressive revolution of generations upon which bourgeois society also depends for its survival. At a time when in France disobedient sons could still be committed to prison by their fathers by the simple use of the notorious *lettres de cachet* (a fate suffered by the thirty-year-old Diderot in 1743), the parental sacrifice motive must have rung true for many a son.

But paradoxically, if parental power is insufficiently strong, it also curtails the generational succession upon which the progress of society depends. For as Theodor Adorno observed, bourgeois society may need tyrannical fathers to give its sons something to kick against; indeed, the bourgeois family 'by repressing the individual . . . also strengthened, perhaps even produced him'.[91] Defoe knew this perfectly well; his Robinson Crusoe describes his decision to disobey his father and leave his home for sea as a necessary sin, a *felix culpa* for which he is richly rewarded.[92] No longer able to rebel against the tyranny of God (who has been proved just and loving) the Enlightenment son had to transfer his rebellion to the alternative sources of authority set up by bourgeois society to replace God.

Something of these contradictions clearly coloured Mozart's own relationship with his father during the composition of *Idomeneo*. Leopold made inordinate sacrificial demands upon his son, loading him with an appalling sense of guilt for his longings for independence, and constantly reminding Wolfgang that God had commanded that 'children must honour their parents', – and that He had supported this command with the sanction of punishments.[93]

In Mozart's revised conclusion to *Idomeneo*, Idamante escapes sacrifice by his father and is made King of Crete by Neptune in his place, a solution to which Idomeneo gracefully accedes, enjoining his people to accept the new dispensation. Thus the painful transition from parental dependence to filial independence is ideally achieved. But it was one which Mozart himself made with more difficulty, and for which he long suffered. Many years after Mozart's death, Constanze Mozart was to recall that on a visit made by Wolfgang and herself to Leopold and Nannerl Mozart in Salzburg in 1783, the family had sung the great quartet from *Idomeneo*. Wolfgang had taken the role of Idamante, the son who must agree to leave his homeland for exile abroad to escape being sacrificed by his father Idomeneo, sung by Leopold. But according to Constanze, Wolfgang 'was so overcome that he burst into tears and quit the chamber'.[94] Surely he must have identified the operatic situation with his own revolt against the overbearing, sacrificial demands of his father, and with the fact that to obtain his freedom he had had to leave Salzburg (his home town, however much he hated it) for Vienna.

PART TWO
VIENNA · THE YEARS OF OPTIMISM
1781–1786

VII

Vienna and the Enlightenment

Among the fifty or so books to be found in Mozart's small personal library after his death there was only one novel.[1] It was entitled *Faustin, oder das philosophische Jahrhundert*, and was by his contemporary and probable friend Johann Pezzl. Pezzl had studied law in Salzburg between 1776 and 1780, a period when Mozart too was based in the city. Between 1781 and 1784, having written an ill-advised satire on monasticism (the one institution which all strands of the Enlightenment were united in condemning) Pezzl found it expedient to take refuge in Protestant Switzerland, where he completed his major novel *Faustin* in 1784 before moving to Vienna, the city in whose praise the novel was written.[2]

Faustin is a Catholic Candide whose tutor Pater Boniface attempts to convince him that in 1748, 'dawn broke in Europe', since when 'there has been the general victory of reason and humanity . . . this has been the enlightened, philosophical century'.[3] Faustin sets off with his tutor to experience the fruits of the philosophical century for himself. But travelling throughout Europe and the New World, Faustin is everywhere disillusioned by the ignorance, superstition and cruelty he encounters. In London, still considered the haven of liberty and toleration in Europe, Boniface is killed in the anti-Catholic Gordon riots of 1780, and an initially enthusiastic visit to Frederick the Great's Berlin is also soured by disillusionment. Faustin finally turns to Vienna, where he is at last convinced of the truth of the lamented Boniface's belief in the triumph of Enlightenment. Here, Pezzl's hero joyfully proclaims, 'under the rule of Joseph, will be the complete victory of reason and humanity. Will be the philosophical century.'

> This long-desired, long-awaited epoch,
> which will raise up all Germany, began in the year
> 1780
> Began with the rule of our beloved Joseph[4]

There is in Faustin's joyous arrival in Vienna a parallel with the turning-point in Mozart's life: his own arrival in Vienna, which was to be his home for ten years, early in 1781. Like Faustin, Mozart had left his native home Salzburg in search of a congenial base, travelling throughout Europe and meeting everywhere with rebuffs, and had at last found his way to Vienna at exactly the moment when it seemed to promise everything. Within a month of his arrival he was writing exuberantly (and not without reason) to his anxious father in Salzburg that Vienna was 'a splendid place – and for my métier the best one in the world. Everyone will tell you the same.'[5] Before long he had engineered his dismissal from his restricting post with the Archbishop of Salzburg and had launched himself upon the dynamic musical free market of Vienna, at the same time plunging into a frenzy of social, intellectual and cultural activity.

Vienna, the largest and – thanks to the reforms of Maria Theresa and her son Joseph – by 1780 one of richest cities in Germany,[6] offered the twenty-four-year-old Mozart at last a worthy forum for his talents. But Mozart's journeys had been spurred by more than a need for a suitable market; they were the expression of a troubled search for his identity as a man and artist. Arrival in Vienna was in many respects the homecoming of which he had dreamt for so long. Under Joseph, for a few brief, feverish years, Vienna became the freest, most open, liberal and tolerant city in Europe, guided by the purposeful vision and forthright hand of the emperor himself. Vienna also promised to become the seat of a renewed German culture in which theatre and opera played a central role. And at the core of Joseph II's very personal vision of an enlightened society was a strong devotion to a reformed Catholic faith.

THE ENLIGHTENED DESPOT

It is impossible to over-emphasize the excitement with which Joseph II's accession to the throne as sole ruler of the Habsburg territories in November 1780 was greeted by those in Austria and elsewhere in Europe dedicated to the ideals of the Enlightenment, a euphoria which is well conveyed in Pezzl's breathless hyperbole. Expectations of Joseph were high. His reputation as a son of the Enlightenment had been well trailed; as early as 1769 Voltaire was assured by Grimm that the young emperor was 'one of us'.[7] He and his brother Leopold (subsequently ruler of Tuscany) had been educated according to the best rationalist principles, and in the doctrines of natural law; in Pompeo Batoni's double portrait of the young Joseph and Leopold a copy of Montesquieu's *L'esprit des lois* rests on the table beside them. In 1777 Joseph had made a conspicuously incognito visit to Paris, where he met and engaged with many of the most prominent *philosophes*.

Within a very short time, Joseph introduced a series of measures that appeared to meet in one fell swoop all the main demands of the Enlightenment, and that did indeed bring Austria into the front rank of progressive nations. Press freedom was introduced, and literary censorship was greatly relaxed. The number of prohibited books declined from almost 5,000 to 900 (mainly papal, atheist and pornographic books).[8] Religious toleration was granted, and monasteries were dissolved. By the end of the decade feudal serfdom had been abolished, and the principle of complete equality of the citizen before the law was finally established. In 1787 the death penalty was abolished in Habsburg territories at a time when, in the land of freedom, the English Parliament was frenetically adding crimes that warranted hanging to the statute book: some 200 by 1800, including sheep-stealing.[9] Joseph's programme seemed to encapsulate everything the Enlightenment had fought for so vigorously over the past century. Austria under Joseph was where the dream of Voltaire and Montesquieu, of Rousseau and Lessing, and of so many others, seemed finally to have come to fruition.

This was not an image which Austria had hitherto enjoyed. For most of the eighteenth century Vienna had been considered the capital of an obscurantist backwater. It was viewed as the bastion of the Counter-Reformation north of the Alps, socially and economically primitive, and hag-ridden by the favourite target of Enlightenment demonology, the Jesuits. Until their abolition in 1774 virtually all education in Austria was controlled by the Jesuits, and until 1751, when the task was taken over by the government, they had also controlled censorship. In 1774 the list of books on the government's censorship files was longer than the papal index, and included most of the major texts of the English and French Enlightenment. Maria Theresa, notorious for her piety and primness, had blocked the efforts of her great Chancellor Kaunitz to introduce Protestant scholars from northern Germany to Austrian universities, and she banned the teaching of English writers, whom she considered uniformly subversive of religion and morality.[10] In the late 1770s an English visitor to Vienna could report that 'Natural philosophy has scarcely made greater progress in Vienna, than sound reason and real religion',[11] and estimated that some 3000 alchemists were at work in the city seeking the philosopher's stone. Already by the mid-century, traditional education in Austria had fallen so far behind the needs of a modern state that many of the lesser aristocracy were sending their sons to Protestant universities in northern Germany or Holland to be educated.

Unlike northern Germany and Switzerland, Austria had at Joseph's accession made no significant contribution to the Enlightenment, and appeared culturally isolated from the rest of Europe. But Joseph's programme was no sudden aberration (as later historians often implied). His mother Maria Theresa was devout and conservative. But she and her advisers, particularly her Chancellor Kaunitz, were also aware of the desperate need for administrative and economic reforms within her terri- tories if the widespread Habsburg inheritance, threatened with disinte- gration at the beginning of her reign, was to remain intact. As a result, Maria Theresa (ruling from 1765 with her son) had presided over a whole series of measures designed to push a sluggish society towards the economic growth upon which the survival of the Habsburg Empire depended.

The pragmatic rather than ideological considerations which lie behind this programme are clear. From his reading of Voltaire and Montesquieu, Joseph had gained a shrewd understanding of the relationship between economic growth and social and religious freedoms. In 1774 he wrote to his mother in angry response to her efforts to force her Protestant subjects in Bohemia to conform to the Roman Church or leave the country: 'Things cannot be done by halves. Either complete freedom of religion, or you must drive out of your lands everyone who does not believe as you do . . . To drive away the living, good farmers and excellent subjects, in order to save the souls of the dead – what arrogance of power!'[12] 'For industry, for commerce,' he wrote elsewhere, 'nothing is more necessary than liberty, nothing more harmful than privileges and monopolies.'[13]

As absolutist monarchs had done before them, Maria Theresa and her son launched a virulent campaign against the feudal powers and the social and financial privileges of the nobility and Estates (the representative provincial bodies of the nobility), aimed at 'humbling the nobles' and destroying their power.[14] Both Maria Theresa and Joseph refused to rule through the Hungarian and Bohemian Diets in which the nobility traditionally exercised power, or to acknowledge the claims of the Estates beyond the minimal formalities required. The law was progressively re- codified to introduce the principle of legal equality and the nobility – to their horror – found themselves subjected to the same penalties as com- moners for crimes, and eventually to the same taxation.

To support these reforms the monarchy had encouraged the introduc- tion of the latest rationalist thinking; most particularly, the theories of rational natural law of the school of Pufendorf and Wolff, introduced from northern Germany with the establishment of chairs of natural law and political economy (*Cameralwissenchaft*)[15] at Vienna University. But unofficial contacts with the wider Enlightenment were also evident. Vienna was at the hub of an empire stretching from Italy to the Nether- lands (modern-day Belgium), a fact that gave it an extraordinary breadth of cultural and intellectual influence. Despite the Jesuits' control of the official organs of intellectual discourse in Austria until the mid-century, there were many who were able to make contact with centres of radical dissent in Holland and, just across the water from the Austrian Netherlands, England. The great military commander Prince Eugene of Savoy, who had been based in The Hague before being appointed Governor of the Austrian Netherlands in 1724, had cultivated Locke's pupil, the radical English Deist John Toland, who sent the prince copies of all of his most daring works; Eugene was also the dedicatee of Leibniz's *Monadolia*. Eugene's court in Vienna was an important centre for the perpetuation of the most innovative ideas of the early Enlightenment, and his library (eventually to constitute the foundation for the imperial library, still housed in Fischer von Erlach's baroque masterpiece in the Hofburg) was famous for the scope of its contents.

The dissemination of officially forbidden literature amongst an educated élite in many eighteenth-century states was not only tolerated, but was even tacitly encouraged by reforming rulers. The flourishing clandestine international book trade of the eighteenth century, whose centre was Holland, ensured that most books could be obtained by those with money. Works by Montesquieu and Voltaire, supposedly forbidden in Austria, were to be found in the libraries of most educated people. Joseph II himself is reported to have had a sneaking regard for the utilitarian theories of writers like Helvétius and Holbach[16] (banned in Austria for their atheism), and Joseph's wife, Isabella of Parma, a woman in whom religious devotion was combined with an enormously wide intellectual learning had, like most literate people in Europe, read Rousseau's *La nouvelle Héloïse*.[17] The library of Haydn's patron Prince Nikolaus Esterházy contained a number of English and French novels, including *La nouvelle Héloïse*, ordered from booksellers in Holland, and by 1772 the influx of English books was so great that the imperial censor Gerhard van Swieten insisted that at least one member of the censorship commission should be able to read English. It is clear from a perusal of Joseph von Sonnenfels's weekly journal *Der Mann ohne Vorurtheil* that novels by Defoe and Richardson were commonly read in Austria in the 1760s, and Sonnenfels was able to cite both Voltaire and Rousseau (describing himself as 'ein anderer Rousseau' in 1765)[18] in the journal, with the clear expectation that his readers would know what he was talking about.

Sonnenfels's was the most prominent voice in promoting the ideals of the Enlightenment during the years of Joseph II's co-rule with his mother. He was primarily a jurist (the new Professor of *Cameralwissenschaft* at the University) who believed that a powerful state, dedicated to the rationalization of society, would encourage prosperity and progress. But he also recognized that the necessary weakening of religious authority and of the hierarchical structures of feudal society were likely to create social instability. Sonnenfels's writings in the 1760s and 1770s show that the reforms of Maria Theresa and Joseph had borne fruit in the emergence of a significant bourgeoisie in Vienna. For his primary preoccupation was with the problem of how the desires of this new class of people (those of 'mittleren Klassen') with wealth and individualist aspirations might be brought into harmony with the wider needs of the state.[19]

THE PUBLIC SPHERE

One of the most characteristic features of the bourgeois Enlightenment was the identification of an autonomous sphere for the dissemination of the new social consensus. Hobbes, the apologist for absolutism, had argued that there could be no security outside the strong state,[20] but John Locke, the apologist for the bourgeoisie, had suggested that between 'Divine Law' (manifested by revelation or the light of nature – not by the Church, we may note), which determines metaphysical good and evil, and 'Civil Law' (the law of the state) there existed a third sphere of social influence, the 'Law of opinion or reputation', legislating for those areas of human activity not covered by the divine or civil law, and by which men judge what is commonly known as 'virtue and vice'. The judgement of moral virtue and vice Locke considered to pertain to 'society' rather than to God or the state.[21] For Rousseau, the moral law of society was of far greater importance and influence than either civil, political or criminal law. The moral law, he writes, 'is not graven on tablets of marble or brass, but on the hearts of citizens. This forms the real constitution of the State, takes on every day new powers, when other laws decay or die out, restores them or takes their place, keeps a people in the ways in which it was meant to go, and insensibly replaces authority by the forces of habit.'[22]

The sphere of opinion that Locke had identified as secret and tacit soon becomes public and manipulable. The development of what we now call public opinion is one of the most notable attributes of eighteenth-century society, and of the Enlightenment itself. The Enlightenment set its sights on very specific and carefully selected targets, and laid patient siege to institutions of influence and power. And it understood supremely well the importance of capturing and manipulating public opinion; setting agendas and of forcing debate to be conducted on its own terms. 'What was not to be done towards their great end by any direct or immediate act, might be wrought by a longer process through the medium of opinion',[23] complained the great English Tory Edmund Burke, on the successful manipulation of public opinion by the *encyclopédistes* in France. In 1775 Sonnenfels, emulating his own mentors, succeeded in getting torture abolished in Austria after a virulent campaign to convince Viennese public opinion of its iniquity.

'It was said of Socrates, that he brought Philosophy down from Heaven, to inhabit among Men; and I shall be ambitious to have it said of me, that I have brought Philosophy out of Closets and Libraries, Schools and Colleges, to dwell in Clubs and Assemblies, at Tea Tables and in Coffee Houses,' wrote Joseph Addison in an early edition of the *Spectator*.[24] Seventy years later in Vienna one of Addison's spiritual heirs, the playwright and satirist Josef Richter, similarly claimed that his *A. B. C. Buch für grosse Kinder* was 'a philosophical dictionary aimed at the man in the coffee house'.[25] The influence of public opinion went hand-in-hand with the creation and development of the familiar institutions of eighteenth-century urban society that constituted what has been called 'the public sphere'. Hence there sprang up the parks and pleasure gardens that played so large a part in eighteenth-century urban society (the Ranelagh or Vauxhall Gardens in London – depicted as Arcadian idylls by Gainsborough – in which so many incidents of social confusion take place in Fanny Burney's novels). Public assembly rooms and concert halls met the leisure demands of an expanding bourgeoisie, while in coffee-shops, reading rooms and salons, political, social and intellectual gossip might be traded. It is not without reason that historians have often looked back on the eighteenth century as the pre-eminently sociable age.

The public sphere is a supposedly neutral ground, free of the partisanship of politics, religion or class, where opinions may be disseminated in safety, divorced from the real power relationships or economic realities of society. Here people of different caste and status could mix freely without violating the essential social hierarchies. This is the new heterogeneous society characterized by Lord Chesterfield as 'Good Company' which 'consists chiefly (but by no means without exception) of people of considerable birth, rank and character; for people of neither birth nor rank are frequently, and very justly, admitted into it, if distinguished by any particular merit, or eminency in any liberal art or science'.[26]

In Queen Anne's London, the old partisan pamphlets and broadsides of an age of violent political conflict were replaced by the new moral weekly journals, primarily the *Tatler* and the *Spectator*, whose purpose was to forge a consensus of opinion regarding taste in the arts, and behaviour and manners in society. The *Tatler* and the *Spectator* make a claim for an urbane impartiality,[27] appealing to reasonable common sense and courtesy rather than precepts or rules, let alone the postures of dogmatic prejudice.

The *Tatler* and *Spectator* aimed to domesticate the unruly aristocracy of the Restoration, and to endow the rougher edges of the new bourgeoisie with civilized social graces and a sense of social responsibility derived from the best of aristocratic culture. If the minutiae of civilized social exchange could be charted and presented in a way agreeable to all parties, what did it matter about the internal state of a man's soul, or the ruthless and cut-throat exploitations of commerce and industry necessary to sustain society in its civilizing pursuits?

The influence of the English moral weekly spread throughout Europe. In Germany and Switzerland there are estimated to have been some 500 imitations of the *Spectator*,[28] many of which reprinted articles directly from the English original, and by the 1760s moral weeklies were also appearing in Vienna. The longest-lived and most influential of these was Sonnenfels's journal *Der Mann ohne Vorurtheil*, which first appeared in 1767. The journal's title (The Man without Prejudice), and Sonnenfels's own description of himself in the journal as the *Beobachter* (spectator, observer)[29] pay obvious homage to Addison. Sonnenfels's articles from the journal were republished in 1784 in an edition of his complete works, of which the first four volumes (in which the *Mann ohne Vorurtheil* articles reappear) were owned by Mozart.

Sonnenfels recognized that, as Spinoza said, human nature 'will not submit to unlimited coercion'.[30] Laws can only achieve so much. The bourgeoisie must be wooed and educated to recognize their duty and the greater good of society. 'An enlightened people obeys because it wants to; one led by prejudice because it must.'[31] Underlying the pleasing mixture of social commentary, critical reviews and gossip of *Der Mann ohne Vorurtheil* is a message for the rising Viennese bourgeoisie, persuading it to conform to a new ideal of moral and social responsibility. Unable to find a suitable phrase to convey his idea in German, he adapts an English phrase: 'This "Spirit Public" '.[32] Sonnenfels considered the creation of this enlightened 'spirit public' to be the most important task facing the modern legislator, educator and artist: 'Therefore it must be recognized that the most important aim is to ensure the uniting of the individual with the general good ... through which the individual citizen is bonded to society as a whole, bringing the understanding of the honourable citizen to enlightenment, and at the same time, ensuring that his own desires are met.'[33]

Sonnenfels's journal suffered frequently from censorship during Maria Theresa's reign, since he incurred the implacable hostility of the Viennese Archbishop Migazzi. But when in 1780 Joseph II was left as sole ruler, he and his advisers clearly took Sonnenfels's words of advice to heart in their determination to create an informed and enlightened public, and to promote a consensus of modern social morality.

Joseph's relaxation of literary and press censorship unleashed a torrent of publications, including some 1200 pamphlets and brochures within the space of one year.[34] Most of these were trivial and ephemeral – much to the emperor's disappointment. But to Aloys Blumauer, poet, member of the new liberal censorship commission, and friend and colleague of Mozart, their function was clear and valuable: it was to perform for the middle and lower orders what books and sophisticated moral weeklies did for the more highly educated classes – to bring about, once again 'True Enlightenment, whose purpose . . . is to bring the individual happiness of the citizen into the closest and most pleasurable relationship with his duty towards God and the State'.[35]

In the wake of the ephemera came more durable gains – the development of a Viennese publishing industry in particular. In 1780 there were six publishers in Vienna, but by 1787 there were twenty-one operating 114 presses, and the economic value of the export of books from Vienna leapt from 135,000 taler per annum in 1773 to 3,260,000 taler in 1792. In the 1730s Vienna, the largest German city, ranked forty-sixth in the table of book-producing German cities; by 1800 she ranked third.[36] As in London at the beginning of the century, booksellers and lending libraries sprang up in response to the new industry, creating new forums for intellectual discussion and the exchange of ideas. The most successful of the Viennese publishers, the millionaire property developer Trattner (of whom Mozart was for a while a tenant in the Trattnerhof near the Graben, and who was godfather to one of Mozart's children) was himself forced to open a reading-room of his own, where readers could peruse the Trattner titles without having to buy them, to counter the success of the other public reading-rooms in Vienna.

During the 1780s there was also an efflorescence of public coffee-houses in Vienna: some seventy by 1790 in a city of around 215,000 inhabitants.[37] A historian of the Viennese coffee-house has written that the coffee-house was to become during this period a virtual substitute for parliament in a country which had no official forums for political debate.[38] 'One doesn't just drink coffee here,' Pezzl tells us in his *Skizze von Wien*, 'one studies, plays, applauds, sleeps, negotiates, haggles, advertises, intrigues, reads papers and journals'.[39] As in London, certain coffee-houses became identified with particular circles of Viennese society: Kramer's on the Graben was well known to be the best place to get hold of international journals, and hence became the most familiar literary meeting place; the Café Stierbock in the Leopoldstadt suburb was a popular masonic haunt, where in 1785 a reception was held for Lafayette, the French hero of the American Revolution.[40]

These developments were an indication of the new liveliness of Viennese intellectual and literary life in the early years of Joseph II's reign, prompting Blumauer to exclaim in 1782, 'Is not Vienna now the sun around which Germany's smaller and lesser planets orbit? Is it not the focus for the whole of Europe? Have philosophy and science themselves ever had such a wide influence?'[41] And this intellectual liveliness was complemented by the deliberately egalitarian openness of Joseph II's own social vision. The imperial gardens, the Prater and the Augarten (in the grounds of which Joseph himself lived quite modestly) were thrown open to the Viennese public, and there, sections of society, from the emperor down, intermingled in social harmony. (Mozart himself promoted a successful series of concerts in the Augarten.) The great ballroom, the Redoutensaal, formerly the preserve of the aristocracy, was made available to all classes at carnival time, and Joseph himself sometimes admitted the public to imperial balls.

'VIENNA SHOULD BE TO GERMANY WHAT PARIS IS TO FRANCE'

But it was the importance of theatre in Viennese life which was to be of greatest significance to Mozart. The promotion of the theatre had been part of the political programme of Maria Theresa and her Chancellor Kaunitz. Their aim was to modernize the Viennese theatre to counteract what was considered the deleterious effect of both the popular, improvised Hanswurst theatre – often scabrous, satirical and of dubious moral taste – and the magical baroque dramas of the Jesuits. For Sonnenfels and his enlightened literary colleagues of the 1760s and 1770s such as Tobias von Gebler, the reform of the Austrian theatre to make it a worthy 'Schule der Sitten' ('school for morals')[42] was to be undertaken in the approved fashion through transfusions of French classical drama and the more recent examples of French sentimental moral drama. Sonnenfels's Gottschedian *Briefe über die wienerische Schaubühne* of 1767–9, outlining his agenda for the reform of Viennese drama, were signed by 'a Frenchman',[43] and initiated his ferocious campaign against the Hanswurst theatre. In 1770, during a brief spell as theatre censor, he succeeded in banning improvisation (so difficult to supervise) from the stage of the Burgtheater altogether.

But as Sonnenfels soon realized, the effect of this promotion of French drama was simply to encourage the development of a new form of aristocratic culture from which all but the French-speaking aristocracy were excluded. It was not what Joseph II or Sonnenfels wanted, and in 1772

Joseph exerted his powers to obtain the withdrawal of the subsidy of the French company in anticipation of his establishment of a German national theatre in Vienna, aimed at the growing bourgeoisie. Joseph's personal interest in the theatre was extraordinary. As an historian of Josephinism has written, 'Joseph saw in the school, the pulpit, and the theatre the three media for the fashioning of public opinion'.[44] He involved himself in the day-to-day running of the two court theatres (until 1776 the only theatres in Vienna) stipulating what kind of works could be performed on certain days of the week,[45] the times of performance, and the minutiae of contracts.

In the course of his frequent journeys outside Vienna Joseph was assiduous in talent-spotting for his theatres. On a visit to Pressburg in 1784 Joseph saw Schikaneder's company perform Schikaneder's new moralistic play, *Kinder, reizet eure Eltern, und Eltern eure Kinder nicht* ('Children, don't annoy your parents, and parents, don't annoy your children') which greatly appealed to him, and prompted him to invite Schikaneder to take over the management of the second court theatre, the Kärntnerthortheater. Joseph also maintained a continuous correspondence with his court theatre director Count Orsini-Rosenberg, in which the emperor gave details of his theatrical visits (often sending plays and opera librettos back for consideration), and requested the latest theatrical news and gossip from home.[46] (This correspondence was even maintained from the front line during Joseph's war with the Turks in 1788.)

Joseph succeeded in establishing a German-speaking National Theatre in Vienna in 1776, an event that caused enormous excitement throughout Germany, and fuelled the hope that German culture, for so long fragmented and dominated by foreign influences, might regain its identity once Vienna became a new cultural capital. 'Vienna,' wrote Wieland, 'should be to Germany what Paris is to France, and we should be in Vienna.'[47] Like many mid-eighteenth-century German writers Wieland had (unsuccessfully) courted patronage in the imperial city. In 1769 Klopstock (Germany's first self-consciously patriotic writer, who had been refused employment in Berlin by Frederick the Great) proposed the foundation of an Academy for German Art in Vienna. The dedication of his proposal to the emperor was accepted by Joseph,[48] although the academy never materialized. At the same period Lessing, still raw from his disappointment at the failure of the German National Theatre in Hamburg, began to entertain plans for a second attempt in Vienna.

The news of Joseph's foundation of a national theatre in Vienna filled German writers with patriotic jubilation. Writing to the leader of the Berlin Enlightenment Friedrich Nicolai, Gebler (who had been Lessing's host in Vienna the year before) proclaimed his enthusiasm: 'Every patriot must rejoice that our German Joseph has designated his court theatre as the national stage.'[49] Lessing wrote in response a letter in praise of Joseph: 'I honour your Kaiser, he is a great man! Without doubt he can give us Germans a national theatre, a patriotic theatre which the king in Berlin merely tolerates and takes no interest in, as does your ruler.'[50] Even Goethe greeted 'the latest literary news from the capital city of our fatherland', and wrote in praise of 'our German Joseph'.[51] 'Give us what we thirst after, a German fatherland, and a law and a beautiful language and sincere religion,'[52] Herder urged in an Ode of 1778, underlining the inordinate expectations the German Enlightenment projected onto Joseph II.

Within two years of the founding of the German National Theatre in Vienna, Joseph had also established a German Opera in the city, to meet the demands of the rising bourgeoisie. For Mozart, German musician in exile, the promised land was clearly beckoning.

VIII

Mozart's arrival in Vienna

The news of Joseph's accession reached Mozart in Munich, where, although he was deep in work on *Idomeneo*, his thoughts turned instantly to the uncompleted German opera *Zaide*. But it was not an obvious reaction. The German Opera in Vienna had been established for some two years, and Joseph's accession made no immediate difference to the situation; indeed, as Leopold had to remind him, the period of mourning for Maria Theresa's death had closed the theatres of Vienna. Mozart's response seems to have been triggered by something more profound: a sense perhaps that with the death of his mother Joseph had now attained his patrimony and could become in his own right a suitable paternal substitute for Mozart's filial emotions.

Mozart had long displayed a tendency to seek out and make strong emotional attachments to father-substitutes, with whom he would then invariably (perhaps necessarily) be cruelly disappointed. In Mannheim he had allowed himself to be adopted by the family of the flautist Wendling, and then suddenly broke off the attachment, but within a short time he had formed a new attachment to another musician Fridolin Weber. In Paris he underwent the same process with Grimm, placing unrealistic hopes on Grimm's support, and then raining torrents of bitter abuse on his head when these were disappointed.

There is no doubt that Joseph II fascinated the Mozart family. Their letters are full of gossipy reports on seemingly inconsequential details of Joseph's activities, foibles, travels, even health. In Wolfgang's letters it is as if he were mentally shadowing the emperor from afar. When, in March 1781, he was summoned from Munich (where performances of *Idomeneo* were still running), to attend Archbishop Colloredo in Vienna, Mozart's attentions turned instantly to the new ruler. Within a week of arriving in Vienna Mozart was writing to his father, 'Well, my chief object here is to introduce myself to the Emperor in some becoming way, for I am absolutely determined that he shall get to know me.' It is as if he nursed the Freudian belief that Joseph would instantly recognize him as his long-lost son.[1]

For all Joseph's famed accessibility (he dispensed with court etiquette, and often mixed freely in public company) Mozart found the emperor elusive. A curious comment in one of his letters hints at a secret belief in the emperor's omnipotence. He recounts the incident of a fire in a side chapel in St Stephen's Cathedral, and then reports on the efforts to put it out: 'It is said that no such disgraceful lack of organization has ever been seen since Vienna was a city. The Emperor is not here, of course.'[2] That apparently inconsequential rider implies an almost childlike belief in the power of the emperor to put all things right, and a magical fear of things going wrong when the emperor was away.

Joseph himself encouraged his subjects to view him in this dependent, paternal light. He preferred to describe himself as the 'Father of his people',[3] and had books published to promote the image of a wise, just, beneficent and indulgent ruler. A substantial mythology grew up on the subject of his secret acts of charity, often supposed to have been undertaken as he wandered around Vienna incognito. Mozart owned a copy of one of these books, the *Skizzen aus dem Charakter und dem Handlungen Josephs II*, a compilation of anecdotes published in 1783. Many years later Constanze told the Novellos that Mozart was so much attached to the emperor that when he was offered a post by the King of Prussia he preferred to remain with the emperor, even though he received no salary from him.[4]

If filial transference to Joseph at last gave Mozart the courage to break free of both his real father and his oppressive employer, Mozart's path to independence was made easier by the flourishing musical scene he found in Vienna. Like most Habsburgs, Joseph II was a competent musician who took a lively and informed interest in music in Vienna. Although the life of exemplary, almost monastic, austerity he lived precluded the sort of festal pomp that kept musicians in full-time work at other courts throughout Europe, Vienna was capital of a large empire whose greater aristocracy – even keener to maintain the outward tokens of their status as their real power was eroded – all maintained palaces for their winter residence in the city. They, and the growing number of lesser aristocracy (who were often ennobled as reward for administrative service), held lavish private entertainments affording numerous opportunities for a freelance composer and musician like Mozart. The new aristocracy, like the bourgeoisie, were eager to acquire civilizing graces to confirm their new status, and had insatiable call for private music lessons for its younger generation. The leisure demands of the recently enriched bourgeoisie had also brought into being a fledgling public concert life that Mozart was quick to exploit.

Mozart's response was instantaneous and joyous. Here, at last, was a forum in which his talents could find both worthy expression and proper reward. For a single concert, playing in the palace of a nobleman, he could earn 50 florins – half his miserable annual salary in Salzburg.[5] The newly established public concert life soon embraced the young virtuoso. Within a few weeks Mozart had clearly already persuaded himself that Vienna was the place for him, and was preparing Leopold for the imminent shock of rupture from Salzburg by describing the rich rewards he could expect in the city.

It was not simply the financial and career opportunities that so enticed Mozart. Within an extraordinarily short time of his arrival he was swept along by the new whirlwind of social and intellectual activity whipped up by Joseph's reforms. And for the first time in his life, Mozart found himself being accorded the respect that he and his father had so long sought for him. 'All possible honour is shown me,'[6] he informed Leopold. His *entrée* into Viennese social and intellectual life was via the salon of the Countess Wilhelmine Thun, wife of Count Franz-Joseph Thun. The Thun-Hohenstein family belonged to the greater aristocracy, and Franz-Joseph and his wife were intimate friends of the emperor. But as supporters of the Viennese Enlightenment they extended their largesse regardless of class or status, welcoming statesmen, intellectuals, artists and masons alike into their home, confirming Johann Pezzl's observations in his *Skizze von Wien*, that the greater aristocracy 'estimated bourgeois intellectuals, artists and businessmen incomparably more than the unproductive minor nobility'.[7]

The Mozart family had made the acquaintance of the Thuns on previous visits to Vienna, and in accordance with Leopold's practice, Wolfgang made speedy contact when he arrived in 1781. Within a week of setting foot in Vienna he was able to write to his father that he had already lunched twice with the countess, and that he was visiting her house almost every day. He remained close to the Thuns throughout the rest of his life, staying with Franz-Joseph's father in Linz in 1783 (where he wrote the *Linz* Symphony), accompanying Franz-Joseph on a visit to Baden in 1784, staying at the Thun palace in Prague in 1787, and accompanying their son-in-law Prince Lichnowsky on a secret mission to Berlin in 1789.

The salon, a social institution imported to Vienna from France, was the preserve of the society hostess, and so influential were the great Parisian society hostesses – Madame du Deffand, Madame Geoffrin, Madame d'Epinay – that one of Rousseau's characters could suggest that 'A point of morals would not be better discussed in a society of philosophers than in that of a pretty woman of Paris'.[8] Pezzl tells us that the Viennese salon hostess was an educator and muse, and that a salon evening was as 'educative and tasteful as it is charming'.[9] The Countess

Thun's salon clearly deserved this encomium, and was recognized as the most important informal meeting place for the adherents of the Viennese Enlightenment. Several accounts of the countess's salon have survived, all of which attest to the role it played in Viennese cultural and intellectual life, in particular as a natural point of gravitation for foreign visitors. From the diary of Georg Forster,[10] who visited Vienna in 1784, it is clear that the Countess Thun was highly regarded: 'everyone with any knowledge and opinion gives her this praise; the Emperor, Kaunitz, English people who are staying here, often visit her circle'.[11] Forster also gives us an idea of the activities at the countess's evenings: intellectual discussions, of course, but also literary pastimes, such as reading aloud from Gray's *Elegy*, or Pope's *Eloisa to Abelard*.

There Mozart met and engaged with the most prominent members of the Viennese Enlightenment, men who often combined their activities as writers and intellectuals with careers as statesmen. Even before he settled in Vienna in 1781 Mozart was known to one such, Tobias von Gebler, a frequent visitor at the Thun salon. By April 1781 Mozart was able to write that he had also met the great Sonnenfels there, and in December of the same year he was intimate enough with Sonnenfels to suggest to his anxious father that if Leopold had any doubts as to the esteem Wolfgang enjoyed in Vienna, he should write to Sonnenfels for a reference.[12] Sonnenfels's name is also to be found on the 1784 list of Mozart's concert subscribers.[13]

It was at the Thun household, too, that Mozart met Gottfried van Swieten. Today best remembered as the librettist of Haydn's two oratorios *The Creation* and *The Seasons*, van Swieten is usually described as the imperial librarian. But he was much more than that. The son of Maria Theresa's personal physician and closest confidant Gerhard van Swieten (the man who had gently nudged the Queen along some of her most liberal paths), Gottfried had been Ambassador in Berlin in the 1770s (where he absorbed many of Frederick the Great's principles of government), and subsequently became a trusted favourite of Joseph II. The emperor made van Swieten a Councillor of State and Director of the State Education Commission in 1781, and eventually in 1782, Director of the new Censorship Commission. He was without doubt the most politically influential member of the Viennese Enlightenment during the 1780s (Joseph disliked the vain and prickly Sonnenfels) and, through the Education and Censorship Commissions, controlled much of the official intellectual and cultural life of Austria throughout the Josephine era.

But van Swieten also found time to indulge a passion for music (he was himself an amateur composer), and held regular Sunday musical meetings for his friends. By April 1782 Mozart was attending these weekly.[14] Van Swieten remained Mozart's most important and loyal patron. In 1789 he was the only person to put his name to a concert subscription list circulated by Mozart in a desperate attempt to salvage his flailing freelance career. On the day of Mozart's death van Swieten was dismissed from his official posts by the new Emperor Leopold, but the following day he nonetheless hastened to relieve the distraught Constanze of Mozart's funeral arrangements. In the circumstances, subsequent reproaches that he might have done better by the dead Mozart seem misplaced.

Mozart, the young composer who had known Grimm and Diderot, was therefore almost instantly accepted into the most distinguished circles of the Viennese *Aufklärung*. Indeed, acquaintance with the Thuns promised to give him access to the emperor himself, for Joseph used to attend private parties there. A mere three weeks after his arrival in Vienna, Mozart missed meeting Joseph at a private concert given by the Thuns because of the domestic demands of Archbishop Colloredo, a fact that almost certainly decided him to seize the earliest opportunity to provoke an argument with his employer and hand in his notice of resignation (which was in fact never formally accepted by Colloredo). Two months after arriving in Vienna he had at last liberated himself from the company of the Archbishop's kitchen-staff with whom he was forced to dine, and from his colleagues – the 'coarse and dirty' violinist Brunetti, and the bloated and ignorant castrato Ceccarelli – with whom he was required to linger in the Archbishop's anterooms in anticipation of Colloredo's sudden wish for some music to distract him.[15]

Despite the fast and furious pace of cultural life (Mozart spent every possible spare evening at the theatre, his greatest delight) Mozart had not forgotten that Vienna provided the opportunity to write the long-anticipated German opera. He lost no time. Already in April he was able to report that the popular playwright Gottlieb Stephanie (known as Stephanie the Younger) had looked over *Zaide* for possible performance by the German Opera, but had decided that Mozart should start from scratch with a new libretto. By June Joseph's court theatre director, Count Orsini-Rosenberg, had commissioned the resident playwright of the court theatre Friedrich Ludwig Schröder[16] to hunt out a libretto for Mozart. Shortly afterwards, having secured the agreement of Stephanie to work on the chosen libretto, and having being assured of Orsini-Rosenberg's approval, Mozart set to work on the new opera, *Die Entführung aus dem Serail*. It was to be his most deliberately *Josephine* opera, written in the full flush of the new ideals of the rationalist Austrian Enlightenment.

IX

Die Entführung aus dem Serail

The libretto for *Die Entführung aus dem Serail*, adapted by Stephanie from a play with songs written in 1780 by the Leipzig merchant and dramatist Christoph Friedrich Bretzner, is one of the weakest Mozart ever set. It is conspicuously short on plot and action, and long on the padding of comic business. (The best joke in the opera is purely musical: that of giving the eunuch harem-keeper Osmin one of the lowest bass roles in the operatic repertory.) On Mozart's insistence Stephanie added a number of arias, but the obvious opportunity the story offers for an extended dramatic scene (the abduction itself) is ignored. Mozart also insisted on one important structural change (moving the ensemble now at the end of Act II from Act III) but this in turn created dramaturgical problems for the third act. Why did Mozart, who had lavished such care and attention upon the text for *Idomeneo*, accept this feeble effort?

There are a number of reasons. Mozart was in a desperate hurry to make a mark in Vienna. Almost all other work was abandoned during the composition of *Die Entführung*; the major works of the Vienna period (in particular the great series of piano concertos) were only begun in the autumn of 1782, after the performances of the opera were over: a sure indication of the importance Mozart attached to the opera. The libretto at least gave him the opportunity to display his musical wares to the Viennese public. As a result, the opera is almost wilfully eclectic in style; 'an Italian bravura aria'[1] for the aristocratic lovers of vocal display; sentimental arias in the vein of German Pietism for the new bourgeois audience; simple strophic songs for the more popular audience encouraged by the emperor's new theatre policies; and plenty of ear-catching Turkish music to please everyone. Not until the time he came to write *Die Zauberflöte* ten years later could even Mozart have made such a mishmash into a coherent work of art.

JOSEPHINE PROPAGANDA

But there was a more important reason for working on the libretto offered to him by Schröder and Stephanie. Not only was he anxious to please these influential luminaries of the National Theatre (expressing his anxiety at offending Schröder should the libretto prove unsatisfactory).[2] But they themselves had chosen the libretto with the express purpose of pleasing Joseph II by having something ready for the entertainments expected for the planned state visit of Grand Duke Paul of Russia in September 1781.[3] In fact, although Rosenberg had told Schröder to look out a libretto for Mozart in June, he and the emperor were abroad when the text was chosen. So keen was Mozart to make his mark that he actually set to work on the opera without having received Rosenberg's final go-ahead, urged by Stephanie to do so, in order that the work might be a *fait accompli* in time for the Grand Duke's arrival. The text of *Die Entführung aus dem Serail*, chosen to appeal to the emperor, is accordingly the work in which Mozart declares his support for the dynamic promise of Enlightened absolutism, the aims of which would have been exhaustively discussed in the circle of senior Josephine statesman in which he was mixing at the time.

The *turquerie* of *Die Entführung* reflects the eighteenth century's delight in exoticism, through which it was able to liberate itself from the tyranny of classical rules. This new aesthetic gave sanction for more natural modes of expression whose universality was confirmed by their existence in other cultures and civilizations. Oriental art provided an excuse for the Enlightenment's freer and more subjective pursuits. Along with the landscapes of Claude, Chinese gardens were often cited as the authority for the new style of English garden, and domestic *chinoiserie* and *turquerie* inspired rococo art throughout Europe.

But *Die Entführung* reflects more than simple rococo exoticism. For as the Palestinian–American critic Edward Said has pointed out, the West has always used the East as a means of defining itself: as a place where all those aspects of its own behaviour which it prefers to deny can be metaphorically dumped, and where those things forbidden but desired can be vicariously enjoyed.[4] Hence the dual image of the East as both cruel and despotic, but also exotic and sensual (although, of course, the images are frequently combined in more lurid Western fantasies). The more cruel and lascivious the portrayal of political and sexual despotism in the orient, the milder such despotisms appeared in the West. In comparison to the oriental tyrant of popular imagination, even Louis XV could be made to look like a good Parisian bourgeois.

In *Die Entführung aus dem Serail* Konstanze duly informs her captor the Pasha that the Western woman is happier than her oriental counterpart, and her maid Blonde makes great play of the contrast between the position of the Western maiden, 'zum freyheit geboren' ('born to freedom') and the Eastern wife confined to the harem. To make the point explicit Blonde is identified as being English; even a lowly English servant is freer than the wife of an oriental potentate. The American Revolution notwithstanding, England was still considered in Austria and Germany the guardian of freedom. 'Oh most fortunate Albion, adorned not oppressed by the throne of a restricted King, from you is slavery banished,' wrote Mozart's colleague Johann Baptiste von Alxinger in his poem *Die Freyheit* of 1784.[5] 'I am an out and out Englishman,' Mozart himself once wrote.[6]

In addition, although the Turks had ceased to be a real threat to Europe since the Seige of Vienna in 1683, the eighteenth-century European powers had a true understanding of the cold-war stratagem of maintaining their subjects in a state of perpetual vigilance against the imagined enemy at the gates. Constant, almost symbolic hostilities were kept up with the Turks throughout the eighteenth century, culminating in the futile and disastrous war into which Joseph II entered in 1788. Eighteenth-century orientalists often helped to perpetuate the old myth of the vicious Turk, and to reinforce the idea that the Ottoman Empire, hunched on the borders of Austria and Hungary and already the Sick Man of Europe, continued to embody the worst fears of European civilization. Cartoons produced in Vienna by the caricaturist Lösenkohl in the 1780s frequently depicted the Turks as cruel and ignorant.

This needs to be borne in mind when we consider the fashion for *turquerie* in eighteenth-century Viennese music. For even if memories of the swathe of terror which the Turks had cut to the gates of Vienna a century earlier had faded by the 1780s, interest in Turkish music was not a sign of genial Austrian complaisance towards a benign neighbour, as is often argued. It was expedient for Joseph to keep the Turks in the public eye as bogeymen in anticipation of the right moment to seize possession of one or other of the chunks of territory which were crumbling from the fringes of the Ottoman Empire. Indeed, at the time *Die Entführung* was being written, Joseph was concluding a devious treaty with Russia to carve up of some of the more accessible corners of the Turkish Empire. The occasion on which Mozart and Stephanie originally hoped that *Die Entführung* would be performed was no less than the visit to Vienna of the Grand Duke Paul as Catherine the Great's emissary to conclude the treaty.

In these circumstances it would be frankly surprising if interest in Turkish music, and the representation of the Turks in *Die Entführung*, was well-intentioned; there has never been a ruling power in history which was happy to encourage its people in favourable attitudes to a potential enemy, real or imagined. If Joseph II was willing to countenance Turkish music, it must have been because it was considered a just representation of the Turks themselves, its clashing and jangling aptly suggestive of the supposed barbarism of the oriental bogeyman. When Gluck in *Iphigénie en Tauride*, written three years before *Die Entführung*, had come to portray the barbarian, human-sacrificing Scythians (whom Voltaire had suggested were the ancestors of the modern-day Turks)[7] he gave them 'Turkish' music for their bloodthirsty rituals. To our ears it may sound comically rustic; but Gluck intended his Scythians to be frightening representations of primitive, savage unreason. And this is certainly how the Viennese audience would have heard the Turkish music in *Die Entführung*: comic, yes, but nonetheless crude and barbaric. In the event it was, significantly, *Iphigénie en Tauride* in a German translation which was performed, at the emperor's express command, during the festivities to greet the Grand Duke, rather than *Die Entführung*, which was not ready in time. (Mozart paid his own homage to Gluck's opera by quoting it in Konstanze's aria 'Traurigkeit'.)

The libretto for *Die Entführung* was almost certainly chosen not, as is so often suggested, as an expression of the bourgeois Enlightenment's more liberal vision of universal humanity and tolerance, but as a story that would serve the emperor's propagandist campaign against the Turks. The representation of the two Turkish characters in *Die Entführung* vividly upholds this picture. Pasha Selim and his harem-keeper Osmin, both lascivious and cruel, bear the standard features of the barbarian in Western literature, stretching back to Euripides' King Thoas, although the plot deploys the device of dividing the character between master and servant, allowing the worst attributes to be loaded onto the latter. The Pasha's love for Konstanze is shadowed by the inordinate lust of his alter-ego for her maid Blonde (although Mozart cannot resist giving Osmin's longing a touch of comic pathos); and the Pasha's threats of torture to make Konstanze relent are elaborated with grotesque and manic relish by Osmin, to the accompaniment of much Turkish crashing and banging. Only at the end of the opera is the Pasha allowed to redeem himself.

THE FAMILY UNDERMINED

The opera also reveals its Josephine intentions in its espousal of the principles of absolutist rationalism. At the end of Bretzner's play Belmonte and Constanze escape punishment for their attempted flight when it is revealed that Belmonte is none other than the Pasha's long-lost son (the Pasha in fact being a Western renegade). The reunion of long-lost families is an old cliché of Western literature, offering a reassurance that however isolated the individual may feel, he or she may always discover lost relatives even in far-flung corners of the globe. But in the eighteenth century the 'family reconciled in the Orient' cliché had assumed far greater significance. For if, as Lessing had claimed, 'the whole human race is one family' (see p. 79), anyone in the world may be someone else's relation, and since the family is assumed (against all possible evidence to the contrary) to be the seat of love and unity, the discovery of lost relatives becomes the recipe for the restoration of harmony in society.

Family relationships may even overcome religious difference, to demonstrate the arbitrariness of religious faith against the claims of universal human love. In Voltaire's play *Zaïre* the Turkish princess Zaïre, loved by both a Muslim prince and a Christian knight, is revealed (too late – the play is a tragedy) to be the sister of the latter. In Lessing's play *Nathan der Weise* reconciliation is brought about more satisfactorily by discovery that the foster-daughter of the Jewish Nathan, and the Christian Templar Knight who falls in love with her, are brother and sister, the nephew and niece of the Muslim Saladin.

The most significant alteration made by Mozart and Stephanie to their libretto, however, was to excise the sentimental familial ending to the story. Belmonte is recognized to be the son of the Pasha's mortal enemy, rather than his own son as in Bretzner's play. The change reflects a more demanding notion of civic virtue and social duty which began to emerge during the course of the eighteenth century as it became evident that sentimental morality, or the bonds of the family alone, were inadequate to constrain the forces of social individualism. By the 1770s even Diderot had felt impelled to concede what the earlier Enlightenment had striven so hard to deny: that ultimately, social virtue – the only kind of virtue that mattered – did indeed entail a degree of self-sacrifice, a sentiment fully in accord with Joseph II's own absolutist perception of the loyal citizen's first duty to the state.

Furthermore, the strength of the bourgeois family was increasingly recognized to present too strong and independent an alternative to public authority. In Voltaire's play *Le mort de César* (1768) Brutus is reminded that duty to the state overrides familial feelings: 'Un vrai républicain n'a pour père et fils/Que la vertu, les dieux, les lois et son pays.' ('A true republican has for father and son only virtue, the gods, the laws and his country.')[8] A few years later, the utilitarian Helvétius was ominously to suggest that to prevent the conflict between family and state arising at all, the Spartan custom of handing children over to the state for upbringing might be adopted,[9] a plan revived by Saint-Just in the French Revolution, and by many subsequent totalitarian systems.

The conflict between these two areas of loyalty is vividly illustrated in David's two greatest paintings of the 1780s, *The Oath of the Horatii* and

Brutus. Both pictures represent a scene of family sacrifice made for the greater good of the state: the sons of Horatius who swear an oath to fight against the Curatii, to whom they are related by marriage; Brutus (not the assassin of Caesar, but the founder of the Roman Republic) who has been forced to condemn his own sons to death for betraying the republic. Each painting portrays in spatial terms the irreconcilable tension between the rigid male world of unrelenting public duty and the emotional female world of the family, the grief-stricken wives, sisters and mothers of those who are to be sacrificed to the state.

Sonnenfels had already identified precisely this conflict of interests between the strength of the family and the wider interests of the state in contemporary Austria in the 1760s. Might not the 'bourgeois housefather', in his devotion to his family, be putting the interests of his family before his duty to the state, Sonnenfels asked?[10] Nothing must come between the citizen and his public duty. A few years later Chancellor Kaunitz specifically enjoined the subjects of the Habsburg territories to transfer all of their familial feelings to the monarch ('as their common father') and the country ('as the mother who nurses them').[11]

THE LAW OF NATURE AND THE LAW OF THE STATE

In both *Idomeneo* and Schiller's *Don Carlos* the implications of the conflict between family and state are clearly raised. Both King Philip and Idomeneo appeal to the superior law of nature in their revulsion at the religious command to sacrifice their own sons. But what happens, as Voltaire recognized in his own play *Brutus*, when the demands of the state override that very same law of nature? If society or the state assume the omnipotence once attributed to God alone (service to God was inseparable from service to the state, Joseph II claimed), and if all natural law derives from the Deity, then a conflict arises between the natural law of familial love and one's duty to the state. Idomeneo is finally forced to concede to the sacrifice of Idamante because unless he does so his people will continue to suffer the torments of plagues and monsters; his public duty as king overrides his paternal feelings. When Joseph II abolished the death penalty in the Habsburg territories, the one crime for which it remained a sanction, for which the individual would still have to be sacrificed, was – as in Rousseau's ideal state in *Du contrat social* – treason.

The claims of the bourgeois family were deliberately undermined in Joseph II's Austria in order to promote the absolute claims of the state. Any conflict between 'natural law' and the law of the state was to be overcome by the re-codification of the law of the state according to the perceived principles of natural law. And natural law made positive in the state was now to be supreme. The enlightened monarch's acknowledgment of the superiority of the law is crucial to his claims to authority. In France the *Encyclopédie* had presented the claims of the laws of nature as a challenge to the arbitrary power of the monarch.[12] But the absolute monarch of the later eighteenth century no longer claimed, as had Louis XIV, that his or her power was derived from God and resided in his or her person. He or she claimed instead to be simply the 'administrator' of the state and the executor of the law (albeit a law that may have been personally decreed); 'The first servant of the state', in Frederick the Great's own words, who governs – as Frederick's minister Hartzburg argued – 'in accordance with the fundamental laws'.[13] Idomeneo reveals himself to be just such an enlightened monarch when he accedes at the end of the opera to Neptune's commands and enjoins his people to obey, for 'that is the law'. In plays of the Josephine period the providential *deus ex machina* who arrives to dispense justice is the monarch himself (specifically Joseph in one play), now the fount of the law.

ORIENTALISM AND THE LAW OF NATURE

'The doctrine of natural law in its eighteenth-century form provided thus the legal basis for the enlightened absolutism whose truest type was the reign of Joseph II,' writes one historian of Josephinism.[14] Natural law, the rational Enlightenment believed, was, in Hobbes's words, 'immutable and eternall',[15] and systematic enquiry of other cultures and religions was exhaustively undertaken to prove this thesis. Anthropology and comparative religion did not fill Enlightenment thinkers with doubts about the permanence of laws because of their relativity, but with confidence in their universality. 'However many religions there are, there is only one moral law,' claimed Georg Forster,[16] expressing the widespread Deist belief that behind all forms of religion there lay a common moral command. Thus the Abbé Raynal, Grimm's colleague on the *Correspondance littéraire* and one of the age's most assiduous students of comparative religion, suggested of Confucius (a favourite honorary *philosophe*) that 'His code is only Natural Law . . . Reason, says Confucius, is an emanation of Divinity; the supreme law is only the accord of nature and reason.'[17] Karl Anton Martini, Professor of Natural Law at Vienna University for forty years (and one of Mozart's 1784 patrons) drew confidently upon sources as varied as the Bible and Tacitus when drawing up his own codification of the Austrian civil law in his *Lehrbegriff*.

The crucial thing, Voltaire argued in *Questions sur l'Encyclopédie*, was to distinguish between 'Laws of convention, arbitrary usages, fashions which pass,' and 'the essential [which] remains for ever'.[18] This endeavour is what unites Montesquieu's two outwardly very different, but in fact cohesive, masterpieces: *Les lettres persanes*, the archetypal work of Enlightenment orientalism, and *L'esprit des lois*. Montesquieu is best known for his sociological explanations for the development of cultural differences, in which he demonstrated how various forms of political society (monarchical, republican, etc.) operated according to distinctive underlying principles determined by geographical and historical circumstances. Thus he suggests that despotic government is innate to oriental societies. But underlying Montesquieu's project was the desire to prove the existence of a universal natural law beyond historical and geographical conditions.

Les lettres persanes is a fictional exploration of these problems, which wittily depicts the mistakes and confusions that arise when Usbek, a Persian aristocrat, visits Europe. The book is in part a satire upon contemporary Parisian society, and employs a favourite device of viewing one's own society through the eyes of an innocent outsider. The book encourages the reader to distinguish between what is merely conventional and what derives from universal, natural principles, and it does so by contrasting the two different societies of East and West. Montesquieu's Persians accordingly find it most curious that in Paris it is men who wear trousers and women who wear skirts. But counterpointing the story of Usbek's visit to Europe is also the account of a revolt in his harem back home. And Montesquieu's suggestion is that, although the despotic government characterized by Usbek and his Persian harem is intrinsic to oriental cultures, it must, by the universal law of nature, be considered unnatural – an argument which he puts into the mouth of the slave Roxane, the leader of the revolt, who claims in her final letter to Usbek that her deception of Usbek is mitigated since in rebelling she has 'amended your laws according to the laws of nature'.[19]

Die Entführung quite clearly continues Montesquieu's strain of Enlightened orientalism, for the new ending which Mozart and Stephanie appended to their opera confirms the existence of the rational law of nature upon which Joseph II based his reforms. The Pasha's immediate reflex on discovering that Belmonte is the son of his greatest enemy is a desire to exact revenge for the wrongdoings inflicted on him by Belmonte's father. But he overcomes this atavistic desire and, with a heavy heart, releases the lovers. 'The abandonment of acts of revenge lies at the heart of the developing public system of jurisdiction', writes one historian,[20] and as in *Idomeneo*, the crucial step from the feudal ethos of familial honour and tribal vendetta to a modern state system of law has taken place. 'Nothing is so hateful as revenge' sing the grateful lovers at the end of *Die Entführung*, lines suddenly set, amidst the general merriment of the finale, to heavily weighted, minor key music to emphasize the import of the opera's moral.

Like the heroes of seventeeth-century Cartesian drama, the Pasha has to overcome his own passions to recognize the true law (and, by implication, the greater good of the state). The captives in *Die Entführung* are not Konstanze and Blonde, but the Pasha and Osmin, who are enslaved by the triple passions of lust, cruelty and desire for vengeance – Osmin comically, the Pasha tragically. 'You are our slaves,' Blonde cheekily tells Osmin; 'You are truly to be pitied,' says Konstanze to the Pasha; 'You imprison the objects of your desires, and are content to pay for your lusts.'

Both Blonde and Konstanze display typically rationalist arts in fending off the attentions of their importunate admirers. One strategem of seventeenth-century rationalists to counter the debilitating effects of sexual passion had been to develop the art of erotic gallantry, whose elaborately constructed artifice, with its intricate codes and rules, was evolved in an effort to distance, control and aestheticize the greedy impulses of sexual desire. And the rules of erotic gallantry, with their complex strategems of attack and feint, counter-attack and retreat, are to sexuality as the codes of duelling to aggression, and the obsessive artifice of vocal *fioritura* to the intoxicating powers of song. Blonde therefore attempts to instruct the impatient Osmin in the arts of gallantry in her first aria 'Durch Zärtlichkeit und Schmeicheln' ('Through tenderness and flattery'), while Konstanze, like her rationalist sister Fiordiligi in *Così fan tutte* (Sense to Dorabella's Sensibility), fences the Pasha's sexual threats with the defensive shield and fancy footwork of rapier-like coloratura in her monstrous aria 'Marten aller Arten'.[21]

In *Idomeneo* Elettra had been unable to overcome her passions and was consumed by madness, and Osmin is clearly Elettra's comic brother in unreason, his passionate jealousy leading to an overwhelming desire for revenge that ends in insanity. The warning of Elettra's instability was supplied by Mozart in her tempestuous vengeance aria in which, in the sonata-form recapitulation, Elettra returns to her original theme in a wildly wrong key (C minor to the aria's D minor). Similarly, Osmin's vengeance aria 'Solche hergelaufne Laffen' (the text for which was dictated by Mozart to Stephanie after Mozart had written the music) leaps at its conclusion into a quite different key from that in which it began.

Osmin is unable to overcome his passions, and is eventually consumed by a whirling dervish-like frenzy of madness. The Pasha, on the other hand (who is, after all, really a Westerner), is able to put his reason to work to recognize the superior law of nature, which tells him (as certainly as it told Ilia) that vengeance cannot be exacted from the descendants and heirs of the original transgressor. Quelling his passionate desire for Konstanze, and his fearsome longing for vengeance, with magnanimous forbearance he allows the lovers to leave, and thus demonstrates the Cartesian theory that the suppression of the passions automatically leads to right-doing. Is this perhaps why the Pasha is portrayed in a speaking role? We have seen already that eighteenth-century aesthetics represented music as the language of the passions in contrast to the rational discourse of spoken language.

THE REDEMPTIVE HEROINE

Numerous versions of the *Die Entführung aus dem Serail* story exist in eighteenth-century art; in novels, poems (Wieland's *Oberon*), plays and operas – including examples by both Gluck and Haydn, as well as Mozart's *Zaide*. But the story is in fact – outside mythology and fable – one of the oldest and most popular stories in all European literature. It is the basis for the Western prose romance as invented in Hellenistic Greece, and it survives in a number of medieval romances, and in several Renaissance novellas, including a version of the story in the *Decamaron* in which Boccaccio introduces us to the appropriate, and familiar, name for the heroine of the story – Costanza. In England it appears in the seventeenth century in the second part of Thomas Heywood's romance-comedy *The Fair Maid of the West* of 1631.

It is a story which invariably re-emerges in periods when secure, enclosed social structures are giving way to expanding worlds and more individualistic cultures: the transition of the closed Greek city state to the fluid and unstable Hellenistic world; the rise of a new individualism which has so often been noted in twelfth-century Europe; renaissance Italy and seventeenth-century England; eighteenth-century Germany. In these unsettling periods, in which the newly liberated individual often feels adrift, unsure of his status and position, and senses that he grows smaller as the world grows larger, the story of the constant woman who remains steadfast while the hero roams the world in search of her provides both a promise of ultimate security, and confirmation of the uniqueness of the individual lover, for whom no substitute will suffice for the patiently waiting mistress.

Mozart's and Stephanie's alteration to the conclusion of the *Entführung* story was not unprecedented. For already in a twelfth-century version of the tale, *Floire et Blanchefleur*, the Emir who holds the lovely Blanchefleur in his harem, and who has apprehended the escaping lovers, is so moved by the constancy of their love for each other that he sets them free.[22] In

The Fair Maid of the West the same conclusion recurs. The lovers play a trick upon the 'Mullisheg' to effect their escape, are apprehended, and returned for punishment. But like the Saracen Emir and the Pasha Selim, the Mullisheg changes his mind:

> You have waken'd in me an heroic spirit.
> Lust shall not conquer vertue. Till this hour
> We grac'd thee for thy beauty, English woman,
> But now we wonder at thy constancy.[23]

As these precedents show, the theme of constancy is central to the story. In the medieval and Jacobean romances the allegorical meaning of constancy, personified in the heroine of the story, is explained by the dictionary definition of the term: 'the state or quality of being unmoved in mind; steadfastness, firmness, fortitude'.[24] It is an appropriate virtue for societies in flux, lamenting the loss of traditional certainties. But during the eighteenth century the moral emphasis of constancy underwent a significant shift that led it to assume an almost entirely passive, sexual connotation.

This shift of emphasis arose from the bourgeois Enlightenment's desire to redefine and relocate morality in the domestic sphere, where it may be promoted without interfering with the essential freedom of commerce and industry to pursue their own goals. Economic activity was beneficial to man, the Enlightenment argued; that was self-evident. But it was in itself 'neither morally good nor bad', as Thomas Paine (whose political libertarianism was combined with ardent free-market principles) insisted, and could therefore suffer no ethical reproaches.[25] Increasingly divorced from the 'real' world of business, the domestic sphere is allowed to shoulder the burden of morality in a capitalist society, and since the home is the province of women, it is above all women who are made to carry the load. In medieval society women had often been closely involved in economic and business activities; by the eighteenth century, bourgeois women, cultivating the indolence of the aristocratic lady, had been relegated to the home as the guardians of society's virtue.

In Athenian ethics, women had been excluded from the possibility of moral maturity since morality was believed to be only attainable in public life, from which women (like slaves and children) were excluded. The separation of public and domestic spheres in the eighteenth century, however, had the opposite purpose: economic and political activities were now the amoral activities from which women as the new guardians of morality had to be protected. 'There are no good morals for women outside of a withdrawn and domestic life,'[26] claimed Rousseau. Women were to be excluded from the exercise of what were considered to be the public, civic virtues such as justice (even though paradoxically, they always represented such virtues allegorically). Richardson, who had a curious belief in the vicarious reality of his characters beyond the confines of his novels, criticized his heroine Clarissa for her determination to hold so steadfastly to her own concepts of duty and justice. But he approved of her decision not to go to civil litigation against her tyrannical father, 'since she would not have had the glorious Merit which she triumphed in, of a resigned and patient Sufferer'.[27] 'Man strives for freedom, woman for morality,' wrote Goethe,[28] clearly demarcating the permissible areas of sexual influence.

Denied the exercise of public virtues, women are left to nurture the domestic virtues that underpin bourgeois society's moral reassurance, in particular sexual continence. According to Rousseau, chastity was the greatest virtue to which a woman could aspire.[29] There is, of course, an obvious practical reason why female continence was encouraged, since it safeguarded the security of property inheritance. 'Consider of what importance to society the chastity of women is. Upon that all the property in the world depends,' Dr Johnson had declared with more candour than was usual in these matters.[30] It was for this reason that eighteenth-century moralists could argue that what in men might be accounted a misdemeanour must be branded a crime and a sin in women, giving rise to a notorious double standard for male and female sexual behaviour. Hume considered that the moral obligation of men to chastity was patently less than that of women,[31] and in *Tom Jones*, Fielding allowed a clear distinction to be made between Tom's true moral virtues of benevolent good-heartedness and his erring but morally unimportant sexual ways.

Writing at the very beginning of the nineteenth century, Walter Scott found that he could forgive Fielding and Smollet their 'indifferent taste' in portraying 'rakes and debauchees', but objected when novelists extended the licence to the personal purity of women, for 'to insinuate a doubt of its real value, is wilfully to remove the broadest corner-stone on which civil society rests'.[32] The virtuous woman is the repository and guarantor of moral values in a society secretly troubled by its moral legitimacy. The woman who allows her virtue to slip fatally undermines the stability of society and the peace of the good bourgeois merchant abed at night, dreaming of ruthless deals and cut-throat competition.

'How good in this Light, how careful of their Conduct ought Young Ladies to be',[33] advises Richardson. In his moral weekly *Der Weltmann* Mozart's friend Otto von Gemmingen anxiously ponders the weakness of Eve and 'the array of innumerable dangerous enticements'[34] confronting the young woman who is about to enter society – the typical experience of Fanny Burney's contemporary heroines in England. Woman is frail and vulnerable, and the disturbingly secret stirrings of her sexual desire (so graphically depicted by Diderot) offer constant provocation to those who wait to pounce, lurking in the shadows like Monostotos to violate the sleeping Pamina in *Die Zauberflöte*. In Fuseli's painting *The Nightmare* of 1781 it is uncertain whether the hordes of the night which haunt the female figure sleeping in obvious sexual abandon may not actually have been engendered by their victim.[35]

The terrifying significance placed upon sexual constancy led to an obsessive need to put female virtue to the test. Indeed, it became almost a moral imperative to do so. Hence the pervading theme of seduction in Enlightenment art, and especially in Mozart's operas. In the century's great epic of seduction, *Clarissa*, the anti-hero Lovelace's relentless pursuit and destruction of Clarissa is a joyless affair, driven not by pleasure, but by an almost puritan desire to test Clarissa's perfection and 'prove her to be either woman or angel'.[36] 'Is it not monstrous that our seducers should be our accusers?' justly complained an Englishwoman who had fallen victim to the same ploy.[37]

In Enlightenment art sexual constancy is the supreme virtue for which women will sacrifice everything else. The centrality of this theme in the *Entführung* story explains much of the story's popularity during the eighteenth century. In one English version, dating from 1721, the reader is left in no doubt by the (female) author about the real moral of 'a Story where Divine Providence manifests itself in every Transaction, where Vertue is try'd with Misfortunes, and rewarded with Blessings . . . where men behave themselves as Christians, and Women are really virtuous, and such as we ought to imitate . . . I hope the World is not grown so abandon'd to Vice, as to believe that there is no such Ladies to be found, as would prefer Death to Infamy.'[38]

Mozart's Konstanze certainly prefers death to infamy, and spares no opportunity to tell us so. 'Kill me Selim, kill me!' she pleads to the Pasha, seeking in an instant the secular martyrdom to virtue which her forebear Clarissa had attained so laboriously. Konstanze's music is shot through with the sublimated eroticism of baroque religious art. In her heroic aria 'Marten aller Arten' she joyously anticipates torture and death at the hands of the Pasha, relishing the thought of every stroke of the bastinado which will be earned in preservation of her virtue. Beside Konstanze's ecstatic tones Belmonte's placid arias of devotion seem beautiful but pallid (as does so much of Mozart's tenor music.)

Once martyrdom had been transferred from the religious to the secular sphere, women in Enlightenment art, paragons of (and martyrs to) virtue, were endowed with the power – and responsibility – to redeem the sins of male bourgeois society. Ilia's last-minute offer of self-sacrifice to save Idamante in *Idomeneo* anticipates a whole string of redeeming heroines stretching forward into nineteenth-century Romantic art, and culminating in Wagner's operatic heroines: Senta, Elisabeth, Brünnhilde and Kundry. In the languishing death-wishes of Konstanze, who is willing to die to save Belmonte when the truth of his parentage is revealed and he is threatened with death, we may be reminded of Wagner's own comment to Liszt concerning the end of Wagner's impassioned love-affair with Mathilde Wesendonck: 'The love of a tender woman has made me happy; she dared to throw herself into the sea of suffering and agony so that she should be able to say to me "I love you!" No one who does not know all her tenderness can judge how much she had to suffer. We were spared nothing – but as a consequence I am redeemed and she is blessedly happy because of it.'[39]

Only an artist, and perhaps only Wagner, could write in those terms. But as Mozart was writing *Die Entführung* he was courting his own Constanze. Her selfless dedication to the domestic virtues provided Mozart with precisely the security he needed to undertake his own more exalted work, as her sexual prudence (he never ceased reminding her) upheld his own 'honour'.

In Bretzner's original play *Belmonte und Constanze*, it is revealed that the Pasha is a Western renegade, a fact that explains his relationship with Belmonte. The particular line in the dialogue in which Pedrillo hints at the Pasha's background was allowed to remain in Mozart's and Stephanie's version, and a contemporary critic reviewing the first performances of the opera in Vienna for a Graz newspaper considered that Mozart and Stephanie had not properly thought through their changes, and had left some loose ends untied. Objecting to the alteration of the original sentimental ending, he complained that the excision of the family reunion meant that 'Bretzner's reason for making the Pasha a renegade is entirely removed, and the alteration made all the more absurd thereby'.[40]

Or was it? As we have seen, Mozart worked for almost a year on the opera, and in his determination to succeed with it was unlikely to have been so careless. There may be an explanation for the decision to leave the Pasha as a renegade other than oversight. I have found a little-known early English masonic drama called *The Generous Freemason* (1731),[41] which is based on the *Entführung* story, although it follows the *Zaide* variant in which a captain of the Pasha's Royal Guard, not the Pasha himself, turns out to be the European renegade who helps the lovers to escape. In this version of the story, the Western lovers are an English couple Sebastian and Maria. Sebastian is a freemason, and the renegade Mirza reveals that he too is a mason. Has perhaps something of this reading of the story filtered through to *Die Entführung aus dem Serail?* It would explain why it was necessary for the Pasha to remain a renegade even though he was no longer to be discovered to be the father of Belmonte. Perhaps there is also a masonic connection in the curiously bourgeois profession with which the noble Spaniard Belmonte is encumbered. Pedrillo introduces him to the Pasha as a *Baumeister*, an architect, the master profession of masonry.

X

Freemasonry and the Catholic Enlightenment

Mozart was not a freemason when he wrote *Die Entführung aus dem Serail* (although Stephanie was). But in 1784 Sonnenfels, as vice-master of the masonic lodge 'Zur wahren Eintracht', wrote a masonic essay 'On the Influence of Masonry on Civil Society', in which he claimed that free-masonry had been the chief vehicle for the propagation and dissemination of the ideals of the Enlightenment in Austria.[1] The Austrian literary historian Leslie Bodi adds: 'It is certain that virtually all representatives of the Austrian Enlightenment, whether writers or civil servants, aristo-crats or bourgeois, German or Hungarian, Bohemian, Polish and Italian, belonged to one or another of the Lodges.'[2] It has been estimated that some eighty per cent of the Austrian higher bureaucracy were masons during the 1780s.[3] Freemasonry undoubtedly attained the peak of its historical influence in Josephine Vienna.

Sonnenfels envisaged freemasonry as a natural arm of the Josephine reform programme. But eighteenth-century freemasonry is better under-stood as typifying the bourgeois Enlightenment's concept of society as an autonomous, self-regulating sphere beyond the jurisdiction of the state. (The fundamental contradiction between these two positions would become increasingly apparent during the course of the Josephine decade.) Where Hobbes in the seventeenth century had argued that there could be no such thing as human society without the guarantees of the strong state, by the end of the eighteenth century bourgeois radicals like William Godwin and Thomas Paine could draw a clear distinction between society ('a blessing') and government ('a necessary evil').[4] Freemasonry is the bourgeois Enlightenment's institutionalized answer to its need for a form of society capable of dissipating the crude power-relationships which otherwise existed between the individual and the state, and of mediating between the rampant desires of the individual and the constraining demands of society. It is above all the microcosm of an enlightened society of free individuals guided by no more than secular virtue.

In the Christianized society of the Middle Ages morality had been inseparable from obedience to the will of God as dictated by the Church. But during the Reformation the idea of the Church as the sole representa-tive of God's revelation on earth, the interpreter and judge of God's command, had been challenged. The reformers had thrown up the unset-tling possibility that there might be different sources of religious authority: the Bible, or man's inner consciousness of grace, as much as the Roman Church. Which path to heaven should the discerning Christian choose when there were suddenly so many on offer?

The problem was compounded as explorers discovered new cultures and civilizations in distant parts of the globe, while scholarly interest in the ethical systems of ancient Greece and Rome (in particular Stoicism) contributed to the realization that Christianity might not have a monopoly on moral truth or authority. Indeed, people increasingly came to consider that Christianity itself had been responsible for too many of the crimes of Western civilization,[5] and that, rather than encouraging acceptable social behaviour, Christianity had simply fostered superstition, ignorance, and blind obedience to the rules and dogmas of the Church. And as Lessing argued, 'What is the good of having the right beliefs if we do not live rightly?'[6] Socially beneficial morality was not necessarily synony-mous with religion. 'Morals and religion, far from being inseparable, are completely independent of each other. A man can be moral without being religious,'[7] wrote the seventeenth-century religious controversialist Pierre Bayle, who even went so far as to suggest that 'A society of atheists would practise civil and moral actions just as well as other societies'.[8]

For those who believed that the Church had fatally compromised its claim to guide people's behaviour (and in this the reformed Churches, often as guilty of fanaticism and obscurantism as the Roman Church, were included), the task was to map out an alternative morality. If bour-geois society was to conduct its affairs without recourse to the oppressive power of the state, it had to lay down a satisfactory code by which Bayle's 'society of atheists' might conduct their 'civil and moral actions' according to a moral law of nature established with the same certainty as the hidden physical laws of nature which Newton had revealed. Hence Hume's assertion that morality was the most important of all subjects, upon which the very peace of society depended.[9] Significantly, before unleashing upon the world his justification of unrestrained economic individualism in *The Wealth of Nations*, Adam Smith, Professor of Moral Philosophy at Glasgow University, had prudently prepared the ground for its devastating effects in a volume of moral philosophy, in which he reassured his age that the natural laws of social morality were at work to restore order within the whirling fragments of the market.[10]

The objective common to all Enlightenment projects was the establish-ment of what we now recognize to be a secular system of social ethics – or what the historian J. L. Talmon described with deliberate paradox as a 'secular religion'. 'Eighteenth-century philosophes were never in doubt that they were preaching a new religion,' writes Talmon:

They faced a mighty challenge ... The Church accused secular philosophy of destroying these two most essential conditions of private and public morality, and thereby undermining the very basis of ethics, and indeed society itself. If there is no God, and no transcendental sanction, why should men act virtuously? Eighteenth-century philosophy not only accepted the challenge, but turned the accusation against the Church itself.[11]

Writing to Voltaire, Diderot asserted that 'It is not enough to know more than they do, it must be shown that we are better than they are, and that philosophy can make more people good than grace'.[12]

Freemasonry was the bourgeois Enlightenment's most persuasive vision of a society guided by such a secular religion of morality. Indeed, Lessing could suggest, freemasonry was itself the very pre-condition for bourgeois society. 'Freemasonry is nothing arbitrary, nothing superfluous,' he wrote in his masonic dialogues *Ernst und Falk*; 'Rather it is something necessary, which is grounded in the nature of man and of civil society ... Freemasonry existed always ... Essentially Freemasonry is as old as civil [*bürgerlich*: the congruity between the two meanings – civil/bourgeois – is itself significant] society. Each can only arise with the other, since civil society may even be no more than an offspring of Freemasonry.'[13]

Freemasonry created a deliberately neutral area of discourse, banishing politics and religion as topics of discussion in the masonic lodge, and laying claim to an egalitarian classlessness (although, of course, its members were carefully vetted, and anyone who was not at least a member of Lord Chesterfield's 'Good Company' would not be admitted except as servants). Early English freemasonry was particularly preoccupied with the propagation of the new secular morality. 'A Mason is oblig'd by his Tenure, to obey the moral Law', enjoin the Institutes of the Grand Lodge of 1723; 'But though in ancient Times Masons were charg'd in every Country to be of the Religion of the Country or Nation, whatever it was, yet 'tis now thought more expedient only to oblige them to that Religion with which all Men agree, having their particular opinion to themselves.'[14] 'You see now what is our Profession; it is the law of Nature', claimed a masonic text of 1722.[15]

Freemasonry existed to bridge the gap between personal and public morality, for as even Kant (whose own ethical system carried the ideal of the individual's personal moral responsibility to its height) was to argue:

The highest moral good cannot be achieved merely by the exertions of the single individual towards his own moral perfection, but requires a union of such individuals into a whole toward the same goal ... A union of men under merely moral laws, patterned on the above idea, may be called an *ethical* ... society, or an *ethical commonwealth*. It can exist in the midst of a political commonwealth.[16]

Kant was no freemason, but this was certainly the ideal of freemasonry. Lessing believed that the day might come when, if everyone obeyed the masonic moral law, the 'inevitable evils' of the civil state might be transcended altogether.[17] 'Morality is the art which teaches man to enter on manhood and to do without princes,' wrote Adolphe von Knigge, recruiting master for the most radical form of late eighteenth-century German freemasonry, the Illuminati. 'Morality alone can secure liberty.'[18] Like William Godwin at the same period, later eighteenth-century German freemasonry envisaged an essentially anarchist society which would be able to dispense with the state altogether.

FREEMASONRY IN VIENNA

Modern freemasonry had been founded in England in the second decade of the eighteenth century as a clear vehicle for the dissemination of the new, post-revolutionary Whig consensus. During the 1720s it spread to the rest of Europe, pursuing the natural development of bourgeois society on the Continent, emerging alongside the reading-rooms, gentlemen's clubs and moral weeklies of eighteenth-century urban society. Although the first official record of a masonic lodge in Vienna dates from 1742, there is some evidence to suggest that freemasonry reached Vienna in the 1730s directly from England as an element in the strategy of Walpole's Whig government to build a system of anti-French alliances across Europe.[19] The founder and tireless recruiting sergeant of Whig freemasonry, Dr Thomas Desaguliers, travelled abroad frequently, enlisting prominent European members for the new movement. One of his catches was Francis-Stephen of Lorraine, the future husband of Maria Theresa and Holy Roman Emperor, who was initiated into freemasonry at Walpole's country seat, Houghton, in Norfolk in 1731. Masonic formulas were incorporated into Francis-Stephen's coronation ceremonies, and it was owing to his protection that freemasonry in Austria survived the papal bans of 1738 and 1751. By the mid-eighteenth century a number of prominent Austrian officials in the Netherlands, only a short boat trip across the water from England, had also been recruited to English freemasonry, including the uncle of Count Coblenzl, one of Mozart's most important patrons.

During the course of its journey throughout Europe freemasonry had picked up numerous accretions. In France, a more hierarchical society than England, higher grades were added to the original egalitarian three grades of English freemasonry. In Germany, where the cosmopolitan fraternity of freemasonry was initially greeted as a force with the potential to unite the German bourgeoisie, the movement soon fell victim to regionalism and national feuds. Different sects and groupings rapidly emerged. Dominant among these by the 1770s was the 'reformed' German sect known as 'Strict Observance', which claimed that German freemasons were the true inheritors of the medieval Templars, and which developed arcane rituals and elaborate paraphernalia to match its pretensions.

By the 1780s most of the Viennese lodges, which came under the jurisdiction of a parent lodge in Berlin, had been 'rectified' according to the tenets of the Strict Observance. But they were also infiltrated by a second strain of German freemasonry, that of Rosicrucianism, which in the 1770s had introduced to freemasonry mystical and occult practices that had enjoyed an enormous vogue in a country in which most people were denied access to any meaningful public life or political expression. The Grand Master of the Viennese lodges, Count Dietrichstein (whose name appears on Mozart's subscription list of 1784), was known to be interested in Rosicrucianism, and several of the Viennese lodges had a predominantly Rosicrucian membership.[20] (Most masonic activity was, until 1781, semi-clandestine.)

In late 1781 the distinguished metallurgist Ignaz von Born took over the mastership of a small and insignificant lodge known as 'Zur wahren Eintracht', and rapidly turned it into the central meeting point of the Viennese bourgeois Enlightenment. Born himself had previously belonged to an English lodge in Prague which he left when it went over to the Strict Observance, and he fought vigorously against the growing influence of reactionary mysticism and occultism within Viennese freemasonry. His purpose at 'Zur wahren Eintracht' was to fulfil a long-held dream to create in Vienna an academy of intellectual and scientific enquiry to match the famous Royal Society in London, which had itself, through Desaguliers, been closely involved in early English freemasonry and Newtonian Deism.

Though physically a sick and weak man who had been poisoned during the course of his own chemical experiments, Born had a charismatic personality, a wide circle of contacts, and worked tirelessly for his lodge. By 1785, under his inspired guidance, 'Zur wahren Eintracht' had 197 members made up of the intellectual, scientific and artistic élite of Vienna.[21] The lodge produced a serious scientific journal,[22] with contributors from all over Europe, and the *Journal für Freymaurer*, which combined masonic news and reports with a series of learned articles on historical aspects of ancient science and religion, to demonstrate the existence of quasi-masonic groups in all cultures and ages. The lodge was also closely associated with the literary journal *Die wiener Realzeitung*, remarkable for the breadth of its survey of contemporary developments in the European Enlightenment. The journal was edited by the poet Joseph Franz Ratschky, and then between 1783 and 1786 by Aloys Blumauer, poet and member of the new liberal Censorship Commission headed by Gottfried van Swieten and Born's closest lieutenant. 'Zur wahren Eintracht' also contained a significant library of some 1900 volumes.[23]

The important role that 'Zur wahren Eintracht' played in Josephine Vienna is testified by a series of visitors to the city who reported on its activities. One such visitor, the Danish clergyman and freemason Friedrich Münter, who visited Vienna in 1784 to report back to Germany on the extent of Rosicrucian infiltration of the Viennese lodges, wrote that 'The whole Bornian [lodge] is a sort of Academy of Science'.[24] Another northern visitor, Georg Forster, confirms this impression in the same year: 'The best Viennese heads amongst scholars, and the best writers, are members.'[25] At Born's own home the intellectual and social activity continued; lectures and seminars were held here, and according to Münter, the house was 'The meeting place of the brothers of his Lodge; and here are where the most interesting people in the whole of Vienna are collected.'[26]

The Born circle also worked hard to establish links with the northern German Enlightenment. Aloys Blumauer maintained a regular correspondence with Wieland, and in 1784 the poet Johann Baptiste von Alxinger made a tour of northern Germany, visiting Lessing's colleague Friedrich Nicolai in Berlin and Wieland in Weimar. Even closer contacts were established with Weimar by another former member of Born's group, Karl Leonhard Reinhold, who settled in Weimar and married Wieland's daughter. From Weimar he continued to contribute to the *Realzeitung* and Gemmingen's *Magazin für Wissenschaften*, and maintained a prolific correspondence with Born, Alxinger, and the poets Ratschky and Gottlieb Leon. He was a close friend of Schiller, and immersed himself in Kant (whose writings were still unobtainable in Vienna in 1786), serving as a successful popularizer, whose efforts were applauded by Kant himself. In 1789 he dedicated a book to 'seinen vaterlichen Freunden Ignaz von Born in Wien, Immanuel Kant in Königsberg und Christoph Martin Wieland in Weimar'.[27] A telling constellation of names linking Mozart's Vienna, Königsberg, and the Weimar of Wieland, Goethe and Schiller.

Wieland graciously accepted the dedication with the words, 'I find myself in the company of two of the greatest men in Germany.'[28]

Beyond its intellectual activities, 'Zur wahren Eintracht' also fulfilled the second important function of freemasonry, serving as a focus for the dissemination of secular morality among the newly independent Viennese bourgeoisie, promoting, in Born's words, 'sympathy, harmony, beneficence, and all the social virtues',[29] and acting as 'a school for men's hearts, and as a mediator between the Law and true inner Morality'.[30] 'Happy are we, honoured Brothers,' wrote Born in his lodge's *Journal für Freymaurer*, 'to think of the Freedom and Equality of natural law as the true foundation of our honourable Lodge, and that in our free and spiritual republic we have no Pope.'[31]

The Born circle was a close, tight-knit group, most of whom were, like Mozart, in their twenties at the dawning of the Josephine era. (Born himself was only thirty-eight in 1780). They considered themselves to be the revolutionary vanguard of the Josephine Enlightenment, and in time became its revolutionary conscience. While keenly supporting the Josephine reforms, they demonstrated a more obviously bourgeois independence, and were more critical of them than men like Sonnenfels and van Swieten, who were closer to the government. Alxinger's poem *Die Duldung* ('Toleration')[32] complained that Joseph's Toleration Edict (officially tolerating only Orthodoxy and Protestantism) had not gone far enough, a sentiment that echoes Paine's complaint that 'toleration is the counterfeit of intolerance'.[33] Van Swieten, who would not countenance any attacks whatsoever upon enlightened reforms, banned the poem, a gesture that highlights the potential for conflict between the aims of Josephine absolutism and those of the bourgeois Enlightenment.

MOZART AND FREEMASONRY

Mozart's initial contacts with the Viennese Enlightenment had been with establishment figures like Sonnenfels and van Swieten. But Mozart must also soon have come into contact with the Born group, for it is clear that socially the circles of Born and Mozart's Countess Thun were virtually interchangeable. It was at a gathering at the house of the countess that Georg Forster first met Gemmingen (who had arrived in Vienna from Mannheim in 1783), Sonnenfels, Blumauer, Gebler and Born himself one evening in 1784; a few days later he paid a visit to Born at his own home, and then accompanied Born and Blumauer (who lodged with Born) again to the Thun salon.[34]

In May 1785 *Die Maurerfreude*, a masonic cantata in honour of Born's scientific achievements, with music by Mozart (K. 471) was performed at the lodge 'Zur gekrönten Hoffnung'. By this date Mozart was intimate enough with Born for the latter to arrange for himself and Blumauer to stay with Leopold Mozart (who had been admitted to a lodge earlier in the year) in Salzburg while passing through the city. Mozart was also well acquainted with many of the other members of Born's circle, including the freemasons Alxinger, Lorenz Leopold Haschka[35] and Leon, with whom Mozart shared the somewhat dubious privilege of being an occasional private tutor to Karoline, the daughter of a senior member of the Josephine administration, the Hofrat Anton von Greiner.[36] Verses by Ratschky, another member of the circle, and by Blumauer, (the 1784 edition of whose poems Mozart owned), were set to music by Mozart.[37]

The names all recur together in 1787, in the autograph album of a less prominent fellow freemason, the teacher Johann Georg Kronauer; Mozart's signature (with a tag written in English) appears alongside those of the familiar intimates: Gemmingen, Born, Alxinger, Blumauer, Ratschky.[38] In that year Mozart worked with Alxinger (who he had previously hoped might make a German translation of *Idomeneo*) when Alxinger undertook the German translation for Mozart's reorchestrated edition of Handel's *Acis and Galatea*, commissioned by Gottfried van Swieten. Born's name appears again in Mozart's own visiting book in the same year.[39]

Mozart was also frequently associated with activities at 'Zur wahren Eintracht'. Indeed, the records of the lodge tell us that in 1785 he attended a number of meetings as a visitor.[40] Yet although Mozart was in contact with the Born circle by 1782, and may even have had previous masonic contacts in Salzburg,[41] and although *Die Entführung aus dem Serail* itself carries a possible masonic message, Mozart delayed joining a masonic lodge until December 1784. When he did so, although 'Zur wahren Eintracht' was the most significant lodge for the Viennese Enlightenment (and the lodge which Joseph Haydn was to enter in 1785), Mozart instead joined another, lesser lodge, 'Zur Wohltätigkeit'.

This lodge had been founded by his former colleague in Mannheim, Otto von Gemmingen, in February 1783. The lodge was recognized as second only to 'Zur wahren Eintracht' as a centre of the Viennese Enlightenment.[42] As a sister-lodge of 'Zur wahren Eintracht', it shared premises and facilities, and Mozart himself was raised to the second and third degrees of freemasonry at meetings of 'Zur wahren Eintracht'. However, there was a significant difference between these, the two centres of Viennese Enlightenment. Examination of the small membership of 'Zur Wohltätigkeit' (some thirty members only) indicates that it was quite specifically the meeting place for those who believed in a *Catholic* Enlightenment in Vienna. It was, undoubtedly, for this reason that Mozart chose to join Gemmingen's lodge rather than the more radical and secular 'Zur wahren Eintracht'.

THE CATHOLIC ENLIGHTENMENT

The idea of a Catholic Enlightenment was, of course, anathema to most Enlightenment thinkers. 'To the *philosophes* who marched under the banner of *écrasez l'infame*', one historian has written, 'the notion of an Enlightenment in Catholic Germany was a contradiction in terms, a monstrous hybrid analogous to grafting a *philosophe*'s head and torso on to the hind quarters of a fat and malodorous sow'.[43] In 1781 the self-appointed guardian of the Berlin Enlightenment Friedrich Nicolai undertook a self-congratulatory tour of Germany to assess the progress of the Enlightenment outside Prussia. To no one's surprise, he came to the widely publicized conclusion that, for all Joseph II's manifest virtues, there could be no such thing as Enlightenment in a fundamentally Catholic country like Austria.[44] Nicolai was a Protestant chauvinist who believed that the north German *Aufklärung* was a natural development of the Protestant Reformation, and that as long as Catholicism continued to flourish in places like Vienna, the achievements of the Enlightenment elsewhere would never be secure.

Nicolai's attack prompted a flurry of indignation in Vienna, where numerous writers, including Alxinger and Blumauer, sprang to patriotic defence of the Austrian Enlightenment. But there were many who recognized that Nicolai's observations about the Josephine Enlightenment had some validity, for as one historian has suggested of Joseph, 'His reforming zeal had a distinctly religious quality'.[45] 'If I could make my whole country Catholic, I would,' Joseph once declared;[46] and Frederick the Great sneeringly dubbed him, 'My cousin the sacristan'.[47] In 1785 Alxinger himself, disillusioned with Joseph's reforms and perceiving that it was in the Protestant northern states of Germany that his own ideal of Enlightenment and literature had flourished, wrote to Nicolai agreeing, reluctantly, that Protestantism *was* perhaps a precondition for true Enlightenment.[48]

Religion was indeed an important part of Joseph II's programme. Before his accession the reform of the Church in Austria had played a central role in the pious Maria Theresa's own modernizing intentions. But increasingly during Maria Theresa's rule the papacy had blocked Habsburg efforts to reform the Church, and the monarchy had found itself forced to assert its independence from Rome. Under Joseph, the Austrian Church was brought directly under the control of the state, and the authority of the pope was denied altogether; Joseph's Censorship

Commission was instructed to be as vigilant in its guard against papal propaganda as it was to be against atheistical works.[49] In 1781 the state issued its own Catechism outlining the duties of the virtuous citizen, and the clergy were effectively transformed into functionaries of the state, to act, as the Lutheran pastor Herder observed in Frederick the Great's Prussia, 'as a moral teacher, a farmer, a list maker, a secret agent of the police'.[50]

Maria Theresa's reforms were often guided by the teachings of Italian Catholic reformers such as Giannone and Gravina, who had found refuge in Vienna, and most influentially, Ludovico Muratori. His ideals of a church dedicated to rational devotion and practical good works and charity were especially favoured by the empress, who encouraged a Muratori circle in Vienna, and many of Joseph's religious reforms were also guided by the Muratorian ideal. Religious ceremony and all forms of mysticism and superstition were discouraged, and in 1786 an imperial decree even banned loud choral music in church, on the pretext that it had been medically proven to be a serious health hazard, and ordered that it should be replaced by quiet singing or, better still, silent prayer.[51] Monasteries and convents that served no practical or charitable purpose were dissolved, and the new Josephine seminaries were dedicated to training a pastoral clergy. Joseph himself stressed the importance of the New Testament, and above all of the 'simple teaching of Jesus'.[52]

Maria Theresa had fought fierce battles with Joseph over the question of religious toleration, and one of Joseph's earliest and most widely applauded acts upon acceding to the throne had been the introduction of an Edict of Toleration. But Joseph himself retained orthodox religious beliefs. For all his utilitarian statism, he believed that it was the job of the Holy Ghost and not the state to 'change the hearts of men'.[53] Atheism he deplored, and his toleration stopped short of Deism.[54] Despite many arguments by Austrian church reformers for the abolition of clerical celibacy, Joseph resolutely refused even to discuss the possibility.

Among those who sprang to the defence of the Catholic Enlightenment in Austria was Johann Pezzl. And his novel *Faustin*, written in praise of Joseph II, has a polemical subtext which carries an important message. Pezzl's purpose in the book was not simply to laud the achievement of the Enlightenment in Josephine Vienna. It was also to counter the imputations of Protestant chauvinists like Nicolai that Enlightenment could only happen in Protestant Germany. Faustin's journeys throughout Europe demonstrate that intolerance and bigotry have no monopoly in Catholic countries; it is in the anti-Catholic Gordon riots in London that Faustin's tutor Pater Boniface is killed (a deliberately ironic comment on the death of Candide's tutor Pangloss at the hands of the Inquisition in Portugal), and in Prussia Faustin learns from the example of Frederick the Great that religious indifference may itself be as intolerant as religious faith. Although Pezzl was himself more Deist than Catholic, for his pains as a defender of the Josephine Enlightenment, he earned himself the accusation from Nicolai of fronting nothing less than a stealthy Jesuit conspiracy to extend the Counter-Reformation north of the Alps.[55] Like Mozart, Pezzl was a member of the lodge 'Zur Wohltätigkeit', whose founder and Master, Otto von Gemmingen, was also a committed Catholic. Gemmingen's moral journal *Der Weltmann* was firmly religious, dedicated to promoting 'The highest and most righteous feeling for Religion'.[56]

Among the lodge's other members were Joseph Eybel, canon lawyer and propagandist for Joseph's Church reforms, and Marc Anton Wittola, editor of the most important Catholic newspaper in Josephine Vienna, the *Wiener Kirchenzeitung*. Wittola was doctrinally conservative; he was a vehement opponent of northern German rationalism and of what he dubbed the 'wild rampant plague' of Voltaireanism.[57] But he saw no contradiction between his own faith and Joseph's reforms, declaring his ideal to be that of a 'Christian Enlightenment'.[58] On Joseph himself he lavished the warmest praise. 'He is a most marvellous ruler,' wrote Wittola at Joseph's accession. 'God has endowed him with such love of truth and justice, with such tireless diligence, with remarkable and all embracing devotion to the poor, that he draws all hearts to him.'[59]

Wittola has been described as 'Austria's first pro-Josephine church publicist',[60] and the importance of 'Zur Wohltätigkeit' was that it undoubtedly served as a centre for the reformist Muratorian Catholicism promoted by Joseph himself. The lodge's very name 'Zur Wohltätigkeit' – Beneficence[61] – hints at its dedication to the Muratorian ideal of salvation through charitable activities (justification by deeds rather than faith).

The members of 'Zur Wohltätigkeit' would readily have equated their religious beliefs with the broad aims of freemasonry. The fact that the pope had twice condemned freemasonry would have carried little weight with Josephine Catholics; 'Romsdruckender Despotismus' was how Gemmingen characterized papal pretensions to authority.[62] Scholars like the former Jesuit and custodian of the University Library in Vienna, Karl Michaeler, who published a pamphlet in defence of masonry against the papal bulls, even went so far as to argue that early Christianity, operating like a secret society of initiates, was itself comparable to freemasonry, and that it shared the same aims: 'Donations for the poor, alms for the elderly, foster homes for the helpless orphan'.[63]

The masonic funeral oration delivered in Mozart's honour after his death quite explicitly commended the lamented brother for having practised as a freemason 'living in virtue, that he may die as a Mason, as a Christian'.[64] Mozart had been brought up in essentially Muratorian beliefs by Leopold Mozart (see pp. 9–10) who once commended his son's notable 'desire to help the oppressed' as having been inherited from his father.[65] 'Do not be too devout,' Mozart inscribed as a gentle reproof in his wife Constanze's prayer book,[66] a reminder that religious piety was better expressed in deeds than in contemplation or self-mortification. And he reproached his father for insinuating that he was allowing the welfare of his soul to lapse, pointing out that true faith could not be judged by the mere outward tokens of religious observance.[67] He often visited the church of the Piarists, a teaching order that based its work upon the New Testament, and he made considerable efforts to secure a place in the Piarist school for his son Karl.

Mozart's own letters are full of little homilies to 'kindness', to the importance of the 'heart', or what French Catholic Enlighteners called 'La religion du cœur'. In Mozart's 'commonplace' album his friend Gottfried von Jacquin writes 'True genius without heart is a thing of naught – for not great understanding alone, nor imagination alone, nor both together, make genius – Love – Love – Love! That is the soul of genius.'[68] These sentimental effusions find their way into Mozart's own funeral oration, which lays great emphasis upon his charitable activities. 'However much propriety demands that we recall to mind his artistic talents, by so much the less should we forget to render a fitting offering to his excellent heart.' Couched in the effusive language of the period, the Ode itself exhorts its readers to recall the good deeds of the lamented composer:

> And think of him who to poor widows' dwellings
> Innumerable gifts did bear;
> Who built his happiness on orphan's blessings
> And gave his coat to shivering poverty . . . [69]

One of the more surprising books in Mozart's exiguous library was English, a copy of *Automathes. The Capacity and Extent of the Human Understanding* by Edward Gibbon's tutor John Kirkby. *Automathes*, described by Gibbon himself as 'a philosophical fiction',[70] is an extended paean to the love and beneficence of God, and to Man's delight in imitating God's love in works of 'benefaction and charity'. But despite his claims of finding evidence of God's authorship of nature in every natural occurrence, Kirkby is no pure Deist. Supernatural revelation survives alongside natural revelation as the most certain evidence of God; and faith, rather than reason, remains the ultimate channel between Man and God. In Kirkby's utopian kingdom the boundaries of state and Church are fluid; temporal laws comply with spiritual laws, even though the Church makes no attempt to dictate these, and instead, concentrates on charity and education, a remarkable blueprint for Josephine Catholicism.[71]

For Mozart too, beneficence was not a substitute for religion (as for the secular moralist) but an expression of it. Mozart's letters tell us of more conventional signs of devotion – attendance at Mass, saying the rosary in thanks for some happy event – which are interwoven in the texture of Mozart's life in a very Catholic fashion; a commingling of religious observance with everyday, profane activities that might have shocked a devout Protestant. But Muratorian Catholicism, like Latitudinarian Anglicanism, was full of reassurances that religious duty was propitious to Man's pursuit of earthly happiness.[72]

The true evidence for Mozart's religious faith is in his works. Romantic and Victorian critics, mistaking religiosity for religious expression, complained that Mozart's church music was lacking in religious feeling. (E. T. A. Hoffmann always maintained that Mozart's church music was his weakest.) But Mozart wrote church music as a natural extension of his other activities, making no distinction between different forms of musical expression other than that required by liturgical convention. His talent, as Leopold never ceased to remind him, was a gift from God – indeed, a token of Divine Grace[73] – and in every act of composition he was fulfilling his duty to God. After he left Salzburg Mozart had little outlet for religious music, because of the new restrictions on the use of music in churches. (Haydn also produced no Masses during a comparable period between 1782 and 1796). This makes the composition of the magnificent but unfinished Mass in C minor (K. 427/417A), begun in late 1782, after the performances of *Die Entführung*, to fulfil a private vow made to God for the recovery of Constanze from illness, all the more revealing as an act of personal, rather than statutory, devotion.[74] It is a remarkable testament to Mozart's inner faith (as well as to his love for Constanze).

But remarkable as it is, neither the C minor Mass nor perhaps even the Requiem, the other large-scale liturgical composition of his maturity, provide the truest measure of Mozart's Christian belief and profoundly religious temperament. This is more clearly revealed in his later operas from *Le nozze di Figaro* onwards, in which he was able to give voice to his understanding of the Christian doctrine as it applied to life itself.

XI

The return to Italian opera

Despite its shortcomings, *Die Entführung aus dem Serail* was an enormous success with the Viennese public. It was regularly performed during an eight month period from July 1782 to February 1783, and provided Mozart with just the springboard he needed to launch his career in Vienna as a composer-performer. The next five years were to be his most prolific and financially successful, and contained the greatest concentration of masterpieces. But it was more than three years before he was able to work on an opera again, and only a month after the triumphant première of *Die Entführung* in July 1782 Mozart was writing angrily to his father that he was considering leaving Vienna. 'If Germany, my beloved fatherland, of which, as you know, I am proud, will not accept me, then in God's name let France or England become richer by another talented German, to the disgrace of the German nation.'[1] What had gone wrong?

The immediate cause of disappointment was the emperor himself, who had failed to offer Mozart the official post the composer believed he merited. Joseph's parsimony was legendary, and Mozart had already had cause to comment on his niggardliness.[2] Although Mozart's early biographers liked to portray him as the victim of cabals and intrigues within the court, in particular on the part of a jealous Italian faction, the real problem lay with Joseph himself, as Mozart recognized. Joseph had no conception of the artist's role beyond the merely practical one of proselytizing his reforms and encouraging civic virtue. He was completely lacking in understanding of the independent needs of creative artists, whom he considered, like his clergy, as no better than glorified civil servants.[3] When in 1784 van Swieten proposed to introduce a copyright law that would undoubtedly have made Mozart's career as an independent composer viable, the emperor refused on the grounds that it would restrict the number of actual items published and sold in Austria.[4]

In 1787 the satirist Josef Richter published a pamphlet entitled *Warum wird Kaiser Josef nicht von seinem Volke geliebt?* ('Why will Emperor Joseph not be loved by his people?'), a catalogue of complaints against the emperor, of which one was that he had completely failed to support the artists and writers in his capital. Like Joseph, Sonnenfels made much of the importance of raising national poets, but in the same breath he could suggest that such poets should not expect 'purses filled with gold and diamond rings ... A single word in praise of the poet by Kaunitz, a smile of the benevolent Liechtenstein must be considered as more of an incentive, more of a reward than all the gold in the world.'[5] Mozart received many words of praise from the great Kaunitz, as he himself acknowledged. But loyalty to Joseph and words of praise from Kaunitz did not pay the rent and feed the children.

Like so many Germans of his generation, Mozart had looked to Vienna at the accession of Joseph II as the centre for a major regeneration of German culture in which he could play a part as a German musician. But their expectations were founded upon false assumptions about Joseph's cultural aims. For Joseph II, the holding-together of his disparate kingdoms was of far greater importance than any quasi-imperial pretensions to forge a German cultural identity. Despite Joseph's obsessive interest in the theatre, he had little understanding of the value of cultural life beyond the strictly utilitarian.

For Josephines like Sonnenfels and Gemmingen, the reform of Austrian culture was perceived as no more than a part of the greater effort (characterized by moves such as the enforced Germanization of the non-Austrian territories in 1784) to unify and homogenize the Habsburg territories, and to create a sense of national allegiance to the monarchy. It was in furthering the interests of the Habsburg rulers of Bohemia, Hungary, Italy and the Netherlands that Sonnenfels developed the concept of *Vaterlandsliebe* in the 1760s, and promoted it with increasing stridency. Similarly, Gemmingen in *Der Weltmann* attacked the cultural cosmopolitanism of an aristocracy which he considered insufficiently patriotic, and proposed that the fashionable 'Weltbürgerschaft and Menschenliebe' of the 1760s and 1770s should be replaced by a new nationalism. His prescriptions, however, took no account of indigenous Austrian cultural traditions.[6]

The failure of the Josephines to understand the historical nature of cultural development, and their belief that an instant Austrian national culture could be created by state rationalization of the arts, was compounded by the notion that Austrian culture could be 'reformed' by the simple importation of suitable models from abroad. The cultural leaders of the Austrian Enlightenment were convinced that its success depended upon being able to drag Viennese culture away from its roots in baroque, Catholic art. They were acutely sensitive to the comments of critics like Friedrich Nicolai who argued that Vienna was far from being ready to assume the mantle of German letters and culture so hastily thrown around its shoulders by the accession of Joseph II. Vienna, he argued, might excel in the non-discursive (and, for Nicolai, essentially non-rational) arts of music, architecture and painting, but Austria was in no state to be entrusted with the wider furtherance of German literary culture.[7]

Protestant northern Germany, with its proud, free cities and its great universities, had long looked on Viennese culture as sensual and frivolous, and a baffling mixture of courtly, populist and religious elements. Nicolai was delighted to be able to score a point against both Goethe (whose youthful *Sturm und Drang* works he hated) and Viennese literary taste by reporting that in Vienna Goethe's novel *Werther* had served as the theme for a firework display. Even Austrian music was dismissed with condescension by northern critics. In the 1770s a series of articles was launched in newspapers in cities like Hamburg and Leipzig attacking the music of Haydn on the grounds that it was frivolous, rustic, exotic and unlearned.[8] Even Leopold Mozart, good bourgeois to the last, considered Viennese cultural life to be excessively hedonistic, lowbrow, and given over to 'foolish stuff, dances, devils, ghosts, magic, clowns ... witches[9] and apparitions.[10]

The main aim of those who sought to implement the ideals of the Enlightenment in Vienna was, accordingly, to suppress traditional Viennese culture so as to establish a modern literary culture in Austria that would stand alongside those of England, France and – increasingly – northern Germany. In 1761 the young Sonnenfels founded a Deutsche Gesellschaft in Vienna, in order to disseminate works by contemporary northern (and Swiss) writers and critics. By the end of the 1760s a mounting pile of these books had been republished in Vienna (thus circumventing the censorship of imported books by the customs), and Austrian writers themselves were making consistent efforts to model their efforts upon those of their German peers. Contact with Weimar was deliberately cultivated by members of the Born circle.

Viennese writers kept their fingers closely on the pulse of cultural developments in Vienna as they nursed Austrian literature into manhood, nervously monitoring its progress. In 1782 both Gemmingen and Blumauer published articles assessing the developments that had taken place since the freeing of the press and the relaxation of censorship (which gave Vienna a significant advantage over Berlin, as Lessing had conceded). Blumauer was still hopeful that the new freedom would in time produce something more substantial; Gemmingen considered that the Viennese theatre was still 'nicht viel besser als Hanswurst's Jackte'[11] ('not much better than pantomime farce'), but looked forward to the 'beautiful dawn which glimmers not much farther away'.[12] But only a year later Blumauer published an article in the *Realzeitung*, in which he praised Goethe for having liberated German literature from foreign influences, and regretted that Austrian literature had failed to keep pace.[13] In his letter of 1785 to Nicolai, Alxinger agreed with his diagnosis that the traditional baroque-Catholic culture of Austria was inimical to the development of a great literary tradition,[14] and by 1787, Leon, another member of the Born circle, was writing sadly to Reinhold in Weimar, 'I entirely doubt, whether Austrian literature will ever attain the level of a true culture'.[15]

To this day, Vienna's relationship to German literary culture remains ambiguous. Statues of Goethe and Schiller are prominently placed on opposite sides of the Opera Ring in Vienna; on the façade of the Burg-theater the busts of Grillparzer and his Austrian colleagues are relegated to a side portal, and the central position is again occupied by Goethe, flanked by Lessing and Schiller. Only on the portals of the Volkstheater is Grillparzer allowed to assume a central position, supported by the quintessential Viennese playwrights Nestroy and Raimund who brought to literary fruition in the early nineteenth century the indigenous elements of Austrian culture – populist, satirical, farcical, magical – which those committed to the concept of a reformed national culture had chosen to ignore.

The traditional Viennese theatre had been based upon a lively mish-mash of influences drawn from Jesuit sacred drama and the popular improvised drama of the Hanswurst (which itself often drew upon *commedia dell'arte* and *opera buffa*, or parodied Italian *opera seria* and Jesuit drama). Viennese *Volksstücke* dominated the Kärntnerthortheater, the second of the two official theatres in Vienna. It was the traditions of popular theatre that Kaunitz and Sonnenfels were determined to sup-press; they banished the Hanswurst from the court theatre and encour-aged in its place the importation of French drama. The inevitable effect of these reforms had been to create a vacuum within the official Viennese theatre. Even during the 1770s, when Joseph was insisting on plays being performed in German, they were invariably translations or imitations of French and acceptable northern German plays, often by writers of non-Austrian origin such as Gebler, Stephanie, Schröder, Gemmingen or Schikaneder. When in 1777 a competition was held for new plays for the recently established National Theatre very little local talent was forth-coming.[16] Much the same had occurred with the German Singspiel, a bourgeois art form deliberately modelled on the French *opéra comique*. Simple, naïve and sentimental, Singspiel eschewed the dramatic and musical extravagance of Italian opera (even sentimental *opera buffa* was musically more demanding than *opéra comique* or Singspiel), and in so doing, created a form that was bland and monotonous.

But the traditions of Viennese theatre, as indeed of Viennese Catholic culture in general, had not died altogether. Baroque elements survive quite clearly in late eighteenth-century Viennese classical art. In the church of St Michael at the Michaelerthor there is a sculpted altarpiece of 1781 which represents a tableau of six larger than life-size figures of the evangelists and archangels, who draw the worshipper's gaze to the name of Jesus. Neo-classical in form, but clearly baroque in sentiment, the work is an extraordinary fusion of apparently contradictory elements, designed, as a contemporary admirer wrote, to 'move the heart of the pure observer' and guide him 'to the genuine truths of Christianity'.[17] It is a religious work of art unlike anything in European art of the period.

The baroque-Catholic element in Viennese art also survived in Viennese theatre, despite the efforts of Sonnenfels and the Josephines.[18] In the 1760s the playwright Philip Hafner had written dramas that retained many elements of the improvised theatre, and the religious-metaphysical trait in Viennese drama survived even in the works of writers who otherwise toed the official 'reformed' line. Gebler's play *Thamos*, with a significant musical contribution from Mozart himself, was admired by Wieland but received criticism from him for its supernatural elements.[19] The highly popular playwright Paul Weidmann, strict Catholic, civil-servant and author of numerous dramas based on the current French model, wrote an allegorical 'Faust' drama, complete with demons and angels, performed in Prague in 1777.

But it was in the popular theatres of the suburbs that the indigenous traditions of Viennese theatre were ultimately to survive and triumph. In 1776 the first licences were granted for independent theatres, and in 1781 the theatre director Karl Marinelli took over the theatre in the Leopoldstadt, where he drew with eclectic abandon on all the traditions of Viennese theatre, creating dramas that were satirical, magical, parodistic and (increasingly during the course of the decade) musical. Despite Joseph II's reservations about the development, by the second half of the 1780s Viennese Singspiel had found its niche in Marinelli's theatre, and attracted large, enthusiastic audiences. By 1786 a number of artists had defected to Marinelli's theatre from the official National Singspiel, which soon died of its own worthy dullness. In 1787 a second theatre opened in the suburbs, the Freihaus Theater auf der Wieden, which was taken over by Schikaneder in 1790. Abandoning his earlier penchant for Josephine moral dramas, Schikaneder made an instant bid to rival Marinelli. It was here, finally, that Mozart would be able to fulfil his lifelong desire to write a true German opera.

But when Mozart was kicking his heels after the lack of commissions following the success of *Die Entführung*, Marinelli's new theatre in the Leopoldstadt suburb had only recently opened, and its fare was considered coarse, primitive and lowbrow by official opinion. The problems Mozart faced in trying to establish his identity as a composer within Viennese culture can therefore be imagined. Habsburg nationalism, together with a narrow definition of civic virtue – the real impetus behind Joseph's theatre reforms – could be of no interest for Mozart. And the aggressively literary preferences of the Born circle clearly excluded musicians. Significantly, Blumauer's *Realzeitung*, the unofficial cultural organ of 'Zur wahren Eintracht', contains no discussion of music (or painting). Music (and hence Mozart himself) is nowhere mentioned in the published correspondence of Alxinger or Ratschky, and the *Journal für Freymaurer* merely deigns to publish a few masonic ditties for use by other brothers. Those Viennese *Aufklärer* who hoped, like Mozart, that Vienna might become the centre for a broader revival of German culture were studiously turning their back on the very traditions of indigenous Viennese culture that might have given Mozart a *raison d'être* as a specifically Viennese composer: Catholic church music; a lively, colourful and spectacular theatre. In their place Mozart was left with a wretchedly immature and anaemic form, the German Singspiel.

If in *Die Entführung* Mozart had hoped to woo Joseph by writing an ideologically Josephine opera, he had set about it the wrong way. The emperor's caustic comment on *Die Entführung*, 'Too many notes, my dear Mozart',[20] was cannier than we recognize. Often dismissed as apocryphal, it is entirely in accord with Joseph's better-documented opinions that Mozart's music was in general too complex and difficult. For Joseph had seen that Mozart's new opera had gone against all the current declared aims of German opera – aimed at the new bourgeoisie – to be simple and direct. 'I hope that you will get something to do in Mannheim where they are always performing German operas,' Leopold had written to his son in 1777. 'If you do, you know that I need not urge you to imitate the natural and popular style.'[21] There is therefore a deliberate cussedness in Mozart's flouting of the conventional expectations of German Singspiel in *Die Entführung*. In the musical excesses of Konstanze's 'Marten aller Arten' (quite the largest and most elaborate aria which Mozart was ever to write, for which no dramaturgical explanation can possibly serve) we hear Mozart throwing down his gauntlet to the destiny of German opera and saying 'that's what German opera *should* be'. The Quartet which concludes Act II is one of the most complex and intricate pieces of dramatic music he ever wrote.[22] As soon as he heard *Die Entführung* Goethe instantly recognized that it had rendered his own Weimar experiments in producing Singspiels in the approved 'simple and economic style' quite futile.[23]

Mozart had no doubts about where the paucity of the official Singspiel would eventually lead. His letters of late 1782 and early 1783 are full of impatient judgements on the amateurish efforts of composers like Umlauf and Gassmann, and he foresaw the closure of the German National Singspiel in Vienna in March 1783.[24] (It was revived again in 1785 before being finally closed in 1787.) Mozart's insistence on putting his own musical and dramatic priorities before ideologically sound texts had already meant that in December 1782 he had refused to consider setting a worthless bit of patriotic tub-thumping by Frederick the Great's favourite writer Ayrenhoff entitled *Welches ist die beste Nation?*[25]

The Josephine concept of German culture as a patriotric Habsburg culture could hold no attraction for Mozart. In May 1785 he turned down an offer to set a libretto by Anton von Klein, whose stuffy Metastasian text for *Günther von Schwarzburg* he had so soundly condemned in Mannheim a few years previously (see p. 54). Klein had offered no definite commission for performance of the opera; but undoubtedly Mozart was also repelled by the nature of the crudely rhetorical libretto; *Kaiser Rudolf von Habsburg* is a piece of blatant Habsburg propaganda about the founder of the Habsburg dynasty (never, in fact, emperor), famed in history for his modesty and decency, and portrayed in Klein's play as a proto-Enlightenment forebear of Joseph II. Furthermore, the widely held idea that a pure German art had to cultivate a deliberate primitivism that eschewed complexity as alien (as advocated by Klopstock's literary followers, and by the Berlin *Liederschulen*) had nothing to offer him.

If he was to write German opera it would have to be for himself, or for an ideal audience à la Wagner. 'I prefer German opera, even though it means more trouble for me. Every nation has its own opera, and why not Germany... Very well then! I am now writing a German opera for myself,' he wrote to Leopold in February 1783 – an extraordinary declaration.[26] But tellingly, the libretto he had chosen for himself was based upon Goldoni's structurally complex masterpiece *Il servitore di due padroni*.

A month before this letter Mozart had accepted a suggestion from Count Orsini-Rosenberg that he might consider writing an Italian opera (in anticipation of the assembly of a new Italian company in Vienna). He threw himself into the project with feverish energy. By May 1783 he was scouring every possible source for an Italian libretto (claiming to have read a hundred possible texts), and was soon to start work on a new Italian opera with Varesco (the unfinished *L'oca del Cairo*). He was at the same time considering another libretto he had received, and had opened negotiations with Lorenzo da Ponte for a completely new libretto, to be written to Mozart's own specifications. (Sometimes assumed to be a second unfinished work, *Lo sposo deluso*, although the text betrays none of Da Ponte's customary dexterity or felicity.)

Having come to fulfil his dream of writing German opera, within a short while he was plunged into work on Italian operas. In part this change of direction was purely pragmatic; the German opera was suspended in 1783, and Joseph gave way to court pressure to reassemble an Italian company. But there was in Mozart's decision to return to Italian opera a more fundamental artistic consideration. German opera was 'more trouble' for Mozart because it was a primitive and ill-defined genre, and as such, was unable to provide him with the pre-existent forms and schemata with which to mediate his own experience and expressive response to the world: the short cuts and fallbacks upon which any artist relies; the patterns of shared expectation which establish a common meeting ground between audience and artist. For this reason *Die Entführung aus dem Serail* is in many respects a less assured work than his adolescent opera *La finta giardiniera*. In the absence of a German tradition capable of fulfilling his needs, Mozart returned to *opera buffa*. It was an artistic step comparable, in some ways, to his decision to affirm his religious position by joining the Catholic lodge 'Zur Wohltätigkeit'; evidence of a desire to belong; to be part of a tradition or community.

Works of art engage with historical circumstances. But they also engage with each other. Thus one critic, having carefully analysed the social context of the eighteenth-century French novel, reminds us that 'if we turn to the novels of Diderot and, later, Laclos for confirmation of these social facts, we must also remember that they reveal as much about their literary origins as about their social environment'.[27] This is especially true of eighteenth-century art, in which the apparent liberation of art-forms from traditional genres and formulas, to engage more directly with social reality, can be deceptive. Hogarth's paintings, long accepted as the first consistent attempt to portray modern urban life in England, derive much of their meaning from reference not to the 'real life' of Hogarth's London, but from elaborate parodic or ironic references to other works of art.

Generic forms provided the eighteenth-century artist with the structual framework and the referential systems which gave depth to his art. The significance of such formal genres struck Goethe and Schiller during the 1780s and 1790s, when much of their invigorating correspondence was taken up with the problems of the classical genres in art. For as both writers recognized, the classical genres offered to the artist who found his own culture lacking in historical depth or continuity a tradition from which he might draw strength. Goethe specifically lamented in *Wilhelm Meisters theatralische Sendung* that Gottsched had – like Sonnenfels in Vienna – instigated the expulsion of the Hanswurst traditions from the German stage. In the absence of a deeply rooted native German literary culture, both Goethe and Schiller turned back to classical forms.

Comparably, *opera buffa* offered to Mozart a well-founded genre with fertile (but not too unshakeably ossified) traditions of performance and practice, an enormous variety of styles and – by the 1780s – some sophistication. Musically it had developed far from its simplistic origins, and had absorbed on the way both the social interests of Goldoni and the satirical influence of Gozzi, as well as sensibility and novelistic plots. It reached its peak in the hands of librettists such as Giovanni Bertati, Giambattista Casti and Lorenzo Da Ponte whose talents were often far greater than those of the composers whom they served.

Lorenzo Da Ponte, disgraced abbé, adventurer, intriguer and philanderer, makes an apparently curious partner for the upright young bourgeois musician Mozart. But it was in some ways a complementary partnership, Da Ponte's robust realism tempering Mozart's more idealistic inclinations. There is even a sense in which Da Ponte can be seen as Mozart's spiritual twin. For all his would-be Casanovan bravado, Da Ponte was, like Mozart, a man in search of identity, security and acceptance. Born a Jew (a fact of which his memoirs significantly make no mention) he had been able to leave the ghetto when his family had converted to Catholicism, and he had subsequently entered the Church. Having disgraced himself as an abbé and been expelled from Venice for adultery, Da Ponte found his way to Vienna.

Like Rousseau, Da Ponte appears to have suffered guilty anxiety for his rejection of both the faith of his forefathers and the paternal embrace of the Catholic Church. Unlike Casanova, he was not a true adventurer relishing his footloose quest for new horizons of pleasure, but a man in search of certainties. Alongside the evidence of his philandering, the *Memoirs* reveal a desire for domestic respectability. Above all, in his dedicated affectation of the role of man of letters, Da Ponte reveals a longing to lay claim to the great inheritance of Italian literature, the only church which would accept the prodigal son, and also confirm that he had indeed escaped the ghetto of Ceneda.

Lorenzo Da Ponte may not have been a great thinker or an original writer, but he was highly educated, and was steeped in the intellectual traditions of classical and Renaissance Italian literature. An elegant and pointed versifier, he wrote librettos that are full of witty verbal play and allusion. Each has a distinctive linguistic timbre, to which Mozart instinctively responded. For *Le nozze di Figaro* Da Ponte turned Beaumarchais's racy comedy, with its strikingly earthy language, into an elegiac romance suffused with poetic reminiscences of Petrarch and Dante, and with the tropes of the *arcadia* movement that had dominated eighteenth-century Italian literature. In *Don Giovanni* the characters, whether comic or serious, are all swept up into the linguistic world of baroque revenge tragedy, the text shot through with images of sensuousness and violence, sometimes to darkly comic effect. (Da Ponte himself claimed to have written *Don Giovanni* with Dante's *Inferno* in mind.)[28] *Così fan tutte* combines classical allusion and Metastasian parody in a text that is constantly undercutting and destabilizing its own reality.

Only within *opera buffa* could Mozart create the dazzling play of musical allusion, parody and irony which gives his mature art such complexity and ambiguity. And most certainly only within *opera buffa*, whose origins in the symbiotic relationship of parody between the *seria* and the *buffa*, of conflict between masters and servants, had survived throughout its history, was it possible in 1785 for Mozart to consider turning Beaumarchais's recent *succès de scandale, Le mariage de Figaro*, into a music-drama.

XII

Le nozze di Figaro

Mozart probably began work on *Le nozze di Figaro* in the late summer of 1785, barely a year after the scandalous but triumphant première of Beaumarchais's play in Paris. For the most part written before the decisive turning of the tide against the Josephine Enlightenment in 1786, *Le nozze di Figaro* represents Mozart's most completely balanced vision of society, a world where individualism need no longer be constrained by (and eventually sacrificed to) the imperatives of the all-powerful state, and whose citizens are free, autonomous individuals learning to interact harmoniously with each other. It combines social realism with a radiant moral idealism and a truly Catholic sense of the everyday immanence of the spiritual in the material world.

Le nozze di Figaro is a comedy in the sense implied by Dante when he entitled his great poem a *Commedia* (only later called the *Divine* Comedy), the purpose of which was 'to remove those living in this life from the state of misery and lead them to the state of bliss'.[1] But for Mozart, bliss is sought in this life rather than in heaven, and is founded upon the earthly institution of marriage. As Vanbrugh's Constant observes: 'Though marriage be a lottery, in which there are wondrous many blanks, yet there's one inestimable lot in which the only heaven on earth is written'.[2] And if felicity is to be sought on earth, then, as *Le nozze di Figaro* recognizes, the forms of actual human society and the search for their perfection assumes far greater importance.

REGAINING PARADISE

Few operas begin with a more mundane, less exalted opening: the servant Figaro measuring a room with a yardstick and calling out figures; his bride-to-be Susanna celebrating her present happiness in the humble pleasure of trying on her bridal bonnet. 'Ora son contento' 'Now I am happy' she sings with simple pleasure. But such innocent bliss cannot last, and to the extent that it would have prevented humankind from aspiring beyond its primal condition in Eden, it is even undesirable.[3] Hence Goethe's Faust is forbidden to desire that any moment of pleasure or ease may last for ever.[4] Figaro's and Susanna's simple happiness is no sooner established than it is ruptured by Susanna's announcement that the Count has designs on her. Knowledge of good and evil has been introduced into the world.

The loss of bliss – of innocence, of peace with oneself, of harmony with nature – runs as a theme throughout *Le nozze di Figaro*, pervading the opera's characters, and suffusing much of the opera's music with nostalgia. The Countess looks back to a time when she imagined herself happy, and in her aria 'Dove sono' laments the vanished 'bei momenti', ('moments'), asking, 'Why has the memory of that happiness not faded from my breast?' The Count is violently tormented by the knowledge that his servant Figaro will enjoy the bliss with Susanna which he is denied: 'Must I see, while I live, a servant of mine happy!' Cherubino is no less racked by his barely understood sexual longings, the objects of which remain forever beyond his reach. His desires are as yet innocent, but having gained illicit knowledge of the Count's guilty *amours*, Cherubino is to be banished from the cosseting cradle of the castle, where the promise of felicity – the Countess – resides, and thrust out into the real world. In his aria 'Non più andrai' Figaro torments Cherubino with his picture of the harsh, adult world which he must now enter; a battlefield of hardship and toil where there is little happiness. Most poignant of all is Barbarina's achingly wistful little cavatina at the beginning of Act IV. 'L'ho perduta' ('I have lost it'), she sings, searching for the pin that betokens the Count's acceptance of Susanna's supposed assignation with him. The ribald innuendos of Figaro and Marcellina as they suggest she has lost more than a pin are only partly to the point: Barbarina laments a whole fallen world of lost innocence.

In his essay *Über naive und sentimentalische Dichtung* ('Concerning Naïve and Sentimental Literature') Schiller identified humankind's fall from Eden (and its subsequent consciousness of loss and disjunction from its former unity with nature) as its primary existential experience. Sentimental art is a result of that loss, an expression of modern humanity's longing to regain its unity with nature: elegiac art laments the loss, idyllic art attempts to restore nature to man. *Le nozze di Figaro* is at times both elegiac and idyllic. But the truest function of art, Schiller suggests, is to maintain the ideal before men's eyes; to ensure that Man does not take the easy option of regressive indulgence of the senses. 'In civilized society nature exists only as an ideal. Harmony and unity are ideal.' The artist's task, therefore, is 'to raise reality to the ideal . . . to *re-present the ideal*'.[5]

The restoration of bliss and harmony is the predominant theme of *Le nozze di Figaro*. But the opera also recognizes that humankind sustains itself as much by the hope of future promise as by transitory present happiness. 'Vieni gioia bella' ('Come, lovely joy'), sings Susanna in her garden aria 'Deh vieni', projecting her longings for felicity beyond herself and her immediate circumstances. At the end of the opera, even as earthly harmony is restored for the present, the characters prefer to look forward to future bliss. 'Tutti contenti *saremo*' ('We *shall* all be happy'), they sing.

But the lesson of the Enlightenment for those at the end of the eighteenth century was that the ideal or transcendent unrelated to the real – the speculative divorced from experience, hope extended beyond the bounds of possibility – turns into the tyranny of abstractions (to which Benjamin Constant was later so memorably to complain that the individual had been finally sacrificed in the French Revolution), or the bitterness of disappointment. 'True happiness consists in decreasing the difference between our desires and our powers' wrote Rousseau,[6] and late Enlightenment artists were constantly reminding their age that whatever we choose to call transcendent arises from the orbit of human possibilities. 'Yet at the heart, the power of the nobler creation is contained in the holy circle of the living formation,' writes Goethe in his poem *Metamorphosen der Tiere*: 'No god can extend these bounds which nature honours: For only thus limited was the perfect ever possible.'[7] Even Schiller, the perennial idealist to Goethe's realist, warns of the dangers of false illusions, 'when an idea is carried so far that not only no experience corresponds to it . . . but also that it is repugnant to the conditions of all possible experience, so that, in order to realize it, one must leave human nature altogether.'[8]

THE END OF SENTIMENTALISM

Le nozze de Figaro eschews such false idealism. But it also rejects the sentimental delusions which had sustained earlier bourgeois Enlightenment thinking. In *La nouvelle Héloïse* Rousseau's doomed heroine Julie had vainly dreamt of a society resembling a large household, cemented by no more than 'inseparable couples, the zeal of domestic attentions and paternal and maternal love'.[9] In some ways this is just the society to which the eccentric household of Aguasfrescas, in which *Le nozze di Figaro* takes place, aspires: a household which contains all classes of society, held together by marriage, by domestic loyalty between classes, and by the dissolution of enmities in the discovery of familial relationships. However, the opera recognizes – as Julie was tragically unable to do – that in the real world social and emotional relationships have to be made rather than taken as read; conjugal inseparability, domestic loyalty and family love have to be worked for, and even then do not guarantee social harmony.

In *Le nozze di Figaro* family reconciliation is therefore not simply avoided, as in *Die Entführung aus dem Serail*, but deliberately subverted.

Beaumarchais's Figaro does indeed find that virtually all his problems are solved when his two mortal enemies, Marcellina and Bartolo, turn out to be his mother and father. But the cliché whereby the natural ties of nature, the *voix du sang*, are always recognized is turned upside down by Beaumarchais, for the voices of nature speak so strongly to Marcellina that she misreads them, only narrowly avoiding committing incest with her own son. 'Didn't nature tell you it a thousand times over?' she asks Figaro, forgetting that what nature seemed to tell her was not quite proper. 'Never' he replies firmly. Beaumarchais's recognition and reconciliation scene is pure comic parody of the genre (of which Voltaire's *Zaïre* was the *locus classicus*), and is beautifully realized in Mozart's musical presentation in the contrast between the over-effusiveness of Marcellina's response (every child's nightmare of public displays of maternal affection) and the less-than-enthusiastic hesitancy of Bartolo's acceptance of his new-found paternity.

If everyone may be someone else's relative (as the sentimental myth liked to pretend), then indeed, incest is a dangerous possibility, and fear of incest became a recurrent shadow in later eighteenth-century art. 'I would venture, in a word, that incest ought to be every government's law – every government whose basis is fraternity,' writes de Sade in *La philosophie dans le boudoir*,[10] issuing a warning worthy of Swift of the dangers of elevating the laws of nature above their proper place, and exposing the Enlightenment's familial myth with the imperturbable logic that characterizes his most outrageous suggestions. At the end of Matthew Lewis's Gothic shocker *The Monk* of 1796 (much admired by de Sade) the reunited family cliché achieves its ultimate incestuous subversion when the novel's diabolic anti-hero discovers that he has raped his own long-lost sister and murdered his mother. This accorded with de Sade's own prescription that in the modern republican state all forms of maternal and familial love should be replaced by love of the fatherland, and that maternal love which threatens the state should be punished and overthrown by rape and murder of the mother. Figaro, fortunately, is spared such excesses. But only just.

Even less sentimental is the representation of the struggle that takes place between Count Almaviva and his valet Figaro. In eighteenth-century society servants were highly visible, and in the great cities, before the industrial age, they made up a significant proportion of the population. Ideally eighteenth-century masters would have preferred their servants to be invisible: the eighteenth-century house was designed to keep servants relegated to the basement and attic, so that they crept up and down concealed staircases and performed their ministrations from secret closets and cubbyholes. However, fractious and insubordinate servants will not conveniently erase themselves from most eighteenth-century art any more than they were dumb or invisible in life.

In fact the eighteenth century reckoned that it had a servant problem, and a considerable mythology grew up around it. Diaries and letters (Mozart's included; he found it especially annoying to have to deal with the country girls employed as maidservants when his wife was away from home) are full of complaints about the sloppiness, laziness and insubordination of modern-day servants.[11] Swift's *Directions to Servants* methodically lists every subversive and devious trick of the domestic trade. Among the ephemera that flooded the market when Joseph II lifted press restrictions in Vienna was a popular sub-genre which earned itself its own name: *Stubenmädchenbroschuren*. These addressed the servant problem with lurid stories warning the upright young bourgeois son of the house against the alluring wiles of servant girls who sought to emulate Richardson's Pamela and seduce their way to becoming mistress of the house.[12] The penalties for servants who broke the trust of their masters were, significantly, especially severe in eighteenth-century society; in France, the sole burning at the stake during the century was of a servant who had broken open his mistress's desk and then set fire to the house to conceal his crime.[13]

What the eighteenth century masters were frightened of was the new independence of servants. 'The movement of the progressive societies has been uniform in one respect. Through all its course it has been distinguished by the gradual dissolution of family dependency and the growth of individual obligation in its place,' wrote Henry Maine, referring to the household *famulus* of feudal society. 'Thus the status of the slave has disappeared – it has been superseded by the contractual relation of the servant to his master.'[14] Figaro, as we know from his great autobiographical monologue in Beaumarchais's play, is representative of this new breed of servant: the individualist freebooter, touchy about his honour and dignity, who enters into a waged agreement with his master, rather than the serf born upon the seigneurial estate and destined to lifelong servitude. One of the Austrian aristocracy's most vehement complaints against Joseph II's abolition of feudal ties in the Habsburg territories was that masters no longer had any effective control over their servants. Joseph's characteristic response, a classic example of the authoritarian backlash that invariably followed the dissolution of traditional social structures, was to forbid any form of collective wage-bargaining by servants, or agreements amongst servants not to take posts made vacant by another's dismissal.[15]

The earlier Enlightenment's more typical response to the troubling new status of servants had been to present a vision of paternalistic masters and sickeningly loyal and grateful servants living together in neo-feudal harmony. *Le nozze di Figaro* deliberately subverts the comforts of this sentimental delusion. The relationship between the Countess and Susanna, however affectionate, is one of expediency brought about by a common threat rather than genuine sisterly sentiment. In the grand accompanied recitative to her aria 'Dove sono', the Countess lists with mounting indignation the catalogue of cruelties and wrongs inflicted upon her by her husband. The greatest of these, announced at the recitative's emphatic climax, is that she has been 'forced to seek help from one of my own servants' – not, surely, the language of sisterly solidarity; the Countess was herself, after all, not so long ago merely Rosina, the ward of Dr Bartolo.

Equally, the relationship between Figaro and the Count reminds us (and more particularly the Count) that in modern society, those who engage in contractual agreements do so as legal if not social equals, undertaking mutual responsibilities to which both partners are beholden. Figaro's contract of service with the Count does not give the Count rights over Figaro's essential liberties (which, Rousseau had argued in *Du contrat social*, can never be alienated in a contractual agreement);[16] nor can it automatically command sentimental loyalty or dependent gratitude from Figaro.

THE PRESERVATION OF HIERARCHY

'Comedy and pastoral celebrate what individuals share in common beneath the skin, and proclaim that this is ultimately more significant than what divides them,' writes Terry Eagleton.[17] This may be a revolutionary or a profoundly un-revolutionary perception, depending on what action one takes upon it. For the Enlightenment, whatever individuals share as equals goes no further than the legal equality necessary for society's new contractual relationships. Figaro and Susanna will gain legal independence in the opera, but servants do not aspire to social or political equality with their masters. For this reason the conflict in *Le nozze di Figaro* remains one between masters and servants rather than aristocracy and bourgeoisie. Servants do not represent an independent social class; they are too symbiotically wedded to their masters, and valets rarely lead revolutions, whatever Napoleon may have said about *Le mariage de Figaro* being the first stone flung in the French Revolution.[18]

Both Beaumarchais's play and Mozart's and Da Ponte's opera are unrevolutionary, even conservative, works: evidence of a modest desire to reform, but not transform, existing social relationships. For unlike the conflict between bourgeoisie and aristocracy, that between servant and master is fought over an unbridgeable social gulf that maintains the essential hierarchies of society. Furthermore, by concentrating on the issue of seduction, one of the most insistent themes in eighteenth-century bourgeois art, artists were deliberately sidestepping the real issues of confrontation. 'Tyranny . . . what men call tyranny is nothing; the seducer is the true tyrant,'[19] exclaims Lessing's Emilia Galotti in a play often performed in Vienna in the 1780s.

The enlightened bourgeoisie had a highly ambivalent attitude to the aristocracy. For all its espousal of liberty and equality, the Enlightenment retained an essentially structured vision of the universe. Wieland's 1793 definition of freedom and equality is a classic statement of this limited bourgeois understanding of these potentially explosive concepts. Freedom is no more than freedom of the individual against outside constraint. As for equality: 'By equality I do not understand the right of absolute equality, which overthrows all distinctions in civil society between classes and estates, between rich and poor, educated and raw; but only, that every citizen of the state shall be without exception equal before the law.'[20] The importance of being content with the pre-ordained structure of the universe runs as a theme throughout the Enlightenment. Rousseau warned against the 'shifting of rank and fortune amongst citizens',[21] and urged that 'To be discontented with my lot is to wish that things were not as they are, it is to wish for disorder and evil'.[22] Schiller's play *Die Räuber*, the last and greatest of the *Sturm und Drang*'s adolescent rebellions against bourgeois and aristocratic society, concludes with a fervent renunciation of all idealistic human efforts to tamper with divine providence in the name of social justice.[23]

If the eighteenth century ended in revolutions it was certainly not because they had been on the Enlightenment agenda. The basic hierarchies of society were considered to be God-given bulwarks, embedded in nature, against the mischievous forces which the Enlightenment had set free elsewhere. If Man was naturally superior to the beasts, why should the aristocrat not be naturally superior to the Third Estate? Many of the absolutist rulers who so systematically undermined the traditional power of the aristocracy were uneasily aware of the nostrum, reiterated by Montesquieu, that without nobility there could be no monarchy.[24]

For the bourgeoisie, however much they might resent the rights and privileges of the aristocracy, however much they might disapprove of the frivolity and ostentation of aristocratic culture, and however much they might reject the aristocrat's adherence to a code of familial honour rather than to social virtue, the existence of the aristocracy afforded a sort of guarantee of their own status. The tacit acknowledgement of the immutability of the class above provided justification for the repression of the class below; it was dangerous to press egalitarian claims against the aristocracy too far lest they be pressed in turn against the bourgeoisie. In the 1789 edition of the *Skizze von Wien*, Pezzl urges bourgeois theatre audiences to show more respect to the aristocracy. With 'Turkish uncouthness', theatre audiences (perhaps attending a performance of *Le nozze di Figaro?*) have become accustomed to cheer and applaud when some mishap befalls an aristocratic character, he complains. Although some members of the aristocracy are guilty of idiocies, the caste in general is worthy of honour and respect.[25]

In this light we can understand the howls of outrage raised by *Pamela* (the classic bourgeois fairy story of the servant who marries her master) and the invariable revelation of Pamela's noble birth in subsequent adaptations. The eighteenth century's emphasis upon blood and inheritance was, of course, quite mythical. In reality the continental aristocracies were permanently re-created from below – from those who had enriched the state through commerce or finance, or those who had served the monarch. Social mobility during most of the eighteenth century was rapid: by the end of the century, one quarter of the entire French nobility had been ennobled during the course of the eighteenth century alone,[26] and the Habsburgs created thirty to forty new titles a year.[27] The aristocratic circles in which Mozart mixed with such ease in Vienna were largely drawn from the newly ennobled administrative classes. But if the value of nobility as a guarantor of natural hierarchy was to be preserved, the myth of its inviolable status had to be bolstered. The reward of ennoblement for the continental Pamela cannot be made by elevation to the aristocracy, therefore, for that would give the game away; so it is made by discovery. The discovery of lost parents or patents of nobility made by the continental Pamelas and, less exaltedly, by Figaro, offers reassurance that the structures of society have, after all, remained intact.

The very mobility of eighteenth-century society gave rise to pressure for a stricter set of rules, of obligations and responsibilities. In 1768 Sonnenfels was obliged to remind young members of the Viennese nobility that continued respect by the new bourgeoisie depended on the example the nobility set; only then would the bourgeois be prepared to accept the 'unchangeable nature of conditions' with equanimity, and 'modestly take the place assigned to him'.[28] Gemmingen's *Der Weltmann* was specifically aimed at reminding those of the higher classes of society of their responsibilities; while lamenting the modern German aristocracy's adoption of foreign morals and manners, it insisted that the natural aristocratic qualities of body and spirit (courage, generosity, etc.) were inherited and could never be lost.[29]

The extraordinary ambivalence of the bourgeois Enlightenment's artistic representation of the aristocracy is evident in Voltaire's now-forgotten play *Le droit de seigneur*,[30] from which Beaumarchais drew for *Le mariage de Figaro*. First performed in Paris in 1762, Voltaire's play is a typical example of the Enlightenment's tendency to project the effects of the eighteenth century's own social uncertainty back upon the Middle Ages. His choice of the *jus primae noctis* to characterize the ills of feudalism is, however, tendentious, for despite much research there is little evidence to suggest that the practice has ever existed other than as a tenacious myth. Voltaire's *droit de seigneur* is no more than a token ritual consisting of a brief interview and an opportunity for moral exhortation and the dispensing of gifts. Feudalism itself is not the culprit. It is not the seigneur (in love with Acante but too honourable to take advantage of his power over her) who is the villain of the story, but his licentious relative, the footloose Chevalier who abducts her – an aristocrat who possesses privileges without concomitant feudal responsibilities, and who has no respect for the new moral status of marriage. And for every licentious aristocrat in Enlightenment art upon whom was projected the guilt of the bourgeoisie's own social libertinism, there are to be found a host of aristocrats (in plays like Diderot's *Le père de famille* and Gemmingen's *Der deutsche Hausvater*) who uphold the respect of their caste by conforming to bourgeois moral ideals.

Beaumarchais's retelling of the story is more provocative than that of Voltaire, for he updates his story to contemporary France during a period in which a wholesale revival of feudal rights and dues was taking place. Significantly, however, Beaumarchais also focuses on a right that he and his audience would know to be obsolete, if not actually mythical. Like Voltaire, Beaumarchais does not launch an attack upon the aristocracy as such, but upon the Count's undermining of the authority of his caste by the abuse of his position. Beaumarchais himself was no revolutionary. For all the rage at the injustice of social privilege and wealth which he put into the mouth of his hero Figaro (excised by Mozart and Da Ponte), Beaumarchais retained a typical distrust of social licence; but unlike his literary hero Voltaire, he located that licence more accurately. 'The unhappy people of England, with its restless craving for liberty would inspire something like compassion in anyone who considered their condition. They despise us as slaves because we obey voluntarily . . . but the licentious passion which the English call liberty never gives this untameable people a moment of happiness or true repose.'[31]

When Mozart and Da Ponte decided on *Le mariage de Figaro*, performances of a German translation of the play had just been personally banned by the emperor on the grounds that it was 'offensive'.[32] Joseph's subsequent decision to permit Mozart and Da Ponte to make their own adaptation has therefore caused puzzlement. But it had a logic of its own, comparable to the rationale which banned the works of Voltaire in German translation in Vienna, but allowed them to be imported in French. Performed in spoken German, *Figaros Hochzeit* would have been seen by the largely bourgeois audience who attended plays given by the German National Theatre (for which seat prices were also lower). Joseph was unwilling to expose this audience to works which might foment any social discontent.[33] But the audience for an Italian opera would have been largely aristocratic, just the audience against whose privileges Joseph was waging a virulent campaign, and to whom he would not have been sorry to point out a few uncomfortable home truths. *Le mariage de Figaro* had been seen by the unimaginative Louis XVI (and most subsequent critics) as an attack upon the *ancien régime* itself; *Le nozze di Figaro* was recognized by Joseph II as a useful weapon to aim at the aristocracy. He was, Da Ponte informs us, far more concerned about the offensiveness of the play's moral, rather than its political, content.[34]

In the world of *Le nozze di Figaro* (as opposed to the *real* world), the underlying distinctions of hierarchy must be seen to be maintained. The Count's attentions to Susanna are as much an affront to his own class – now more dependent on the symbolical distinctions of caste than before – as to bourgeois morality. In submitting to his feelings of jealousy against Figaro in the aria 'Vedrò mentr'io sospiro', and in summoning the old gods of vengeance to his aid, the Count is unwittingly demeaning himself. Joseph II had subjected his nobility to a rigorous egalitarianism (forcing them to pay the same taxes as the ordinary citizen, and in 1787 to suffer the same humiliating punishments for crimes), but in art, class distinctions could be upheld.

MARRIAGE: THE TRANSCENDENT PROMISE

The conflicts that arise in *Le nozze di Figaro* demand no radical alteration of society for their resolution; simply the renegotiation of relationships according to the new rules of contract between the legally free and equal individuals brought into being by modern society. The opera celebrates the ideal of marriage in bourgeois society as the central, non-political, contractual instititition of the new order, 'the all-subsuming, all-organizing, all-containing contract'.[35] Bourgeois marriage is central to Mozart's moral world, as it is for Rousseau, Kant and Goethe, mediating the conflicting interests of the individual, the family, religion and the state. But for the post-Rousseauvian Enlightenment marriage is not simply a means of legitimizing erotic attraction to suit society; it now also serves to affirm the autonomy and moral dignity of the individual.

In the great series of works that Rousseau produced in the 1750s and 1760s, he had painted an acute picture of the 'man of our day, a Frenchman, an Englishman, one of the great middle classes. Ever at war with himself, hesitating between his wishes and his duties . . . neither a man nor a citizen.'[36] In place of this debilitating conflict Rousseau had proposed a higher, spiritual freedom in which Man transcended his natural needs and learned to dictate his own moral ideals and imperatives, 'which alone makes him truly master of himself; for the mere impulse of appetite is slavery, while obedience to a law which we prescribe to ourselves is liberty'.[37] In such a society, Rousseau imagined, the conflict between personal integrity and social conformity would no longer exist. Man would freely enter into self-determined social relationships, and for Rousseau (as for Kierkegaard later) marriage was the primary institution in which men and women were able to exercise their power to make autonomous ethical decisions. The theme is addressed in *La nouvelle Héloïse*. Here the passionate love between Julie and her tutor Saint-Preux is blessed by nature but not, it seems, by society; and Julie, conforming to the wishes of her tyrannical father, submits to her duty and to a loveless marriage. The reality of the conflict between passion and duty (which Julie tries to deny) is made clear in her creation of an English garden, designed with consummate skill to give the illusion of nature. According to Julie, those who love nature but cannot seek it in faraway places (like Saint-Preux, who has retreated to the mountains) 'are reduced to doing it violence, to forcing it in some manner to come and dwell with them',[38] a revealing choice of words. But her efforts to create a compensatory substitute through art are bound to fail. Julie's garden, ominously named Elysium, is a deathly place, and the novel ends not in the domestic harmony and bliss through which Julie seeks to abolish all the contradictions of society, but in the death of Julie and her child. For Rousseau, the idyll of the bourgeois garden is a delusion.

Read superficially, the novel is a passionate vindication of natural love over the hypocrisies imposed by social convention or familial duty. But earlier in the novel Saint-Preux tries to assuage Julie's feelings of guilt for her passion by persuading her that real virtue resides in upholding the moral obligations of the 'sacred bonds' of mutual love, the promises that constitute the primary law of nature, rather than in submitting to a dutiful marriage.[39]

It is not simply natural erotic attraction that gives the love of Julie and Saint-Preux its legitimacy, but the freedom with which their promises were made. Her failure to uphold the moral bonds of mutual love, and her submission to the duties of an arranged marriage, lead to her death. For Rousseau, the promises of mutual love create their own *natural* obligation, and are superior to any merely social conditions that may be placed upon marriage. Similarly, when Da Ponte's Count is publicly forced to confirm his abolition of the *droit de seigneur* he describes the abolition of so unjust a right as 'restoring to nature and duty their rights'.[40]

THE SOUND GROUNDS FOR MARRIAGE

If marriage was to assume its transcendent contractual role in society, it was essential to establish grounds as certain as those that the Enlightenment had sought to establish for social and commercial contracts: people must be certain of the necessary conditions for entering into marriage agreements, and society must guarantee their ability to do so. 'With every nation in the world marriage is a sort of contract which can have any sort of conditions attached to it', wrote Montesquieu in *Les lettres persanes*,[41] and the conditions which late eighteenth-century bourgeois society came to insist upon for the legitimacy of the marriage contract were freedom and love.

There is much argument about when it was in Western culture that love became recognized as the primary ground for marriage. But there is no doubt that ever since the Middle Ages, whether because of capitalism or Protestantism, Sensibility or Romanticism, mutual love and affection have become increasingly accepted as the basis for marriage in the West. In 1549 Cranmer's prayerbook already enjoins that, apart from the traditional functions of procreation and avoidance of fornication, marriage is founded upon 'mutual society, help and comfort',[42] and in the famous seventeenth-century English moral chapbook *The New Whole Duty of Man*, the case is even more clearly stated: 'No law obliges a man to marry; but he is obliged to love the woman whom he has taken in marriage . . . the husband first promises to love his wife, before she promises to obey him: and consequently as his love is the condition of her obedience she need only obey if he is loving.'[43]

This last condition introduces a key factor: the admission that if either side reneges on the agreement the contract becomes null and void. The traditional religious view of marriage sees its commitments as indissoluble vows made to God. The newer attitude insisted that vows be replaced by mutual agreements made between two partners. This is what lies at the heart of Milton's radical arguments for divorce, and during the seventeenth century in England, claims for the *de facto* nullification of the marriage contract when one partner or the other defaulted on his or her promises became common.[44] Among the most radical and controversial aspects of Joseph-II's *Ehepatent* (Marriage Law) of 1783 was the affirmation that marriage was essentially a 'civil contract'.[45] For the first time in modern Europe divorce was legalized, a move that acknowledged the priority of affective ties in marriage over religious obligation or property considerations.[46]

In his study of the relationship between the modern family and capitalism, Engels recognized the link between the rights demanded for both social and marital contracts in bourgeois society. Freedom and equality were the prerequisites of commercial contracts, he noted, 'But how did this fit in with the hitherto existing practice in the arrangement of marriages? Marriage according to the bourgeois conception was a contract, a legal transaction, and the most important one of all because it disposed of two human beings, body and mind, for life.'[47] If marriage was a contract, it presupposed the individual freedom of the partners on which all contracts depend.

Arranged marriages, made for dynastic or financial reasons, were accordingly angrily denounced by Milton, the first theorist of bourgeois marriage. Aphra Behn compared such marriages to the enforced vows of the reluctant nun. Milton was adamant that the partners of a marriage should give their 'full, free and mutual consent'[48] to the arrangement. Parents, guardians, even employers could put enormous physical, moral and economic pressure on children to obey their marital plans for them, but if the children refused to give the crucial words of assent – like Diderot's nun at the altar – the marriage could not take place. In eighteenth-century treatments of the conflict between the marital desires of children and parents, the parent who attempts to arrange the choice of a marital partner for a child is always proved to be wrong. It makes no difference whether the arrangement is carried out under duress, as in the attempts of Clarissa's parents to enforce her match with the loathsome Solmes, or whether the children themselves acquiesce in a loveless marraige, as in the disastrous *Marriage-à-la-Mode* of Hogarth's famous cycle of narrative paintings, which opens with the signing of an arranged marriage contract drawn up between the son of a spendthrift duke and the daughter of a rich but parsimonious merchant. Such marriages are always morally nullified.[49]

Most rationalist moralists considered marriage founded upon sexual desire to be equally slavish. Lady Mary Wortley Montague, who defied her parents to run away with the man she loved, preferred to talk of 'freindship' [*sic*] rather than love as the basis of marriage, since for her love signified 'a Passion rather founded on Fancy than Reason';[50] Fielding in *Shamela* warned strongly against entering into marriage for 'the transient Satisfaction of Passion'.[51] And although the mid-eighteenth century renounced the strict rationalist anathema against sexual desire, it merely shifted its attention to the equally unhealthy claims of romantic love, which conservative moralists saw being reared by the climate of sensibility, and propagandized through the novel. Later Enlightenment thinkers considered romantic (as opposed to affective) love to be as transiently delusive a basis for marriage as pure lust had been. In *Rasselas*, Dr Johnson warns: 'Such is the common process of marriage. A youth or maiden meeting by chance, or brought together by artifice, exchange dances, reciprocate civilities, go home, and dream of one another . . . find themselves uneasy when they are apart, and therefore conclude that they shall be happy together.'[52] By the end of the century, it was recognized as being in society's best interests to ensure that the marriage contract was entered into freely and autonomously, 'without constraint either from the passions or from persons' as a French jurist insisted.[53]

MOZART ON MARRIAGE

The significance attached by Beaumarchais to marriage is clear from its central role in *Le mariage de Figaro*. In his preface to an earlier play, the tediously worthy *drame bourgeois*, *Eugénie*, he had written, 'The subject of my drama is the despair to which the imprudence or the malice of another can lead a young person in the most important action [i.e. marriage] of human life.'[54] Two letters written by Mozart, some ten years apart, convey with great succinctness the central social and ethical role of marriage in late eighteenth-century bourgeois society. In the first, written from Munich in 1778, Mozart asks his father to send his congratulations to a Salzburg friend who had recently got married. But the bourgeois Mozart cannot refrain from casting somewhat prim aspersions: 'I wish him joy with my whole heart; but his, I daresay, is again one of those money matches and nothing else. I should not like to marry in this way; I want to make my wife happy, but not to become rich by her means . . . Herr von Schiedenhofen was obliged to choose a rich wife; his title demanded it. People of noble birth must never marry from inclination or love, but only from interest and all kinds of secondary considerations. Again, it would not at all suit a grandee to love his wife after she had done her duty and brought into the world a bouncing son and heir. But we poor humble people can not only choose a wife whom we love and who loves us, but we may, can and do take such a one, because we are neither noble nor highly born, nor aristocratic, nor rich.'[55]

What Mozart meant (or did not mean) by love is indicated in a second letter, written in 1787 to his 'restless' younger friend Baron Gottfried von Jacquin, and replete with the sententiousness conferred by five years of domestic stability and marital contentment, and ten years' seniority: 'Well dearest friend, how are you? I trust that you are all as fit and well as we are. You cannot fail to be happy, dearest friend, for you possess everything that you can wish for at your age and in your position, particularly as you now seem to be entirely giving up your former rather restless way of living. Surely you are becoming every day more convinced of the truth of the little lectures I used to inflict upon you? Surely the pleasure of a transient, capricious infatuation is as far removed as heaven from earth from the blessed happiness of a deep and true affection?'[56]

This opposition of affection to infatuation, and his earlier insistence upon freely contracted marriage based upon love rather than financial considerations, affirms the dual requirements of enlightened bourgeois marriage. Mozart himself had a realistic appraisal of marital expectation, which excluded both sexual infatuation and romantic idealization. His description of his intended bride Constanze might not satisfy the expectations of contemporary commercial romanticizers of marriage, but demonstrates that for Mozart the 'golden-mean' was as relevant to his domestic life as to his music. Constanze 'is not ugly, but at the same time far from beautiful . . . She has no wit, but she has enough common sense to enable her to fulfil her duties as a wife and mother . . . she would like to be neatly and cleanly dressed, but not smartly . . .' But most important, the condition without which these virtues and Mozart's understanding of the moral meaning of marriage would be meaningless, is love: 'I love her and she loves me with all her heart. Tell me whether I could wish myself a better wife?'[57]

Like Goethe with the simple Christine Vulpius, Mozart kept faith with the terms of his love for his wife. The letters he wrote to her while he was away from her, or she from him, in the last two years of his life are among the most affecting testaments of marital love ever written, all the more touching and believable for their simple naïvety and complete absence of self-conscious composition: 'Every other moment I look at your portrait – and weep partly for joy, partly for sorrow.'[58] 'My consolation is that soon letters will no longer be necessary, for we shall be able to talk to each other and kiss and press each other to our hearts.'[59] 'As soon as my business here is over, I shall be with you, for I mean to take a rest in your arms.'[60]

You can't imagine how I have been aching for you all this long while. I can't describe what I have been feeling – a kind of emptiness, which hurts me dreadfully – a kind of longing, which is never satisfied, which never ceases, and which persists, nay rather increases daily. When I think how merry we were together at Baden – like children – and what sad, weary hours I am spending here! Even my work gives me no pleasure, because I am accustomed to stop working now and then and exchange a few words with you. Alas! this is no longer possible. If I go to the piano and sing something out of my opera, I have to stop at once, for this stirs my emotions too deeply.[61]

In the face of such evidence of devotion, it is difficult to fathom Alfred Einstein's and Wolfgang Hildesheimer's assertions that Constanze was unworthy of Mozart, and that Mozart cannot have found true love in his marriage![62]

THE MARRIAGES OF *FIGARO*

The opera to which Mozart would have turned for consolation at the piano in 1791, and which stirred his heart too deeply, was *Die Zauberflöte*, Mozart's spiritual apotheosis of marriage. But the opera that contains the most profound exploration of marriage as a human and social institution is *Le nozze di Figaro*. Here marriage becomes, *inter alia*, the symbolic battleground for that unsettling transition from a feudal to a modern contractual society. By updating Voltaire's feudal *droit de seigneur* from the Middle Ages to the eighteenth century, Beaumarchais had been able to compress the historical process of several centuries into the space of one day (*La folle journée*); for Mozart, that compression reflected the real experience of his society. Those who like to describe *Figaro* as a revolutionary work should note that it encapsulates the history of a non-political, non-revolutionary transition, fully in accord with the ideals of bourgeois liberalism.

Mozart's marriage to Constanze, undertaken without Leopold's consent, had demonstrated his filial independence. As a free man Figaro also demands the right to make his own arrangements and marry the woman he chooses and loves. The demand was not without topical controversy in 1780s Vienna. The *droit de seigneur* may have been a mythical right in late eighteenth-century society, but the seigneur's right to withhold permission for servants to marry was, in central Europe at least, a reality. Despite the Church's increasing concern about the exercise of this power,[63] numerous civil laws in southern Germany and Austria protected the master's power over his servants' marital freedom, denying former servants who had married without their master's consent the right to settle or find work in towns, and in some cases empowering the authorities to return servants who had absconded in order to marry. These laws had indeed been repealed along with other feudal powers in 1781, but Joseph II's Serfdom Patent, which placed great emphasis upon the freedom of marriage for servants, still only allowed them a limited autonomy; the lord of the manor could still refuse permission for marriage when there were 'good reasons'.[64] The Count may not win in the end, but he seems to have no difficulty in finding numerous 'good reasons' for delaying the marriage of Figaro and Susanna.

The struggle of Figaro and Susanna for autonomous determination of their marriage is, then, a historical struggle that takes place against the background of a series of marriages sought – or already based – upon some of the false contractual grounds outlined earlier in this chapter. In the bizarre episode of Figaro's contract with Marcellina, it is revealed that Figaro has in the past incurred debts with Marcellina, and at one point rashly committed his hand in marriage as surety for the loan. Since Figaro has defaulted upon the debt, Marcellina has a clear legal right to demand that he marry her. No better example could be given of ill-advised contract-making – and no better vindication of the Rousseauist view that the exchange of mutual affection carries far greater weight as a true moral condition for marriage than any legal conditions. Don Curzio, as representative of the civil law, rules that the contract is valid; Rousseau-ist natural law rules that it must be invalid, and nature lets us know of its abhorrence of such a match by the fact that, were Figaro to marry Marcellina, he would be marrying his own mother.

The marriage of Count and Countess Almaviva is profoundly flawed because it is based upon mutually false expectations. On the Countess's side the delusion is that of romantic love, an ideal that is pathetically unrealistic. Her very first words are addressed to Amor, a plea for him to restore the Count's love to her or else allow her to die. But we should be wary of taking the Countess and her sentimental appeal to love at face value. It is all very well to talk, as many do, of Mozart bringing added seriousness and pathos to Beaumarchais's characterization of the Count-ess (who, incidentally, was played by a well-known tragic actress in Beau-marchais's first performances) in translating the play into an opera, but Mozart was also drawing attention to the self-deluding powers of senti-mental love. An eighteenth-century audience was accustomed to the *opera seria* pretensions of aristocratic characters being parodied in *opera buffa* (as in *La finta giardiniera*), and Mozart would have played upon this ambiguity. The exalted fusion of love and death is appropriate to an heroic character like Konstanze facing real death in *Die Entführung aus dem Serail*. It is less so to the Countess, who is in fact a familiar figure in the late eighteenth-century literature written in reaction to the excesses of Sensibility: the deserted wife, steeped in indolent self-pity and comforting herself with dreams from romantic novelettes.[65] When Susanna comes to fetch the Countess's smelling salts from the Count (a pretext for arranging an assignation) she pointedly comments that the Countess is suffering from 'her usual vapours'.

Mozart's ironic intentions are made entirely clear in the Countess's second aria 'Dove sono'. In the heroic *opera seria* recitative which precedes the aria, we recall that the greatest indignity inflicted upon her, announced at the solemn climax of the music, is that of having to 'seek the help of a servant'. Heard without words we might take the music to represent the purest expression of tragic suffering, but if this is really all the Countess has to complain of, it is difficult to take her affectations quite as seriously as she herself patently does (which is precisely what Mozart intended).

No marriage based upon such grandiose romantic delusions could possibly have survived. For as Beaumarchais's Count makes clear when he is attempting to seduce his own wife under the impression that she is Susanna, what he requires above all, within or outside marriage, is sexual adventure. 'What about love?' asks the Countess, perhaps somewhat wistfully. 'Love is just a novel of the heart: it is pleasure which is the true story,' replies the Count. The Countess has her wits about her, and extracts from the Count his requirements for a wife. They are, it seems, 'to maintain our desire, to renew it through love, to reanimate, so to speak, the charm of their possession with that of variety'; to which the Countess replies, with somewhat justifiable sourness, 'So they have to do everything?' The Count, true to form, agrees: 'It is too often forgotten' – 'Not by me any longer', answers the Countess to herself, and from the other women concealed in the darkness, Marcellina and Susanna, comes the echo 'Ni moi . . . Ni moi'.

The scene is a perfect illustration of the contemporary aristocratic conception of marriage, described by Montesquieu's Persian visitors to Paris with evident distaste: 'After what I have told you of the way of life in this country, you will easily imagine that the French do not exactly make a point of being faithful. They believe that it is as ludicrous to swear eternal love to a woman as to assert that one will always be healthy, or always happy. When they promise to love a woman for ever, they assume on her side a promise to be always attractive; and if she breaks her word, they consider themselves no longer bound by theirs.'[66] Accordingly, the solution Beaumarchais gives his Countess is to suggest that she may be better equipped henceforth to play the Count at his own game and engage with him on a more equal footing, and thus to renegotiate the terms of the marriage more realistically. This crucial little scene is missing, however, from Da Ponte's libretto, and as a result it is often suggested that the refulgence that Mozart's music bestows on the reconciliation between Count and Countess at the end of the opera is perhaps too perfunctorily achieved. We may feel that not enough has changed to justify such radiant understanding, and that despite all the affirmations of repentance and forgiveness (heard not for the first time in the day) life will probably soon return to normal.

But in purely musical terms Mozart did in fact take care to plot the equivalent of the Beaumarchais scene into his score, in the Act III duet in which the Countess dictates to Susanna a letter of assignation with the Count. The text of the letter is in fact no more than the briefest three lines of arcadian verse, a teasingly incomplete and seemingly inconsequential canzonetta: 'Che soave zefiretto/ Questa sera spirera/ Sotto i pini del boschetto' ('What gentle breezes/ Will breathe this evening/ Beneath the pines in the grove'). But it will be enough; 'The rest he will understand.' If the text is elusive, however, the music with which the Countess conveys it to Susanna is far from being so; it is in the richest idyllic mode, attributed by Schiller to the sentimental artist who longs to regain his unity with pre-lapsarian nature, and it is suffused with the Countess's familiar nostalgic longings. As she softly hints at the assignation in the woods, we know that the gentle breezes in the pines are full of painfully redolent memories – of times past when it was with Rosina herself that the Count used to make such nocturnal assignations, perhaps. Certainly the Countess does not need to complete the lines of the 'canzonetta carried on the air' (like Ilia's messages of love in *Idomeneo*) to be sure that the Count will get the message: perhaps the memories are too bitter-sweet to be recalled any further, or too personal to confide even to the faithful Susanna.

The audience is by now forewarned, and perhaps prepared to see through the beauty of the music to the dangerously romantic self-delusion behind it, were it not for the fact that Mozart retains the power of his irony to turn the tables. The advent of irony represents the key step, according to Kierkegaard, in humankind's progression from sensual innocence to ethical maturity; it marks the painful moment in which the disjunction between appearance and reality, reality and the possible, first becomes apparent. For now the Countess is herself employing her own sentimental language manipulatively, still believing in its potency and effectiveness, but able to distance herself enough both to share it with Susanna, and commit it to a letter designed to deceive the Count.

Recognized for what it is, the pastoral idyll loses its intoxicating and regressive powers of delusion. There can be no return to the innocence of nature, as Rousseau had so clearly forwarned (see pp. 33–4). But now the Countess is projecting her nostalgic longings into the future, where they no longer have the power to sap her resolve: 'questa sera *spirera*' ('*Will* breathe this evening'). It may be that beneath the pines in the garden the natural feelings of love for Rosina that had once inspired the Count may stir again. And the garden exists here and now, not simply in the past in which the Countess has hitherto lived her emotional life. Having filled herself with new resolve in the ecstatic concluding section of her previous aria, the Countess appears no longer a pathetically abandoned wife but a character capable of taking her destiny into her own hands and renegotiating her terms with a new realism and maturity. If Beaumarchais's Count is to be believed, from henceforth Mozart's Countess will earn not just expedient contrition from her husband, but also respect.

For the Almavivas, lost felicity has to be restored, and the end of the opera will bring about that restoration. But Figaro and Susanna are starting from the beginning, and it is in their progress towards marriage, the actual subject of the opera, that the possibility of founding marriage upon true terms is explored. The marriage of Figaro and Susanna is a portrait of a marriage that will be stable and secure, based upon freedom and true love, firmly rooted in sound understanding and proper contractual commitments, and free of romantic or sentimental delusion.

Susanna herself understands the nature of contractual promises quite clearly, and reveals her instinctive respect for them in her duet with the Count at the beginning of Act III. She has undertaken to arrange an assignation with the Count that will lure him into a trap, and to do so, has to persuade him that she has overcome her reluctance to entertain his advances. In an ecstasy of anticipation at the fulfilment of his desires, the Count obsessively makes Susanna repeat her promises. 'Then I'll see you in the garden? you won't forget . . . I'll see you . . . won't forget . . . so I'll see. . . ?' Like a bride at the altar, Susanna repeats the vows of this profane catechism; in full at first, until the Count's ardour mounts, his questions come faster, and his impatience curtails Susanna's responses to a simple, breathless 'si . . . no . . . no'. The duet captures the rhythms of the longed-for sexual act itself, the Count blissfully swooning into a post-coital A major (Mozart's favourite key for sensuality) as she gives her promise. But, whether through conscious or unconscious revulsion, Susanna rebels against the Count's attempt to confirm the lascivious contract by endless repetition, and at last cannot prevent the wrong answer from slipping out, betraying her innate sense of the impropriety of playing with the promises which will shortly bind her in marriage.

Unlike Rousseau's Julie, who imagines that it is possible to construct a world in which social relationships are transparent, and human beings can infallibly read each other's hearts, Susanna is well-versed in the skills of social deception. She knows how to survive in a fallen world in which many people one encounters, such as Don Basilio, can only live by the adoption of guises – as he makes clear in the rather pathetic Act IV aria that does much to humanize this otherwise unlikeable character. Susanna may contrast herself to Marcellina, the 'old pedant' who considers herself superior to Susanna 'because she has read a few books', and she easily exposes the hypocrisies which underlie conventional social manners in the second *Duettino* in Act I, in which she and Marcellina hiss insults at each other under the guise of social courtesies. But in her Act IV aria 'Deh vieni', Susanna too practises the art of deception for her own ends, while Mozart demonstrates the full sophistication of his ironic procedures.[67]

Susanna's Act IV aria is a nocturne of ravishing stillness amidst the chaotic bustle, sung as if by a dryad of the castle garden who can command not only the breezes (like Ilia), but the very earth and sky themselves to respond to her love. The bustling human world falls silent at Susanna's artful bidding (literally artful, since her aria is properly a song, a serenade). Nothing can detract from the sheer beauty of the aria itself, the melody swaying over gently plucked strings (hinting, perhaps, at a guitar accompaniment), beatified by tender woodwind. But Mozart, like Susanna, is no sentimentalist believing (as did Rousseau) that music is somehow magically exempt from the duplicity of linguistic communication. For Susanna is in fact enticing the Count to his fate, and her siren-song consciously employs all the tricks of seductive allurement.

Furthermore, she is fully aware that lurking miserably in the darkness is Figaro, hearing with his own ears the evidence that Susanna is betraying him. The poignancy of the situation lies in the fact that while we are ravished by the aria, itself intended to deceive the Count, we are also aware (and should be able to see) that poor, foolish Figaro is suffering agonies of jealous torment, and that what is giving us such pleasure is wounding the honest (if unworthy) Figaro to the quick. Yes, the aria is beautiful, but it is also exquisitely cruel – that is, unless we subscribe to the view that the sheer unaffected beauty of the song (its buoyant accompaniment making it quite different from the drooping, languid sentimentality of the Countess's arias) reveals an essential sincerity at its core. For underneath its double deception, the aria can also be heard as Susanna's true love song to Figaro, every word and note transcending the bog of subterfuge and deceit in which they are mired. (After all, the obstacles to Susanna's happiness were all resolved at the end of the sextet in Act III, and it is only out of loyalty to her mistress (and perhaps reverence for the state of matrimony) that she is still engaged in intrigue. Susanna anticipates a time when love can at last be freely enjoyed; when as Schiller hoped, 'what we experience now as beauty will one day approach us as truth', and bliss will reside on earth again.[68]

The attainment of the long-desired marriage between Figaro and Susanna is not achieved without internal as well as external trials, pain and even punishment. But it is not in spite of, but because of, such moments of necessary misunderstanding (their two opening duets are Pinteresque studies in mutual inattention and incomprehension that bode far from well) that self-knowledge is gained. Figaro's great outburst of bitter disappointment at the supposed fickleness of women in his Act IV aria is unjust; both Susanna and the Countess are models of redemptive female constancy. But it will ensure that he, at least, will never again be tempted to put women on pedestals as goddesses. This realism gives the conclusion of the opera its sense of achieved, rather than imposed, resolution. Beaumarchais's play ends with a good chuckle all round, and a merrily pointed song sung by the victors as the aristocratic couple look on with paternal indulgence. Mozart's opera ends in a promise by everyone, servant and master, victor and vanquished, to celebrate the all-healing power of true love. But although Mozart apotheosizes the reconciliation between the Count and Countess in the closing pages of the opera, it is a reconciliation aided by the steadfastness of Figaro's and Susanna's own reverence for marriage, based upon a solid, pragmatic relationship, healthily sexual instincts, and a clear understanding of how the world works.

MARRIAGE AND THE COMMUNITY

Le nozze di Figaro retraces the progression of relations in modern society from those based upon pre-ordained status to those negotiated by contract. But in promoting the ideals of a contractual society, the opera is not simply proclaiming the triumph of untramelled bourgeois individualism: promises imply commitments and limitations of absolute freedom. Furthermore, *Figaro* clearly recognizes the limited efficacy of contractual relations alone to establish anything more than a purely abstract legal equality in society; from the outset it is evident how easily the Count himself can manipulate the terms of a contractual society to his own advantage in sexual matters.

In the opening scene of Act II the Countess quizzes Susanna about the Count's overtures to her, and asks, rhetorically: 'So, he wishes to seduce you?' Susanna's reply shows how clear-sighted she is about these matters. 'Oh, my lord the Count doesn't dispense compliments to women of my estate; with them it's a matter of financial contracts.' ('contratti di danari'). In other words, if the Count cannot possess Susanna through his feudal right then he will not waste his time with the blandishments and endearments of seduction, the arts of erotic gallantry which are reserved for women of his own class; he will have her through the simpler expedient of buying her. This is contract as understood in the crudest mechanisms of the market, according to which anything may become a commodity which can then be sold and bought. Susanna promises to sell herself to the Count so that she shall receive the dowry money with which to pay off Marcellina and liberate Figaro from his debt – economic necessity means that people may always be forced to sell what is of greatest value to them.

Susanna's sharp observation to the Countess exposes the reality behind the myth of contract: that in moving from social relations based on status to those created by contract, privilege and class will be abolished, and replaced by a society of equals. But the truth is, of course, quite otherwise. As Engels insisted, the capitalist contract is a con, in which legal equality is no guarantee of true equality. 'The labour contract is to be freely entered into by both partners. But it is considered to have been freely entered into as soon as the law makes both parties equal *on paper*. The power conferred on the one party by the difference of class position the pressure thereby brought to bear on the other party – the real economic position of both – that is not the law's business . . . As regards the legal equality of husband and wife in marriage the position is no better.'[69] Women never enter the marital contract on equal terms with men, and even in a world where social relationships are ordered by financial trans- actions rather than status, the Count retains his power to command his desires by exchanging the control offered by status and privilege to that offered by money. Ultimately, the freedom of Susanna and Figaro (as was the freedom of Mozart) is actually achieved with economic indepen- dence, so that Susanna no longer needs to sell herself.

But in the end, the world of Aguasfrescas is not really that of the new bourgeois market. It is, rather, a deliberately anachronistic community, a microcosm of a cosy neo-feudal society in which servants and masters, familial dependants and professional household staff live and work in each other's pockets; the sort of society that Romantics were soon to evoke with such fond imagination. With its nostalgia for the old order, this society sees rampant bourgeois individualism as destructive of the organic network of interrelationships upon which it depends. Figaro's and Susanna's escape from repressive feudal tutelage to marital freedom takes place in the context of traditional social customs, and celebrates the function of marriage not only as a consolidator of social relationships, but also as an institution of communal cohesion and stability; the point of engagement not simply between isolated individuals, but also between individuals and the history, traditions, culture and values of society at large.

This function of marriage is supported by Beaumarchais's introduction into his play of the problematic group of peasants. Who are they, and what are they doing in this comedy of social manners? They seem in some respects strangely out of place, not just in Figaro's and Susanna's bedroom, but as a quaintly rococo presence within a play that in other respects appears rooted in social reality. But clearly, Beaumarchais would not have introduced these tongue-tied rustics unless he had some important function for them to play in the drama, even though he was unable to overcome the perennial problem of the 'chorus' in spoken drama.

The peasants assume their role more happily in the opera, where a natural place is provided for them in the chorus. But they are not there simply to provide picturesque and tuneful interludes to the intrigue of the real drama, as in most *opere buffe*. In Act I the chorus is introduced to the scene by Figaro himself, and in Act IV they appear as the necessary witnesses to the formal ceremony of Figaro's and Susanna's betrothal. In traditional cultures the communal witnessing and celebration of such ceremonies is of the greatest importance. In Mozart's time, most rural societies also had public courtship rituals at which courtship was supervised collectively (although this did not imply that marriages were arranged). In his *Lettre à d'Alembert* Rousseau took the opportunity of affirming his belief that since marital fidelity was 'the root of all social order',[70] soundly contracted marriages were too important to be left to the fickle whims of inexperienced young people. In the ideal republic he suggests that there would be public dances arranged to allow prospective couples to meet 'with propriety and circumspection ... in a gathering where the eyes of the public are constantly open and upon them ... Can a more decent way of not deceiving one another, at least as to their persons, be imagined?'[71]

In traditional societies, this communal interest in marriage did not stop at courtship and betrothal; many rural communities also operated a primitive policing system for the marriage state itself, to ensure that its condition within the community was properly maintained and its status respected. There were penalties for all sorts of derelictions of the recognized codes of marital duty, sexual continence, or patriarchal authority. It is in the light of these codes that the imprecations against the cuckolded husband that are so common in eighteenth-century *opera buffa* (recalled in the angrily baying horns of Figaro's Act IV aria) must be understood; not only would the seducer be punished for his crime, but also the husband, who was considered equally guilty of having undermined the status both of marriage, and of patriarchal authority in society (for the same reason, hen-pecked husbands were also punished, usually by ridicule). The public humiliation of the cuckolded husband was a feature of many continental rural societies well into the nineteenth century, despite the fact that eighteenth-century authorities had legislated against the custom.

As Philippe Ariès wrote regarding the policing of marriage by what he described as the rural community's sexual vigilantes, 'The *stabilitas* of the community seemed to depend on the *stabilitas* of marriage, and society had to make sure this was strictly observed'.[72] This is why the superficially somewhat incongruous chorus of peasants is of such significance in both play and opera, and why Figaro forces their introduction into the private domestic space of the household with such vigour. The Count prefers to pursue his *amours* in secret corners and under cover of darkness, away from the public acknowledgement of sexuality and the commitments demanded by marriage. Marriage thereby loses its function as an institution of social *stabilitas*, and it is in fact the conventional marriage of the the Count and Countess, and not that of their progressive servants, that is so isolated and lacking in the traditional support of communal blessing.

To ensure that his own marriage is fortified by this public affirmation, Figaro brings the chorus into the house as witness. Thus in Act I the Count is forced to make public acknowledgment of his renunciation of a right that does so much to undermine marriage. Figaro sweeps the peasants into the Count and Countess's very ante-room, and puts them through paces that he has quite clearly rehearsed with them beforehand. 'Cos'è questa commedia?' ('What is this comedy?') the Count demands angrily after the chorus has left, showing that he recognizes what Figaro is up to. The touching little ceremony of gratitude to the gracious seigneur who has renounced his rights was no picturesque rococo tableau from Lancret or Pater, but Figaro's first real challenge to the Count – a challenge all the more menacing for the pastoral insouciance of the music, elusively mocking but quite beyond the reach of the Count's wrath.

In Act III the introduction of the chorus is even more significant. Once again it interrupts a petty intrigue with Cherubino, and Figaro subverts the resolution of the scene (which would have resulted in further punishment for Cherubino) by announcing the wedding march which we hear in the distance. This time the music that accompanies the chorus has resonances of both battle (aggression is never far away in *Figaro*, and there are frequent moments of angry confrontation in the opera) and public ceremonial, as the chorus pushes its way into the private domestic space of the household to perform as a public witness to the betrothal of Figaro and Susanna. Figaro will win his battle with the Count not because he is an individual representative of the soon-to-be-triumphant bourgeoisie, but because his escape from feudal servitude acknowledges traditional communal values.

THE 'ORGANIC' SOCIETY

In appealing to the customs and values of community, *Le nozze di Figaro* conveys the growing desire of an increasing number of thinkers, such as Burke in England and Herder and Goethe in Germany, to affirm an organic vision of society which recognized the validity of social custom and historical tradition as opposed to the increasingly abstract rationalism of the absolutist Enlightenment or the fragmenting implications of free-market individualism. In Vienna by the mid-1780s the arbitrariness of many of Joseph II's reforms was becoming apparent. In his rationalization of law, Joseph indiscriminately overrode not only the reactionary rights and powers of the feudal nobility and Estates, but also many harmless (but, so far as Joseph could see, irrational and unproductive) traditional social customs. Thus as feudal authority was loosened the government introduced a growing number of laws regarding public order in rural areas, including restrictions and controls upon peasant festivals. As early as 1771 rural wedding festivities, great feasts of joyous licence and indulgence which in good years could stretch on for days until the celebrants dropped or the victuals ran out, were restricted by edict to no more than one day.[73]

Joseph's chilly, utilitarian vision of society was not met with the same fervent enthusiasm by his less self-righteously rational subjects. In his pamphlet *Warum wird Kaiser Joseph von seinem Volke nicht geliebt?* of 1787 Josef Richter suggested that 'The best among people would wish that the Emperor may be more patient with the lesser faults of men and with their weaknessess'.[74] Joseph's Cartesian expectations that once people were shown the rationality of his reforms they would automatically accept them were increasingly being confounded. The optimistic assumptions of human rationalism which *Die Entführung*, Mozart's most Josephine opera, had so enthusiastically espoused had not been fulfilled. 'He failed to take into account the weaknesses of human nature' was to be Herder's epitaph on Joseph.[75]

'We are afraid to put men to live and trade each on his own private stock of reason,' wrote Edmund Burke, one of the fathers of modern conservatism, 'because we suspect that this stock in each man is small, and that the individuals would do better to avail themselves of the general bank and capital of nations, and of ages.'[76] Hence the increasing tendency of the age to assert the value of social customs rooted in historical continuity and tradition. This form of conservatism drew its intellectual authority from a new understanding of history and historical processes, and recognized that human society is not simply an abstraction to be manipulated at will, or merely an aggregate of isolated contractual agreements between individuals. Human beings are born, as Burke insisted, into a partnership 'not only between those who are living, but between those who are living, those who are dead, and those who are to be born'.[77]

Goethe more than anyone understood this concept of society as a living, developing organism given shape and meaning by the historical continuity of inherited custom and shared value. In his play *Egmont* (1787), which concerns the Revolt of the Netherlands, Egmont mediates the conflict between the brutal, repressive tyranny of Spain and the abstract rights and liberties of man claimed by the Dutch rebels with his defence of the ancient rights and customs of his nation. 'You know how delighted I am at every prospect of improvement the future offers us,' said Goethe to Eckermann in 1825, 'But, as I said, I hate all violent and sudden transitions with all my soul, for they are not natural.'[78] Goethe's own preferred image of the development of nature and society was 'metamorphosis'. His Weimar colleague Herder was to dismiss the legislative efforts of Joseph II, arguing that the laws evolved through custom and experience could lay greater claim to being 'natural' than rationally constructed 'laws of nature',[79] and the Austrian historian Hormayr, writing shortly after Joseph's death, specifically reproached the emperor for having done violence to nature by applying mechanical reforms to an organism as complex as the Austrian state.[80] Between the centrifugal dynamics of bourgeois individualism and the rationalist, utilitarian statism of Joseph II, *Le nozze di Figaro* affirms the alternative values of community and tradition, and offers marriage as a symbol not only of contractual relationships between free and autonomous individuals, but between individuals and their community.[81]

MARRIAGE AND CHRISTIAN FORGIVENESS

Religion is among the most effective institutions for the transmission of social and cultural values, and only shortly before writing *Le nozze di Figaro* Mozart had joined the Catholic lodge 'Zur Wohltätigkeit'. *Le nozze di Figaro* is the opera that most confidently conveys his new masonic vision of a self-regulating society of people guided by the moral principles of Christianity.

In his study of Austrian literature, *La réalité, royaume de Dieu*, Roger Bauer suggested that Austrian culture of the eighteenth century had remained rooted in the Catholic belief that the material world, imperfect though it might be, reflected the divine cosmos, and that all human actions on earth carried an emblematic relationship to the divine. In 1786 Goethe recorded his admiration for a Jesuit drama he saw in Regensburg, with its combination of spiritual and 'wordly wisdom';[82] and the joyous mundanity of Catholic art (a reflection of the Catholic insistence that grace is attained through man's efforts on earth) was unmistakably carried forward into the Muratorian Austrian Catholicism of the 1780s.

Enlightenment theologians (of whom there were a surprising number) in general turned their attention away from the mysteries of faith or grace, sin or redemption, to what had been for St Paul the greatest of the theological virtues: charity, or love.[83] In theological love, and its social counterpart charity (*bienfaisance* or *Wohltätigkeit*), the Christian Enlightenment recognized the affinity between the bourgeois Enlightenment's ideal of moral autonomy, and the rejection of Judaic legalism (salvation through observance of the law) by St Paul and Jesus himself.[84] Diderot had a clear understanding of the way in which, in the past, humankind had alienated humanly conceived concepts of God and turned them into the idols of distant divinity and the tablets of law: 'Men have banished divinity from their midst; they have relegated it to a sanctuary; the walls of a temple are the limits of its view; beyond these walls it does not exist ... Madmen that you are, destroy these enclosures which obstruct your horizon; liberate God; see him everywhere where He actually is, or else say that He does not exist at all.'[85] More specifically, the Abbé Morelly, one of the modern originators of the principle of communism, wrote that it was the idea of human *bienfaisance* itself, rather than nature, which 'raises men to a conception of God, at an earlier date and with more certainty than the spectacle of the universe would have done'.[86]

In much later-Enlightenment thinking a vision of an essentially religious society which has dispensed with the Church altogether became increasingly common. In his late work *Religion within the Limits of Reason Alone*

Kant anticipated a 'divine ethical state' which would be no less than the Kingdom of God on earth.[87] But although Kant's kingdom requires God as an expression of the absolute form of Man's pursuit of the good, it remains strictly ethical. In contrast, Mozart's religious kingdom on earth is much more clearly a Christian – and even particularly a Catholic – kingdom, founded upon the gospel of forgiveness.

'There is not one Moral Virtue that Jesus Inculcated but Plato & Cicero did Inculcate before him; what then did Christ Inculcate?' asked William Blake in his aphoristic text *The Everlasting Gospel*: 'Forgiveness of Sins. That alone is the Gospel.'[88] For the gospel of *Wohltätigkeit* may also be extended to embrace the virtue of forgiveness, the most specifically Christian virtue, and the one that transcends the unconditional rules of morality and justice. 'The negation or anulling of sin is the negation of abstract moral rectitude – the positing of love, mercy, feeling', Ludwig Feuerbach was to observe.[89] And for Blake, who rejected the purely ethical religion of later Enlightenment thinkers like Kant, it was precisely this transcending power of forgiveness which distinguished Christianity from mere practical ethics.

> It was when Jesus said to Me,
> 'Thy Sins are all forgiven thee.'
> The Christian trumpets loud proclaim
> Thro' all the World in Jesus' name
> Mutual forgiveness of each Vice,
> And oped the Gates of Paradise.[90]

In *Le nozze di Figaro* the meaning of forgiveness is explored in some depth. In Act I Doctor Bartolo, having been tricked out of his anticipated marriage to Rosina in *Le barbier de Seville*, sings stentoriously of his desire for vengeance upon Figaro. To forget insults is 'low and base', he bellows, in accordance with the old retributive notion of justice. As Hobbes suggested, since both revenge and forgiveness are 'hateful' to the wrongdoer,[91] modern societies transfer the dispensing of justice to the impersonal realm of the state. But between the primitive desire for personal vengeance, and the abstract majesty and rigour of the law, the Christian Enlightenment recognizes that society can only operate effectively if human beings are also able both to apologize and to forgive.

Thus in *Le nozze di Figaro* Cherubino begs the Count's pardon for having twice unintentionally overheard the Count's indiscretions with Barbarina and Susanna. But despite the appeals of all of those present, Cherubino is denied forgiveness by the Count (until, that is, Cherubino threatens to reveal the Count's own misdemeanours, whereupon the

Count's pardon is purely expedient, and still results in Cherubino's banishment). The Count's refusal to forgive runs like a leitmotif through the opera. Furious at the Countess's confession that Cherubino is lurking hidden in her closet the Count refuses all her pleas for pardon. A few moments later the tables are turned, for it is Susanna and not Cherubino who emerges from the closet. The Count has been made to appear a jealous and unforgiving bully, and in turns pleads for forgiveness. The Countess's forgiveness is not given lightly ('my heart cannot bear so great a wrong'), and she recognizes that the too ready forgiveness forever expected of women in society weakens dignity and justice: 'Who would ever believe in a woman's fury?' she asks. But eventually she weakens and relents, admonishing the Count with the words, 'He who cannot forgive others doesn't deserve to be forgiven'. These words were specifically added by Mozart and Da Ponte to the scene, and are drawn directly from the Christian injunction that only those who are willing to pardon others can hope for ultimate pardon for themselves.

That assurance of ultimate forgiveness is fundamental to Mozart's profoundly religious view but is lacking in the secularized, rational religion of the Enlightenment, in which religious discourse (such as that of Muratorian Catholicism) has been reduced to what Hobbes called 'Humane Politics'.[92]

But people living in a secularized, ethical society do not lose their awareness of sin, the underlying sense of 'dread' which Kierkegaard identified as the primary consciousness of our separation or alienation from a former wholeness and unity – be it God, nature, or human society itself. The 'nameless crimes' so often hinted at in Romantic art, the guilt with which all human beings are stricken for their shortcomings haunt even the most rational. Furthermore, so powerful is the human longing for evidence of moral order and purpose in the universe that people often prefer to believe that injustice and unhappiness must be no more than the wages of their own sins and transgressions against a just and loving God. Christianity, which acknowledges the profundity of these feelings in its teachings on original sin, also offers to every human being the promise of redemption and forgiveness.

Banished from religious discourse in the eighteenth century, these profound existential themes inevitably reappear in eighteenth-century art. The three great novels of the English bourgeois Enlightenment, Defoe's *Robinson Crusoe*, Richardson's *Clarissa* and Fielding's *Tom Jones*, all re-enact (beneath their deceptively naturalistic exteriors) the story of Man's original sin, his expulsion from Paradise, and hope of eventual return home and ultimate reacceptance. Richardson specifically wrote *Clarissa* as a 'religious novel', claiming to have 'investigated the great doctrines of Christianity under the fashionable guise of an amusement'.[93]

All Mozart's operas deal with the theme of ultimate forgiveness in one form or another, charting a passage from transgression of some sort (usually betrayal of trust, or faith,) to a desire for vengeance and thence to forgiveness. In *Idomeneo* that forgiveness still comes from heaven, an indication of the existence of divine justice. In *Die Entführung* forgiveness has been brought down to earth, but the hierarchical relationship between God and humanity is retained in the relationship between the Pasha and his captives. Mozart's Pasha exercises the grace which is his by virtue of the absolute power he possesses over Belmonte and Konstanze; it is more correctly described as mercy rather than Christian forgiveness,[94] made in rational recognition of a greater justice.

In *Le nozze di Figaro* theological grace becomes truly immanent. The *Dea ex machina* who descends to dispense pardon (the musical phrase which follows her bestowal of forgiveness seems to float down from above) upon the Count is the Countess. She has no real earthly power over the Count and is not simply exercising a prerogative of mercy, but rather, true Christian forgiveness, which she is empowered to do by virtue of the Count's own contrition and desire to receive pardon. In the closet scene in Act II (the previous occasion on which the Count had besought pardon) he had done so with a crucial reservation (specific to Mozart and Da Ponte), 'If I did wrong, I beg your forgiveness.' That *if* is a typical weasel word which implies that he does not really accept full moral guilt; and for her part, the Countess's forgiveness had been offered more out of the weakness of her own desire for approval than true moral strength.

It is hateful to our self-esteem, Hobbes observed, to have to receive pardon from those whose superiority we do not acknowledge; 'But to have received benefits from one, whom we acknowledge for superior, enclines to love'.[95] By the final scene of the opera the Countess has attained the stature which allows the Count to recognize his own degraded status, and to wish to receive her forgiveness. The Count is brought to recognize his wrongdoing by the marital constancy of his wife, a theme introduced very specifically by Mozart and Da Ponte into *Le nozze di Figaro*.

It is only 'love toward a thing eternal and infinite [which] fill the mind wholly with bliss,' wrote Spinoza,[96] and all human beings need the promise of something unconditional and unchanging to live by. In the Bible the metaphor of marriage is frequently used for Man's relationship with God, and sin is often equated with unfaithfulness and estrangement from God. According to the modern theologian Paul Tillich, 'the concern of faith is

identical with the desire of love: reunion with that to which one belongs.'[97]
The desire for forgiveness is the desire for reconciliation; atonement –
the repentance of sin – means literally reconciliation and 'at-one-ment'.
St Paul himself describes God's forgiveness as 'reconciling the world
unto himself, not imputing their trespasses unto them.'[98]

It is through her unconditional fidelity that Mozart's and Da Ponte's
Countess is able to reconcile the erring Count to herself. Beaumarchais's
Countess indicates that she will rely upon the power of renewed sexual
attraction through dalliance and flirtation to regain her husband's interest,
and she is never herself absolutely above sexual reproach (hinted at in
her obvious *tendresse* for Cherubino, which Beaumarchais will expose as
more than *tendresse* in *La mère coupable*.). In her own first aria in Mozart's
and Da Ponte's opera, the Countess makes a similar plea to Amor (erotic
attraction) to restore her husband to her. But in the second half of 'Dove
sono', she implores a different divinity to aid her, making an ecstatic
appeal instead to the power of constancy to help regain her husband's
'ungrateful heart.'

Where the earlier Enlightenment had promoted a purely sexual notion
of constancy, the moral focus has now shifted. Constancy has regained
its medieval connotations, attested to no longer by trials of seduction, but
by inner steadfastness. It remains a female virtue, that has the power to
redeem the unsettled, improvident male worlds of business and politics
with its promise of transcendent certainty and ultimate forgiveness. The
marital fidelity upheld by the Countess in *Le nozze di Figaro* is an emblem
of God's own covenant to keep faith with mankind. Stendhal was quite
correct when he described the hymnlike music which follows the Count's
contrition and abasement and the Countess's serene bestowal of grace as
'le plus beau chant d'église qu'il soit possible d'entendre.'[99]

XIII

The meaning of classicism

Le nozze di Figaro is Mozart's most classical opera; a balanced reconciliation of the aching human dualisms of feeling and reason, of the individual
and society, of nature and culture, of freedom and necessity, and of the
material and the spiritual, which was fleetingly glimpsed by a handful of
late eighteenth-century artists before the advent of political and industrial
revolution.

The ideals of late eighteenth-century classicism derive from Rousseau,
whose search for an ethics that reconciled individual freedom and social
necessity had led him to propose that Man's highest freedom was achieved
through the ability to make his own moral laws, lifting him out of his
subjection to material, sensual instincts. Obedience to self-legislated laws
as a higher freedom reappears in the moral system of Kant, Rousseau's
most assiduous reader. But both recognized the dangerous potential for
self-legislated laws to disintegrate into complete moral relativity, and
consequently, for society itself to collapse. Rousseau proposed (by shaky
sleight of hand) that the individual might submit to the collective social
law of the General Will without losing his freedom. Kant externalized his
moral law by proposing that any valid moral law must be able to be
universalized, its autonomy being maintained by Kant's insistence that a
moral law should always be an end in itself, rather than a means to an
ulterior end (such as salvation, or the needs of the state).

WEIMAR CLASSICISM

The years during which Kant was working on the last of his three Critiques
(1787–8) were the years during which Goethe and Schiller were forming
their extraordinary creative collaboration. One of their major bones of
contention was Kant himself, whose transcendent idealism went against
all Goethe's deepest feelings about the immanence of the ideal in the
real world of things. Nonetheless, Goethe's own classical formulations
frequently reflect his understanding of Kant.

In Werther Goethe had unwittingly unleashed a monster, for he had
never intended that people should read his novel as an encomium to
destructive individualism. He was appalled by the way in which readers
adopted Werther as a model (in 1778 a young woman was found drowned

in the river near Weimar with a copy of *Werther* in her possession)[1] and angered at their inability to see the warnings in the book. Werther is self-pityingly indulgent, full of second-hand emotions based on the windy bardic writings of Klopstock and Ossian (the phoney Homer of the North invented by the Scotsman James Macpherson). 'No one remarked that while Werther is in his senses he talks about Homer and only after he goes mad is in love with Ossian,' complained Goethe, many years later.[2] Mozart was equally scornful of the craze, rampant in Vienna in the 1770s, for lofty bardic poetry. In 1782 he accepted a commission to set an ode on the recent British capture of Gibraltar by the Viennese poet Michael Denis, who liked to style himself 'Sined the Bard'. But Mozart found the text 'too exaggerated and pompous', and never finished it.[3]

'Be a man, and do not follow my path,' Goethe pointedly prefaced the second edition of *Werther*, and shortly afterwards accepted a civil-service post at the court of Weimar, where for ten years he was occupied with administrative jobs in the small Duchy. It was an indication of the former rebel's desire for social responsibility and commitment. In many of the occasional pieces Goethe wrote for the Weimar theatre he attacked the absurd affectations of sentimentalism, and in his more personal work during this period he became increasingly interested in the discipline, serenity and balance of classical art. In 1786 he left Weimar for a two-year visit to one of its founts, Rome. There, amongst other things, he completed his great classical drama *Iphigenie*.

Goethe's commitment to classicism in the 1780s was evidence of a search for a more mature balance between subjective individual expression (of which Goethe was the master) and objective reality. 'So long as he [the writer] merely expresses his limited range of subjective feelings, he is still no true poet,' he wrote in 1826, surveying the new subjectivity of Romantic art with distaste, 'but he becomes one as soon as he can make the world his own and express that.'[4] But how was the artist to make the world his own? Kant, who was also concerned with the philosophical gulf between subjective experience and objective reality, addressed this problem in his theory of knowledge.

According to Kant, the gulf is bridged through the mediation of space and time, and the universal categories of perception common to everyone, which enable us as individuals to grasp and order what would otherwise be the merely chaotic experience of our senses.[5] Above all, it is aesthetic activity that affirms man's relationship with nature. Aesthetic experience, for Kant, represented the workings of nature within man, not merely a relationship *between* man and nature. Goethe's classicism was similarly a response to the recognition that the artist's best means of sorting the welter of inchoate experience that the outside world presents is through the inherited structures of classical form, which prevent the work of art degenerating into either incommunicable solipsism or slavery to the randomness of material perception. As Goethe's scientific studies had shown, nature had its own 'will-to-form', and in his sonnet *Natur und Kunst*, Goethe explained how the artist, like the Rousseauvian individual, willingly acknowledges the objective laws of form because, once they are internalized and made his own, they allow him to transcend the gulf between the freedom of the subject and determined necessity of the object:

> Wer Grosses will, muss sich zusammenraffen;
> In der Beschränkung zeigt sich erst der Meister,
> Und das Gesetz nur kann uns Freiheit geben.

[He who wills great things must gird up his loins; only in limitation is mastery revealed, and the law alone can give us freedom.][6]

Artistic genius, Goethe was to write, was 'that power in man which, by its actions, gives laws and rules'.[7]

For Goethe and Schiller, classicism was the artistic expression of a *social* vision of man. 'True art is like good company,' Goethe tells us in *Wilhelm Meister*: 'it constrains us in the most delightful way to recognize the measure by which, and up to which, our inward nature has been shaped by culture'.[8] 'Every individual human being is less a human being by just so much as he is an individual,' wrote Schiller; 'every way of feeling is just so much less essentially and purely human as it is peculiar to one particular object. Only . . . in pure expression of the essential does the great style lie.'[9] And for Schiller, music above all the arts was capable of reaching to the essential, since music was the most formal, least imitative, of the arts. The musicologist Friedrich Blume suggested that in Schiller's understanding of music, 'The antinomy of necessity and freedom is surmounted and conquered in the classic work of art through the analogy of inner feeling and outward form'.[10]

VIENNESE CLASSICISM

Viennese musical classicism has been aptly named, and the frequently made comparison with Weimar classicism is no less appropriate, for in the music of the great Viennese masters there is clear evidence of the kind of aesthetic social vision that lies at the heart of Weimar classicism. As with the early works of Goethe and Schiller in the context of contemporary German literature, Viennese musical classicism evolved from the confusion of musical styles prevalent in the mid-eighteenth century.

These ranged from the bland pleasantries of the 1750s *galant* style (impersonal to a fault) to the more individualistic musical forms that had sprung up in the 1760s and 1770s: the sentimentalism of Italian opera composers like Piccinni; the expressive style (known by the German term for sensibility as *Empfindsamkeit*) of C. P. E. Bach, with dramatic extremes that are sometimes so violent that they lead to musical incoherence; the powerful emotional naturalism of Gluck; and the attention-grabbing pyrotechnics of the Mannheim school of composers. Both Mozart (and to a lesser extent, Haydn) demonstrate a thorough acquaintance with each of these languages. A number of Haydn's more expressive works of the late 1760s and early 1770s have been dubbed '*Sturm und Drang*', and the young Mozart, more widely travelled and more receptive to external influences than Haydn, easily assimilated the various languages of musical sensibility.

Mozart's absorption of the individualistic musical styles of his contemporaries was naturally tempered by a respect for the formal rules of his art. He was contemptuous of composers like Vogler in Mannheim, whose crude efforts to surprise an audience led to violent changes of tempo and dynamic, and unprepared modulations that Mozart considered to be no more than 'clumsy plunging'.[11] The fullest statement of Mozart's musical aesthetics is to be found in a famous letter written to his father concerning the composition of *Die Entführung aus dem Serail*. It is well known, but deserves to be quoted again in the light of our understanding of late eighteenth-century classicism.

Mozart is describing his approach to setting to music Osmin's comic vengeance aria. He records the sudden plunge at the end of the aria which is in 'a totally different tempo and in a different key. This is bound to be very effective, for, just as a man in a towering rage oversteps all the bounds of order, moderation and propriety, and completely forgets himself, so too must the music forget itself.' Expressivity must, however, respect the bounds of form: 'But as the passions, whether violent or not, must never be expressed in such a way as to disgust, and as music, even in the most terrible situations, must never offend the ear, I have gone from F (the key in which the aria is written) not into a remote key but into a related one: not its nearest relative, D minor, however, but the more remote A minor.'[12]

Although Mozart refused to be bound by pedantic rules (as he explained in the same letter), like Goethe, he increasingly came to value the paradoxical freedom afforded him by his complete mastery of formal constraints. One of the most exciting moments in his musical career was the discovery, under the guidance of Gottfried van Swieten, of the music of

J. S. Bach and Handel in 1782. Like any composer of the period who wrote church music, Mozart had been schooled in the 'learned' style traditionally considered appropriate for certain sections of the Mass. But for secular music, composers of the mid-eighteenth century had rejected the complex polyphony of baroque composers. J. S. Bach's music was considered by many to be scholastic and 'unnatural', and a divergence had developed between the sacred/learned (contrapuntal) and the secular/ galant (melodic) styles. For Mozart, the discovery of contrapuntal music as an expressive vehicle, rather than a dutiful tradition, in the hands of Bach and Handel was a revelation.[13] The sudden delight he took in writing fugues from this moment indicates a new joy in pure form for its own sake.[14] But more significant was Mozart's growing tendency to interpolate passages in the contrapuntal style within his secular music, thus bridging the gap between the expressive and learned styles so evident in his Salzburg Masses (and even in the great Mass in C minor) where jaunty Italianate arias sit side by side with strict polyphonic choruses.[15]

Contrapuntal music may have carried symbolic significance for Mozart. In baroque polyphony the individual elements are often rationally subordinated by homogeneity of tempo and rhythm to the overall dictates of the whole; an apt paradigm for the procedures of the absolutist state. But in Mozart's use of counterpoint, the superabundance of individual melodic themes precludes their submergence and loss of identity within a despotic polyphonic texture; counterpoint becomes analagous to the interrelationship of free and equal individuals in society.

It was through his ability to handle counterpoint expressively that Mozart was also able to transfigure the often inflexible language of traditional opera seria, with its succession of largely homophonic arias conveying stereotyped emotions in fixed keys. It was against this rigid and impersonal approach to expression that Gluck had rebelled, arguing that the human emotions were not static and bounded, but fluid and changeable; music, he insisted, must be as 'various and many sided as feeling itself'.[16] Mozart, however, was not willing to follow the subjective implications of Gluck's approach. Indeed, in his own day he was often to be accused of being too learned and complex, and of ignoring the heart in favour of the mind. Although he explored Gluck's use of large-scale, through-composed musical structures in Idomeneo, and attempted in that opera to break down the unnatural distinction between recitative and aria which Gluck had so deplored, he was not prepared to allow musical form to be determined solely by the meanderings of human emotions.

Gluck had essayed a subjectivist, naturalistic response to the limitations of opera seria, a response that reflected the heroic phase of bourgeois

individualism; there are few ensembles in Gluck, whose most characteristic representation of the relationship between individual and society is
the grand tableau in which an isolated soloist stands out from the anonymous mass of the chorus. Mozart sought musical modes of expression
more analogous to the social interaction of individuals with each other,
as envisaged in the masonic ideal of society. Out of this the dramatic
ensemble arose more naturally, and was to be endowed by Mozart with
unequalled invention.

In Mozart's operatic ensembles society is no longer perceived as a pre-
existent totality from which the individual must extricate him or herself,
but as a complex web of interdependent relationships. (In his *Memoirs*
Da Ponte tells us that this complexity was deliberately aimed for in the
fashioning of the libretto for *Le nozze di Figaro*).[17] Such a model of society
contradicted the inflexible hierarchies of *opera seria*, and Mozart's efforts
to introduce ensembles into *Idomeneo* met with stonewall hostility from
the original singers, who considered it a threat to their individual status.
Nonetheless, the first thing Mozart did on being given Metastasio's sorely
old-fashioned text for *La clemenza di Tito* in 1791 was to ensure that it
was turned into a 'real opera' by the addition of ensembles. It was,
however, in *opera buffa* that Mozart found the operatic genre that most
truly matched his classical aspirations.

'Musique ne sait pas dialoguer',[18] Boileau had complained to Racine
the great master of classical dialectics, on being asked to write an opera
libretto, and almost a hundred years later Wieland in his *Versuch* could
still claim that the problem with opera was that 'action cannot be sung'.[19]
But the development of sonata form in later eighteenth-century music
offered dramatic opportunities to Mozart that allowed him to reveal in
his *opere buffe* not only the interrelationship of individuals, but the possibility of some sort of dynamic and progressive interaction between them,
unfolding towards the ever-implied promise of an ideal resolution.

In an age which had recently developed narrative theories of music (as
in the programmatic symphonies of Vanhal or Dittersdorf) it is not
fanciful to hear in Mozart's piano concertos a representation of this
dynamic relationship; a progressive dialogue between the individual
expressive voice of the soloist and the wider 'community' of the orchestra,
the former distinguished from the latter, yet frequently drawing from
the same fountainhead of ideas, and both ultimately uniting in joyous
unanimity.[20] But the classical ideal of individual fulfilment through social
integration expressed in so many of the piano concertos attains its richest
expression in Mozart's operas. Here Goethe's insistence that the individual must engage with reality by coming to grips with its inner formal

workings, and Schiller's Kantian belief that humanity's slavery to material necessity could be transcended by aspiring to the ideal, are reconciled. For Mozart's operas, most especially *Le nozze di Figaro*, represent the consummation of the Enlightenment's dream of a self-regulating society in which social order and ethical truth manifest themselves as aesthetic beauty.

THE AESTHETIC MODEL OF SOCIETY

At the beginning of the century the Earl of Shaftesbury first observed that in making aesthetic judgements, although our response is based upon subjective taste, there is none the less an extraordinary degree of unaminity of opinion about what is beautiful or ugly in nature. In other words, that there is a correlation between our subjective sense that something is beautiful, and the objective, natural order of things in the world. 'The law appearing in phenomena', explained Goethe, one of Shaftesbury's many German admirers, 'produces, in the greatest freedom and in accordance with its own conditions, the objectively beautiful'.[21]

This aesthetic observation was applied by Shaftesbury to ethics. The social manners and graces of civilized society are no less the objectified expression of natural ethical than of aesthetic values. 'No sooner are actions viewed, no sooner the human affections and passions discerned ... than straight an inward eye distinguishes and sees the fair and shapely, the amiable and admirable, apart from the deform'd, the foul, the odious or the despicable. How is it possible therefore not to own that as these distinctions have their foundation in nature, the discernment itself is natural and from nature alone.' To philosophize was 'to learn what is *just* in society, and *beautiful* in Nature, and the order of the world'.[22]

The beauty of the equation of ethics and aesthetics was that it answered the bourgeois desire to reconcile subjective freedom and objective necessity; it provided, as Kant recognized, 'lawfulness without a law'.[23] Furthermore, it persuaded people that, in spite of all evidence to the contrary, the outer laws of the universe might be in accord with their own lonely efforts towards moral perfection. Contemplating the beauty and order of the starry heavens above, in Kant's famous phrase (which so moved Beethoven), Man finds assurance of the objective truth of the moral law within.

At the end of *Die Zauberflöte*, Tamino and Pamina are offered 'the eternal crown of Beauty and Wisdom'. The true wearer of the crown is, of course, Mozart, whose operas ring with the assurance of an aesthetic, and hence moral, order to the universe. In Mozart's comic operas, in particular, there is a powerful sense that the characters exist within the material world, and that, in their quest for dignity and freedom, they are subject to all the material forces that can beset us: instinctual desires and physical needs; vulnerability to chance and fate; entrapment to misconceived aims and misdirected ends; and ignorance of the ultimate truth of things. But underlying this world is the inner logic, clarity and grace of Mozart's music, structuring events to persuade us – at least subliminally – that there *is* order and purpose behind the flux and chaos perceived by our mere senses, and that Man's search for the inner freedom bestowed by ethical choice is blessed by the aesthetic beauty and order of the outer world.

But if Mozart's music offered us no more than a formal ordering of experience, our sense of its moral as well as aesthetic rightness would be limited. The necessities of form can sometimes intrude too forcefully and arbitrarily upon experience, and compromise truth. Numerous composers, including Mozart himself, in setting the Mass found themselves obliged to follow time-honoured conventions which bore little relation to the expressive meaning of the text. Thus the need to end a Mass with an uplifting 'finale' often meant setting its concluding text, the 'Dona nobis pacem', to rousing music which was entirely inappropriate ('liturgically impertinent' it has even been suggested),[24] a clear example of a disjunction between form and expressive truth. As Goethe argued, valid form arises from the internal necessity of phenomena, not from external rules. What allows the mature Mozart to fulfil our aesthetic need for intimations of a moral order in the world is that the formal discipline of his music is combined with a respect for the variety of individual experience, which dispels any sense of the imposition of an arbitrary or reductive order upon events. 'A political constitution will be very imperfect if it is able to achieve unity only by suppressing variety,' as Schiller writes in the *Letters on the Aesthetic Education of Man*,[25] drawing an explicit parallel between the relationship of aesthetic reason (which demands unity) and nature (which demands multiplicity), and the relationship of the absolutist state to bourgeois society. However, Mozart's music takes us beyond the aesthetic ordering of social complexity. According to Schiller, it is only by analogy that external beauty mirrors and appears to confirm the internal moral sphere in Kant's aesthetics: there is no bridge between the two. In his *Aesthetic Education* Schiller sets out to find a way of reuniting through art the liberated inner world of the Kantian individual and the sensuous, material world. Schiller pointed out that the condition of Kantian autonomy 'was completely absent of content', and that man cannot live in a sphere of pure rationality, completely divorced from the real world. 'The determination he has received through sensation must therefore be pre-served, because there must be no loss of reality.'[26] Schiller identified the real world as being embodied aesthetically in the 'sense drive', and the rational in the 'form drive'. 'The sense drive insists upon absolute reality; [Man] is to turn everything which is mere form into world, and make all his potentialities fully manifest. The [formal drive] insists upon absolute formality: he is to destroy everything in himself which is real world, and bring harmony into all his changes. In other words, he is to externalize all that is within him, and give form to all that is outside him.'[27]

As a philosopher, Schiller loses the rhetorical clarity that distinguishes his drama and verse, and wrestles with the abstractions that so dogged Kant. But how apt, none the less, is Schiller's description to our experi-ence of Mozart's operas. For along with its formal mastery, Mozart's music has a sensuousness quite its own, that distinguishes it from that of Haydn and Beethoven. There is nothing emotionally abstract about Moz-art's music; for all its formal perfection, it communicates with a physical expressiveness that reunites the world of form and order with the sensual world of real human feeling, transforming – as Schiller required – 'every-thing that is mere form into reality'. The ideal in Mozart's music is not achieved by the subjection of the material and the sensual to the rational and formal, but by their seamless integration. Goethe, otherwise notori-ously obtuse in his comments upon music, understood something of this in his suggestion that the perfect music would combine the instinctive sensuality of southern art with the rationality of northern art (in fact, his solution to all artistic endeavour). It was a fusion which perhaps only an 'Austrian' composer like Mozart could have achieved.

Schiller believed that this transcendence of the dualism of the rational/ formal and the material/sensual was the precondition for the life of aesthetic freedom which was Man's highest aim. (It has to be said that Schiller was ambiguous, if even confused, on this, and that he sometimes regarded aesthetic freedom as a precondition for an ultimate, moral freedom.) He characterized aesthetic freedom, famously, as play – an activity which is entirely self-fulfilling, and hence completely free, yet which takes place within the material, rather than the ideal, world. For Schiller, play was the ultimate expression of the 'purposeful purposeless-ness' of aesthetic freedom.

In Schiller's definition of play we reach the summit of the classical ideal of an aesthetic social order. 'But does such an Aesthetic state really exist, and if so, where is it to be found?' asked Schiller in the closing paragraph of his *Aesthetic Education*. 'We are likely to find it, like the pure Church and pure Republic, only in a few chosen circles, where conduct

1. Early influences. i Ludovico Muratori (1672–1750). Catholic reformer influential in Salzburg; writings by Muratori were owned by Leopold Mozart. ii Christian Fürchtegott Gellert (1715–69). Poet and sentimental hymnist; correspondent of Leopold Mozart. iii Baron Friedrich Melchior Grimm (1723–1807). *Encyclopédiste*, close colleague of Diderot, colleague, then enemy, of Rousseau; Mozart's patron and host in Paris. iv Christoph Martin Wieland (1733–1813). Poet, novelist and critic; doyen of Weimar. Favourite author of the Mozart family; Wolfgang met him in Mannheim in 1777.

2. Joseph II and his brother, Leopold of Tuscany (later Leopold II), in Rome in 1769, by Pompeo Batoni. On the table beside them is Montesquieu's *L'esprit des lois*.

3. Josephine statesmen. i Karl Anton Martini (1726–1800). Jurist, Professor of Natural Law at Vienna University; subscriber to Mozart's 1784 concert series. ii Tobias von Gebler (1726–86). Senior civil servant and Josephine reformer; playwright and friend of Lessing; author of *Thamos, König in Ägypten* (incidental music by Mozart); prominent freemason. iii Joseph von Sonnenfels (1733–1817). Jurist and journalist; mentor of the Viennese Enlightenment; supporter of Mozart and prominent mason. iv Gottfried van Swieten (1734–1803). President of Joseph's Education and Censorship Commissions; amateur composer; friend and patron of Mozart; possible mason.

4. Count Franz Joseph Thun (1734–1800), portrayed on the frontispiece to the esoteric work *Protokoll über den Spiritus familiaris Gabiodone,* 1787; enlightened aristocrat, noted occultist and mason; friend, patron and lodge brother of Mozart.

5. Friends and patrons. i Countess Maria Wilhelmine Thun (1744–1800). Wife of Franz Joseph Thun; famous for her intellectual salon and three beautiful daughters; adored patron of Mozart. ii Franz Sales von Greiner (1730–98). Senior Josephine civil servant; literary salon host; father of Karoline Pichler, prolific novelist, pupil and memorialist of Mozart; mason. iii Prince Karl Lichnowsky (1756–1814). Enlightened aristocrat and early Viennese Kantian, who travelled with Mozart on a secret mission to Berlin in 1789; Beethoven's most loyal patron; mason.

6. Luminaries of the Viennese theatre. i Franz von Heufeld (1731–95). Playwright and director of the German Theatre in Vienna in the 1770s; friend of the Mozart family. ii Friedrich Ludwig Schröder (1744–1816). Playwright and Shakespearean actor; most influential figure in Viennese theatre during the early 1780s; recommended the text of *Die Entführung aus dem Serail* to Mozart. iii Gottlieb Stephanie the Younger (1741–1800). Playwright, actor and stage manager of the German Theatre in Vienna; adapted libretto of *Die Entführung* for Mozart; mason. iv Karl Friedrich Hensler (1759–1825). Playwright of Viennese Volksstücke (popular plays); director of the Leopoldstadt Theatre; author of masonic memorial oration for Mozart.

7. Radicals and Deists: the 'Zur wahren Eintracht' lodge. i Ignaz von Born (1742–91). Metallurgist; master of the radical masonic lodge 'Zur wahren Eintracht'. ii Aloys Blumauer (1755–98). Poet, satirist and journalist; close lieutenant of Ignaz von Born; member of van Swieten's censorship commission; colleague of Mozart, who set one of his poems to music. iii Karl Leonhard Reinhold (1758–1823). Former monk forced to flee Austria for breaking vows; close friend of Born; son-in-law of Wieland; popularizer of Kant. iv Johann Baptiste Alxinger (1755–97). Aristocrat and epic poet; advocate of northern German Enlightenment; colleague of Mozart.

Faustin,

oder, das

philosophische

Jahrhundert.

1780

Dritte vermehrte und verbesserte Ausgabe.

1785.

8. Frontispiece to the Josephine novel *Faustin* by Johann Pezzl
(1756–1823), the only novel in Mozart's library.

Otto Freih v Gemmingen

L. A. Hoffmann.
Professor der deutschen
Sprache in Pest

9. Josephines and Catholics: the 'Zur Wohltätigkeit' lodge. i Otto von Gemmingen (1755–1836).
Playwright, dramaturg and essayist; Josephine civil servant; founder and master of the Catholic 'Zur
Wohltätigkeit' lodge; friend and colleague of Mozart. ii Leopold Aloys Hoffmann (1748–1806). Secretary
to Chancellor Kaunitz; masonic pamphleteer; later professor of enforced German in Pest. iii Marc
Anton Wittola (d. 1797). Vigorous publicist of Josephine church reforms.

10. i Wolfgang Heribert von Dalberg (1749–1806). Playwright and Director of the Mannheim National
Theatre; masonic controversialist. ii Franz Anton Mesmer (1734–1815). Founder of the pseudo-
science of animal magnetism; patron of the Mozart family in Vienna in 1768. iii Christian Gottfried
Körner (1756–1831). Life-long friend and musical amanuensis of Schiller (brother-in-law of Dora
Stock, portraitist of Mozart on his visit to Dresden in 1789).

POLITISCHE SPAZIERFAHRT.

London in the Newport Street No. 89.

Charleson del.   *Birmingham sc.*

11. i The English Garden of Count Coblenzl at Reisenberg; engraving by Johann Ziegler, from a view by Lorenz Jauschka. ii Catherine the Great of Russia takes Joseph II for a ride during the Turkish War; caricature, *c.* 1788.

12. Allegorical representation of Joseph II's Tolerance Patent of 1781.

13. Print from Johann Mansfeld's *Gallery of Catholic Abuses*: a church service in Vienna satirized as a concert. Joseph II was to abolish such impieties.

14. The ceremonies for the Coronation of Leopold II
as King of Hungary, 1792.

15. Frontispiece to the libretto of *Die Zauberflöte*,
engraved by Ignaz Alberti, Vienna 1791.

MAURERREDE
AUF
MOZARTS TOD.

VORGELESEN

BEY EINER

MEISTERAUFNAHME

IN DER

SEHR EHRW. ST. JOH. ☐

ZUR

GEKRÖNTEN HOFFNUNG

IM ORIENT VON WIEN

VOM

Bdr. H. . . . . r.

WIEN,
GEDRUCKT BEYM BR. IGNAZ ALBERTI.
1792.

16. Title page of Karl Friedrich Hensler's masonic memorial oration on Mozart's death, published by Alberti, Vienna 1792.

is governed, not by some soulless imitation of the manners and morals of others, but by the aesthetic nature we have made our own; where men make their way, with undismayed simplicity and tranquil innocence, through even the most involved and complex situations, free alike of the compulsion to infringe the freedom of others in order to assert their own, as of the necessity to shed their Dignity in order to manifest Grace.'[28] Schiller's image recalls his memory of watching an English country figure dance (the contredanse which was so popular in bourgeois circles in Mozart's Vienna), and marvelling at its combination of freedom with order, energy with grace. In his poem *Der Tanz* he conveyed his delight in the whirling scene, in which rollicking steps are ordered into social dance by 'the mighty divinity of wellbeing',[29] in words which anyone who has for a moment experienced the exhilaration of harnessing the physical expenditure of dance to the discipline of formal steps and patterns would recognize.

Perhaps Schiller's reminiscence of a humble social dance elevated to a symbol of spiritual grace in the human world explains our intimation of moral harmony in Mozart's own aesthetic world. For Mozart's music is (as Schiller proposed all true aesthetic activity should be) founded upon the very principle of play. Mozart himself, we are told, particularly loved dancing, and as Wagner observed, dance underlies much classical music.[30]

Mid-eighteenth-century musicians and theorists such as Algarotti and C. P. E. Bach (who banished the minuet from the symphony) had tried to expunge dance-forms from serious music. Yet the multifarious languages of dance – of the minuet, sarabande, passepied, gigue, and siciliano; of the bourrée, gavotte, march, musette or contredanse – survive in Mozart's music, hinting at hidden patterns of social relationship and communication, and arousing physical recollections of characteristic mood and emotion for the eighteenth-century audience. In his cavatina 'Se vuol ballare', addressed to the absent Count, Figaro shows that he who recognizes society to be a dance (and can command the different forms of the dance) has the upper hand. If the Count wishes to make those around him dance, Figaro will play the tune. Lulled into a false sense of security by the reassuring measures of the aristocratic minuet, the imaginary Count is suddenly jerked into a *capriola*, forced to execute undignified hops and leaps before being swept into a bourgeois contredanse, in which the likes of Figaro will always sweep the floor. We are clearly reminded of Figaro's intentions when, in the Act II Finale, it is to the disarming measures of a minuet that Susanna emerges calmly but triumphantly from the closet, and engages the Count in her own teasing mockery of his stately dance. In the Act III Finale, dance itself takes over; the whole society of Aguasfrescas is drawn into a fandango, at once graceful and edgy, whose minor key and exotic trills remind us that beneath the apparent resolution of events lurk unresolved tensions.

But in the exalted or the grotesque, the tragic or the comic, the rhythms and gestures of dance also weave their way more imperceptibly through Mozart's operatic scores, drawing events in their wake, reconciling the rational and the sensual, and raising Mozart's characters, foolish and bewildered as they are, beyond their subjection to the material world which forever threatens to consume them, or the jostling community of fellow-beings who threaten to crush them, into the transcendent world of play and freedom.

THE SUBLIME AND TRANSCENDENT

In his *Memoirs* Lorenzo Da Ponte recalled that in looking for a suitable comic text for Mozart, one of his considerations had been to supply Mozart with something 'sublime'.[31] It is an unexpected word to find in relation to an *opera buffa*. But Da Ponte's intuition about the nature of Mozart's genius was acute, for in *Le nozze de Figaro* Mozart was indeed able to give expression to the later Enlightenment's understanding of the sublime and transcendent sphere in human activity.

For the earlier Enlightenment the dictates of earthly society had outweighed all other considerations. The Enlightenment made persistent efforts to diminish the influence of the unknowable (metaphysical truth, divine grace) in peoples' lives, and many of the questions which had hitherto been answered by religion were now to be addressed to Man in society. God was banished as a distant abstraction to a quiet corner of his universe, and religion was relegated to Sunday churchgoing, or became indistinguishable from secular morality, a mere instrument of social education (Hobbes's 'humane politics'). The most certain way of pleasing God, wrote Montesquieu, is 'without any doubt to observe the rules of society and the duties of humanity'.[32] To Joseph II there was no distinction between the citizen's duty to God and his duty to the state.[33] For the *philosophe*, wrote Diderot, 'Civil society, is, so to speak, a divinity on earth ... he worships it'.[34] This divinization of secular society was to reach its apogee in the French Revolution, in which the church of St Geneviève was deconsecrated and turned into a pantheon, literally a 'place for the gods', and dedicated to the Revolution's own saints and martyrs, upon whom was conferred the secular immortality of fame.

But conversely, as Rabbi Jonathan Sacks has pointed out, the banishment of God, and the secularization of religious discourse leaves an unmistakably God-shaped hole in Man's spiritual ozone layer.[35] And ever since the eighteenth century art has aspired to fill the spaces left by an absent God. More particularly, it has been music, so often understood to be the most spiritual of the arts, which has met this need; it was, after all, the eternal *silence* of the infinite spaces which had filled Pascal with such horror.[36]

In Thomas Mann's novel *Doktor Faustus* the narrator Zeitblom complains that liberal theology 'degrades the religious to a function of the human; the ecstatic and paradoxical elements so essential to the religious genius it waters down to an ethical progressiveness ... it lacks insight into the daemonic character of human existence'.[37] Eighteenth-century aesthetics introduced the concept of the 'sublime' to account for the wayward religious impulses of the daemonic which reason had not been able to expunge from human consciousness. In Burke's definition of the sublime in art and nature, the emotions aroused by sublimity are clearly those that formerly belonged to religious experience: 'Astonishment, admiration, reverence and respect', the attributes of humanity's consciousness of the greater than itself, prompted by 'terror, obscurity, power, privation vastness, infinity, magnitude'.[38]

The art-form that had always maintained a relationship with the numinous was opera, in which Man's relationship with the gods (in whatever form they manifested themselves) had remained a central theme. In the seventeenth century opera had been classified (with doubtful approval) as the genre of the 'merveilleux'. Banished from Metastasian *opera seria*, the numinous made an obvious return to opera in the calculated sublimity of Gluck's operas, and in Mozart's supernatural music for *Idomeneo* and *Don Giovanni*, where it was intended to arouse in the listener Burke's emotions of 'astonishment, admiration, reverence and respect' through the attributes of the musical sublime, identified by Burke as 'loudness, suddenness, intermittence, cries'.[39] In time church music, deprived of its most meaningful, ecstatic employment in an era of rational devotion and practical piety, would rediscover its function by borrowing from the quasi-religious sublimity of secular music. Beethoven's *Missa Solemnis* opens unmistakably with the solemn rituals of *Die Zauberflöte*.

But reaching beyond the need to acknowledge the numinous and the sublime in human experience, the later Enlightenment also developed a new understanding of the meaning of divinity itself. Since Man had banished fairies and romances from his art, Burke observed, he had instead turned for inspiration to 'the marvellous in life'.[40] The later Enlightenment displays a marked tendency to laud the wonder of human aspirations. For Diderot, truth, virtue and beauty were the father, son and holy spirit of a personal trinity of transcendent aspirations, and they are also the subjects of Kant's three great *Critiques* of the 1780s on knowledge (truth), ethics and aesthetics.

To Kant, truth, morality and aesthetic beauty, insofar as they are ultimately unknowable and unattainable on this earth, represented the most our mortal understanding is capable of comprehending of divinity. 'He who loves virtue loves God', wrote Wieland in his *Sympathien*, a work so beloved of the Mozart family, 'and can we love the supreme Being without advancing towards perfection?'[41] As Goethe understood so well, people cannot live without belief in something beyond themselves: without goals or objects of devotion in which to have faith, or without ultimate hope of attaining such goals.[42] The objects of humanity's worship in later Enlightenment art are its own ideals. Goethe's Iphigenia, when she finds herself confronted with a conflict between her supreme conception of truth and the need for deception to save the lives of herself, her brother and Pylades, pleads with the gods to uphold her moral ideals, and her own faith in them: 'Save me, and save your image in my soul',[43] In van Swieten's and Haydn's *Creation* Man is created, as in the biblical account, in the image of God; but in Goethe's poem *Das Göttliche* the gods are themselves remade in Man's image, and Man is urged to be 'generous and good' so that the gods themselves ('those beings of our surmise') may be modelled upon him.[44] 'What man reveres is his innermost humanity turned inside out,' says Goethe in one of his epigrams.[45] 'Thine own humanity learn to adore,' commands Blake's Christ.[46]

Opera came to play an increasingly important role in conveying humanity's transcendent aspirations in later eighteenth-century art. Opera, according to the *Encyclopédie*, was 'the divine of the epic put on stage' (le divin de l'epopée mis en spectacle).[47] and in accordance with the newly conceived divinity of Man, both Goethe and Schiller came to recognize that in opera the fusion of the human and the exalted realized their own aspirations towards the ideal. Schiller had long nursed an antipathy to opera, the result of enforced over-exposure as a boy to the performances of old-fashioned *opere serie* at the Court Theatre in Württemberg. As a young writer he was determined that his own dramas should have no taint of the operatic in them, and he criticized Goethe for his use of music in the visionary closing scene of *Egmont:* 'a perilous leap into the world of opera'.[48]

But increasingly Schiller came to believe that music was the art most capable of reaching beyond the tyranny of the material towards the ideal. The purpose of music, Schiller was persuaded by his friend and musical amanuensis Körner (who was the first theoretician to attempt to apply the terms of Kantian idealism to musical aesthetics), was 'to raise us from our lowly, circumscribed state of dependence and represent to us the infinite'.[49] In the funeral oration that was delivered to Mozart's mourning masonic colleagues after his death the sentiment is similarly expressed that through his music Mozart himself 'lifts our aspirations to a higher goal'.[50]

Michael Tippett once observed that whenever dramatic writers such as Goethe, Schiller and Yeats have wanted to convey some form of transcendence, they have found themselves turning first to verse, and then to music.[51] By the time Schiller came to write *Don Carlos* in 1783, he had found the need to use dramatic verse for the first time. At a similar moment Goethe felt impelled to put his prose drama *Iphigenie* into verse. In each case the writers were responding to a need for less naturalistic forms to convey their moral and aesthetic idealism, an idea given complete expression by Schiller in his 1805 essay on 'The Use of Chorus in Tragedy' (1805), in which he proposed 'openly and honourably to declare war on all naturalism in art'.[52]

Converted by performances of Gluck's *Iphigénie en Tauride* in Weimar in 1796, Schiller came to believe that opera might be 'the avenue by which the ideal can steal its way back into the theatre'.[53] Reports of performance practices at the theatre in Weimar during the 1790s also confirm the new operatic aspirations of Goethe, who was said to have trained the casts of his plays as if he were running an opera rehearsal, conducting the verse as though it were song, and 'constantly appealing to the analogy of music in his instruction'. He described Part One of *Faust* as a tragedy, but Part Two was 'in part an opera'.[54]

The burgeoning theatrical idealism of Goethe and Schiller had been quite clearly anticipated by Mozart. The spiritual aspirations of *Die Zauberflöte*, with its assertions of human divinity, are unmistakable. But as Schumann once said, 'The greatest skill in art is that of spiritualizing the material,'[55] and, as we have seen, in *Le nozze di Figaro* Mozart miraculously achieved that ideal, firmly rooting the spiritual in the earthly humanity of comedy. In 1789 the French writer Quatremère de Quincy wrote an essay on opera in which, laying emphasis upon the new ideality of music, he argued that the very sublimity of music rendered it unsuitable for comedy: 'Associated with comedy, it [music] rejects all the light transitions which nuance roles, all the delicacy, lightness, all the finesses of reasoning, all that string of varied interests ... The chords of its lyre are tuned too high to accord with any other sphere: she dips her brush in colours that are too strong to ally herself with the light nuances of comedy'. With a subtle misquoting of Aristotle, Quatremère claimed that 'The model of comedy is man as he is; that of opera man as he might be'.[56]

Quatremère's prognostications had already been confounded by Mozart, whose music was more than competent to depict the nuances and finesses of comedy. But more to the point, it was precisely through comedy within opera that Mozart was able to affirm in *Le nozze di Figaro* that men and women as they *are* and men and women as they *might be* exist together, in conflict perhaps, but the one always contained within the other. 'The desires of man are infinite', wrote Blake,[57] to which Goethe would have riposted with his famous rule: 'If you wish to advance into the infinite, explore the finite in all directions.'[58] And it was Schiller, the great idealist, who believed that comedy was the truest art of the ideal, allowing man 'to take a calm and lucid survey of all that surrounds him . . . ultimately smiling at the absurdities rather than shedding tears and feeling anger at the sight of the wickedness of man'.[59]

In his poem *Die Götter Griechenlandes*, Schiller had suggested that the essential quality of Greek classicism was that it reflected an era when humankind had lived in accord not only with material nature, but also with the gods alongside whom it had shared its world. *Le nozze di Figaro* is the most radiant expression of late Enlightenment classicism's reconciliation of the spiritual with the material. In medieval cosmology the secret harmonies of the spheres had sung the praises of God's creation, and had been drawn down from heaven to echo in Man's earthly praise of God. In the later Enlightenment the voice of the artist himself ascends upon the wings of his own song to re-occupy the vacant corridors of heaven and sing the praises of humanity from above.

PART THREE

THE YEARS OF RETREAT

1786-1791

XIV

The collapse of Josephinism

In December 1785, while Mozart was at work on *Le nozze di Figaro*, Joseph II issued an edict to 'reform' Austrian freemasonry. Its purpose was to bring freemasonry under closer supervision by the state. The numerous Viennese lodges, already forbidden to have contact with organizations outside the Habsburg territories, were now to be amalgamated into three official lodges, government supervised, whose members were to be registered with the police. Viennese freemasonry was no longer to be an autonomous institution.

Joseph's high-handed masonic edict was deliberately offensive towards what he termed the '*gaukeley*' (mumbo jumbo) of the freemasons, and threw Viennese freemasonry into a crisis from which it never recovered.[1] As early as 1786 Gottlieb Senn, himself a freemason, wrote to Reinhold in Weimar, commenting that Viennese freemasonry 'so gut als eine Null ist' ('is as good as nought').[2] The edict was also a sign of the new authoritarianism which was becoming evident in Joseph's rule. He had grown increasingly wary of the independent activities of Viennese freemasons, suspicious of their allegiances to authorities beyond his control (such as the Berlin Grand Lodge, and the Bavarian Illuminati), and was concerned at the growing influence of both the reactionary Rosicrucians and the radical Illuminati within Viennese freemasonry. The edict marked the beginning of a general paranoia about the efflorescence of secret societies in late eighteenth-century Europe, a paranoia that by the beginning of the next decade would bring widespread accusations that the freemasons had been responsible for nothing less than plotting the French Revolution.

More generally, Joseph's edict reflected increasing alarm at what was perceived in many quarters as a growing individualism and social libertarianism in Vienna, that had arisen out of the very reforms Joseph had himself introduced at the beginning of the decade. By 1785 Joseph too had become disappointed and embittered by the failure of his people to respond more positively (and more responsibly) to his liberalizing programme. According to his brother the Archduke Leopold, ruler of Tuscany, Joseph had as early as 1784 started to regret some of his reforming zeal, repenting in particular the fact that his Church reforms and the relaxation of censorship had not encouraged reasoned debate and enlightened morality in Austria, but instead moral libertinism and lack of concern for public welfare. His own apparent cynicism had promoted an unfortunate image: 'He himself gave the appearance of having little religion and few morals, and that has set a bad example and encouraged libertinism; now he wishes he hadn't, but it's too late.'[3]

The image which Josephine Vienna projected was of a society rife with moral uncertainty and laxity, selfishness, materialism, and growing disaffection with its autocratic ruler. The English musical historian Dr Burney, who remembered Vienna in the good old days of Maria Theresa, was to look back on those days with affection. 'Her piety has been thought to border on bigotry, but if we may judge of its effect by the tranquillity, happiness and affection of her people with their turbulence, discontent and detestation of her unprincipled, philosophical, and disorganizing successor, we suppose that too much religion is less mischievous in a sovereign than too little.[4] Mozart's song *Die Alte*, K.517 (1787), is a comic expression of these attitudes, sung by an old woman looking back to the good old days 'zu meiner Zeit' ('in my times') when everything was different and better.

The famous *Stubenmädchenbroschuren* (see p.144) were an early sign of the opposition that arose to the relaxation of social distinctions encouraged by Joseph's reforms; but by the second half of the decade even former supporters of Joseph's reforms such as Johann Pezzl had become disillusioned and crusty. In his *Abduls Erzerum* (1787) Pezzl painted a bleak picture of a contemporary society given over to brutish licentiousness. Tempted to redefine the meaning of *Aufklärung* in his *Skizze von Wien*, a few years after Kant's more famous effort, Pezzl claimed that the term *Aufklärung* had been brought into disrepute since many people thought that it simply meant being anti-religious. On the contrary, Enlightenment, according to Pezzl, was having regular habits, a good diet, taking care of one's health, and submitting one's own interests to those of the public good.[5]

As Joseph kept up the pace of reform on the one hand (pressing on with his legal reforms and his campaign against the nobility) he began to reverse many of his earlier liberalizations, which he now considered 'to undermine all religion, morality, and social order'.[6] A characteristic decree of the second half of the decade was the outlawing in 1787 of prostitution (for which Vienna was infamous) as a crime against the state – presumably on the grounds that it went against the populationist principles in which he believed. Supervision of publications became prevalent from 1784 onwards, when a deposit had to be paid to the Censorship Commission on all brochures and pamphlets printed, and by 1790 full censorship of newspapers had been reintroduced.

Although these steps were initially taken to police the morals and religion of the population rather than the security of the state, in 1786 a confidential instruction from Joseph outlined plans for a secret police system to deal with the growing number of malcontents and disruptive social forces in the empire, and increasingly censorship itself was put in the hands of the police. When in 1786 Ignaz von Born (in a surprisingly unenlightened gesture) applied to have a pamphlet suppressed that criticized his handling of the masonic crisis brought about by Joseph's reform, it was to the police rather than the Censorship Commission that he applied.[7] In 1787 Joseph wrote to his minister in Belgium, where discontent with religious reform had boiled over into open revolt, that 'scribblers and publishers who indulge in libels must be severely punished. Those who oppose us with ridicule and threats must be arrested, whipped and kept in jail',[8] a clear indication of the repressive bent of Joseph's mind at this date.

ATHEISTS AND MATERIALISTS

Among Joseph's foremost concerns was the spread of atheistical tendencies in Vienna. In her voluminous memoirs, published in 1844, the novelist Karoline Pichler[9] recalled that during the 1780s there had existed two intellectual camps in Vienna. One comprised people who were, as she described them, '*Materialisten und Atheisten*', who were influenced by writings imported from France and Protestant Germany,[10] and who were 'neither true Catholics nor true Austrians'[11] – the characteristics which therefore identified the second group. It is clear that the main division between the two camps occurred between the members of the two leading masonic lodges of the Viennese Enlightenment: Ignaz von Born's lodge 'Zur wahren Eintracht' and Mozart's 'Zur Wohltätigkeit'.

The religious tenor of the lodge 'Zur wahren Eintracht' was essentially Deist, and maintained the intellectual inheritance of the early English Enlightenment, reminding us of the relationship between early English freemasonry and the London Royal Society. The first recruiter of freemasonry, Dr Thomas Desaguliers, Newton's secretary, was himself a scientist and scientific popularizer like Born. Many early lodge meetings were given over to scientific lectures and demonstrations, and Desaguliers wrote a poetic treatise entitled *The Newtonian System of the World, the Best Model of Government*:

What made the Planets in such Order move,
He said, was Harmony and mutual Love.
The Musick of the Spheres did represent
Their ancient Harmony of Government.[12]

The name 'Zur wahren Eintracht' itself means 'true harmony' a clear indication of its Newtonian loyalties.

The complex beauty of the Newtonian system indicated rather than denied a God; such balance of forces kept in perfect harmony seemed to demand a prime mover and overseer, and the little wrinkles in the system which Newton had been unable to iron out simply proved the necessity of a deity to make occasional running adjustments. Since God worked through nature, knowledge of nature and discovery of her laws was the surest way of attaining knowledge of God himself. For a militant Deist like Paine, writing at the time that Born's lodge was active in Vienna, 'The principles of science lead to this knowledge; for the Creator of Man is the Creator of science, and it is through this medium that man can see God, as it were, face to face'.[13]

But the development of science in the eighteenth century had in fact consistently led to a questioning of the place of God in the universe, and eventually to an atheistic materialism. In particular, biological research forced an awareness that nature was not static and orderly; that there were vital living forces at work in matter itself, constantly bringing change and transmutation (recognition of which led several eighteenth-century thinkers, including Diderot, to arrive at the uncertain shores of an evolutionary theory). The work of biologists like Needham and Buffon which had hinted at the possibility of spontaneous generation led to a realization that nature carried within it the seeds of its own generation. If this was the case, there was no need to believe that the material atoms of which Man was constituted required a soul to animate them, as Descartes had argued, or that the universe itself required a prime moving deity.

The implications of scientific materialism spread into other areas of human enquiry. The French materialists, La Mettrie, Holbach, Helvétius, and (reluctantly) Diderot, argued that explanation for all human actions must be traced back to physical or biological functions, Human beings were simply biological machines (L'homme machine was the title of the genial La Mettrie's infamous little book, much admired by Frederick the Great), all of whose spheres of activity could be mechanistically explained; 'physical sensibility is the sole cause of our actions, thoughts, passions and feelings', claimed Helvetius.[14] People were entirely determined by their physical makeup and its interaction with the environment.

Holbach and Helvétius were banned in Austria for their arrant atheism, but they provided intellectual inspiration for Adam Weishaupt, a former Jesuit at the Bavarian University of Ingolstadt. Inspired by his reading of these, and by the Scottish school of social scientists and political economists that included Francis Hutcheson, Adam Ferguson and Adam Smith, in 1776 Weishaupt founded a secret society that was to act as an élite group within freemasonry, dedicated to the rational reform of society based upon materialist, scientific and utilitarian principles. Known as the Illuminati, its most significant following was in Vienna, where 'Zur wahren Eintracht' also functioned as a radical Illuminati cell within Viennese freemasonry, and where its most prominent members included Born, Sonnenfels, Alxinger, Blumauer (and possibly, van Swieten).[15]

Through the Illuminati, and through contact with current developments in scientific enquiry, it is very likely that there were members of 'Zur wahren Eintracht' who might have espoused that materialism and atheism which Karoline Pichler complained had been 'introduced from abroad' into Vienna. There is evidence that there was indeed anxiety about the extremes of rationalist freethinking to which intellectual enquiry within 'Zur wahren Eintracht' had led. Friedrich Münter, later to become a distinguished Lutheran bishop, had been full of praise in 1784 for the fact that the lodge had eschewed all the paraphernalia of higher grades and masonic oaths and what he called the 'hokus pokus' of Rosicrucianism.[16] But he confided to his diary certain misgivings about the anti-Christian tendencies of the lodge:

A consequence of former Catholicism,[17] [is that] the majority reject the whole of Christianity, and treat the [lodge] as the place where they can preach openly about these matters. I listened to several lectures of this sort, which more or less implied, to those who so could so interpret it, and would as soon they were given the slightest opportunity, that all practical Religion is Priestcraft.[18]

Two years later, after Joseph II's masonic edict, Leopold Aloys Hoffmann, a member of Mozart's lodge 'Zur Wohltätigkeit', wrote a pamphlet in defence of Joseph's reform, in which he argued that Viennese freemasonry had fallen into irreparable strife and bickering. Hoffmann identified two sides in the confrontation, and blamed both equally, criticizing those who had become involved in mystical activities, and were seeking the philosopher's stone and conjuring ghosts, and those who had lapsed into *Freygeisterei* (freethinking) and who believed in the 'Project of a general human-equality', a clear reference to the aims of the Illuminati. In a second pamphlet, he accused Born and Sonnenfels of having gone too far in their rationalism, citing Sonnenfels's apparent mockery of the masonic oath, and Born's belief that everything could be explained by science.[19]

Mozart would undoubtedly have shared his fellow lodge-member Hoffmann's attitudes. Alongside his father's hostility to the Roman Church (which he would have shared with most Josephine Catholics) he had also inherited a profound distrust of religious *freigeister* and moral libertinism. The oboist Ramm in Mannheim was described by Mozart as a 'libertine',[20] and the Wendling family had been rejected by Mozart because of their licentious lifestyle. Mozart refused to travel to Paris with them; claiming that they were without morals because they were lacking in religion, and 'friends who have no religion cannot be our friends for long'.[21] Mozart's rather prim attitude was apparently unfashionable in Mannheim. 'Most people here have no religion and are out-and-out freethinkers,' wrote his anxious mother; 'No one knows that this is the reason why Wolfgang has not gone off with them, for if it were known he would be laughed at.'[22]

An even more important part of Mozart's religious faith included a fervent belief in an immortal soul and in an afterlife. Not only did he affirm in 1777 that he expected to meet his mother again in heaven, but ten years later he expressed the hope of meeting his friend Sigmund Barisani 'in a better world and never more to part'.[23] The materialist's scornful dismissal of the soul as an 'occult power'[24] horrified him. For Mozart, possession of a soul was the guarantee of man's spirituality, the attribute at the heart of Mozart's vision of humanity. One of the books in his library was Moses Mendelssohn's neo-platonic *Phädon*, a reworking of Plato's dialogue on the soul, from which Mozart virtually quoted when writing his own thoughts on death and immortality to his father in 1787.

Mendelssohn argued that our knowledge of the eternal absolutes of truth, beauty, goodness and perfection depend upon our own possession of an eternal soul. Virtue and beauty ('harmony, symmetry, proportion') must have been implanted in matter by God, and can therefore only be perceived by man's spiritual faculties. 'If our soul is mortal . . . then whatever we think beautiful, sublime, or moral is no impression of God's accomplishments . . . Then we are sent here like the beasts to look about for food and die.'[25] 'You say that I must remember that I have an immortal soul,' writes Mozart to his father in 1781. 'Not only do I think it, but I firmly believe it. If it were not so, wherein would consist the difference between men and beasts?'[26]

Mozart's decision to join 'Zur Wohltätigkeit' in 1784 implies, therefore, not merely an affirmation of his belief in a moral, enlightened Catholicism. It was undoubtedly also made in response to his own alarm and hostility to the increasingly widespread materialism and atheism endemic among the more radical Viennese Enlightenment thinkers associated with the lodge 'Zur wahren Eintracht'. Mozart was, in Karoline Pichler's terms, choosing to be an Austrian and a Catholic.

Beyond the conflict in Viennese freemasonry between materialists and Catholics, Joseph II's 1785 reform opened a second inherent source of division, and laid bare the inevitable contradiction between the absolutist and the bourgeois conception of modernization and reform. On the one side were those like Sonnenfels who had considered freemasonry as a legitimate target for Joseph's plans for enlightened reform which would ensure that 'through the means of the Order itself the number of virtuous citizens should be increased', and that 'Human sympathy [*Menschenliebe*] and civic duty [*Bürgerpflicht*] should be brought into a closer relationship'.[27] On the other side were those in the Born circle for whom freemasonry represented the culmination of the bourgeois Enlightenment's efforts to create an autonomous community independent of the state, guided by the principles of secular morality alone; a Kantian 'ethical commonwealth' existing within the political commonwealth, a society in which eventually, as the Illuminati proclaimed, the need for princes and rulers would simply fall away as mankind learnt to regulate its affairs by scientific and utilitarian principles.

It was this latter conception of freemasonry that Joseph and the Josephines could not tolerate. In his 1784 article on freemasonry in the *Journal für Freymaurer*, Sonnenfels had warned against the dangers of encouraging anti-state tendencies within freemasonry, and had even insisted that it was a freemason's duty to reveal to the authorities any plots against the state.[28] Interestingly, Friedrich Münter, reporting at the time of the masonic crisis in 1786, hints at fierce arguments between Born and Sonnenfels, and tells of accusations against Sonnenfels for having betrayed the movement by encouraging Joseph to undertake his reforms.[29]

Like his fellow 'Zur Wohltätigkeit' lodge member Pezzl, Hoffmann, who supported the emperor's reform, was employed as a secretary to the Chancellor Kaunitz. It is clear that in general the members of the lodge 'Zur Wohltätigkeit', both intellectually and socially more conservative than the Born circle, were closer to the Josephine administration, and more inclined to view the emperor's growing alarm at the signs of social and moral libertarianism in Vienna with sympathy. Significantly, the only member of the Born circle who supported Joseph's masonic reforms was Aloys Blumauer, who worked as a member of van Swieten's Censorship Commission, and whose major poetic work was a parody of Virgil's *Aeneid*, a satire on contemporary Viennese society in which he inserted eight entirely serious strophes in praise of the emperor. Blumauer joined Hoffmann in writing poems in praise of Joseph's masonic reform (specifically warning of the dangers of creating 'a state within a state')[30] for which he was bitterly reproached by many of his colleagues in 'Zur wahren Eintracht'.

This small group of masonic works in support of Joseph's reform includes Mozart's two songs *Zerfliesset heut* ('For the Opening of the Lodge'), K.483, and *Ihr unsre neuen Leiter* ('For the Closing of the Lodge'), K.484. On 19 December 1785 the members of 'Zur Wohltätigkeit' had met with the members of 'Zur wahren Eintracht' to discuss the new lodge amalgamations commanded by Joseph's edict. Gemmingen and twenty members of his lodge, including Mozart, decided to join with members of 'Zur gekrönte Hoffnung' to form the amalgamated lodge 'Zur neugekrönte Hoffnung', rather than the amalgamated lodge 'Zur Wahrheit' (of which Born was, briefly, to become master, before abandoning freemasonry altogether at the end of 1786).[31] The songs were written in January 1786 to commemorate the closing of Mozart's former lodge 'Zur Wohltätigkeit', and the opening of 'Zur neugekrönte Hoffnung'. The text of the former lauds the emperor's efforts to reform freemasonry: 'Joseph's beneficence has crowned us, in whose breast a threefold fire burns, with new Hope. Let this song of praise be sung by heart and tongue together, to the father, who binds us more closely.'[32] In January 1786 Mozart clearly still believed that the policies of the emperor might restrain the rising tide of social, moral and religious licentiousness. The desire for order was beginning to outweigh the prerogative of freedom.

XV

Don Giovanni

Don Giovanni was written in 1787 for Prague, where performances of *Le nozze di Figaro* had enjoyed enormous success early in that year, giving rise to a commission for a new opera. After the glowing humanity of *Le nozze di Figaro*, and its blessing upon the Christian gospel of forgiveness, *Don Giovanni*, the story of the *dissoluto punito* ('the libertine punished', the opera's primary title) has been seen by critics and commentators as a puzzlingly anti-Enlightened work.

THE PROBLEM OF GIOVANNI'S DAMNATION

The question it inevitably raises is: how seriously are we to take the damnation of Don Giovanni? Did Da Ponte or Mozart, or their audiences, believe in Don Giovanni's hellish fate? The Enlightenment had, after all, made determined efforts to liberate people from the demeaning fear of death which had given the medieval Church such power over benighted Christians. Lessing's famous essay *Wie die Alten den Tod gebildet* ('How the ancients depicted death') of 1769, with its classical image of Death as the serene brother of Sleep, was intended to drive the old skeletons and cadavers from tombs and churches. It was widely influential, and its image of Death and Sleep as beautiful youths appeared on Canova's neo-classical monument to Clement XIII in St Peter's, on which Canova started work in the year of *Don Giovanni*. The Enlightenment had also rejected the image of the jealous and angry God of the Old Testament. In late seventeenth-century England the conservative Dryden had with scornful irony ridiculed the new image of a liberal God:

> That lets the world and human kind alone;
> A jolly God that passes hours too well
> To promise Heav'n, or threaten us with Hell.[1]

Voltaire considered it ridiculous that, if indeed God existed, He could possibly wish to 'occupy himself for an eternity of centuries in roasting a poor devil'.[2] Both Moses Mendelssohn in *Phädon* and Otto von Gemmingen (who believed in a more conventional God than Voltaire), also dismissed the idea of eternal damnation and torment. 'The angry and vengeful God, are not these false ideas which have been allowed to grow up; for do we not abhor anger and vengeance in men?' writes Gemmingen in *Der Weltmann*.[3]

In most commentaries upon the opera the final damnation of Don Giovanni is the one issue writers fail to address. Joseph Kerman considered it a bit of unwarranted theology that Mozart found 'thrust at him at the end of *Don Giovanni* – right at the end, when things were getting rushed, as usual'.[4] Brigid Brophy thought the only possible explanation was the effect of the psychological trauma upon the otherwise enlightened Mozart of the death of his father during the composition of the opera: the judgement scene was a guilty projection of Mozart's own fear of retribution for his rebellion against his dead father (for whose death he felt subconsciously guilty).[5] Irving Singer suggests that the terror at the end of the opera represents human fear of death in general, rather than fear of damnation;[6] surely wrong, when one recalls that during the very composition of the opera Mozart had written in consolatory terms of death: 'the true goal of our existence, I have formed during the last few years such close relations with this best and truest friend of mankind, that his image is not only no longer terrifying to me, but is indeed very soothing and consoling.'[7]

Don Giovanni's tremendous damnation, one of the most thrilling scenes in all drama, cannot simply be brushed aside as an aberration on the part of a panicky composer looking at his watch in the small hours of the morning, or rationalized away as either psycho-drama or existential angst. It is central to our understanding of the whole opera. For the Enlightenment's attitude to the supernatural was, as in so many things, ambivalent. Dedicated to eradicating medieval superstition, the Enlightenment tended to rationalize human intimations of the supernatural (as in Gothic horror novels, which excelled in creating shivers of terror, only to explain the ghostly pheonomena away as natural occurrences), or aestheticize them (as in Burke's explanation of the sublime (see p.183)). But the Enlightenment also fervently believed in a just universe, and reserving its judgement of heaven and hell, was frequently tempted to invoke a little divine intervention on earth (as in *Idomeneo*) to uphold its belief in a just God. In Goldoni's version of *Don Juan* (a story which he himself called 'that wretched Spanish tragicomedy')[8] the worst aspects of the old story are carefully rationalized to ensure that the reprobate's divine punishment may be put down to natural causes if desired; a strictly non-attributable lightning bolt strikes him dead, with no hint of heaven or hell.

But even such intervention, with its suggestion that God might have to suspend the laws of nature on earth to manifest his justice, offended the

Newtonian sensibilities of the more rationalist Enlightenment thinkers, who preferred to convey the notion of divine justice through material rewards on earth. Wieland wrote to Tobias von Gebler that although he much admired his play *Thamos*, Gebler should excise the divine lightning bolt meted out to the criminal conspirators at the end of the story on the grounds that such supernatural intervention trivialized God.[9] In *Justine*, de Sade used a divine thunderbolt to blast the impeccably virtuous heroine, to discredit what he considered to be the fiction of a just and moral God.

Actual depictions of hell, however, were considered inappropriate in eighteenth-century high art. Henry Fielding was in no doubt that belief in hell belonged to 'the days of superstition', and pointed out that 'the whole furniture of the infernal regions hath long been appropriated by the managers of playhouses, who seem lately to have laid them by as rubbish, capable only of affecting the upper gallery – a place in which few of our readers ever sit'.[10] Antonio Eximeno, a Spanish Jesuit, wrote in 1774 of the Don Juan play: 'it is no excuse that educated persons are well aware of the improprieties of such comedies which please only the ignorant lower classes; for in the theatre the taste of the common people upheld by the educated classes is the national taste'.[11] By the eighteenth century the old morality tale of Don Juan had indeed become the subject-matter of just such popular farce. Don Juan was a pantomime buffoon carried to hell by squealing devils in crinkled catsuits. 'We have all seen him in the pantomime/ Sent to the Devil ere his time,'[12] writes Byron of the hero of his own irreverent comic epic on the story. In the introduction to an operatic version of the Don Juan story by the librettist Giovanni Bertati and composer Giuseppe Gazzaniga, which was performed in Venice in January 1787 (and upon which Da Ponte drew heavily for his own libretto), the members of an Italian touring opera company about to perform the old story agree amongst themselves that it is no more than vulgar farce, 'una bella e stupenda porcheria',[13] and just the thing for provincial German audiences. For precisely these reasons, Da Ponte has himself been accused of opportunistic pandering to popular taste in choosing for the provincial capital Prague the discredited old story of Don Juan, and retaining its most populist feature, the uproarious fate of Don Giovanni himself. The accusation carries some weight when we recall that the Venetian police files tell us that, while still a priest, Da Ponte had been caught *in flagrante delicto* with a married woman, and had brazenly protested his innocence with the oath, 'May God strike me down while I celebrate the mass.'[14]

The most common complaint against *Don Giovanni* in its own day was that Mozart's divine art was wasted on such vulgar nonsense. 'Oh had'st thou not squandered the power of thy spirit! Had thine sentiments been more in harmony with thine imagination and had not led thee to take such unclean steps to greatness!' wrote one Mozart admirer on the occasion of the opera's revival in Berlin in 1791.[15] But Mozart's decision to accept Don Giovanni's fate, neither rationalizing it (as had Goldoni), nor trivializing it into mockery or parody, was entirely deliberate. He could easily have insisted that Da Ponte alter the ending, had he wished. But everything about the music for Don Giovanni's damnation tells us that Mozart intended his audience to be shattered by it. His reasons for this can only be understood in relation to his perception of the seriousness of Don Giovanni's transgressions. Very simply: the punishment fits the crime, and, for Mozart, so serious are Don Giovanni's crimes that only the ultimate punishment can serve. So only when we have properly understood the enormity of Giovanni's crimes can we assess the appropriateness of his punishment.

WHO IS DON GIOVANNI?

The problem with which Don Giovanni presents us is one of identification: he is almost impossible to collar. And neither the eighteenth century's customary depiction of Don Juan as a bungling boulevard *farceur* forever caught with his trousers around his ankles, nor the nineteenth century's idealization of the Don as romantic hero, can explain Mozart's dangerously elusive anti-hero. Don Giovanni, as many have noticed, is a 'nonperson'; a bundle of drives without apparent pyschological motivation. Who is Don Giovanni? No one can tell; at least, not from the opera itself: 'Who I am you shall never know', he sings in his very first statement as he wrestles with the (literally) furious Donna Anna ('una furia disperata', as she describes herself).

Unlike Molière's Don Juan, who is a garrulous rationalist forever engaging in philosophical dispute about his puerile principles, Mozart's Don is virtually without self-reflection. His arias provide no insights into his psyche (his third aria is in fact sung in the guise of Leporello), and his biography is so numbingly repetitive that it can represent no history of real human growth and development. In place of the confessional *Diary of a Seducer* of Kierkegaard's Don Juan, Don Giovanni has no more than an enumerative list kept by his salacious appointments secretary. It is precisely this anonymity that has prompted Don Giovanni's later would-be biographers, all of whom recognize Mozart's Don to be somehow the quintessential Don Juan, to attempt to reconstruct him from the history of his previous and subsequent manifestations, and from analysis of the eighteenth-century seducer. They hope, in vain, that Mozart's evanescent

Don Giovanni will assume human form at the point where these histories intersect.

But the emphasis which the Romantics placed upon Don Giovanni's erotic quest, and the energy which the twentieth century has devoted to the psychology of the obsessive seducer, is misplaced. It is an understandable emphasis, since it is impossible not to be seduced in turn by Mozart's music in this opera, and to forget how pervasively that erotic charge runs throughout his works. Is Giovanni's music any more suggestive than Zerlina's? (Together, of course, the combination is irresistible; the duet 'Là ci darem' is one of the most erotically charged moments in all art.)

Giovanni's list of conquests is, no denying it, quite staggering. But it is patently comic too (the absurdly accurate figure for his Spanish conquests to date, 'mille e tre', is obviously meant to be funny), and provides no real grounds for psychological speculation. Only when Don Juan's repetitive couplings are seen as sublimated expressions of something else can they furnish material for psychological investigation, and there are no grounds for this in the opera itself. Don Giovanni's impulsive and opportunist escapades are quite unlike the compulsive quest of Richardson's Lovelace in *Clarissa*, in which one seduction alone furnishes the material for a domestic epic of tragic obsession; or the vindictive strategies of Laclos's Valmont, a typically rational sensualist, who insists until too late that he is driven by principle rather than passion, and pretends that he can eradicate natural impulses from his desiccated world.[16] Routine seduction of the kind in which Giovanni engages is, in the end, simply banal. Even with Mozart to supply him, Don Giovanni has only one tune up his sleeve when it comes to serenading his victims: the tune heard in the Act II Trio in which Giovanni so cruelly deceives the gullible Elvira, reappears, adorned but scarcely disguised, with the mechanical tinklings of a mandolin, as a yearning serenade to her maid.

THE SENSUALIST AND TRICKSTER

Don Giovanni is in fact a cheap sensualist rather than a true erotic seducer. Indeed, he is thoroughly impatient with the elaborate stratagems of erotic play that characterize the pursuits of Valmont; he grows petulant with Zerlina's coy hesitations, and attempts rape for the second time within the opera. Giovanni's sexual appetites are indistinguishable from his other gross physical appetites. He is a glutton and toper, and in the final scene mocks Elvira's deluded belief in the moral power of love by toasting 'women and fine wine' in one rousing breath as the common 'sustenance and glory of humanity'. To Giovanni, women are no more than objects for consumption to satisfy physical need. Giovanni's three solo numbers are more like the mono-affective expressions of the passions of baroque opera than the self-revelatory *Credo* with which Verdi and Boito furnished another apparently motiveless villain, Iago. In baroque terms, Don Giovanni is simply the personification of Appetite, Lust and Violence.

In each of his arias the opportunity for modulation of emotion or tone is denied. Giovanni launches himself into 'Fin ch'han vino', never pausing for respite or breath until he has completed his obsessive, repetitive list of the physical pleasures of food, drink, dance, song and, almost as an afterthought, sex. The serenade 'Deh vieni' is an endless cantilena, lacking repose until it relapses into mere strophic repetition, at which point one imagines that Giovanni will probably keep going like an automaton, churning out verses until he has attained his purpose. His third aria 'Metà di voi' is a crude incitement to violence, an indication of the true baseness of Giovanni's nature.

In a sense, Don Giovanni's career as a sexual libertine is only incidental, a token more of the bourgeois obsession with the morality of sex than of the significance Giovanni himself attaches to his seductions. If extra-marital sex is the most grievous sin in a naughty world, then to represent a naughty man he must, for the bourgeois, be represented as a libertine. But in fact, the meaning of the word libertine originally implied religious rather than sexual freethinking, and the sexual libertinism of Molière's *Don Juan* (a text which Da Ponte most certainly kept at his elbow as he was writing Don Giovanni) is really a secondary feature of his religious revolt. Indeed, Molière's rationalist libertine explicitly revolts against religion in the name of reason rather than sex.

But Kierkegaard's distinction between the unreflective operatic Don Giovanni, who is only interested in the immediate satisfaction of sensual desire, and the reflective Don Juan of Molière, who relishes and savours the cunning of his deceptions is, though true, only partially useful.[17] For while Mozart's Don Giovanni is certainly a sensualist, he also retains many of the characteristics of his forebear, the original Don Juan in Tirso de Molina's play: he is a *burlador*, a comic trickster whose sexual obsessions are combined with a delight in childish escapades and in the chaos and confusion they bring in their wake. Giovanni's comic wooing of Elvira whilst disguised as Leporello is a pointless deception, undertaken out of a sheer devilry which, as Leporello recognizes, quite outweighs the ostensible need to get Elvira out of the way to allow access to her maid. Even more gratuitous is Giovanni's deception of Masetto and his band of peasant vigilantes when, still in disguise, he sends them off in pursuit of the real Leporello and Elvira. Like all true tricksters, he relishes the frisson of danger he courts in inciting them to 'fire upon' the villain Don Giovanni.

THE THREAT TO SOCIETY

If the rationalist libertine of Molière's age had concentrated on rebellion against God, it was natural that the Enlightened libertine of Mozart's age should attack the new divinity of the era, society. And it is as a threat to society, as an embodiment of the forces of social disruption and moral licentiousness Mozart and his contemporaries saw all around them, that Don Giovanni must be judged. Most particularly, as an embodiment of these forces, Don Giovanni threatens the sort of humane society based upon free contractual agreements and guided by the moral principles of Christianity envisaged in *Le nozze di Figaro*.

Mozart sometimes wrote works in pairs, contrasting two works in the same form by major and minor keys.[18] This pattern is repeated in the relationship of *Don Giovanni* to *Le nozze di Figaro*, in which the former may be seen as a demonic minor-key subversion of the latter, since both works are framed by the tonality of D. The world of *Don Giovanni* is the negative of the portrait of the luminous society of *Le nozze di Figaro*: a world in which custom and tradition have reverted to their dark, tribal origins of murder and revenge; in which the stable values of hierarchy and status are persistently undermined; in which the promises – in particular the marital promises – that make a free society based on contractual agreements possible, are no longer honoured or respected; in which morality, Christian or otherwise, is no longer adequate as a basis for human solidarity; and in which the unyielding hierarchies of heaven and earth, optimistically abolished in *Figaro*, have in the end to be restored.

Don Giovanni is a harbinger of chaos; a lord of misrule turning the world into a permanent carnival of transgression. He releases in other characters appetites and energies hitherto unknown, spinning them like tops into a frenzy of dislocated motion, and sending them out to whirl into each other in the darkened streets of Seville. Even stone statues come to life as he draws near. In the Finale of Act I, the dances that had underpinned the orderly intertwining of individuals in the classical vision of society are superimposed in a scene of steadily mounting rhythmic tension and confusion. The *menuetto, follia* and *allemanna* to which the characters dance have been specifically commanded by Don Giovanni in 'Fin ch'han vino', and are associated with the three social classes: aristocracy (the aristocratic masqueraders are invited to the ball by Leporello to the reassuring sounds of a minuet being played in the background), peasantry and bourgeoisie, classes who should remain forever discrete.

Mozart's *tour de force* of organized disorganization demonstrates the social chaos to which libertarian egalitarianism gives rise.

In *Le nozze di Figaro* the *seria* and the *buffo* characters merged seamlessly in the *mezze carattere* who were allowed in *opera semiseria* to assert a common humanity, in spite of the necessary distinction of class and status. (Lessing speaks of the whole human race 'as one family, the high and low, the rich and the poor', with no implication that fraternity implies equality.) Both Figaro and Susanna are endowed with the full-scale *recitativo accompagnato* normally reserved for *seria* characters. But in *Don Giovanni* the *seria* and *buffa*, as exemplified by Anna and Zerlina, are trapped within their own straitjackets of convention, only to be forcibly and uncomfortably thrown into each other's unwanted company. In Giovanni's ballroom their stratified dances, thrust together, grind and jar in horrible social disharmony.

Mozart had himself witnessed the effects of such enforced egalitarianism some years earlier. In December 1781 he wrote to his father about a public ball he had attended at the imperial palace. As was his wont, Joseph II had opened his doors wide, and the occasion had been infiltrated, Mozart complained, by 'friseurs and housemaids'. None other than Figaro and Susanna, of course, who are heroes and heroines in their place, but are not welcome when they overstep the bounds of their status. At one point in the evening, the common people had pushed themselves so roughly into a dance that the emperor and his guest, the Grand Duchess of Russia, had been jostled by the crowd. Mozart had the scorn of a spiritual aristocrat for the emperor's well-known affectations of egalitarianism. 'All I can say is that it serves him right. For what can you expect from a mob?'[19]

Don Giovanni further elides the class distinctions which maintain society by the indiscriminacy of his seductions. A Valmont, like Count Almaviva, at least takes professional pride in matching his strategems to the character and status of his victims; a virtuous married woman is approached in a different way from an *ingénue* fresh from convent school. But to Giovanni all women are the same: 'peasant girls, maidservants, city girls, countesses, baronesses, marchionesses, princesses'; as long as they wear a skirt they are ready game for Don Giovanni. How humiliating for an aristocratic lady to know that, to Don Giovanni, she is no different from a peasant girl. The Countess at least has the hollow comfort of knowing that the Count's courtship of her maidservant differs from his courtship of herself.

THE INFAMOUS PROMISCUITY

Through his lack of sexual discrimination, Giovanni destroys not only status distinctions, but the very individuality that lies at the heart of the bourgeois world. In so doing, he threatens to draw society back to the inchoate mass from which the Enlightenment sought to rescue it. The imperatives of economic development in modern society demand an individualistic base, and the eighteenth century (and subsequent bourgeois societies), in creating the free and equal individuals required by capitalism, had therefore to be convinced of the pristine intactness of the individual before he or she entered society. The individual had to be abstracted from the collective and vigilantly fenced about to curtail any desire to merge back into the comforting mass. According to the French historian Michel Foucault, the development of modern social individualism is paralleled in the crucial structural distinction between Renaissance and classical modes of thinking.[20] The former had explained phenomena by the principle of resemblance and correspondence; the classic mode insisted upon replacing analogy with the separating and taxonomizing process of analysis, represented by the great classical projects such as Linnaean botany, Dr Johnson's *Dictionary*, and the *Encyclopédie*.

In his distrust of the linguistic metaphor, Dr Johnson displayed the eighteenth-century insistence upon distinctness as the necessary basis of coherent order. This insistence is echoed by the eighteenth century's wider anxiety about human and social forces that threaten to undermine the distinction between individuals in society – above all, sexuality. For Giambattista Vico, the great Neapolitan historian and founder of modern anthropology, social chaos is characterized by precisely the confusion and bestiality which derives from the 'infamous promiscuity of things and women' in the pre-social state of nature,[21] a promiscuity that can only be terminated by the selectivity of property and marriage in civilized society.

The Enlightenment therefore found itself torn between its desire to celebrate the liberating pleasures of sexuality, and its concern both at the fragmenting implications of that sexual individualism, and the regressive power of sexuality to undermine individuality and to return society to the confusion threated by a Don Giovanni. Without 'preference', or attachment to 'particulars', Burke insists, 'the passion which belongs to generation, merely as such, is lust only'.[22] The Enlightenment would not represent sexuality itself as reprehensible, or suggest that it must be suppressed, but it consistently conveyed its anxiety about sexuality that is neither individuated nor clearly directed. Rousseau talks of the dangers of having as a youth been 'intoxicated with love that lacked an object',[23] and Mozart's adolescent Cherubino displays just such a promiscuity of undirected impulses, as he flitters from one focus of desire to the next, alighting indiscriminately on the fetishistic substitutes so wantonly scattered throughout eighteenth-century literature and art.[24] (In his double cross-dressing – woman to man to woman – Cherubino further disturbingly blurs the boundaries of gender and identity so crucial to the Enlightenment. Acknowledging the relationship between Freudian sexual fetishism and Marxist commodity fetishism, the recent production of *Don Giovanni* by Ruth Berghaus for Welsh National Opera depicted Don Giovanni himself as a shoe-fetishist, but hinted that for Giovanni, women were themselves merely fetishistic substitutes for his unfocused desires.[25]

The dangerous confusions of this regressive, infantile sexuality are especially evident in the hedonistic paintings of Boucher, who endowed every object in his paintings with sexual potential; his world reflects the animistic materialism of those *philosophes* who taught that every atom of the universe was jigging with sexual desire, and he irresponsibly dissolves the necessary boundaries between nature and culture as if they had never existed. His boudoirs erupt in the wanton disarray of nature, and his forests are as safe as boudoirs; his adults engage in childish games, whilst his children occupy themselves with the more serious business of sex. Boucher (like Fragonard) celebrates the liberating pleasures of sex, apparently oblivious to the dangers of such erotic excesses. But the limitations of such inchoate sexuality are quite evident in Boucher's mythological paintings, where his gods and goddesses are undifferentiated and indistinguishable; plump objects of indiscriminate desire that resist any attempt to focus the desire they arouse. Don Giovanni merely raises Boucher's heedlessness into an absolute principle.

DECEPTIVE APPEARANCES

In his abuse of disguises Don Giovanni confirms a further lingering Enlightenment fear of a society in which the conventional signs and codes of social position and personality can no longer be relied upon. The earlier Enlightenment had often celebrated the crowded anonymity of the modern city and its public institutions. Thus Montesquieu's Persian visitors to Paris rejoice in the freedom the city offers to those who wish to relinquish the conventional marks of birth and status. Tired of the attention his exotic costume attracts, Rica puts off his outfit and dresses like a European, and discovers that he is now accepted for who he is rather than what he appears.[26]

As we have seen, the Enlightenment recognized the paradox that to relinquish the outwards signs of natural status often required the adoption of a different persona, and that dishonesty might be the quickest path to the truth. Casanova tells us that Catherine the Great of Russia used to pass incognito amongst crowds to listen to what was said about her.[27] In the plays of Marivaux the prince often dresses as a servant to ensure that the woman he is courting loves him for his true self and not simply for his status or for his wealth.[28] Count Almaviva in *Le barbier de Séville* ensures the attention, and tests the true love, of Rosina when he serenades her as a penniless student; and ironically, the only way that Rosina as the Countess can expose her husband's bad faith is, in turn, by disguising herself as a servant and encouraging her husband to seduce her. In *Così fan tutte*, it is through disguise that Ferrando and Guglielmo are able to expose the shallowness of their mistresses' vaunted fidelity.

But if masquerades and disguises are gauges of social freedom to be celebrated, they are just as potent provokers of anxiety among those who fear the effects of a relaxation of hierarchies and status in society. For, as Defoe pointed out, in modern society the freedom accorded people in their outward display meant that it was increasingly difficult to determine peoples' true position in society: 'It is a hard matter now to know the Mistress from the Maid by their Dress, nay very often the maid shall be much the finer of the two,'[29] he complained, reminding us of the ease with which Susanna and the Countess exchange costumes and roles in *Le nozze di Figaro*, and the more insidious interchangeability of Don Giovanni and Leporello (roles played by identical twins in Peter Sellars's 1980s production). In the works of the post-revolutionary generation of English moralists the masquerade often became a symbol of the moral corruption brought about by too much social freedom; Hogarth's paintings are consistently preoccupied with the dangers of the masquerade, and in the novels of Richardson, Fielding and Fanny Burney, the masquerade is represented as a merry-go-round of social and moral confusion. Jane Austen shows her most conservative colours when, in *Mansfield Park*, the decision to indulge in amateur dramatics brings the final catastrophe upon those who have undermined the social stability and moral structure of the household.

From the very opening of the opera, Don Giovanni insists upon anonymity as Donna Anna attempts to unmask her assailant.[30] Giovanni has clearly perfected the art of concealment. To Ottavio and Anna he is known as a gentleman, a fellow member of their own class. His observance of the customary proprieties of that class – courteous manners, the tokens of aristocractic honour he dedicates to the service of Donna Anna (and which reveal, in their absurd effusiveness, the hollowness of such tokens) – seem to confirm that he is worthy of esteem. Montesquieu in *L'esprit des lois* suggested that the prerogatives of honour (self-esteem or Rousseau's *amour-propre*) might serve as a brake to the anti-social desires of the individual not adequately constrained by virtue alone. But honour is a quality that is entirely dependent upon outer perceptions of behaviour. As long as society believes one's honour to be intact it may be considered to be so. Honour and virtue may coincide, but not necessarily. And in the hands of Don Giovanni, honour is an easily abused attribute (he has already demonstrated that he *has* no honour by breaking an oath sworn 'sul mio onore').

For how can we tell the worth of a person from their appearance when they may be adopting a disguise of some sort? 'The honesty of true nobility is seen in the eyes,' Giovanni reassures Zerlina, endorsing the popular idea that nobility is transmitted in the genes. But just as Giovanni is bent ingratiatingly over Anna's hand, Elvira bursts upon the scene and instantly throws such certainties into confusion. In the Quartet which ensues Elvira warns Anna and Ottavio that Giovanni is a deceiver and betrayer. She herself looks and behaves, initially at least, like a noble-woman; they commend her 'noble appearance and sweet majesty'. Indeed, she *is* an aristocrat, but her increasingly extravagant and unseemly be-haviour seems to belie her appearance, and throws Anna and Ottavio into a comic dither of uncertainty, as they are suddenly faced with a break-down of recognized codes, and the possibility of making a social *faux pas*.

The confusion into which Don Giovanni throws the world is high-lighted by the ambiguity of Elvira's status in the opera. She is an aristocrat, and her music, rhetorical and florid, clearly belongs to the *opera seria* conventions of Anna and Ottavio. But she undoubtedly also fills Mozart's demand for a *mezza carattera* (semi-comic) role in *opera buffa*. Like Dora-bella in *Così fan tutte*, she was originally denied the accompanied recitatives which would have given her true *opera seria* status (although, significantly, Mozart added one in the indispensable aria 'Mi tradi' he wrote for the Vienna production of the opera, which so increases her status). In the Act I finale Elvira joins her aristocratic peers; but in the opera's epilogue Elvira sings her last farewell with the *buffo* characters before rejoining the aristocrats for the final *stretta*. Her brush (for it was no more than that for him) with Don Giovanni has robbed her of proper social status.

Confronted with these contradictory signs, how should Anna and Otta-vio behave in the Quartet? To disbelieve either Giovanni or Elvira is to impugn the honour of one or the other. 'A chi si credera?' ('Whom can one believe?') they whisper nervously to each other as Giovanni attempts to alleviate their fears with unctuous reassurances that the poor thing is 'pazza' ('loopy'). As the Quartet progresses they struggle to maintain decorum against Elvira's mounting hysteria and the muttering of Giovanni's veiled threats against her. The subsequent discovery of Giovanni's true identity resolves the situation; but it undermines even more shockingly than the murder of the Commendatore the premises upon which the society of Anna and Ottavio is built, for it tells them that appearances can no longer be trusted. Don Ottavio weakly expresses his amazement that a 'gentiluomo' – one who is defined by his observance of the code of honour, according to Rousseau[31] – could behave in such a dishonourable fashion. The effect of Giovanni's deceptions is to force the other characters to abandon openness in turn. To survive in a society based upon deception one must engage in deception oneself and assume a mask. 'I faint!' gasps Anna as she and Ottavio are swept into the maelstrom of Giovanni's ball. 'Pretend!' Don Ottavio mutters to her under his breath.

'I KNOW OF NO PROMISES'

Having shredded the conventions that hold society together, Giovanni also ensures that they will not easily be reconstituted by means of bourgeois contracts. Indeed, Giovanni makes a point of breaking promises, thus making a mockery of one of the very foundations of modern human community. In the scene immediately after the murder of the Commendatore, Giovanni swears to Leporello that he will not get angry with him should Leporello venture to speak his mind about Giovanni's deed. Leporello does so, and immediately Giovanni explodes. 'And your promise?' Leporello reminds him. 'I know of no promise,' replies Giovanni, setting an ominous precedent for what is to come. 'Sir, I promised to marry him,' says Zerlina, as Giovanni dismisses her fiancé Masetto as a dolt. 'That promise means nothing,' replies Giovanni.

That promise, of course, is the most sacred promise of bourgeois society. And it is as a subverter of marriage that Don Giovanni the libertine is most brazen. Like Count Almaviva, Don Giovanni attempts to seduce a girl on the day of her marriage. This attempted seduction of the betrothed but as yet unmarried woman threatens bourgeois institutions at their symbolically weakest point, and undermines not only chastity, but also the family and marriage. Indeed, it is the second time that very day that he has violated these institutions, since Anna, victim of his earlier attempted rape, is betrothed to Don Ottavio. And her father's attempts to defend his daughter's honour lead swiftly to further outrage, as the old man is hacked down by Giovanni.[32]

'The only function I have is to make husbands wild or fathers desperate,' claims Montesquieu's Don Juan.[33] Although women are the ones who are truly damaged by male sexual aggression, male patriarchy considers itself affronted. The eighteenth century had laudably strict laws against rape, but the sternness of the laws reflected the fact that rape was considered a crime against the property of the father or husband rather than an assault upon the integrity and person of the woman herself. The violator of a daughter (particularly an heiress) or of a wife was far more likely to be convicted in court when prosecuted by father or husband than if a woman tried to bring a prosecution herself.[34]

Having abused Donna Anna, and having given the slip to Donna Elvira (whom we are told in Molière's play he has abducted from a convent, and who therefore wears the wedding-ring of Christ on her finger), Don Giovanni knows he is in luck when he chances upon a chorus of peasants merrily singing of the joys of love. The chattering tune, irregularly phrased, conveys the Cherubino-like 'flutterings of the inexperienced heart', and the wanderings of 'light-headed men', about which Zerlina and Masetto sing. But their song, easily misheard as an exhortation to 'gather ye rosebuds while ye may' and enjoy the pleasures of youth while you can (the sort of sentiment we might customarily expect in a pastoral scene of this sort) is in fact telling us the opposite. For the remedy for fluttering hearts and light heads is, so Zerlina and Masetto complacently affirm, to settle down and get married. They look forward to a bucolic but domestic future in which, safely wedded, 'we will enjoy ourselves, sing and dance'.

'Is there a wedding?' asks Giovanni, signalling his interest even before he has set eyes on his victim. In no time he has singled out the bride (her most important recommendation) and set his cap at her. In the scene which follows, Don Giovanni's cavalier attitude to marriage is spectacularly subversive, and reflects one of the eighteenth century's most persistent concerns: that of the unscrupulous seducer who promises marriage to his victim simply to overcome her reluctance to be coaxed into bed. In *Pamela*, Richardson introduces the possibility of just such a specious wedding into the history of the aristocratic Mr B's long siege of Pamela. It is a brilliant device, for it creates in the reader an uncertainty as to whether the conspiratorial wedding that does eventually take place may not be just one more cruel trick played on Pamela.

Don Giovanni, whose attractions are clearly even less resistible than those of Mr B, is even more liberal in his promises of marriage, which are evidently part of his routine. Donna Elvira certainly considers herself to be betrothed to Don Giovanni, and the duet 'Là ci darem la mano' between Giovanni and Zerlina is nothing less than Giovanni's proposition of marriage as he directs Zerlina's wary (she has been warned about *cavaliere* like Don Giovanni) but increasingly wide-eyed gaze towards his 'casinetto', a gloriously sly touch, since his palace, undoubtedly admired by the curious and covetous Zerlina many times in the past, is certainly no cottage. 'There we will be married,' he sings in the last line of recitative, before sliding imperceptibly into the meltingly seductive (and all-too-well-practised) enticements of the duet itself: 'There you will give me your hand, there you will say yes to me.' It is not just her simplicity that makes her unable to resist, and perhaps it is only from the safety of the auditorium that we can recognize the real intent behind Giovanni's alluring offer in the erotic promise with which Mozart's music subverts the reassuring marital proposals of the text.

It is Giovanni's contempt for marriage that finally rouses the Statue of the Commendatore to action. Molière's Statue waits for Juan's insolent invitation to supper before stirring; Mozart's Statue is so incensed by Giovanni's licentious chatter that he interrupts the despoiler of his peace. In the graveyard where the Statue has been erected, Giovanni (who is still in disguise) recounts an adventure with a girl who has apparently taken him for Leporello. 'What if the girl had been my wife?' is Leporello's horrified response. (There has been no mention of Leporello's wife up until now, but suddenly we realize how close Giovanni is to repeating Count Almaviva's outrage against *his* servant Figaro.) 'Better still!' he guffaws. It is at this ultimate profanity against bourgeois society that the Statue's sepulchral voice, accompanied by ghostly trombones from the darkness, cuts off Giovanni's mocking laughter.

In *Le nozze di Figaro* marriage that has been undermined must be restored to health for the good of society. But in *Don Giovanni*, once the promises of contractual society have been dissolved, faith in the possibility of reconstructing society upon such promises is apparently destroyed for ever. As a result, we are left at the end of the opera with a perilously unstable world drained of human fidelity. From Elvira's first appearance it is clear that Giovanni's betrayal has for her undermined all the foundations of normal social exchange. In the Act I Quartet she declares herself to be beyond all social caution and restraint (while Giovanni menacingly cautions her to show more care lest she dishonour herself). At the end of the opera she retreats to the one place where she knows that promises will be kept and vows of constancy will be accepted for ever, the place from which the Enlightenment had so strenuously sought to preserve its daughters: the convent.

Donna Anna too finds herself conspicuously incapable of renewing her own promises to Ottavio, evidence, perhaps, of guilty longings behind her tireless pursuit of Giovanni. Having brought Anna the news that Giovanni will shortly be punished for his crimes and Anna avenged, Ottavio proposes to put the world to rights by marrying her the following day. But for Anna the world cannot be so easily mended, or promises so blithely remade. 'Forse, forse' ('Perhaps, perhaps'), she sings in her aria 'Non mi dir', bleakly reiterating the word which spells disaster for a society founded upon the certainty of promises. Ottavio's fidelity will no longer serve as an earthly substitute for the absolution which, as for Elvira, only heaven can now offer. 'Perhaps one day Heaven will again feel pity for me,' sings Anna, trailing clouds of aimless coloratura which indicate how very far she is from finding the peace she seeks.

GIOVANNI AS BOURGEOIS LIBERTARIAN

Don Giovanni is a destructive force who embodies all the most profound social contradictions underlying the Enlightenment. He is an extreme embodiment of the bourgeois individualist's quest for liberty, but at the same time characterizes the disintegration that is the inevitable consequence of the fulfilment of that quest. The contradiction is manifest in the ambivalence of meaning in the Italian word *libertà*, which Giovanni rousingly summons the guests at his party to toast, and which can mean both 'freedom' and 'licence'; and it is the bourgeois materialist confusion of these two definitions which lies at the heart of *Don Giovanni*. Don Giovanni is, predictably, a sexual libertine and an aristocrat. But he really represents those aspects of the bourgeois Enlightenment's programme that cannot be depicted in their true colours: the bourgeois, rather than the aristocratic, pursuit of libertarian pleasure. Don Giovanni is a man 'free from cock to wig' (as a contemporary pithily described the political radical and notorious lecher John Wilkes).[35] Wilkes also fought for political freedoms, but he and his contemporaries were apt to confuse the ideals of political *libertà* with the enjoyment of sensual and material *libertà*. When James Boswell, another notorious leacher, arrived in London fresh from the stuffy confines of Calvinist Edinburgh, he instantly set off 'like a roaring Lion after girls, blending philosophy and raking',[36] with a will that confirmed de Sade's recognition in *La philosophie dans le boudoir* of the bourgeois materialist's reduction of moral to sexual freedom.

Giovanni carries to its logical fulfilment both the bourgeois materialist's rationalizations of the morality of pleasure (even keeping a ledger of his transactions like any good bourgeois merchant), and the materialist arguments that man attains his truest freedom in the unrestrained satisfaction of his desires. 'True wisdom consists infinitely more in doubling the sum of one's pleasures than in increasing the sum of one's pains,'[37] argued de Sade, a principle to which Giovanni adheres with admirable consistency. In Holbach's *Système de la nature*, Nature addresses Man:

'Oh Man, in following the impulse I have planted in you to strive every instant of your life for happiness, do not resist my sovereign law. Labour to your own felicity . . . You will find the means clearly written in your heart . . . O man, be happy.[38] 'At no matter whose expense', de Sade thoughtfully adds as a rider.[39]

Elvira wildly accuses Giovanni of breaking 'all the holy laws of earth and heaven' in abandoning her. But if the laws of heaven are no more than the laws of nature (as the Enlightenment had always taught) and the laws of earthly society must in their turn concede to the laws of nature, what possible wrong can be imputed to Giovanni? As de Sade was quick to spot, if all Man's impulses were blessed by nature, nothing could be sinful. 'If nature forbade sodomy, incest, pollutions, etc., would she allow us to get so much pleasure from them?' he asks.[40] If everything is natural, everything is permitted. To Giovanni sexuality is as natural and necessary as eating and breathing, as he informs Leporello when his servant attempts to persuade him to give up women. In his *Supplément au voyage de Bougainville* Diderot had argued that there is no moral injunction against sexuality itself. But once this position has been conceded, the only imputation which can be made against Giovanni's appetites is their sheer excessiveness: a question of health and hygiene rather than ethical right and wrong. Only if one takes into consideration the Kantian injunction against treating other people as means rather than ends in themselves can a framework for Giovanni's condemnation be constructed. And bourgeois capitalism, with its penchant for turning people into commodities (as Rousseau had already noted)[41] is not over-anxious to encourage the notion of people as ends in themselves.[42]

Giovanni the materialist has no fear of the laws of heaven or earth. This is not because, like a de Sade or a Baudelaire, he sets out to challenge the Christian God with deliberate blasphemies, but because he acts in accord with nature. If nature is wicked, then so be it; so too must God be, if indeed He exists. As if to confirm Giovanni's self-justification, the opera repeatedly hints at the connivance of Giovanni's victims in their own downfall. The Enlightenment's earlier raped heroines such as Clarissa had invariably been unconscious (hence completely guiltless) at the moment of defilement. But the possibility that Anna had herself issued some sort of invitation to Giovanni is clearly suggested. Zerlina too may not have bargained on rape, but she accedes to Giovanni's offer of marriage with a blatant disregard for conventional proprieties. And Elvira pursues her own humiliations far more purposefully than she pursues Giovanni's downfall. With such women thrown in his path, it is easy enough for Giovanni to persuade himself that he is doing no more than satisfying the 'sweet desires' he supposes every woman to carry 'in the middle of her heart'. Giovanni (and, it would seem, Da Ponte and Mozart) denies women what Laclos's Valmont considered to be the hypocritical Clarissan 'pleasures of vice with the honours of virtue'.[43]

Don Giovanni, natural man, as Kierkegaard and many since have observed, bears all the characteristics of one of Goethe's daemonic spirits ('daemonic', rather than 'demonic', to imply not an occult or moral quality, but an amoral, elemental force of nature, an inner, driving destiny). He is possessed, according to Kierkegaard, of 'the power of nature, the daemonic, which as little tires of seducing ... as the wind is tired of blowing, the sea of billowing, or a waterfall of tumbling downward from the heights'.[44]

What Kierkegaard failed to recognize is that the untameable daemon, Don Giovanni, is the libertarian daemon of capitalism itself, a system that has persuaded itself that its dynamic *economic* pursuits are (as Adam Smith taught) self-motivated forces of nature – as if commerce were driven by the animistic spirits found by primitive man in the rocks and trees, deities quite without moral purpose or imputation. And capitalist libertinism, encouraged by the necessary destruction of traditional social controls, soon turns into the social and moral libertinism recognized by Mozart and his contemporaries within their own society.

THE FAILURE OF BOURGEOIS MORALITY

After his encounter with Don Juan in Paris, Montesquieu's Persian visitor writes home with incredulity: 'What do you think of a country where such people are tolerated, and where a man who follows such a career is allowed to exist? Where faithlessness, treachery, abduction, perfidy and injustice earn respect? Where a man is esteemed for separating a daughter from her father, a wife from her husband, and for breaking the most delightful and most sacred attachments?'[45] Since this was how many Viennese had come to regard their own society by the mid-1780s, the inevitable question was therefore: how can Don Giovanni be stopped? How can the spirit of individualism he represents be controlled without recourse to the unacceptably repressive authority threatened by the absolutism of Joseph II as he attempted to stopper the bottle. *Don Giovanni* demonstrates that the bourgeois Enlightenment's simple moral stratagems of eliding pleasure and virtue, and persuading itself that self-gratification and public welfare were identical (hence legitimizing its desired pursuits), had actually provided a justification for individualism and rampant materialism. As Rousseau had shown in *La nouvelle Héloïse*, the garden in which the bourgeois Enlightenment had sought to readmit and sublimate the impulses of nature was itself a fiction, a sentimental attempt to disguise (rather than transcend) the reality of the contradictions between passion and duty.

One by one Don Giovanni picks off the bourgeois Enlightenment's moral pieties, sentimental or otherwise. He flouts the bourgeois ideal of friendship ('the sacred cloak of friendship' as Ottavio calls it). As in *Le nozze di Figaro*, but with even greater brutality, the sentimentalization of master and servant relations is soundly trounced by Giovanni. He shows no loyalty to poor Leporello; he is perfectly willing to sacrifice him to the wrath of the Maskers to save his own skin by accusing Leporello of attempting to rape Zerlina, and considers it a huge joke to direct Masetto and his gang of thugs to beat up (and indeed, to shoot) Leporello. Leporello, on the other hand, returns as good as he gets, for he lacks entirely the sort of sentimental loyalty recommended for the modern servant. His ties to Giovanni are purely mercenary; he spends most of the opera complaining about his master's antics, but he is always ready to be bought round by a well-filled purse. Like Molière's Sganarelle (who cries, 'What about my wages!' as Don Juan is dragged to hell), Leporello's only thought, having just witnessed the roasting of his master, is to get along to the inn and find another: masters are as expendable as servants, and as easily replaced – as long as they pay.

As we have seen in *La finta giardiniera* and *Idomeneo*, the bourgeois Enlightenment had also tried to convince itself that there was a beneficial connection between erotic sensibility and moral sociability. The confusion implicit in such an attitude is unwittingly apparent in numerous paintings by that master of erotic sensibility, Greuze, whose genre paintings often adopt imagery familiar from the religious eroticism of baroque art to convey the new social sexuality of the Enlightenment. In a painting like his *La mère de famille*, in which an absurdly fecund mother submits with the abandon of Bernini's St Teresa to the physical attentions of her teeming family, moral sentiment is sexualized to the point of perversion.

Don Giovanni offers a horrible warning about the effects of this most dangerous confusion of erotic and moral sensibility. At the beginning of Act II, Giovanni defends his sexual exploits, claiming that they are due to 'an overbundance of sentiment' suggesting, in other words, that his sexual desire is evidence of, indeed motivated by, sentimental feeling. 'He who remains faithful to one is being cruel to the others; I . . . love them all.' This is Giovanni's most reflective moment in the opera; significantly, it is borrowed from Molière. With heavy irony Leporello applauds his master's possession of so much 'beneficence' – the very basis of the bourgeois (and masonic) ethics of feeling.

At the first sighting of Elvira in Seville, Giovanni's overabundance of sexual sentiment moves him to feel what he affects to mistake for pity. As Elvira pours out her torrents of impotent rage against her betrayer, Giovanni, the culprit himself, lurking in the background, beguilingly voices his sympathy and compassion for so much grief. But moral arousal surely cannot be smelt in the air, as Giovanni claims to sniff the scent of femininity which draws him like a dog to Elvira, and which so readily stimulates his 'beneficent' juices. Later, in the gardens of his palace, Giovanni makes his second approach to Zerlina. She, knowing that Masetto is hidden nearby, pleads pitifully with Giovanni to exercise the pity in his own heart. Since his pity is a sexual, rather than a moral, feeling, he has no difficulty in complying. 'Yes my dear,' he answers, oozing instant compassion, 'I am all love.' But his love is that 'sensibility without feeling' that Rousseau perceived as the reality behind the plausible materialist ethics of sensibility. 'It is wrong to feel pity', Elvira sings in the Trio at the beginning of Act II, knowing deep down that the imagined pity she continues to feel for Giovanni, which has prompted her to leave her own home in pursuit of her incorrigible betrayer, is sexual and not truly moral (and hinting too that Giovanni's crimes are beyond mere mortal pity: to continue to feel love for him is in some way to transgress against the greater moral edicts of the universe).

The simplest corrective the opera can offer to Giovanni's insidious confusion of sexuality and sentiment is the unambiguously unsentimental sexuality of Zerlina. Her sexuality really does have restorative powers, but they are unashamedly sensual and no more. In her first aria 'Batti batti', Zerlina uses the same masochistic language of invitation to sexual torture as Konstanze in *Die Entführung*, when she pleads with Masetto to punish her for her misdemeanours. But unlike Konstanze's bid for erotic martyrdom, Zerlina's sexuality is not sublimated in an expression of virtuous resolve. Her appeal is frankly and openly sexual. In her second aria 'Vedrai, carino', Zerlina's sexuality proves itself to have a miraculously medicinal effect, the homeopathy of arousal effectively numbing the sprains and bruises Masetto has received from Giovanni. (At the end of the opera Zerlina and Masetto will find their own way back to equilibrium; a solution which is unabashedly earthly, as befits their status, and none the worse for that. Freed of the scourge of Don Giovanni, their sole desire in the concluding scene is to go home and have a good supper!)

But this still leaves the broader problem of how society is to deal with Don Giovanni. The bourgeois 'morality of the senses', the Enlightenment's preferred solution, has proved that its virtues are double-edged. But Giovanni is also impervious to reasonable argument, and he laughs in the face of direct appeals to his heart. Twice Leporello (no moral paragon himself) states that his master must have a 'soul of bronze' or a 'heart of stone'. For Giovanni, as embodiment of the materialists' 'man-machine', quite simply lacks a conscience. He will never, as did the Count in *Le nozze di Figaro*, recognize his guilt, feel remorse and repent. According to Rousseau, 'Conscience is the voice of the Soul,' the guarantee of Man's spirituality.[46] But the materialist recognizes no such force, deriding it as an occult phantom.

As one of Goethe's amoral forces of nature, the daemonic spirit is quite impervious to normal moral constraint. 'All the moral powers combined are of no avail against them; in vain does the more enlightened portion of mankind attempt to throw suspicion upon them as deceiving if not deceived – the mass is still drawn on by them.'[47] Don Giovanni is dangerous (a danger of which Mozart surely must have been aware) because he acts with such commitment and virtuosity that even though we disapprove, we cannot help admiring him. Even when his efforts actually fail during the course of the opera, there is something heroic about such dogged persistence, which commands respect. Indeed, since he lacks any conscious moral purpose, it is virtually impossible to consider and condemn Giovanni as an evil character. (To call a deed evil, says Kant, requires that it be committed out of evil volition.)[48] He simply is what he is, for better or worse, and is irresistibly seductive for it.

Brick by brick this daemonic force dismantles the carefully constructed ideal that sustained the spiritual vision of human society in *Le nozze di Figaro*. During the course of the opera Elvira, initially possessed by an ancient concept of vengeance, comes to accept the moral imperatives of compassion and forgiveness, a classic Mozartian transition conveyed in her troubled and impassioned aria 'Mi tradì'. But in Don Giovanni's world her forgiveness carries no transcendent power or authority, since grace depends upon the decision of the offender to recognize his guilt and repent. And nothing – not even the whiff of incipient brimstone – can make Giovanni repent. Elvira's last-ditch attempt to save Giovanni is brutally rejected. Indeed, Giovanni gleefully subverts the whole process of repentance. In the Act II Trio he mockingly and extravagantly pleads with Elvira for her pardon, and in so doing, exposes the moral ambiguities which underlie society's facile confessions of penitence and the too-ready bestowal of pardon for unforgivable crimes.

Nor has the redemptive constancy of womankind extolled in *Figaro* the power to redeem a Don Giovanni. Constancy has become an impotent virtue; Elvira is certainly constant in her unwillingness to abandon Giovanni, but the meaning of constancy is problematic when it comes so close to sexual obsession, and is no longer upheld by a conventionally virtuous woman. For Elvira is, by all standards of the age, a fallen woman (and it is not until the age of Dickens, Dostoyevsky and Wagner that the fallen woman will be allowed to assume redemptive powers). And to whom is Anna constant? To the memory of her father? To Ottavio? Or perhaps, covertly, to Don Giovanni himself (as E. T. A. Hoffmann insisted)? In the past, the constant lover, like Ramiro in *La finta giardiniera*, had served as a token of stability and assurance in an uncertain world. But Don Ottavio's tender affirmations of constant love, which should offer a human centre of stability to counterbalance the explosive effect of Don Giovanni, prove weak and ineffectual. In Ottavio's first aria 'Dalla sua pace' (in Da Ponte's most exquisite Metastasian mode) the attributes of the constant lover have become mere self-abnegation:

> Upon her peace mine depends;
> What pleases her gives me life,
> What saddens her is death to me.
> If she sighs, then I too sigh.

Such constancy reduces the lover to a mere shadow of his mistress. Beauty may be truth; the aesthetic may mirror the moral world. But against a Don Giovanni neither can succeed.

What stratagems remain to deploy against the mercurial Giovanni? For if the Don Giovannis of this world cannot adequately be restrained by society, then individuals will inevitably take the law into their own hands. (Witness the disturbing rise of vigilantism in our own age.) The opera therefore presents us with a fearsome portrait of a world in which people pursue wild vendettas through the streets of a Seville mysteriously denuded of the customary presence of the forces of law and order. The language of the opera is consistently violent: we are plunged into a world where a distraught woman sings with relish of tearing out her seducer's heart, or a cuckolded peasant mutters under his breath (like Mime in *Siegfried*) of lopping off his tormentor's head. Elvira persuades herself that 'just heaven' commands her to carry out its vengeance, and there is a sort of logic in this: if the power of mercy and forgiveness has been made immanent in society, so also must be the power of vengeance and punishment. The *opera seria* characters in *Don Giovanni*, representatives of the aristocratic counter-revolution soon to point the finger of accusation at the Emperor Joseph who had so vilely betrayed them, pursue their vindictive roles with deadly purpose. Vengeance is no longer – as in *Figaro* – a subject of comic parody, borrowed by a self-important bourgeois Doctor Bartolo for the occasion; it has been restored to its appropriate aristocratic caste. In the duet which concludes the opening scene of the opera, Ottavio and Anna swear a terrible vow to the gods to avenge the death of Anna's father, and in so doing, violate all the Enlightenment's sternest injunctions (see pp. 67–71). A society so disordered unleashes the atavistic instincts of a more primitive age, represented as ghosts from the past, who wait (as the inscription on the statue of the Commendatore tells) until they can come back to exact their revenge. For ultimately, literally nothing on earth seems to be able to put a stop to Don Giovanni. The combined forces of Anna, Elvira, Zerlina, Ottavio and Masetto (not to mention Masetto's gang of thugs) unite to pursue him, but they are powerless. Cornered and exposed by his pursuers at the end of Act I, Giovanni still slips through their fingers like a sorcerer. Imagining that they have him in their power a second time in the great Sextet in Act II, the man they think to be Giovanni turns out to be Leporello. But on this, the first occasion on which all the characters are brought together without Giovanni, he is an unseen presence informing their every thought and move, yet ever beyond their reach. Ottavio's pledge in his aria 'Il mio tesoro' to seek other help (the forces of law?) and return to Donna Anna only with news of Giovanni's death is just as ineffectual. Who will rid the world of this turbulent spirit?

THE RETURN OF THE PUNISHING GOD

In 1751 the Swiss scientist Albrecht von Haller[49] had written a dire warning of the effects of allowing religious scepticism to flourish in contemporary society. Drawing a vivid picture of the modern materialist, Haller sketches a portrait of Don Giovanni with uncanny prescience:

The sceptic who denies an avenging God, and an eternal life to come, restricts our happiness to the brief period of our terrestrial life, in duration, and to the enjoyment of sensual pleasure in substance . . . The pleasures of love – more especially the animal side of love – and the most refined tickling of our senses are considered man's highest good; they alone make us happy, even if it is happiness without honour and devoid of approval by our fellow men . . . This happiness must never be restrained by that old pedant called VIRTUE . . . The torments of an uneasy conscience, or that sense of guilt which relentlessly pursues us, must be dismissed as a mere prejudice incubated in us through parental blows administered during childhood.[50]

The social consequences of religious scepticism are, according to Haller, that 'honour in commercial transactions would disappear, servants would cease to be loyal to their masters; oaths would become worthless'.[51] In other words, he assumes some form of religious belief to be necessary not in its own right (for example, in pursuit of personal salvation), but to uphold the civil bonds of society. Religion supports the moral virtues of the family, upholds obedience to the state and to authority, and ensures sexual fidelity. But more particularly, belief in an all-powerful God, capable of punishing wrongdoers, is essential as the ultimate means of upholding the proprieties of a modern society.

The Enlightenment had always been surprisingly reluctant to dispense with an all-powerful God. For all their notoriety, there were really very few atheists among its supporters. Though conventional religions had been ostentatiously paraded out of the front door of the house of reason, God was always being quietly slipped in at the back door to lend his support to this or that system. Newton needed the God who had designed the cosmos to carry out running repairs and periodical adjustments to his mechanical universe; Adam Smith needed God to ensure that the free-market economy did indeed remain beneficial to mankind. And from Locke to Kant the Enlightenment had worried about the efficacy of moral laws that carried no power to 'reward the compliance of, and punish deviation from . . .', as Locke said.[52] Writing about the impossibility of deriving moral laws from the exercise of pure reason alone, he concluded that 'If therefore anything be printed on the mind of all men as a law, all men must have a certain and unavoidable knowledge that certain and unavoidable punishment will attend the breach of it'.[53]

Only the promulgation of belief in divine punishment and reward could ensure against human vice, argued Voltaire, 'because a vengeful God is needed to punish in this world or the next the wicked who have avoided human justice'.[54] Bayle's vision of a 'society of atheists', Voltaire was forced to concede, is 'impossible'.[55] If there is no God, everything is permitted, and Sonnenfels quoted with approval Voltaire's famous line, 'If God did not exist, it would be necessary to invent him'.[56] 'Can a people without religion be ruled?' Sonnenfels was to ask in *Der Mann ohne Vorurtheil*,[57] and in his major juristic work he gave the Voltairean answer: 'Religion is the most effective instrument to further moral conditions. Secular legislation will be insufficient on several points if not supported by the bond of religion and its punishments.'[58] (Even those dogmatic dictators of secular virtue, the Jacobins, insisted on introducing the cult of the Supreme Being and his quasi-religious ceremonies of worship into the fast-souring Revolution.)

The conclusiveness of these views is especially evident in the development of Rousseau's thinking. In Rousseau's *Social Contract* Christianity, the true religion of man as conveyed in the Gospel, was the highest form of conventional religion: 'By means of this holy, sublime and real religion all men, being children of one God, recognize one another as brothers'.[59]

This, we might suggest, is the form of religious faith that underlies the premises of *Le nozze di Figaro*. In *Emile* Rousseau had argued against belief in hell: 'What need to seek a hell in the future life? It is here in the breast of the wicked.'[60] But in the *Social Contract* Rousseau issues a caveat to such optimism. 'We are told that a race of true Christians would form the most perfect society imaginable,' he says. But on its own, such a Christian society would only work if every member was indeed a good Christian. Within a society dedicated to the virtues of Christian resignation and charity, there is no means of dealing with 'a self-seeker or hypocrite, a Catiline or Cromwell, for instance'.[61] Or a Don Giovanni, we might add to Rousseau's curious list of villains, in whose wicked breast we detect no intimations of hell.

One of the essential dogmas of Rousseau's new civic replacement for Christianity remains a belief in 'The existence of a mighty, intelligent and beneficent Divinity, possessed of foresight and providence, the life to come, the happiness of the just, the punishment of the wicked'.[62] Belief in the existence of an all-powerful and punishing God had come to be understood as the necessary condition for any sort of social order: the only means of quelling the Don Giovannis of the modern world.

This belief in retribution seems out of tune with Mozart's devotion to the exercise of humanitarian beneficence and the ideals of Christian compassion and forgiveness. But the later Enlightenment had come to recognize that talk of Deism or moral Christianity, let alone atheism or materialism, was only possible among a small, educated and responsible élite; that, in Voltaire's famous words, such matters should not be spoken of in front of the servants. 'My dear fellow, I don't believe any more than you do that hell is eternal,' Voltaire quoted a Protestant Minister as saying; 'but it's a good thing for your maid, your tailor, and even your lawyer to believe it.'[63] John Toland, one of the founders of systematic Deism, directed that his Hymns for Deists should only be sung behind closed doors, when the servants had left the room.[64]

The Enlightenment invented a neat historical myth to explain the apparent contradiction within its religious arguments. It is the notion, known as the theory of the two religions or the two philosophies, that all cultures have sustained an outer, exoteric form of religion for the populace at large, and a secret, esoteric religion for initiates. 'It is important to know', writes Voltaire, 'that among nearly all the nations called idolaters there was sacred theology and popular error, the secret cult and public ceremonies, the religion of the wise and that of the vulgar.'[65] 'The rational and thinking part of mankind', Locke believed, had always worshipped 'one supreme invisible God.' But that knowledge had always proved dangerous in the wrong hands. Christianity itself, he suggested, was a mystery religion, but Jesus had concealed his true message, for to have revealed it would have created 'manifest danger tumult and sedition . . . disturbance in civil societies, and the governments of the world'.[66] The historical importance of ancient Egypt ('the first school of mankind',[67] according to Rousseau) to the Enlightenment was that it was the Egyptians who had first practised monotheism, passing it to the Jews in slavery and hence to Moses (Freud's eccentric thesis on this subject had distinguished antecedents) and with somewhat more grasping at mythical straws, to the mysteries of the Greeks via Orpheus.[68]

This was one of the reasons for the continued exclusivity of freemasonry throughout the eighteenth century, for the often noted contradiction between its universalist social ideals and its clubbish secretiveness. Its secrets were not the secrets of arcane matters, of mystery or magic.[69] They were the more dangerous secrets of the true God of the initiates of secret cults throughout history. Like his masonic brothers, Mozart would have espoused a dual set of values. Within his lodge he and his brethren would have promoted the truth of moral Catholicism, and of the gospel of charity and forgiveness. Outside, they would have continued to affirm the realities of divine retribution for the masses (Goethe's masses, who are so easily deceived and seduced otherwise by the daemonic lure of Don Giovanni).

George Bernard Shaw's Nietzschean complaint that 'Gentlemen who break through the ordinary categories of good and evil . . . do not, as a matter of fact, get called on by statues, and taken straight down through the floor to eternal torments; and to pretend that they do is to shirk the social problem they present,'[70] therefore misses the point entirely. Whether or not this happens, it is advisable, when people like Don Giovanni are abroad, to promote the unassailable belief that it *might* just happen. The wicked are most certainly not always punished on earth; it can do no harm for them to fear that they might be somewhere else. That being the case, the Enlightenment concluded, people would be well-advised to settle for Pascal's wager;[71] to weigh up the possibilities and pursue their lives under the supposition that, whereas there is little to be lost if after all God or eternal life are not true (since they will never know), there is everything to lose if they are, and people have failed to take the necessary precautions.

In Vienna the social and moral unrest of the later Josephine years was particularly important in prompting the reaffirmation of belief in a more conventional, judgmental Christian God. As early as 1784 a significant reversal had taken place in van Swieten's Censorship Commission when the decision to allow a Deist book propounding the message of rational natural religion was overturned by the emperor.[72] A member of that commission was Aloys Blumauer who had often expressed Deistic beliefs in his masonic poems. But Blumauer had kept his distance from the more militantly anti-Catholic members of 'Zur wahren Eintracht', and was notably hostile to Nicolai's criticisms of the Austrian Catholic Enlightenment. During his editorship of the *Realzeitung* a significant section in every edition was dedicated to 'Theologie und Kirchenwesen', and in 1786, in an article on 'Suicide in England', Blumauer suggested that the apparent epidemic of suicides in England (suicide was considered evidence of the worst social dereliction during the eighteenth century) must be blamed upon the insufficient religious sanctions of pure Deism.[73] By 1791 even a former radical like Alxinger in his Arthurian epic poem *Bliomberis* had come to agree that religion was necessary 'to keep the people in order'.[74] The giant with whom the knightly hero Bliomberis himself battles is an allegorical representation of none other than the notorious atheist David Hume.

The damnation of Don Giovanni at the end of the opera is therefore for Mozart both real and not real. It is real to the extent that Mozart and the Enlightenment had come to recognize the importance of belief in God's avenging powers for the very security of society itself; not real to the extent that Mozart and the Enlightenment thinkers, safely within the walls of their masonic lodges and clubs, considered themselves personally exempt from the need for such beliefs for their own moral conduct. It could be said that if *Le nozze di Figaro* is Mozart's esoteric exploration of the themes of enlightened Catholicism, *Don Giovanni* is his exoteric statement, a public response to the real world as he and his enlightened colleagues saw it in the middle years of the reign of Joseph II.

Most significantly for the bourgeois Viennese Enlightenment, belief in a punishing God precluded the need for the increasingly dictatorial powers being exercised by Joseph II to restore control and authority in a restless society. By 1787, the year of *Don Giovanni*, criticisms of Joseph's despotic rule were coming even from those who had supported his programme most ardently. Joseph Richter's *Warum wird Kaiser Joseph nicht von seinem Volke geliebt?* was a catalogue of reproving warnings to Joseph written more in sorrow than anger. But Paul Weidmann's *Der Eroberer* of 1786, written by a former staunch Josephine, was a vehement attack upon personal despotism, and in 1788 *Sydney*, a play about Monmouth's rebellion against James II of England, by another enlightened critic, Ignaz Fessler, was banned after its first performance. The posthumous biography of Joseph written by Johann Pezzl, whose *Faustin* had greeted the Josephine dawn with such optimism, has been described as a blanket condemnation of Joseph,[75] holding the emperor responsible both for the social libertinism of the decade, and the need for authoritarian repression to which it gave rise.

THE FORGIVING GOD

Institutions such as the Church or state make no appearance in *Don Giovanni*; humans conduct their lives in the shadow of God alone, unmediated by earthly institutions. The existence of the eternal world is announced from the very outset of the opera in the awe-inspiring opening chords of the overture. The overture to *Figaro* had begun in an earthly chuckle, and ascended during its course to exuberant heights; the world measured by the span of human aspiration. The human world of *Don Giovanni* is placed immediately in relationship to the divine sphere of heavenly justice, stern and unyielding.[76]

The gods, conspiciously absent in *Le nozze di Figaro*, are constantly invoked by the characters in *Don Giovanni* in recognition of their own human impotence. Vengeance upon Don Giovanni is frequently referred to the gods (curiously pagan in a clearly Christian society, the result of the juxtaposition of the worlds of pagan *opera seria* and modern *opera buffa* in the opera). Intimations of a divine sphere, and of Giovanni's eventual fate, are offered at the end of Act I when the characters sing of the 'thunder of vengeance', and even Leporello and Giovanni acknowledge that a 'terrible storm' is brewing. In her aria 'Mi tradi' Elvira too has forebodings of the imminence of supernatural retribution upon Giovanni.

But Mozart's punishing God is, in fact, not quite Voltaire's expedient *Dieu vengeur*. For an essential, and a very Catholic, element in Da Ponte's and Mozart's presentation of the Don Giovanni story is often overlooked. At the end of the opera Giovanni is most certainly dragged away by demons. But God gives Giovanni every opportunity to repent of his sins and save himself. The Statue's task is to warn Giovanni of his impending death so that he can repent, not, as is so often implied, to carry Giovanni to hell. 'Come and dine with me', is the Statue's invitation. And he quite specifically tells us that he eats at God's board in heaven on 'cibo celeste' ('celestial fare') and not at the barbecue in hell.

Giovanni is being invited to accompany the Statue back to heaven. He is about to do so, despite Leporello's desperate counterpoint of warning (Leporello is, of course, genuinely fearful of death, even if it leads to heaven), when he learns that the price is repentence of his sins, and refuses. The Counter-Reformation version of the Don Juan story by Tirso de Molina warns that the sinner cannot rely upon last-minute repentance; death and damnation may strike at any moment. *Tan largo me lo fiais* is the play's subtitle – Don Juan's catchphrase 'Plenty of time for that' (i.e. repentence), about which he is proved horribly wrong. Mozart's Enlightened Catholic version turns this lesson round. God is all-generous, and offers forgiveness even to the very worst sinner up to the very last moment. In place of vengeance, God offers love and acceptance – even to Don Giovanni.

For Mozart, there is no contradiction between the ultimate sanction of punishment and his belief in the infinite forgiveness of God. In the Requiem we find the two positions united within the context of the Catholic liturgy itself. In the succession of its movements the work ceaselessly alternates terror and consolation, visions of hell and visions of heaven in a way that leaves the listener with no doubt of the terrible reality of the experience of exclusion from God, but offers perpetual hope of unlimited forgiveness.[77]

The forgiveness of Mozart's Catholic God is not discretionary, neither is it reserved for the elect. It is always present for the asking. As the medieval mystic Julian of Norwich insisted, God does not even need to exercise an act of forgiveness towards the sinner. His forgiveness is always there, since God cannot change His mind. It is men who change and turn to God, not the other way round. Indeed, God Himself does not punish; it is sinners who punish themselves in turning away from Him.

But Don Giovanni refuses to repent, and even at the moment of death turns down God's grace. The ostensible message thus proffered is a simple warning to all those who refuse to believe in hell. But Giovanni's refusal also implies something more essential about his condition. For Giovanni, materialist Man immured in the condition of sensuality, experiences no disjunction between himself and nature, or between himself and his aspirations. He is indeed the aptest representative of Kierkegaard's aesthetical condition, and lives in a perpetual present of basic, instinctual fulfilment. It is only when Man aspires to the ethical condition, and in so doing assumes the freedom of dictating his own desires (as Kierkegaard suggests), that he becomes aware of the angst of freedom; of the gap between his aspirations and their fulfilment. Only then does he need to turn to God, the only absolute and eternal thing we can know, for ultimate reconciliation.[78] But Don Giovanni, the simple materialist, has no need of such reconciliation: as Montesquieu observed, 'Every Christian wants to go to paradise, except for a few libertines.'[79]

There is, however, a paradox here, for at the single moment of defiance

Don Giovanni suddenly acquires an heroic consciousness and stature hitherto denied to him. If knowledge of our certain death is one of the things that separates human beings from beasts, and gives the activities of our short span of life their meaningful purpose (as Mozart had himself asserted in his letter to his father on death), then in the moment of death Don Giovanni becomes aware of his humanity. With his desperate, defiant denial he becomes a triumphant yea-sayer, prepared to plead his values of individual freedom at the bar of heaven itself. In this moment, as the scene is written by Mozart, it is almost impossible not to identify with Don Giovanni and adopt him as some sort of existential rebel: a rebel whom Camus was to describe as 'A man who says no: but whose refusal does not imply a renunciation,' and who prefers 'the risk of death to a denial of the rights that he defends'.[80]

THE ARTIST AS CRIMINAL

'Art is an activity which exalts and denies simultaneously', writes Camus in *The Rebel*.[81] Was there perhaps an identification in Mozart's own mind between the rebellion of Don Giovanni and his own subversive artistic spirit? And had Mozart, disillusioned once again in an exalted paternal substitute (Joseph II), finally transferred his need for a figure of paternal authority to God, the only more exalted being who now remained to receive his filial obedience, and whose power was so unshakeable that Mozart the artist could rebel secure in the knowledge that his rebellion would not destroy the framework of the universe, and in the certainty that, stricken with guilt for his subversion, he would receive ultimate forgiveness?

Pushkin recognized the covert identification of Don Giovanni with the artistic spirit of Mozart in his pair of short plays *Mozart and Salieri* and *The Stone Guest*, in which he equated Giovanni's daemonic impulses with Mozart's artistic urge. And as a daemonic spirit, Don Giovanni is perhaps the very daemon to which Socrates had attributed the inspirational madness of the artist. But the Romantic Pushkin deliberately de-criminalized his Giovanni in turning him into an artist, whereas it is the criminal spirit of Giovanni with which Mozart identified his own guilty genius. Like the truest artist, Giovanni is the man who is apparently exempted from the constraints of ordinary morality. Even an arch-materialist like Helvétius had believed that the extraordinary individual, the genius, must be permitted to override the rules of established behaviour if humankind is to progress, and Diderot had been very aware of the confusing aesthetic appeal of great crimes.[82] Shortly after Mozart's death his former colleague, the Salzburg trumpeter Andreas Schachtner, confided his memories of

Mozart to the erstwhile Nannerl Mozart. In one revealing recollection he stated, 'I think that if he had not had the advantageously good education which he enjoyed, he might have become the most wicked villain, so susceptible was he to every attraction, the goodness or badness of which he was not yet able to imagine'.[83]

Like Don Giovanni, the absolute artist remains uncommitted to anything or anyone which will constrain his freedom; he breaks promises and defies threats. Like Giovanni, the artist must adopt chameleon disguises to penetrate into the world of others and assume that 'negative capability' that Keats believed to be so important to the poet. Giovanni is a latter-day Orpheus who, instead of making the mountains sway, brings statues to life; an Orpheus who has switched his allegiances from Apollo to Dionysus and rouses those around him to frenzied dance. The artist too is a lord of misrule who delights in overturning convention and making the familiar unfamiliar, turning life into a permanent carnival. Mozart also loved carnivals, and he delighted in pranks and riddles, in secret codes and languages that upset the conventional order of things and the safe proprieties of language and logic so important in the age of reason and empiricism. His *Zoroastrian Riddles and Proverbs*, written for the Carnival of 1786, are full of the teasing puns and *doubles entendres* with which Mozart loved to thumb his nose at conventional respectability. Barely a week after hearing of the death of his father in June 1787, while he was at work on *Don Giovanni*, he perpetrated his cruellest act of artistic vandalism, the *Musikalischer Spass*, K.522, the work of a Don Giovanni let loose to destroy beauty as well as truth and virtue.

In this context, how are we to take the perfunctory final scene of the opera and its trite moral valediction: 'This is the end of those who do ill'; a scene which can only come as an anti-climax to the apocalypse that has gone before? As a welcome return to normalcy and order, however bleak they may be; a recognition of the necessity of stability, rounded off at last with the assurance of a fugue? Or is it ironic, serving to inform us with a knowing wink that, however destructive Don Giovanni is, life will never be quite the same again; a recognition of the unresolvable tension between every human being's desire for some sort of structure and order, and the implications of attempting to make that order manifest on earth? Except that in *Don Giovanni* justice and order (as well as truth, virtue and beauty) are removed to the safer precincts of heaven, leaving little on earth for humans to aspire to.

But how much greater need is there then for the attitude of irony if people are to survive with self-respect. And there is also a sense, perhaps, in which ultimately the ironic attitude is a religious attitude; a double bluff on Pascal's wager. Consider the following observation by Renan:

There are many chances that the world may be nothing but a fairy pantomime of which no God has care. We must therefore arrange ourselves so that on neither hypothesis we shall be completely wrong. We must listen to the superior voices, but in such a way that if a second hypothesis were true we should not have been completely duped. If in effect the world be not a serious thing, it is the dogmatic people who will be the shallow ones, and the worldly minded whom the theologians now call frivolous will be those who are really wise.

In utrumque paratus then. Be ready for anything – that perhaps is wisdom. Give ourselves up, according to the hour, to confidence, to scepticism, to optimism, to irony, and we may be sure that at certain moments at least we shall be with the truth ... Good-humour is a philosophic state of mind; it seems to say to Nature that we take her no more seriously than she takes us ... We owe it to the Eternal to be virtuous; but we have the right to add to this tribute our irony as a sort of personal reprisal ... Saint Augustine's phrase: *Lord, if we are deceived, it is by thee!* remains a fine one, well suited to our modern feeling. Only we wish the Eternal to know that if we accept the fraud, we accept it knowingly and willingly. We are resigned in advance to losing the interest on our investments of virtue, but we wish not to appear ridiculous by having counted on them too securely.[84]

Mozart was one of the great masters of artistic irony. Lest it lapse into bitter cynicism, however, irony demands an audience, and in relation to the ultimate concerns of the universe the only appropriate audience can be God himself. The innocent worship God with beauty; the honest depict the mess of His creation with truth. But with irony the believer can at one and the same time worship, and acknowledge the worst. The beauty of Susanna's nocturne in *Le nozze di Figaro*, or of the Trio of farewell in *Così fan tutte* is no less real for our knowledge of the ironic circumstances in which they are sung. And that unnerving irony, rarely absent from our consciousness in Mozart's operas, is the evidence that Mozart was as far from being one of Schiller's naïve artists as is possible. The ironic is the acknowledgement of the inescapably divided consciousness of modern man, of his perpetual separation from ultimate truth and knowledge. Mozart's cheerful comic finales, happy expressions of simple affirmation, are unconvincing to many. But it may be that they should not be taken as evidence of the shallowness of eighteenth-century optimism, but as the particular expression of Mozart's attitude of metaphysical irony: affirmative, but ultimately holding his own counsel, like Don Giovanni, even before the bar of heaven.

XVI
Così fan tutte

We are accustomed to thinking of *Così fan tutte* in conjunction with its fellow Da Ponte operas *Le nozze di Figaro* and *Don Giovanni*. But really it should be examined in relation to *Die Zauberflöte*, the opera to which it is much closer in date of composition (and which, I believe, Mozart was already considering in the summer of 1789, before he had started work on *Così fan tutte* in the autumn of that year; see pp. 297). They stand in relation to each other as the works in which Mozart explores two radically opposed ways of looking at human experience: materialist and spiritual. And they share a common structural feature: in both operas an educational programme is undertaken by two pairs of young lovers under the watchful supervision of an educator – respectively, Don Alfonso and Sarastro. So different in genre, *Così* and *Die Zauberflöte* are related nonetheless because both reside at the extreme poles of their respective genres, identified by Northrop Frye in his *Anatomy of Criticism*[1] as comedy and romance. The central theme of romance is the adventurous quest, the journey of search. The essential theme of comedy, Frye suggests, is the attainment of social integration and reconciliation between hostile social groups or generations, invariably achieved through the story of young lovers overcoming obstructions to the fulfilment of their true love in marriage (as occurs in that archetypal comedy *Le nozze di Figaro*).

Così fan tutte belongs to what Frye calls the satiric form of comedy, the least optimistic, coloured by the darker tones of the tragic mode 'in which a humorous society [the society which classical comedy seeks to overthrow or reconcile] triumphs or remains undefeated ... This phase of comedy presents what Renaissance critics called *speculum consuetudinis*, the way of the world, *così fan tutte*.'[2] This represents irony as resignation to, rather than transcendence of, human weakness. *Die Zauberflöte*, on the other hand, reaches towards what Frye calls the *penseroso* phase of comedy and romance in which, instead of aspiring to social integration, 'the social units of comedy become small and esoteric, and even confined to a single individual'.[3] A more secluded and isolated vision of society (an island, a secret community) takes over, and in romance, 'a movement from active to contemplative adventure'.[4]

Both visions of society, the comic-ironic and the romantic-esoteric, represent what may be seen as complementary dramatic responses to the collapse of social and political conditions at the end of the Josephine decade in Vienna. *Così fan tutte* reflects the disillusionment at the failure of material solutions to the problems of society, whereas *Die Zauberflöte* emphasizes spiritual inwardness and mystical esotericism. The worlds of the material and spiritual conjoined in *Figaro* are radically separated.

In mood and texture, *Così* is the most sensuously beautiful of Mozart's operas; the music has a luminosity comparable to a halo glowing around a backlit figure. But this is no numinous radiance; it is a trick of the light, a conjuror's illusion, as fragile as the hopes and promises which it dresses; a warning that sensual beauty can be no substitute for the spiritual beauty extolled in the closing lines of *Die Zauberflöte* (the opera that contains little of Mozart's sensual music). *Così fan tutte* forces us to ask the question, 'What if there is no absolute moral truth or beauty?' Could we really live in a world stripped of the divinity of transcendent aspiration, sustained by no more than the humorous irony enjoined at the end of the opera?

> Fortunate the man who takes everything for the best,
> And in all trials and tribulations allows himself to be guided by reason.
> What usually makes others weep is, for him, cause for laughter,
> And in the world amidst whirlwinds he will find a beauteous calm.

The music to which the characters sing of calm is in fact rousing and turbulent, reminding us that a rare moment of actual stillness in the opera, the prayer for calm sung in the Act I Trio 'Soave sia il vento', is delusory – a prayer founded unknowingly upon a charade. Could we really live so, without believing that the obstinate courage of our irony was somewhere, in the empty spaces of the universe, observed? Without believing that our trials were truly trials (as those in *Die Zauberflöte*) rather than simply accidents (the Italian word *casù* is ambiguous here)? In the purely material world depicted in *Così*, irony becomes just another shield of bravado for a diminished humanity, first cousin to the unpleasant trait of cynicism that is so often the outcome of disappointed illusions. No one, it was often noted at the time, had become more cynical by 1790, when *Così* was performed, than the former supporters of the Josephine Enlightenment.

THE END OF JOSEPHINISM

The last years of Joseph's reign were characterized by widespread social and political unrest, an unrest manifested by rebellion in the Netherlands and Hungary, and increasing internal dissent in Austria itself, where there had been peasant uprisings, and bread riots in the suburbs of Vienna following the disastrous harvests of 1787 and 1788. In 1788 Joseph had embarked upon a disastrous, futile and costly war against the Turks, which had had an instant impact upon the flourishing Austrian economy. An indication of the new economic climate was Joseph's decision in January 1789 to suspend the Italian opera in Vienna since it was losing too much money, and the Italian company was only saved by the ever-resourceful Da Ponte's introduction of a successful new subscription scheme.[5]

These developments had a direct effect upon Mozart's own economic position as a freelance composer-performer, a decline reflected in the painful series of begging letters to his masonic colleague Michael Puchberg from the years 1788 and 1789. We know little of Mozart's activities during these years, and even his trip to Berlin in 1789 is shrouded in mystery. But his previously abundant compositional output began to dwindle, and the few letters which survive from the years 1787–9 tell of ill-health, low spirits, dented hopes, and an obvious falling off in his interest in public and social activities. His own mood was a bitter reflection of what was going on around him.

Joseph attempted to pass the blame for events on to none other than Mozart's most loyal patron Gottfried van Swieten. As President of the Censorship Commission, van Swieten had been more liberal than Joseph was willing to countenance, and in 1789 a protégé of van Swieten, the publisher Wucherer, was arrested and banished from Austria for publishing illegal books. As Minister for Education van Swieten had aimed to strip education of any religious character; he was more concerned about the dangers of religious orthodoxy than heresy, and believed that students should be taught a system of secular values based upon 'philosophy'. [6] But his reforms, which indicated a far more radical rejection of religious education than Joseph was really prepared to accept, had failed. In 1790 Joseph wrote to the Chancellor Kolowrat expressing his discontent: 'Since an essential aspect of the education of young people, namely religion and morality, is treated far too lightly, since the heart is not being educated and no feeling for one's true duties is being developed, the state is deprived of the essential advantages of having raised right-thinking and well-behaved citizens.'[7] We could not have a clearer message from the bunker of the crumbling Enlightenment ideal on the effect of its collapse.

The rationalizing system of Josephine reformers like van Swieten had been essentially utilitarian (Joseph II himself is said to have had some interest in the materialist utilitarianism of Helvétius and Holbach), and its failure was in large part the result of Joseph's lack of sensitivity towards any other than the rational and material dimension of human existence and experience. It is as a critique of the rationalist and materialist outlooks (considered to be contradictory positions by eighteenth-century philosophers, but as both Goethe and Blake recognized, at one when considered against the ideal of Man as spiritual being) that *Così fan tutte* must be considered.

If there was any room left for doubt concerning the premises of Josephinism by 1789 we only have to remind ourselves that both *Così fan tutte* and *Die Zauberflöte* were also written in the shadow of the French Revolution, an event which should be recognized not as the bourgeois antithesis of Enlightened absolutism but in many ways, particularly in its elevation of the absolute obligations of the citizen to the state, as its demotic twin. It is no coincidence that one of the central symbols of the Revolution was the revolutionary oath, an all-subsuming vow overriding all the carefully maintained contractual institutions of bourgeois individualism – but a vow made now to the new deity of the state. The main distinction between Josephinism and Jacobinism was that the Jacobins had a powerful understanding (which Joseph himself quite lacked) of the use of political symbolism to elevate the secular claims of the state to serve Man's need for a sphere of transcendent aspiration and obligation. The revolutionaries talked quite explicitly of the religion of morality, and canonized its own saints and martyrs for secular worship.

According to the British *chargé d'affaires* in Vienna, Joseph II's own response to the news of the fall of the Bastille in July 1789, with revolution in Belgium and Hungary foremost in his mind, was 'transports of passion', uttered with 'the most violent menaces of vengeance'.[8] Marie-Antoinette was, after all, his sister. But Joseph's response was not necessarily characteristic of those who supported his aims. Many who may broadly be characterized as Josephines welcomed the developments in France. The reforms enacted by the new legislative assembly in 1789 had repeated, law for law, the programme Joseph himself had undertaken ten years earlier: dissolution of the monasteries, establishment of a national Church, religious tolerance, abolition of feudal rights, and equality before the law. 'A great many of these things had already been conceived and carried out by me for the public good',[9] as Joseph himself commented.

Thus, paradoxically, many of those who had supported the aims of the absolutist state under Joseph were to become the most vehement supporters of the ideals of the French Revolution, and in particular of Jacobinism. A number of those implicated in the Austrian 'Jacobin conspiracy' of 1795 were former supporters of Joseph's reforms who believed (rightly) that his achievements were under threat from the reactionary government of Franz II: the Hungarian Martinovics, who had worked as a secret agent for Leopold II; the poet and magistrate Prandstätter; Aloys Blumauer; and the former Custodian of the Imperial Library and intimate of van Swieten, the Abbé Strattmann. On being questioned about his political sympathies, Strattmann answered, 'I liked certain aspects of the French Constitution of 1789 . . . because in my opinion our own is much the same, and it is almost entirely based on the principles which have been taught in our universities'.[10] Many of the so-called Austrian Jacobins, members of van Swieten's circle, were almost certainly known to Mozart.

Così fan tutte is often described as if it depicted the wistful and illusory world of a Watteau painting, a world about to be shattered as easily as a fragile piece of Meissen china in the hands of a Parisian *sansculotte*. It is as though Mozart himself, turning his back upon the events in France (which were reported daily, approvingly, in the official Viennese newspapers), was the representative voice of an essentially shallow aristocratic society, a society seen, with hindsight, to be dancing heedlessly on the crust of a volcano. Nearer the mark is the view that the opera is a bittersweet tale of lost innocence. This is perhaps confirmed when we recall that the origin for the story of the man who disguises himself in order to test the fidelity of his wife is to be found in the tale of Cephalus and Procris from Ovid's *Metamorphoses*. For the *Metamorphoses* contains the most resonant account in classical literature of humanity's fall from the Golden Age, when Man, nature and the gods had lived in harmony. The magical transformations of Man into beast, plant and divinity in Ovid's tales are an expression of the longing to restore the concord of that era.

But the lost innocence in *Così fan tutte* is not simply that of men and women in their natural state, nor that of the romantic ideals of young love, nor yet that of a pleasure-loving society. It is also the innocence of the secular Enlightenment itself, and as in *Don Giovanni*, the opera recounts the destruction of that innocence through the Enlightenment's own gnawing contradictions.

THE SCIENCE OF MORALITY

One of the premises of materialism is that man as a machine may be studied with the exactitude of any other machine, and the laws of his behaviour determined with the certainty of Newton's mechanical laws of physics. Such laws might imply no duty or obligation, but they would ascertain precisely how human beings could be expected to behave. The attempt to establish the laws of human behaviour on a scientific basis was of some importance. As we have seen, bourgeois society takes its own preferred social practices and then universalizes them as moral laws; in so doing, it denies the presence of laws beyond existing social structures. The laws of nature are the laws of human nature.

This view led to a form of moral philosophy that had a great deal more to do with psychology than with more conventional modes of philosophical enquiry. Even Kant, who was to be responsible for restoring metaphysical speculation to philosophical discourse, acknowledged that the three major areas of philosophical enquiry, which he identified as metaphysics (what can I know?), ethics (what ought I to do?) and theology (what may I hope for?) were dependent upon a fourth, anthropology (what is man?): 'In the end, all may be reckoned to anthropology, since the first three questions relate to the fourth.'[11] The anthropological approach to ethics was founded upon the assumption that human nature was essentially the same everywhere; that, as Hume claimed, 'It is universally acknowledged that there is a great uniformity among the actions of men, in all nations and ages, and that human nature remains still the same, in its principles and operations. The same motives always produce the same actions.'[12] It was upon this basis that the possibility of discovering the universal moral laws depended.[13]

To do this, it was necessary to believe that human nature might be studied with the same objective detachment, precision and rigour that Newton had brought to mechanical enquiry, and that from such observation might emerge what Hume called 'the science of man'.[14] Newton himself had thrown down a challenge to philosophers when he suggested at the close of his *Opticks* how the experimental method could be extended: 'If natural Philosophy in all its parts by pursuing the inductive method shall at length be perfected, the bounds of moral philosophy will also be enlarged.'[15] Thus, Locke determined 'to place morality amongst the sciences capable of demonstration',[16] and earned himself the praise of d'Alembert (a mathematician before he was a *philosophe*) for his attempt to 'reduce metaphysics to what it ought in fact to be, the experimental physics of the human soul.'[17] But it was the fearless Hume who undertook to lay the definitive groundwork for such a physics: his greatest work, the *Treatise of Human Nature*, carries the subtitle 'an attempt to introduce the experimental method of reasoning into moral subjects'. When proposing his moral theses in the *Treatise*, Hume subjects them to what he describes as 'Experiments to confirm this system'.[18]

A number of eighteenth-century literary figures – Montesquieu, Voltaire, Rousseau, Diderot and Goethe – were engaged in scientific enquiry, and at a time when even the moderately well-educated could still hope to keep abreast of the latest scientific developments Newton was popularized for a wider non-scientific public by several writers, including Voltaire himself. Many eighteenth-century artists believed that art too could be employed as a valid field for quasi-scientific experiment into human behaviour. The basic premise of such enquiry was that human beings could be removed from their customary environment, and, by means of the writer's pen, their behaviour observed with the scientific precision brought by the biologist with his scalpel.

The plays and novels of Marivaux in particular share the spirit of amateur scientific enquiry which occupied the Parisian salons at which Marivaux was a frequent guest. The apparent artlessness of Marivaux's two unfinished novels of social manners, *Marianne* and *Le paysan parvenu*, derives from the fact that narrative structures are dispensed with in favour of the simple accumulation of observed incidents and details, like so much empirical scientific data. Marivaux's plays are, for obvious reasons, not so open-ended, and are intricately plotted. But often these carefully structured plots, manipulated from within the story, give the plays a quality of contrived human experiment. Many take place within an artificial, isolated environment in which the characters are taken out of their natural habitat and placed under close observation, as if under the biologist's microscope. In the three philosophical plays *L'île de la raison*, *L'île des esclaves*, and *La colonie*, the subjects (or victims) of the experiments are shipwrecked on islands where they are stripped of their customary social and sexual status, and then observed as they reveal their supposed human essence.[19]

Marivaux's plays provide the immediate model for *Così fan tutte*, as Charles Rosen first pointed out.[20] But as we have seen, the story of *Così fan tutte* has its origins in Ovid, and it was surely from Ovid (rather than from the tale's many later variants in Italian Renaissance novellas, *Don Quixote*, Shakespeare, or eighteenth-century operas such as Casti's and Salieri's *La grotta di Trofonio* of 1785) that the classically educated Da Ponte drew his initial inspiration. For the tale of Cephalus and Procris appears not only in the *Metamorphoses*, but also in Ovid's dissection of the science of love in the *Ars Amatoria*, a work whose suave, often cynical tone is similar to that of the eighteenth-century's own literary experiments in love. Da Ponte adapted these sources to the experimental genre developed by Marivaux, drawing upon one particular work which uniquely employs all the most important aspects of the *Così* story. It is one of Marivaux's least known plays, *La dispute*.

LA DISPUTE

The dispute in question arises between a prince and a lady of his court as to whether it is men or women who are naturally more inconstant. To test the contrary arguments (and judging by the nature of the experiment, to test the patience of those awaiting an answer), the prince has set up a controlled behaviourist experiment. Four children (two girls and two boys) have been reared from childbirth in an almost totally isolated, natural environment, accompanied only by a pair of black servants (innocent scions of nature), and quite unaware of the existence of an opposite sex. On reaching sexual maturity, the point at which the play begins, the children are at last introduced to each other, the girl Eglé to the boy Azor, the girl Adine to the boy Mesrin. Rapturous love at first sight is followed by almost instant – if confused – transference of affections when the young people are confronted with alternative partners, and the play ends with a swap of partners. The tokens of mutual betrayal are, as in *Così*, the exchange of portraits.

The moral of the play appears to be close to the ostensible moral of *Così fan tutte*: that ideals of human constancy and fidelity may be unrealistic in the face of nature. What is relevant for our argument here is that the quasi-experimental presentation of moral debate in *Così* adopts a mode clearly derived from Marivaux, and most probably from *La dispute*. Marivaux had quite a vogue in Germany and Austria in the mid-eighteenth century at a time when German dramatists were being encouraged to look to French models for their own work. Collections of Marivaux's plays were translated into German and published in the 1740s, and a number of his plays were performed in Vienna during the heyday of the French theatre's influence in the 1760s. But *La dispute* had been withdrawn after the first Paris performance in 1744 following a disastrous reception, and was not performed again in France until 1938. This might seem to make it unlikely as a possible inspiration for *Così fan tutte*. But curiously, the play was translated into German and published in Vienna in 1778,[21] recently enough for it to have been lingering in someone's library, or to have been recalled and brought to the attention of Mozart or Da Ponte some ten years later when they were looking for a subject for their new opera.

THE TEST

Così fan tutte sets out to put to scientific test the bourgeois Enlightenment's vision of a world held together by some form of purely secular morality – be it rational, sentimental or materialist – independent of the customary obligations of social, economic and political relationships in traditional societies, or of the authority of religion. It maps out its terrain with a chilly clarity: 'The opera is constructed according to the principles of self-reference and even within the overture Mozart has created a sense of axiomatic demonstration', one critic writes of its musical construction.[22] Da Ponte's text is remorselessly secular, rejecting the possibility of any sort of divine or metaphysical sphere in relation to human affairs, and allowing its characters no escape into the sort of transcendent human consolation offered in *Le nozze di Figaro*. The only external point of reference is that of the implacable experimenter, Don Alfonso, who warms the crucible and tests the temperature with efficient equanimity.

Up to this point it might be argued that the opera is akin to the novels of Jane Austen, all of which share the same secular outlook, and indeed *Così fan tutte* is often directed in the spirit of an Austen novel. But the opera also cuts itself off from any of the traditional social structures by which people customarily learn to define themselves and gauge how to fulfil their role in society. *Così fan tutte* is curiously unspecific in its definition of social detail in a way that Austen never is. In her novels we always know the precise economic and class status of her characters, and such considerations are usually the mainspring of the action. The narrow social context of the novels serves by exclusion to give us a very clear idea what or whom the heroines should *not* emulate, and how they should *not* behave. They demonstrate the acceptable parameters of moral behaviour so clearly that a lapse into unmannerly rudeness is quite as shocking as the carefully calculated social outrages of a de Sade. Likewise, we know that, however deficient in true moral qualities is the household at Mansfield Park, the alternative of Fanny Price's home in Portsmouth is far worse.

In *Così fan tutte* we know nothing. We do not know who Fiordiligi and Dorabella are, nor why, if they come from Ferrara (as indicated in the *dramatis personae*) they are in Naples.[23] They seem to have no parents (which places them metaphorically in the same position as Jane Austen's notoriously badly-parented heroines, but at the same time deprives them of some crucial co-ordinates of identity), and we have no idea of their economic or social status. There is no real world outside that of the opera: the war to which the men depart is imaginary, and the chorus appears and disappears like rabbits from a conjuror's hat. As a result, there are no objective standards by which we or the characters can judge their actions. The setting of the story – its deliberate artifice and lack of external referents – forces the characters to exist in a world of essences, hermetically sealed from the redeeming inconsistencies of the real world.

This experiment in human behaviour takes place in a sterilized laboratory whose conditions are exaggerated by its carefully contrived mathematical symmetries: three male and three female characters, two pairs of lovers, a clean exchange of partners, and so on. These symmetries provide us with the otherwise missing context of the 'just order of things', the aesthetic condition from which everything commences, by which everything is judged, and to which in the end everything must return. It is, therefore, a nonsense to suggest that at the end of the opera the lovers should exchange their original partners. On the grounds of emotional truth alone this would make no sense, since it was not to Guglielmo that Dorabella transferred her affections, nor Ferrando that Fiordiligi fell in love with, but a pair of exotically mustachioed Albanians named (not very convincingly) Sempronio and Tizio. Fiordiligi may still hanker after Sempronio at the end, but Ferrando will be no substitute. But even if there were no such emotional considerations, the symmetries of the opera require a return to the original order of things, as surely as the demands of social propriety, class or money in the carefully delineated and purposefully mapped-out world of a Jane Austen novel.

The question the opera then asks is whether human beings are capable of making moral decisions of any absolute validity in such an environment? And who better to preside over that world than a *philosophe*, as Don Alfonso is described, the quintessential figure of eighteenth-century culture, its ideal legislator and educator?

THE ROUSSEAUIST EDUCATION

Education was the eighteenth century's great panacea for the cure of individual and social ills. The Enlightenment's faith in the power of education is one of its most lasting bequests to subsequent ages; it is also one of the most telling indications of the Enlightenment's essential conservatism, in which change was to be effected not through the reform of society itself, but through the better adaptation of the individual to the needs of society. The single most popular theme of eighteenth-century fiction is that which deals with the education of the naïve or untamed young individual to social conformity.

The eighteenth-century's optimism about the power of education reached its peak simultaneously among the French materialist *philosophes* and in the statist educational programme of the Habsburgs. The extreme materialist determinism of Helvétius led not (as his opponents argued) to fatalism and nihilism, but to a highly optimistic estimation of what could be achieved through education. If all actions are physically determined, then the intervention of new causes can modify people's actions; men and women could be satisfactorarily conditioned, by the control and manipulation of their environment, and by the stimuli of pleasure and pain, to whatever outcome was desired. In Austria, Kaunitz argued that the sole useful purpose of education was to create dutiful citizens. 'The strength of the state depends on the good fortune of having virtuous citizens' he wrote to Maria Theresa; 'Education can make them in all climates of the world'.[24]

The most influential work on education during the eighteenth century was Rousseau's *Emile*, part educational manual, part novel, part profession of religious faith. In it he attempted to prescribe an educational system which would overcome what he considered to be the dangerous conflict between reason and feeling, and between individual impulses and the demands of society. Reason and feeling teach contradictory messages. At one moment reason may impose the dictates of unwelcome duty upon the desire for self-gratification; at another, natural feelings may speak of 'the common weal' while reason decides to argue instead for the self.[25] How is Man to decide which he is to follow? How is he to choose between the imperatives of the natural man and those of the citizen, a choice which the bourgeois Enlightenment had denied was necessary? According to Rousseau, the educator's task is to demonstrate that the choice between pure reason and brute feeling is a false one; that Man is neither the rationalist's pure mind, nor the materialist's bundle of teeming sensations.

Rousseau agreed with Locke's insistence that "'Tis Virtue, then, direct Virtue, which is the hard and valuable part to be aimed at in Education'.[26] Virtue requires the making of moral choices and decisions, and Rousseau made a clear distinction between natural, innocent goodness (which may be based upon pre-moral sentiments such as compassion, and entails no element of purposive decision) and true virtue, which demands the making of moral choices. But Rousseau departed from Locke by rejecting any attempt to instil ethical precepts into children by the use of reason until they are themselves capable of mature rational decisions.

Education is not, therefore, just a matter of learning rational conformity to the outward rules of social duty, for in these instances 'Our wisdom is slavish prejudice, our customs consist in control, constraint, compulsion'.[27] The purpose of education is to teach true morality to the child – to teach him (and for Rousseau that *him* is deliberate) to distinguish between moral right and wrong, and to act on that distinction. To achieve this he proposes a three-tier programme of moral education, starting with a practical training through the lessons of experience via the senses ('Experience precedes instruction').[28] This is followed by the development of reason (for it is 'reason alone teaches us to know good and evil'),[29] leading to the attainment of full ethical maturity, through which the individual learns to exercise a moral conscience able to 'love and hate' the good and evil that reason could only teach him to know.[30]

Da Ponte, like most educated people of his age, knew his Rousseau well. As a young man he had written a Rousseauist essay on the subject 'Whether Man is happier in an organized society or in a simple state of nature', and *Così fan tutte*, subtitled *The School for Lovers*, bears all the hallmarks of the Rousseauist programme of education, in that it addresses the question of whether men and women are best educated to moral maturity through reason or feeling, or whether there is a sphere of moral truth that exists beyond either of these.

The polarities of reason and feeling, duty and inclination, are crucial to *Così fan tutte*; Fiordiligi and Dorabella are themselves distinguished by the conventional characteristics of reason and feeling (see below). But it is not the gulf between reason and feeling that separates Dorabella and Fiordiligi, or even the men and the women in the opera. In fact, it is made quite clear that the men in *Così* are just as prone to sentimental nonsense as the women. In the opening scene of the opera, Ferrando and Guglielmo display their extravagant passions for their mistresses in music that is exuberantly expressive of their youthful ardour. 'Scioccherie di poeti' ('poetic froth') Don Alfonso scoffs, dismissing their protestations of the eternal fidelity of their beloveds.

It is Don Alfonso who really represents reason (of a sort) in the opera, and who is accordingly endowed by Da Ponte with all the attributes of the popular eighteenth-century image of the *philosophe*, familiar to the age from the famous satirical play *Les philosophes* (1760) by Palissot:[31] disillusioned, cynical, and misanthropic. ('When I was a young fellow I used to think that philosophers were people who said little, seldom laughed and turned a sulky face upon the world in general', wrote Leopold Mozart to his son's patroness Baroness Waldstätten, confirming this popular image.)[32] But Alfonso is presented as a rationalist in the Enlightenment sense of one who combines common sense with pragmatic realism, a characteristic portrayed musically by the fact that he is virtually always dryly accompanied by strings alone.[33]

Don Alfonso is not simply an old cynic (like Mr Bennett in *Pride and Prejudice*), whose callow, irresponsible rationalism comes near to destroying two pairs of vulnerable young lovers. At the beginning of the opera, Don Alfonso tries to use reason and logic with Ferrando and Guglielmo to dissuade them from their over-romantic attitudes. He asks them to consider the arguments for and against the possibility of female constancy, but to no avail. For the two young men are simply too immature (and too infatuated) to listen to the arguments of reason. As Rousseau had pointed out, 'Of all man's capacities, reason, which is, so to speak, compounded of all the rest, is the last and choicest growth, and it is this you would use for the child's early training? ... You begin at the wrong end, you make the end the means. If children understood reason they would not need education.'[34] In Rousseauist terms, Ferrando and Guglielmo are at the pre-rational stage in their moral development, and can only therefore be expected to respond to education through the practical experience which, according to Rousseau, 'precedes instruction'.[35]

Accordingly, Don Alfonso has no choice but to allow Ferrando and Guglielmo to discover the error of their ways through direct and perhaps bitter experience, as Rousseau had directed. 'The duty of the educator is not to avoid error, but to guide the misguided; indeed, to allow him to quaff his error to the full,' advises Goethe's Rousseauist Abbé in *Wilhelm Meister*, 'this is the wisdom of the teacher. He who only samples his error husbands it and delights in it like a rare pleasure; but he who exhausts it completely is bound to recognize it if he is not mad.'[36] Guglielmo and Ferrando are certainly made to quaff their error to the full by having to undergo an otherwise quite unnecessary mock wedding ceremony with their new mistresses (Alfonso's point has actually been proved the moment Fiordiligi submits to Ferrando/Sempronio's pleas of love).

Like Goethe's Abbé, Don Alfonso attempts to ensure that the educative experience of Ferrando and Guglielmo is carefully guided and monitored. The only problem is that the pragmatic rationalist, whose picture of mankind is coloured by his purely materialist assessment of Man's limitations, is unable to see beyond the first stages of Rousseau's educational programme, the purpose of which is to lead the pupil to the point where he or she can be assumed to be rational. Alfonso seems to have achieved this: at the end of the opera the characters unite to sing the unconvincingly cheerful and conventional moral, 'Fortunate is the man who takes everything for the best and . . . allows himself to be led by reason'. (A suitable enough sentiment from the Age of Reason; after all, it was a great deal of irrational silliness by both men and women that led the characters along the path to disaster: unrealistically romantic expectations, sentimental effusions, emotional outbursts, and much else besides.)

But pragmatic rationalism of this sort denies whole areas of human experience which Don Alfonso, as materialist educator and the mentor of Enlightenment ethics, is unable to acknowledge. For sure, his pupils Ferrando and Guglielmo are carefully monitored, but the anguish of the conscience-stricken Fiordiligi as she wrestles with new feelings of guilt and remorse, an anguish for which Alfonso's own limited understanding would not have been able to calculate, takes place out of his sight. As Rousseau had insisted, the attainment of reason is merely the necessary preliminary to the final stage of moral education, the stage in which the newly rational individual learns to exercise moral responsibility. 'Reason alone teaches us to know good and evil. Therefore conscience, which makes us love the one and hate the other, though it is independent of reason, cannot develop without it.'[37] But reason is not sufficient of itself, as Fiordiligi learns to her cost. The true moral experiment of *Così fan tutte* is conducted beyond the blinkered gaze of Don Alfonso (and perhaps, by implication, of Da Ponte; see below).

REASON VERSUS FEELING

Within the demanding framework of *Così fan tutte*'s symmetries (hidden from the characters) Fiordiligi and Dorabella are put through their moral paces, furnished with no more than the instincts of feeling or the most fragile powers of reason. The two attributes are clearly distinguished in the emerging personification of the two sisters themselves. Up until the third scene of the opera the sisters appear identical. But after their lovers have departed for war, differences of temperament emerge. Fiordiligi is presented, like Elinor in *Sense and Sensibility*, as the more sensible and rational of the two sisters, less prone to excessive displays of emotion, more inclined to follow the dictates of reason; like Elinor she possesses 'strength of understanding, and coolness of judgement'; but she is not without emotion.[38] Dorabella, on the other hand, like Austen's Marianne, is quicker to respond to her emotions and to submit her behaviour to the dictates of feeling; 'eager in everything; her sorrows, her joys, could have no moderation'.[39]

Although both sisters react forcefully and extravagantly to the departure of their lovers (just as both Elinor and Marianne suffer with equal intensity when they lose their respective lovers), it is Dorabella who subsequently dissolves into paroxisms of hysterical grief in her aria 'Smanie impacabile', displaying the pathological symptoms of sensibility which are very like those of Marianne when the egregious Mr Willoughby suddenly disappears. On the other hand, when two strangers arrive and promptly start to court the sisters with unmannerly ardour, it is Fiordiligi who rebuffs them with a stern affirmation of unswerving constancy and fidelity that the Konstanze of *Die Entführung* or Leonora of *Fidelio* would surely admire. In her aria 'Come scoglio' she deploys rational arguments with an angularity of expression that might even have satisfied the geometrical demands of the Cartesian classicist Fontenelle, as she fires off impressive volleys of defensive coloratura. But the conviction with which Fiordiligi states her position is simply explained: at this point in the opera there is no disjunction between what Fiordiligi knows by reason to be her duty, and her feelings, which are still firmly attached to her absent lover. As long as reason and feelings, duty and sentiment, do not contradict each other there is no problem.

The problems arise in the following scene, the beginning of the Act I Finale. The girls are still using second-hand novelettish language in bemoaning their absent lovers; but the music, indolent strings trailed by fatuous flutes, tells us that the real problem is boredom.[40] Suddenly the 'Albanians' stagger in with a fine pretence of having poisoned themselves out of unrequited love, and the girls are instantly put in a dilemma. Reason may continue to tell them that the strangers' approaches should not be encouraged, but a stronger feeling, the basic Humean moral sentiment of pity, overrides their reason. 'In such grievous moments who could abandon them?' The men, uncharacteristically percipient, recognize the cause of their weakening and what it must lead to: 'We'll see that their pity will end in love'. For pity, the morality of sensibility, can all too easily be confused with sexual attraction (as Don Giovanni had demonstrated). And so, heedless of the dictates of reason and conventional social propriety, Dorabella and Fiordiligi succumb to their natural instinct for pity as inescapably as they will soon respond to their sexual feelings. When Guglielmo embarks upon his seduction of Dorabella it is for a token of her pity that he pleads; without second thought Dorabella yields him her heart.

THE MESMERIC CURE

To the materialist, sexual feeling and moral pity are related, since they are both rooted in physical sensibility. The supposed physical origins of people's emotions are demonstrated in the maid Despina's experiment in the fashionable science of animal magnetism to cure the foreign suitors of their arsenic poisoning. Disguised as a doctor, Despina dispenses the latest alternative medicine invented by Franz Anton Mesmer in Germany, as she so correctly explains, but subsequently famous in France.

Mesmer claimed to have discovered the invisible life-force which animated matter in the absence of the immortal soul.[41] His discovery was far from implausible in an age which was desperately seeking the material secret of life, and which had also come happily to accept the undeniable existence of apparently occult forces such as Newtonian gravity. If an invisible force such as gravity was able to hold the physical universe together, and if Luigi Galvani could demonstrate the activity of animal electricity (wrongly, it later transpired), why should it be fanciful to suggest that magnetism, an incontrovertible if mysterious power in minerals, should have a comparable animal manifestation? Mesmer believed that animal magnetism was an invisible fluid that animated Man, and drew people together in social attraction; thus he claimed to have discovered scientifically the material cause of man's social instincts.

In Paris, where he had come to settle in the 1780s, Mesmer's followers split into two camps. Many mesmerists embroiled themselves in the numerous forms of spiritual mysticism and magic occultism that flourished at that time in Europe. But others developed the materialist implications of Mesmer's principles, claiming that he had identified 'a morality issuing from the world's general physics',[42] and extending the premises of the mesmeric Society of Harmony to quasi-scientific political conclusions.[43]

A third group explored the medical implications of Mesmerism, in particular the psycho-sexual effects that had gained Mesmer himself so much notoriety (and eventual discredit). A well-known practitioner of this strain of Mesmerism was the Scottish medical student James Graham, who between 1779 and 1784 made a tidy living in London with his famous 'celestial bed',[44] advertised as a cure for female sterility and male impotence. The sufferers were placed on a bed charged with magnetic fluid that appears (given the length of time Graham plied his trade) to have had the effect of curing their problem. Two years after the demise of Graham's experiments, an article in Blumauer's *Realzeitung* of March 1786[45] reported on 'das himmlische Bett des Doktor Graham' to the Viennese, as avid for titillation as today's tabloid readers.

The implications of Despina's mesmeric demonstration are clear. The pseudo-Doctor's faith in the power of the magnetic stone to heal is clearly a materialist's faith. For in the curiously ill-defined world of mesmeric materialism the physical, sexual, moral and social are intertwined as Mesmer's strange but supposedly scientific force extends its powers of attraction through all creation. The Albanians, their poison drawn out of them by the magic lodestone, are brought back to a sort of consciousness by another form of physical magic indistinguishable to the materialist: the reluctant ministrations of Fiordiligi and Dorabella, urged on by Alfonso and Despina. Exercising their pity they unwittingly demonstrate, like Zerlina in *Don Giovanni*, its affinity to the powers of sexual arousal. Feeling is beginning to contradict reason.

The crucial scene in the opera's moral debate takes place at the opening of Act II. Here we begin to see the dangers that arise when feelings (now increasingly identified as sexual) seem to contradict rather than support the norms of moral duty, and may no longer be able to be relied upon to provide a guide to behaviour. The girls have set up for themselves an ideal of sexual constancy as a supreme virtue – an ideal that presented no problems as long as it was in accord with their emotional feelings. (Conversely, it remains possible to believe in the simple morality of the feelings when feelings seem thus so readily to support the objective norms of acceptable behaviour.) But Dorabella and Fiordiligi are soon to learn that reason may itself carry no moral validification or certainty; that it is in fact a neutral agent, capable (sometimes) of distinguishing truth from falsehood, but not capable of decreeing obligatory moral laws, nor of compelling action. As Swift so often demonstrated, reason is a harlot capable of being used for both good and bad ends. When it is not based upon sound empirical observation it is easily abused, and readily turns its hand to the less estimable task of *post-facto* rationalization.

LA PHILOSOPHIE DANS LE BOUDOIR

At the opening of Act II Despina argues with perfect rationality that the girls should take advantage of the opportunity for some diversion that is being offered them by the exotic suitors. She is remarkably *au fait* with fashionable materialist philosophy, basing her remarks upon principles derived from the most progressive sources. Like Don Giovanni, Despina is a sensualist, although with more modest appetites than he. She is first introduced to us slavering over her mistress's morning chocolate. 'Isn't my mouth perhaps like yours?' she asks rhetorically. She no longer, as sentimental servants in the past like Pamela or Sandrina, appeals to the commonality of honour or of the heart, but to the egalitarianism of the taste buds.

In her first aria, in Act I, Despina had informed the sisters that they were wasting their tears for their absent lovers. All men are faithless wretches whom women should repay in kind. This is a principle recognizably derived from rational libertinism, in which sexual behaviour had been seen as a kind of warfare in which all men were sexual predators, and all women potential losers unless they could reciprocate with ruses and stratagems of flirtation and rejection, seduction and betrayal. Such is the terrifying world portrayed in Laclos's novel *Les liaisons dangereuses* in which the villains employ reason with devastating effectiveness to achieve their passionate desires, and in which the novel's horrible but fascinating anti-heroine Mme de Merteuil claims to have drawn authority from studying 'our manners in the novelists, our opinions in the philosophers', no less.[46]

In this world there need be no moral quibbles; all moral considerations are dismissed as pure hypocrisy. This is the world we recognize too from de Sade, who shows the futility of Justine's desire to reconcile her feelings with virtuous and benevolent behaviour. Nature, de Sade tells us (echoing Holbach) has nothing to do with virtue or morality; indeed, even compassion 'perverts the general law: whence it results that pity, far from being a virtue, becomes a real vice once it leads us to interfere with an inequality prescribed by nature's laws'.[47] The only realistic course is to follow the promptings of the instincts and the desire for gratification, and to use reason to ensure the most expedient attainment of such gratification. Justine, a victim of the sentimental delusion of virtue, is destroyed by her sister Juliette, the rationalist who employs her reason with unrelenting acuity to achieve her own sexual ends.

This is just the course of action Despina proposes in her second aria, in which she elaborates the principles hinted at in the first. In a short preamble she suggests that by the age of fifteen there are a number of things a woman should know if she is to survive in the world, including 'what is good and what is bad'. Quite so, nods the Enlightenment moralist, missing the sly little turn on the word *bene* that suggests Despina has other *bene* than virtue in mind. And indeed, the perkily insinuating section that follows is a guileless celebration of hedonism. Despina demonstrates that de Sade's arguments, trimmed of their excesses, can be employed in the politest of drawing rooms without producing more than the slightest frisson. In *Justine* de Sade had written that 'True wisdom consists infinitely more in doubling the sum of one's pleasures than in increasing the sum of one's pains'[48] (by which he meant self-denial in obedience to the rules of conventional morality). Despina, like Don Giovanni, clearly knows that two pleasures are better than one: 'Eat the fig, but don't throw away the apple', she advises the girls.

It is the materialism of Despina and Don Alfonso that underlies the putative moral of the story: human beings can only follow their natural inclinations which, being natural, cannot be denied. If morality is located in the human body, then no natural impulse can be immoral. 'I would just like to know what species of animal these beauties of yours are, if they have, like all of us, flesh bones and skin, if they eat like us, if they wear skirts – in short, if they are goddesses or women,' Don Alfonso asks rhetorically of Ferrando and Guglielmo as they extol the constancy of their mistresses. Despina, the parlour *philosophe*, reiterates the argument at the beginning of Act II when the sisters disingenuously pretend ignorance of what she is suggesting. With no little exasperation she demands, 'Are you of flesh and bones, or what?' As de Sade would have insisted, if women have sexual feelings, these must be natural and therefore right. The eponymous heroine of Mary Wollstonecraft's unfinished novel *Mary* is confronted with a similar problem to that of Fiordiligi and Dorabella and raises the same issue:

Have I desires implanted in me only to make me miserable? Will they never be gratified? Shall I never be happy? . . . With these notions can I conform to the maxims of worldly wisdom? Can I listen to the cold dictates of worldly prudence, and bid my tumultuous passions cease to vex me, be still, find content in grovelling pursuits, and the admiration of the misjudging crowd, when it is only one I wish to please – one who could be all the world to me?[49]

Dorabella's response to Despina's wily proposals shows how the ground is shifting. She questions Despina's suggestion not with a genuine moral objection, but with a more prudent concern for what people will say if she and Fiordiligi pursue Despina's plan. That is, she accepts the terms of Despina's rational calculation, and raises a purely pragmatic counter point in which the value of her reputation must be weighed against any possible pleasure that may accrue from pursuing the plan. This is an indication of the degree to which social definitions of virtue distort any efforts to ascertain the categorical rather than merely contingent principles of ethical behaviour. As sexual honour came to be substituted for moral virtue, reputation came to replace true chastity as the crucial indicator of a woman's virtue.[50]

In Fanny Burney's novel *Evelina* (1778) Evelina's tutor Mr Villars warns her in a letter: 'Remember, my dear Evelina, nothing is so delicate as the reputation of a woman: it is at once the most beautiful and most brittle of all human things.'[51] No wonder that Burney's contemporary Mary Wollstonecraft exclaimed with some impatience that 'reputation' in women was in her day valued more highly than true chastity.[52] Indeed, even Rousseau, the cause of so much of Wollstonecraft's legitimate fury, had suggested that ' "What will people think" is the grave of a man's virtue and the throne of a woman's'.[53]

Having made the easy transition from virtue to honour and thence to reputation, Dorabella is sooner reassured by Despina's sagacity than Fiordiligi, who retains a lingering doubt, and weakly attempts to forestall the inevitable. What will happen to our hearts, to our love for our betrothed? she asks. Dorabella responds with all the confidence of her new-found rationalism: 'They'll stay as they are'. In his *Confessions*, Rousseau recorded a modern *philosophe* telling a married woman, his beloved Mme de Warens, that sexual union 'was an act most unimportant in itself; marital fidelity need merely be kept up in appearance, its moral importance being confined to its effect on public opinion; a wife's sole duty was to preserve her husband's peace of mind; consequently infidelities concealed did not exist for the offending partner, and were non-existent, therefore, to the conscience.'[54]

'So convenient a thing is it to be a reasonable creature', wrote Benjamin Franklin, 'since it enables one to find or make a reason for everything one has a mind to do.'[55] But Fiordiligi has in fact put her finger on the crucial question, for she has unwittingly revealed the existence of ethical questions outside the simple terms of moral debate provided by the arguments of reason or feeling. What moral imperative does sexual fidelity carry? Is fidelity a necessary condition of constancy?[56] Dorabella has persuaded herself that it need not be.

But if fidelity *is* a necessary condition of constancy, is it a sufficient condition? If so, what meaning does the notion of constancy carry that is not contained in the notion of fidelity? For Fiordiligi these questions are simply unanswerable within the limits of pre-Rousseauvian ethical debate, with which the sisters find themselves confronted. The checklist leaves no options. Objectively valid moral decisions can be derived from neither reason nor feeling; human emotions and desires are no more capable of making the crucial step from 'is' to 'ought' than are precepts derived from processes of logical deduction. Social morality demands that outward appearances and conventions be obeyed, but cannot be demonstrated to carry any universal moral obligation; manners are not morals. And if supposed moral absolutes such as chastity and constancy can be shown to be no more than the objectification of certain desired social ends such as the secure transference of property, what moral imperative can they be said to carry? If sexual morality was a mere social artefact, and if it demanded that women obey rules of sexual restraint from which men were exempted, what true universal obligation could such partial rules then carry? Perhaps Fiordiligi should turn instead to utilitarian ethics for help in her dilemma, since utilitarianism judges the moral worth of a deed according to its effect on the happiness of others. It will therefore tell her (as it easily persuades Dorabella, and as Rousseau's *philosophe* attempted to persuade Mme de Warens) that as long as the happiness of the sisters' absent lovers is not affected, there can be no moral harm in their pursuing and enjoying their own pleasures whilst their lovers are away. Utilitarianism simply allows reason to justify a deed for which the imperatives of feeling have already made their own commitment.

The materialist ethics that Fiordiligi is encouraged to follow had carried the implication of a total abandonment of moral responsibility, since – as Holbach and Diderot had observed – people surely cannot garner moral opprobrium for deeds that are physically determined by nature. According to Holbach, people believe in free will, 'but they have not paid attention to the fact that our wishes and desires are necessarily caused by objects or factors which are entirely independent of us'.[57] Man exists as a creature of nature, and nature itself is entirely amoral: 'Men have completely failed to see that this nature, lacking in both good and evil intentions, merely acts in accordance with necessary and immutable laws'.[58] 'E amore un ladroncello', Dorabella will later sing in her second aria; love is a thief, who gives peace and takes it away, and enchains the soul to its demands – a submission which would have overwhelmed the rational moralist of an earlier age with torrents of self-disgust.

It is just such an abnegation of responsibility that Fiordiligi relies on in agreeing at last to follow Dorabella's plan to engage in a little flirtation with the suitors. All right, she says, do what you wish but I don't want to be blamed if things go wrong. In the subsequent duet 'Prendero quel brunettino' the pair vie with each other in disclaiming any serious intentions in the forthcoming flirtations, playfully mocking the amorous afflatus of their new suitors. As they puncture such protestations of undying love Mozart, with the cruellest irony, reminds us of the music of their own previous protestations of perpetual fidelity in their opening duet.

THE ADVENT OF CONSCIENCE

Fiordiligi is to learn that this denial of responsibility, to which the ethical systems of materialism inevitably led, is impossible; that 'infidelities concealed' are not 'non-existent to the conscience'. And she learns it in a scene that is profoundly disturbing, a scene in which she confronts a world without spiritual or moral certainties, without either social validification or human solidarity, and without the possibility even of any transcendent moral choice: the outcome of the debilitating failure of the material alternatives the secular Enlightenment had attempted to provide for itself. As a result, Fiordiligi finds herself at the abyss of nihilism. It was an abyss into which one half of the Enlightenment toppled, plunging into de Sadean anarchy and the reimposition of order through political terror in the Jacobin Revolution (or through absolutist repression in Josephine Austria), and from which the other half recoiled in horror, retreating into certainties of another sort: the transcendental metaphysics of philosophical idealism, spiritual inwardness, or a return to the Romantic myths of feudal society. Through its confrontation with nihilism, the Enlightenment was presented with a vision of hell in many respects quite as terrible as that into which Don Giovanni is dragged, shrieking but defiant.

Let us look more closely at the scene in question. The location has moved from the house to a garden beside the sea. But the garden has now lost its restorative powers. The terrain is precarious – a thin strip of cultivated nature poised between the fragile security of the house, and the boundless and shifting uncertainties of the sea. It is evening. Left alone by Alfonso and Despina, the two pairs of lovers at first engage in inept cocktail-party chit-chat, the sort of social exchange that is clearly no longer adequate in what are far more dangerous circumstances. Ferrando and Fiordiligi go off for a stroll in the woods, leaving Guglielmo and Dorabella alone. Dorabella puts up a spirited pretence of resistance but soon succumbs, and she and Guglielmo retreat discreetly to a more private place. The stage is empty for a moment. Then Fiordiligi bursts in, clearly in the greatest distress, exclaiming that she has just seen 'an asp, a hydra, a basilisk', and begging Ferrando, who is in pursuit, to leave her. Ferrando assumes that she is referring to him, but she is referring instead to her own feelings, which have reared up to torment, and perhaps engulf her, in the dark.

Whatever happened 'amongst these shadows and these trees' (as she sings in the aria which follows) it is not what Fiordiligi herself seems to imply – that she has already yielded to Ferrando – for in the next scene Ferrando is able to report that she is still inviolate. But for Fiordiligi, as with Donna Anna, it is immaterial at this moment whether the sexual act has actually taken place or not. The monsters that have arisen out of the dark are the monsters of guilt and conscience which, as Freud reminds us, will afflict us whether or not we actually carry out the criminal intentions we all secretly nurse.[59] Illicit desires rather than sinful deeds are what afflict Fiordiligi amongst the shadows. And 'the voice of remorse', as Rousseau had put it, comes implacably to perform 'the secret punishment of hidden crimes', a role formerly assumed by the gods.[60]

Conscience cannot be explained in the cosmology of ethical materialism. But the horror and shame that Fiordiligi feels, for which she begs her absent lover's pity and forgiveness in the aria 'Per pietà', forces her to recognize the possible existence of some moral sphere unreachable by either rational deduction or material feeling: a moral sphere that lies beyond the Enlightenment's easy excuses of a moral scepticism; beyond the confusion of pleasure and virtue, or of sexuality and compassion; beyond the limited morality of social conformity and manners; and beyond the moral absolution of determinism.

Fiordiligi has learned that one cannot play games in these matters, that it may not, after all, be possible to eat the fig and keep the apple, and that it is a mistake to imagine that the indulgence of pleasure necessarily brings happiness. 'The first condition of happiness is to feel,' argued La Mettrie, who believed that happiness could only lie in sensual gratification.[61] But sensual pleasure and spiritual happiness are not the same thing. 'We sought pleasure and lost happiness,' Saint-Preux and Julie recognize in the bleak light of the morning after.[62] Nor does one have to commit 'wrong' deeds to inflict the unhappiness of moral guilt upon oneself; inconstancy can take place in the heart as surely as in the sexual act itself. Dorabella had persuaded herself that it was possible to be unfaithful while remaining constant; Fiordiligi discovers that one may be inconstant without even being unfaithful.

Fiordiligi has discovered that the law supplied by conscience is far sterner and more demanding than those she has hitherto been schooled to acknowledge. Her torments of guilt and remorse disprove the materialists, but they offer no comfort to Fiordiligi herself, fighting between the rational dictates of duty and the compulsions of feeling ('Ever at war with herself, hesitating between her wishes and her duties', as Rousseau had put it.) She appeals to courage and constancy in her aria 'Per pietà' with all the fervour of the Countess or Beethoven's Leonora at a similar moment of despair, but without their ability to embrace the transcending power of an ideal such as constancy. 'Per pietà', with the recitative that precedes it, portrays with unbearable poignancy the solitary confrontation of a human being with a world that, stripped of moral or spiritual guidance, seems unable to offer any alternative framework for making choices – precisely the world that the Enlightenment strove so hard to avoid.

The musical language is recognizably related to the complacent assurance of Fiordiligi's first aria, but the wide angular leaps in the vocal line have lost their firm support, becoming exposed and faltering. Unyielding obbligato instruments accompany and shadow every phrase, perhaps the outward expression of the inner moral law tormenting her. The one point of transcendent truth and certainty to which Fiordiligi can appeal is Guglielmo's love for her, and her belief in his fidelity – at the very moment at which he is seducing Dorabella. And it is doubly ironical that her anguished plea for pity and forgiveness will be met by Guglielmo's furious anger, whilst it is Ferrando who will be willing to forgive the far more fickle and easily seduced Dorabella.

Fiordiligi's hopeless attempt to suppress her new feelings by appealing to an ideal that has no certain foundations or justification in her moral world, is exposed in the third scene of Act II. Unable to suppress her sexual promptings Fiordiligi has decided that the only hope is for her and Dorabella to flee and join their lovers at the front. She calls for Ferrando's and Guglielmo's uniforms to be brought to her so that they can disguise themselves as soldiers (as well not to ask what the uniforms were doing in Fiordiligi's wardrobe in the first place). But it is, of course, hopeless. Ferrando arrives, and with an inevitability only delayed by her anguish, Fiordiligi succumbs to his fervent wooing.

Fiordiligi's submission is the logical outcome of the failure of rationalism and materialism to provide for people's human needs. Looking to France in the year the opera was written, commentators would see the old spectre of anarchism and chaos rising out of the precipitate dismantling of the *ancien régime*. The Jacobin Terror, far from being the fulfilment of that chaos, is the logical outcome of the failure of Enlightenment ethics, the imposition of a Rousseauist political system to abolish the possibility of moral ambiguity altogether. Only a couple of years after *Così* Robespierre would reiterate its message that neither reason nor feeling were adequate or reliable indicators of moral behaviour. 'Reason misled by passions is frequently only a sophist pleading their cause . . . it is essential to create in him [the citizen] an instinct for moral things which will enable him to act rapidly to do good and avoid evil'.[63] To escape from this totalitarian nightmare the later Enlightenment turned its attention to the cultivation of a personal, inner transcendence of the materialist dilemma.

FRAILTY AND THE TRANSCENDENT VOW

We are often encouraged to admire *Così fan tutte* for its comic tolerance of human frailty. 'Comedy', writes Terry Eagleton, 'pays its dues to the edifying values of truth, virtue and beauty, but understands how not to permit these admirable goals to terrorize humankind to the point where people's weaknesses become painful to them and their self-esteem dwindles to nothing.'[64] But in *Così fan tutte* this is precisely what fails to happen: Fiordiligi *is* terrorized. And we need to beware of acceding to the opera on its own ostensible terms (or those of Don Alfonso) if we praise its healthy scepticism too readily. For to do so, singing along with Don Alfonso wryly (or even compassionately) '*così fan tutte*', is to accept the materialist's deterministic estimation that neither men nor women can behave in any other way than that in which they are programmed to behave. What value, edifying or otherwise, are we left with when truth, virtue and beauty have been so cruelly trounced as in *Così fan tutte*? At the end of the opera, as we have seen, the chastened lovers unite with their would-be educators Alfonso and Despina to sing in praise of tolerance and reason. But Mozart pointedly undermines their expression of confidence by setting the text to the very same musical phrase to which Fiordiligi had sung, with such rational complacency, of her constancy in 'Come scoglio' – an unfortunate recollection, but one which surely alerts us to Mozart's own reservations about such easy rationalizations.

In *Così fan tutte* Mozart returned to the thematic preoccupations of *Idomeneo*, exploring once again the crucial Enlightenment distinction between vows and contracts, and between sound and unsound contracts, upon which the social cohesion of bourgeois society was believed to depend. As in *Idomeneo*, the plot of *Così* is set in motion by some apparently ill-judged vows that need to be replaced by rationally (and mutually) determined contracts. When in the opening scene of the opera Ferrando and Guglielmo adduce 'giuramenti' (vows) as evidence for their mistresses' unswerving love we should be warned of what is to come. But unlike *Idomeneo*, the conclusion of *Così fan tutte* seems to affirm rather than deny the validity of such vows; to argue that vows, self-determined commitments to ideal courses of action, the late Enlightenment's new divinities, are precisely what raise people out of the trap of material determinism, and create values which affirm dignity and self-esteem. Even Nietzsche, who rejected all traditional ethical commands, conceded the 'extraordinary privileges' conferred on humans by the ability to make promises.[65]

As Romantic composers from Rossini onwards were to discover, thumping vows and oaths make great opera. In *Così fan tutte* Mozart anticipated them, gleefully sending up the conventions of extravagant oath-taking. In their opening duet Fiordiligi and Dorabella, having sung the praises of their lovers, make fervent vows of eternal constancy to them. The double vows are conveyed as one sister sings exaggerated leaps up and down the vocal register against sustained notes sung by the other, notes which are held so long that one feels that the singer's breath must surely run out – a sort of physical test. It is a demonstration (and indeed proof) of the intended determination and constancy of the sisters: 'If ever this heart of mine changes its desire, let Amor make me suffer for it.' The vow is made to the presiding deity of all Mozart's comic operas, Amor or Eros, and it is in the first place through the power of erotic love that the girls do indeed suffer. But their real mistake is that in making their vow they recognize only the power of Eros, rather than any higher ideal of love; their opening expressions of love for Ferrando and Guglielmo are languorously erotic (in obvious contrast to the romantic ardour of Ferrando and Guglielmo's own declarations in the previous scene). It is the god of the higher ideal of love and constancy who returns to exact his retribution so pitilessly.

According to the materialist vision (if it can even be called that) the vows of Fiordiligi and Dorabella are, like Idomeneo's vow, invalid because they are against the law of human nature. 'The first vows sworn by two creatures of flesh and blood were made at the foot of a rock that was crumbling to dust; they called as witness to their constancy a heaven which never stays the same for one moment; everything within them and around them was changing, and they thought their hearts were exempt from vicissitudes. Children!'[66] That is Diderot, sounding very much like Alfonso addressing his own young charges in *Così fan tutte*. 'Can God, who made Man so inconstant and frail, authorize such rash vows?' he asks of his reluctant nun in *La religieuse*. 'Can these vows which run counter to our natural inclinations, ever be properly observed except by a few abnormal creatures in whom the seeds of passion are dried up, and whom we rightly classify as freaks of nature?'[67]

Fiordiligi and Dorabella may not be committing themselves to the chaste incarceration of the convent, but their vows of perpetual fidelity are, according to eighteenth-century materialism, just as unnatural. What this implies, of course, is a severely diminished understanding of the commitments possible between humans, even in the fundamental commitment of marriage. In the *Encyclopédie*, under the heading 'Indissoluble', we find that Diderot accordingly complains that is not possible to base marriage as a contractual agreement upon the premises of constancy. '*Indissoluble* . . . that which cannot be dissolved, broken. Marriage is an *indissoluble* engagement. The legislators who have given man indissoluble laws can hardly have known his natural inconstancy. How many they have thus rendered criminal or unhappy.'[68]

INTERCHANGEABILITY

But *Così fan tutte* – if only by negative implication – affirms the human need for values and commitments beyond those supplied by nature. Fiordiligi experiences this need, but is unable to meet it. Her predicament is compounded by the materialist view of human nature, which denies the possibility of a transcendent human personality. It is no coincidence that the characters in *Così fan tutte* are, initially at least, ill-defined and virtually interchangeable. The two sisters are presented in the opening scenes as identical twins, singing the same music and sharing the same emotions. Customarily cast as soprano and mezzo-soprano today, Mozart did not distinguish them so clearly, occasionally forgetting which sister was which when writing their names in the score. Their lovers are at first only differentiated by the more distinctive vocal characterization implicit in the difference between the lyric tenor of Ferrando and the *buffo* bass of Guglielmo. The blurring of personality threatens the distinctness on which classical society depends. Hence the too ready transference of affections during the course of the opera, a transference that undermines all sense of individual identity and hints at a society in which the confusions threatened by the inchoate longings of a Cherubino or the indiscriminate couplings of a Don Giovanni reign supreme.

Così fan tutte is only one among numerous eighteenth-century works which use a story of interchangeable lovers to deal with the problem of sexual desire that is not securely individuated. The theme is found in many of the plays of Marivaux, in numerous operatic comedies, in

Goethe's play *Stella* (where the hero finds himself genuinely in love with two women between whom he is unable to choose), and in a late novel by Wieland, *Freundschaft und Liebe auf der Probe* in which two couples exchange partners. But it is explored with greatest complexity in Goethe's novel of 1809, *Die Wahlverwandschaften*.

Like *Così fan tutte* (which Goethe knew, and had had performed at Weimar) *Die Wahlverwandschaften* recounts a quasi-scientific experiment in human conduct; its title refers to a chemical process by which, in certain combinations, the basic elements of two distinct materials will separate and re-combine to form new substances – a process which accordingly takes place between two pairs of people in the novel. It occurs against a background in which an almost magical set of pre-classical correspondences seems to prevail, in an inadequately differentiated society peopled by insufficiently individuated characters (all of whom, for instance, curiously carry the root name 'Otto': Otto himself, Otto as the real name of Eduard, Charlotte and Ottolie). It is also a society in which traditional moral maps have lost their authority and have become meaningless rules and precepts; a dislocated and rootless world, like that of *Così fan tutte*, conveyed in the novel by the restless and aimless tinkering constantly undertaken by Eduard and Charlotte on their estate. Landscape gardening has become, as in the novels of Jane Austen, a symbol of instability rather than a token of healthy integration.

The scientific theory of elective affinity hints at the materialist view that in their emotional tangles the characters are doing no more than obeying the dictates of natural laws. Like *Così fan tutte* (and *La nouvelle Héloïse*), *Die Wahlverwandschaften* weighs the relative moral demands of natural sexual passion against the maintenance of empty vows (in this case, of a dead marriage), and questions what moral imperative these can carry. At the centre of the novel is the famous scene of the 'adultery' between husband and wife Eduard and Charlotte. By outward convention, of course, it is no adultery since it takes place within marriage, but during their lovemaking, both Eduard and Charlotte are thinking of the desired absent partners with whom they have fallen in love. Where is the 'crime'[69] which Eduard senses the next morning? In the illicit desires that accompany their legally sanctioned lovemaking, or in the sin of the 'licit' lovemaking against the true love in their hearts?

Goethe does not provide an easy answer. But in his erotic poem *Das Tagebuch* an answer is hinted at. A married traveller spends the night in an inn with a maid, but finds that despite the strength of his passion for the girl, he is unable to consummate his desires. At the poem's conclusion he recognizes that he has been thwarted by the 'compelling power of duty, and infinitely greater power of love'.[70] But true love and marital duty are not mutually exclusive, for as in *La nouvelle Héloïse*, true, mutual love carries its own natural moral obligations. The promises of marriage are both natural and social (as Saint Preux had told Julie); Eduard's guilt after his lovemaking with his wife is the natural guilt of a double violation: of love and marriage sundered, and hence of the moral integrity of the principle of mutual love in marriage.

Something of this wisdom is intuited by Mozart in *Così fan tutte*, even if the text itself does not allow its victory. Fiordiligi has been persuaded, as have Eduard and Charlotte, that love and duty are separable. But working within her, as within Goethe's traveller, is the voice of her conscience. And as Rousseau, horrified at the 'rootless and sterile morality' of the 'ardent missionaries of atheism' so fervently believed,[71] moral conscience was a sign of humankind's spirituality; indeed, 'the voice of the soul'.[72]

Conscience, conscience, divine instinct, immortal and heavenly voice, sure guide to men who, ignorant and blinkered, are still intelligent and free; infallible judge of good and evil who shapes men in the image of God, it is you who form the excellence of man's nature and the morality of his actions; without you I feel nothing within that raises me above the beasts, nothing but the melancholy privilege of straying from error to error, relying on understanding without rule and reason without principle.[73]

'There are no gods speaking; it is your heart which speaks,' insists Goethe's King Thoas in response to Iphigenia's claim that her moral conscience is the voice of God. 'They speak to us only through our hearts,' replies Iphigenia.[74] Fiordiligi's painful access of conscience confutes the materialist premise, and furnishes proof that the gods have not abandoned humans. But there is nothing occult about it. 'He who obeys his conscience is following nature,' says Rousseau,[75] an assertion confirmed by Goethe's impotent traveller. Conscience does not come from on high. But nor is it merely the internalized voice of social injunction; that is bad conscience, as Nietzsche insisted before Freud. True conscience, Nietzsche suggested, arises out of the network of commitments and promises – to oneself or others – undertaken in the course of any human life; the ability to abide by them (assuming they are authentic) confers dignity and self respect.[76]

It may indeed be, as the opera proposes, that mere human affections (especially those founded upon no more than physical desire) are frail, and that social transactions are transitory. As Mozart's already quoted letter (p. 154) to his friend Gottfried von Jaquin shows (and as his autumnal setting of the song *Abendempfindung* K.523 further demonstrates), Mozart had by the later 1780s conceived a pervading sense of the mutability and transience of human life. But the transience of earthly relationships does not annul the commitments – indeed, the vows – human beings make to themselves.

Even if the tormenting voice of conscience fails to placate Fiordiligi's desires, the advent of conscience-stricken feelings about her earlier promises indicates that those promises had legislated their own moral validity beyond the precepts of rational duty. In the serene Canon in the Act II Finale the new partners (with the exception of the unforgiving Guglielmo) toast each other before making their pledges of marriage. Led by Fiordiligi they ask that cares be drowned in their glasses, and that no memory of the past should remain in their hearts. Only, it seems, in oblivion can the memory of past commitments and promises be erased. And at the end of the opera, only the forgiveness and acceptance of their rightful partners can absolve the sisters of their betrayal of their own ideals of truth and virtue.

The elevation of the claims of conscience as ultimate moral arbiter is the outcome of the necessary internalization of bourgeois morality at the end of the eighteenth century. According to Hobbes, the individual's appeals to moral conscience had represented a challenge to the power of the absolutist state, and hence an evil. For this very reason, in the late eighteenth-century absolutist state, monarchic or democratic, conscience becomes the final guarantor of the individual's spiritual uniqueness: the last defence against the encroachments of the worldly realm.

At the conclusion of his *Second Discourse* Rousseau had painted a bleak picture of a society guided by no more than the materialist values of his age. In such a society 'We have only . . . honour without virtue, reason without wisdom, and pleasure without happiness'.[77] It is a cruelly apt description of the world in which the lovers in *Così fan tutte* had found themselves. Rousseau himself proposed a political solution to the dilemmas of his age. German artists and thinkers such as Kant, Goethe, Schiller and Mozart explored instead an inner, spiritual solution to the search for true happiness and wisdom – the theme of *Die Zauberflöte*, the opera which was already in Mozart's mind in the summer of 1789, before he started work on *Così fan tutte*.

XVII

La clemenza di Tito

In the spring of 1791 Mozart began work on his new opera for Emmanuel Schikaneder's suburban Theater auf der Wieden, *Die Zauberflöte*. But his work was interrupted in July by a commission from Domenico Guarda-soni, impresario of the Prague National Theatre, to write an opera for the festivities to accompany the coronation in Prague of Leopold II as King of Bohemia in September 1791. The opera was to be based upon Metastasio's fifty-year-old drama *La clemenza di Tito*.

Mozart was in fact second choice for the opera, earlier approaches having been made to his old rival Salieri, who was too busy with duties in Vienna to undertake the commission. The opera was written in the greatest haste, for the authorities in Prague only issued Guardasoni with the contract on 8 July for an opera, to be performed 'within the first days of September'.[1]

Mozart's facility is legendary; indeed, many of the stories of Mozart's speed of composition (such as Da Ponte's recollection that *Le nozze di Figaro* was written in six weeks) are precisely that, and have been encour-aged to bolster the myth of his divine inspiration. In fact, Mozart's facility was no more than that required of any composer of his period. And unlike Rossini, who evidently preferred to intersperse bouts of frantic composition with periods of leisure (or non-compositional activity), Mozart took no particular pleasure in composing at high speed. Over works about which he truly cared, like the six 'Haydn' string quartets, he was prepared to labour for years. It is therefore impossible not to conclude that, since he was deep in work on *Die Zauberflöte*, an opera of far greater significance to him, Mozart accepted the Prague commission reluctantly; he needed the money, and it offered him an instant showcase to display his talents to the new Emperor, Leopold, who had succeeded his brother Joseph in February 1790.

Although much effort has been devoted to rehabilitating *La clemenza di Tito* in recent years, it shows all the signs of Mozart's haste. Older commentators, writing in the days when Beethoven and Brahms were still gods, were less reverential about every last dot spattered from Mozart's pen; Donald Tovey suggested that *La clemenza di Tito* gave 'the nightmare impression of *Die Zauberflöte* having dried up and gone wrong'.[2] The opera indeed has a thoroughly stolid decorum from which it only rarely escapes. Metastasio relied heavily upon lengthy recitatives to carry the weight of his tortuous plot, and neither the convoluted recitatives, nor the mellifluous abstractions of Metastasio's verse in the lyrical arias, provided Mozart with much to get his teeth into. The music in its turn is often bland and abstract. The anti-heroine Vitellia's first aria, for example, in which she reproaches her dogged lover Sesto for his doubts of her love, is full of melismatic phrases that sound as if they have been lifted straight from the almost contemporary clarinet concerto. Over-similar melodic ideas (such as the identical phrases in the arias 'Deh per questo istante' and 'Non piu di fiori') recur throughout the opera, less the evidence of thematic integration (as in *Così fan tutte*) than of apparent absent-mindedness.

The Saxon court poet Caterino Mazzolà, who was briefly serving as court poet in Vienna, was commissioned to turn Metastasio's libretto into 'a real opera' (Mozart's own words)[3] since there was no time to prepare a new text. But even the substantial cuts made by him to clarify the plot, and the insertion of some duets and ensembles to alleviate the relentless sequence of arias customary in *opera seria*, could not give the opera the internal dramatic structure upon which even the greatest composer relies. Mozart, the master of the grand gesture, wrote three ceremonial scenes for the opera. One, a *Zauberflöte*-like march and hymn of praise for the deliverance of Tito from assassination, has a serene beauty, and the final scene of the opera begins with a magnificent, uplifting march. But although the first of the opera's three public scenes in praise of Tito may have been suitable for the ceremonial occasion of the opera's perform-ance, it comprises ponderous and empty rhetoric. The finale to Act I, in which the attempted assassination takes place and the Capitol is set alight (all off-stage) is the only extended musico-dramatic scene in the opera, and has a sombre grandiloquence.

It was precisely the somewhat bland simplicity of much of the opera's music which restored Mozart to favour with some who had formerly complained at the complexity of most of his music. Its 'Greek simplicity and calm sublimity'[4] were praised by many for whom Goethe's *Iphigenie* had represented the apogee of Weimar classicism. For those Romantics engaged in what has been called the 'raffaelization' of Mozart,[5] *La clemenza di Tito* was truest evidence of Mozart's status as a Romantic classic (or was it classical Romantic?) It is worth recalling that Metastasio, condemned by Calzabigi and Gluck for his cold, sententious moralizing (fully to the fore in *La clemenza di Tito*) was considered by many of his age to be the epitome of Romantic sensibility; his limpid verses were placed by Rousseau, one of his most fervent admirers, at the head of the chapters of *La nouvelle Héloïse*. Metastasio's biographer, Dr Burney, who also praised his famed benevolence and sensibility, lauded the poet for effecting the very revolution that Gluck and Calzabigi would later claim for themselves; that of classicism without classicizing: 'He may be said to write with classic elegance, though he had liberated himself from classic chains.'[6]

THE LACKEY OF ABSOLUTISM

The choice of *La clemenza di Tito* – not Mozart's own – for the coronation in Prague must have seemed fairly obvious, if somewhat uninspired. The text had originally been written in 1743 in honour of the Emperor Karl IV, and had been set some forty times subsequently during the eighteenth century; an obligatory vehicle for those engaged in the flattery of the numerous petty monarchs of Germany. It was the kind of baroque praise with which the austere and incorruptible Joseph II had felt distinctly uncomfortable, and which he had discouraged. But his brother Leopold was quite different. No less enlightened than Joseph, he recognized that politics was, as Hofmannsthal was to say, as much to do with magic as practical statecraft,[7] and understood the purpose of ritual and ceremonial in the popular imagination far better than his prosaic brother. He committed himself to old-fashioned coronation ceremonies in his Hereditary Possessions (the crown of Bohemia was in fact the senior of the Habsburg titles) and expected pomp and circumstance to dignify the occasion.

Metastasio's libretto, one of his most successful and popular (praised by Voltaire as being worthy of Racine) contains his best exposition of the principles of enlightened monarchical absolutism. The Emperor Titus was famed in antiquity for his magnanimity; Suetonius in his biographies of the Roman emperors, from which their subsequent reputations largely derive, cites Titus's famous comment 'diem perdidi' upon realizing that he had not committed a good deed one day. Titus therefore provided a classical model for the wise, just and beneficent ruler (one much approved by the freemasons). As recounted by Suetonius, the opera presents the scene in which, burdened with the tokens of fame and honour by the Romans, Titus refuses to accept them, rejects deification, and insists upon giving the wealth showered upon him to succour the needy victims of an eruption of Vesuvius. Did Joseph II, dubbed by Pezzl the 'German Titus',[8] take lessons from his forebear as Roman emperor when the citizens of Brussels offered to erect a statue to Maria Theresa, and he insisted that instead the money should be spent on charitable projects and the building of a hospital?[9]

Metastasio has often been dismissed as a mindless lackey of absolutism. But he was in fact one of the most politically astute of eighteenth-century writers, with a clearly defined political outlook. Metastasio's egregious flattery of his sovereigns (as exemplified in the dedication to Karl IV that accompanied *La clemenza di Tito*) is indeed nauseating to modern ears. But his devotion to absolutism was principled and considered. In an age that had somewhat hazy notions of the meaning of republicanism,[10] Metastasio saw no contradiction in extolling the self-sacrificing republican virtues ('according to the pagan idea')[11] of the eponymous Roman hero of his drama *Attilio Regolo*, and the new statist ideals of modern absolutism, which demanded of its citizens a similar self-denial for the greater good.

But he objected that true republicanism (government without monarch) was inherently unstable because it depended too much on the individual citizen's virtue. Only the strong government provided by the absolute ruler could provide the necessary stability and authority to combat those tendencies of the age which troubled the cautious Metastasio. 'I am seduced by the venerable example of supreme paternal authority; nor has the axiom that the most simple and uncompounded machines are the most perfect and durable ever been confuted',[12] he wrote. Metastasio's conservatism was remarkably prescient. Already in 1767 he was viewing the developments of his era with disquiet, writing of the reforms being undertaken by Maria Theresa and her consort Joseph that 'all great revolutions and changes of ancient systems (even if it were certain that posterity would be benefited from them) are ever fatal to the unhappy mortals who are condemned to be spectators of the conflict'.[13]

THE PREROGATIVE OF CLEMENCY

Metastasio drew the dramatic meat for his imperial homage in *La clemenza di Tito* from Corneille's play *Cinna*, or *La clémence d'Auguste*, in which Augustus's close confidant Cinna is driven, like Sesto, to conspire against the emperor by his love for the vindictive Emilia, who is impelled by her own desire to avenge the wrongs inflicted upon her father by Augustus. *Cinna* was written in 1640, when Richelieu was launching the modernization of the French monarchy that was to culminate in the exemplary absolutism of Louis XIV. But Richelieu's own reforms prompted political instability (which erupted a few years later into the civil wars of the Fronde between the nobility and monarchy), and Corneille's play is a plea for the authority of the strong but merciful monarch.

The central incident in Corneille's play, the confrontation of Augustus and his would-be assassin Cinna, was itself drawn from Seneca's dialogue *On Clemency*, dedicated with horrible historical irony to his most unclement pupil Nero. Seneca's dialogue is a eulogy to clemency, or mercy, a virtue which is presented as the especial prerogative of the strong ruler, whose hand retains the ultimate power of grace. Seneca's definition survived as an important tradition in Western political thought. It is a recurrent theme in Shakespeare (we recall Portia's ardent plea that Shylock dignify himself by exercising the mercy which 'becomes the throned monarch better than his crown')[14] and Montesquieu considered the exercise of clemency to be *the* distinguishing characteristic of a monarchical system; its best justification. The Western tradition of justice tempered by mercy (often represented together as complementary virtues) recognizes that absolute justice can never be entirely and perfectly embodied in positive laws. And positive justice, both inflexible and fallible, needs mercy, most aptly exercised by the monarch, to temper its stern and impartial sword according to the higher claims of *natural* justice.[15]

The sovereign mercy of Corneille and Montesquieu established a special relationship between the ruler and the aristocracy (who were the invariable recipients of clemency). For this reason not all eighteenth-century absolutist rulers considered clemency to be an entirely desirable attribute. Louis XV, presented with a scheme for a series of paintings to celebrate instances of clemency by famous rulers of the past, vetoed the proposal as unsuitable to his own image of manly kingship.[16] He was clearly unwilling to accept Seneca's distinction between pity ('a vice of weakness'), pardon (offending against justice by the 'remitting of a deserved punishment'), and true mercy.[17]

But with the Enlightenment's increasing insistence upon the absoluteness of the law, and upon equality before the law and impartiality in administering the law, the enlightened state came to consider mercy as an anachronistic and ultimately obsolete virtue. As Seneca himself pointed out, it essentially involves breaking the law in the name of a superior concept of justice. Against the wishes of the imperious Richelieu, who desired to introduce into France the principles of absolute impartiality before the law (in particular for the nobility) and who forbade the pardon of offenders, Louis XIII had insisted upon retaining his distinctive prerogative of mercy.[18] But precisely for this reason, in the summer of 1791, whilst *La clemenza di Tito* was being written, the Constituent Assembly in France was declaring its objections to the arbitrariness of monarchical mercy. Using the arguments of utilitarian jurists such as Bentham, the radical deputy Jerome Pétion insisted that the exercise of mercy was an affront to egalitarian justice. Echoing Shakespeare's Angelo in *Measure for Measure*,[19] he argued that 'The clemency of a nation is to be just'.[20]

Observing the development of events in France from Mainz, Georg

Forster noted that 'The most furious democrat and the most authoritarian despot follow today only one speech; both speak of the preservation and deliverance of the state, and of law and justice'.[21] Unsurprisingly therefore, given the affinity between absolutist and democratic statism, both Joseph II and his brother Leopold were committed to this new concept of legal impartiality in which the ruler became the upholder rather than the mitigator of the law (to mitigate the law was to weaken it, Sonnenfels had argued). In the famous letter Leopold wrote to his sister Marie-Christine, Governess of Belgium, just before acceding to the Habsburg thrones in January 1790, in which he outlined his political philosophy, he adumbrated his commitment to constitutional principles, telling her that the sovereign himself 'must interfere neither directly nor indirectly in civil or criminal justice . . . I believe, in conclusion, that the ruler must rule in accordance with the law' – a direct confutation of the prerogative of sovereign mercy.[22]

NEW IMAGES OF MONARCHY

The development of this new concept of the universality of the law in the late-Enlightenment absolutist state is apparent in changing portrayals of the monarchy in eighteenth-century art. On the Pestsaule in the Graben in Vienna, an exuberant baroque monument erected to give thanks to God for relief from the plague of 1679, the Emperor Leopold I, sceptre and orb in hand, makes his representations to God on behalf of his suffering subjects. Below him a female figure expels the plague, proof of the efficacy of the sovereign's intercession and his position as guarantor of God's grace, from whose proximity he draws his own power and glory. But in *Idomeneo*, a century later, although the king maintains the baroque relationship between monarch and deity, the deity now represents the just law of nature, rather than theological grace. Idomeneo acknowledges the primacy of the law by accepting Neptune's command that he abdicate in favour of Idamante, exhorting his people to obey too.

In H. F. Moller's play *Sophie, oder der gerechte Fürst*, written during the middle years of Joseph's reign, the *deus ex machina* who arrives to dispense justice and set an innocent heroine free from prison is Joseph II himself, now the representative of the sovereign law of the state, who needs no heavenly authority to sanction his power.[23] On the Pestsaule, the illustrative roundels on the base of the monument depict scenes of God's punishment and grace in the Old and New Testaments, evidence of the frailty of Man's own efforts to improve his lot without divine approval mediated by the baroque monarch. But the neo-classical roundels that surround the equestrian monument to Joseph in the Hofburg in Vienna

depict not the grace of God, but the emperor's own exercise of beneficence and justice: his concern for public welfare, his encouragement of
trade and agriculture, his promotion of the sciences.

In view of the later Enlightenment state's insistence upon the absolute
dictates of the law, it may be questioned whether Metastasio's fable of
monarchical clemency from an earlier age was quite so appropriate for
the coronation of the new model monarch Leopold II fifty years later.
But let us consider the context of the opera, for a crucial clue is given to
the true ideological purpose of the opera by the fact that it was commissioned for Leopold's coronation not by the imperial authorities but by
the Bohemian Estates, the representative body of the Bohemian aristocracy.[24] Mozart's *La clemenza di Tito* is not a conventional hymn to enlightened despotism, as is usually claimed, but a missile lobbed in the aristocratic counter-revolution to absolutism.

THE ARISTOCRATIC COUNTER-REVOLUTION

The Habsburgs had traditionally relied heavily upon the support of the
Estates. But as we have seen (p. 88), both Maria Theresa and Joseph II,
like the French monarchs of the seventeenth and eighteenth century, had
refused to acknowledge their claims. The Hungarian Diet (the meeting
of the Estates) was suppressed in 1764, the Bohemian in 1775, and
Joseph had deliberately not been crowned in Hungary and Bohemia to
avoid having to recall them and swear coronation oaths to uphold their
rights. In place of the traditional rights and privileges of the nobility and
the Estates, Maria Theresa and Joseph introduced new codes of state law
whose purpose was to make everyone equal in the sight of the law. 'All
men are equal at birth,' claimed Joseph himself; 'we inherit from our
parents no more than animal life, hence there is not the slightest difference between King, Count, bourgeois and peasant. I find nothing in
divine or natural law to contradict this equality.'[25]

Joseph's egalitarian principles hit the aristocracy hardest through his
implementation of uniform land taxation (from which the nobility had
always been exempt). As a result of his tax proposals of 1785 Joseph met
the first significant aristocratic opposition to his reforms, on the grounds
that the nobility were, 'after all, much more important to the state than
the capitalists'.[26] During the later 1780s Joseph faced increasing hostility
to his programme, from major aristocratic officers of state such as Kaunitz, Kolowrat (Chancellor), Zinzendorf (Chief of the Economic Commission, who was sacked for his opposition in 1788) and Pergen (police
chief). But he also met with obstruction from the provincial nobility upon
whom he was still often dependent for the execution of his decrees. In

February 1789 a new taxation law, aimed at the nobility, gave rise to open aristocratic rebellion in Hungary. In Belgium the Estates went so far as to declare independence.

The aristocratic resistance Joseph met was in part a reflection of a Europe-wide aristocratic counter-offensive against egalitarian absolutism (the right to be equally unfree!). In France, the nobility had from the beginning of the eighteenth century already embarked on a rearguard action to restore the status and privileges lost under Louis XIV; during the course of the century they gradually regained many feudal rights (usually for their financial rather than political value) and managed to restrict entry to the army and higher ranks of the Church to the nobility. In Sweden, where Gustavus III had in 1789 openly sided with the Commons against the nobles, an aristocratic conspiracy assassinated the king in 1792. In Russia Catherine the Great was forced to issue the traditional Russian nobility with a Charter of Nobility granting them, for the first time, the rights and privileges they imagined to be enjoyed by their Western counterparts. In Prussia, where the king had always preferred to rule his militarized state in alliance with the Junker nobility, the notorious General Legal Code of 1794 reasserted 'the natural, inalienable and sacred rights of noblemen'.[27]

It has often been observed that the recalling – for the first time since 1614 – of the Estates General in France in 1789, a move that ushered in the French Revolution, was in fact the last triumph of the aristocratic counter-revolution in France. And it was the reassertion of political, rather than merely social, rights that was to be of the greatest significance in this counter-revolutionary movement throughout Europe. During the eighteenth century a substantial body of political theory grew up to support the claims of the nobility to have a say in government as an estate of the realm. Known in French as the *thèse nobiliaire*, its most famous proponent was (the Baron Secondat de) Montesquieu, who argued that a strong aristocracy was the best defence against despotic absolutism. The *thèse nobiliaire* found its supporters in late 1780s Vienna, where as early as 1787 Franz Kratter (who had formerly supported Joseph's masonic reforms) called for the aristocracy to 'limit the usurped powers of the absolute monarchy'.[28] By the 1790s Sonnenfels, casting a nervous eye on developments in France, was suggesting that they had arisen through a dangerous combination of autocratic monarchy, over-powerful bourgeoisie and weakened aristocracy.

When Leopold II arrived in Vienna in March 1790 he found himself confronted with widespread rebellion by the aristocracy in response to his importunate brother's reforms. To restore order Leopold was forced to reverse the hated taxation laws of 1789, and to agree to recall the Estates. His efforts to gain political control have often been characterized as a reactionary move against the Josephine reforms.[29]. But Leopold himself was committed to progressive reform, having turned Tuscany, his small fiefdom, into a model of the Enlightened state. Although he was forced to make immediate concessions to the nobility in the Habsburg Empire to avert outright revolution, his longer-term plan was undoubtedly to continue his brother's programme (though he died in 1792, before he could achieve his aims).

The nobility could not, therefore, be assured of Leopold's dedication to their cause. In Belgium the Democratic Party (the first political grouping to use this term in modern history) had specifically sought the protection of the new emperor against the reactionary counter-revolution effected by the Belgian Estates. In Hungary, the Peasants' Decretum of 1790 supported the emperor against the aristocratic Diet. The emperor was himself secretly instrumental in the publication of pamphlets, written by Mozart's former fellow lodge-member Leopold Hoffmann, which urged the Hungarian bourgeoisie to oppose the renewal of aristocratic rights.[30]

The coronation of Leopold in Prague in September 1791 was therefore an occasion of immense political importance. It was on Leopold's part a sign of his willingness to acknowledge, if not acceed to, the claims of the Estates; and it was an opportunity for the nobility to assert their position and make their demands to the new emperor.

In the contract issued to Guardasoni for the opera to celebrate Leopold's coronation it was stipulated that the libretto should be written on either of two subjects dictated by the Graf Rottenham, Bohemian Count of the Castle and spokesman for the Bohemian Estates on the matter. Unfortunately, we do not know what these subjects were, but it is clear that Graf Rottenham, and his four aristocratic colleagues who were party to the contract, were determined that they should dictate the subject of the opera, and it was they who insisted that if there was not enough time for a new libretto to be written, then the subject was to be *La clemenza di Tito*.

The reason should now be clear. The libretto offers praise for a sovereign willing to override the implacable dictates of the law to exercise his personal prerogative of mercy. It would have made a pointed appeal to the new emperor to display his own clemency, and to temper his brother's rigid adherence to the abstract majesty of the law, which had done so much to undermine the status of the nobility. As Louis XIII had insisted (against the wishes of Richelieu), and as Montesquieu had reiterated in the widely influential *L'esprit des lois*, the sovereign's prerogative of clemency created a powerful bond between monarch and aristocracy. In presenting *La clemenza di Tito* the Bohemian Estates were making a bid for a renewal of the old alliance between the monarchy and the aristocracy, an alliance they eventually achieved during the years of social reaction and political repression under Leopold's son Franz II.

Whether any of this complex political manoeuvring would have been relevant to Mozart, immersed in the spiritual profundities of *Die Zauberflöte*, is debatable. The evidence of *Così fan tutte* and *Die Zauberflöte* tells us that by 1789 at the latest Mozart, like many Viennese, had lost interest in political programmes and solutions (see next chapter). Joseph II had died virtually friendless and unmourned ('That was good of him,' was Kaunitz's bitterly laconic comment),[31] and it is unlikely that Mozart would have lamented Joseph's lonely demise either ideologically or professionally. Most Austrians, though, however disillusioned with the world of politics, greeted Leopold's accession with wary hope. And Mozart himself, now desperately needing an official salary to enable him to survive after the collapse of the Viennese public concert life, inevitably hoped that Leopold would display more largesse than his brother. In fact, Leopold had little time to devote to cultural matters, and did not attend the theatre in Vienna until September 1790, six months after his arrival.[32] But as with Joseph ten years previously, Mozart laid seige to Leopold, following him to Frankfurt in October 1790 for his coronation as emperor in the hope of attracting his attention – fruitlessly.

Mozart was faced with a dilemma. Largely uninterested in public life by this date (his letters show an impatience with the social demands he knew to be necessary to his career and a preference for solitary theatregoing and time spent with his family),[33] he was none the less reliant upon attracting official interest in his work. He would have welcomed the political stability promised by Leopold II, but (as we shall see in the next chapter), would have regretted Leopold's own inclinations to more egalitarian and democratic forms of government, which might have inclined Mozart to sympathize with the claims of the Bohemian Estates. It may be that the obvious perfunctoriness of *La clemenza di Tito* is a reflection of these ambivalent and unresolvable attitudes.

THE GODLIKE EMPEROR

However, the opera did claim at least some of Mozart's artistic interest, a fact indicated, as so often, in important changes made in refashioning the libretto. For in Mozart's and Mazzolà's alterations to Metastasio's libretto the princely virtue of clemency is clearly transmuted into the Christian virtue of forgiveness; sovereign into divine grace.

But forgiveness and mercy are not necessarily synonymous (see p. 337, n. 94). And mercy can also be offered without forgiveness of the crime itself, since forgiveness implies a form of cancellation of the original sin or crime, rather than simply of the punishment due to it. Above all, forgiveness implies a personal wrong; we cannot properly forgive people ourselves for wrongs done to another person.

The act of insurrection that Sesto undertakes should properly be viewed as a crime against the state. But in Metastasio's paternalistic concept of Enlightened absolutism Sesto's crime is considered a personal affront to the monarch. The sins laid by Tito at Sesto's feet ('Rome in turmoil, the throne offended, the laws violated, friendship betrayed') are all personalized by Tito as offences against himself. As such Tito offers Sesto personal forgiveness rather than merely monarchical clemency after he has been tried and found guilty by the Senate. When Sesto, unwilling to betray Vitellia, refuses to exonerate himself or accept the proffered hand, Tito announces that he is now Sesto's judge rather than his friend.

There is something godlike in Tito's position as dispenser of both justice and mercy. Indeed, we become aware throughout the opera that the relationship of many of the characters in the opera to Tito recalls that of human beings towards the Christian God. In the opening scene, Vitellia reproaches Sesto for his doubts of her love: 'He who has blind belief is bound to keep faith.' But faith is only due to those who, unlike Vitellia, are themselves unconditionally faithful to their covenants. Blind belief in false idols is destructive. Tito refuses to be turned into an object of idolatry, and prefers truth to flattery. He commands through love rather than fear, relying upon loyalty and devotion, and upon the moral conscience that loyalty and trust inspire. Those who betray that trust inflict upon themselves the pangs of estrangement and guilt. The guilty Sesto is ushered into Tito's aweful presence ('his customary gentleness gone'); he trembles and falters; he is commanded to approach, and offered the opportunity to confess and repent. Proudly he declares before leaving, like Don Giovanni, that death does not afright him. But Tito's grace is, like God's, unconditional.

Meanwhile, Vitellia is suffering, for the first time, the torments of a guilty conscience for having sent Sesto to his death, the signs that even she is not beyond redemption. But, as Sesto's sister Servilia reproaches, her conscience-stricken pity is not enough. Only true confession of guilt for the crime can save Sesto and relieve her of the burden of her sin. 'Non più di fiori', Vitellia sings as she recognizes that she must relinquish her hopes of marriage to Tito (which were based upon lust for power, not love) and the false bliss she had vainly believed this would bring. Like Ilia and Konstanze, Vitellia throws herself at the judge's feet to save the man who loves her. Determined to show the absolute constancy of his own mercy, Tito absolves everyone, and in one of the most significant additions to Metastasio's original text, sings that 'True repentance . . . is worth more than constant fidelity'. It is a direct reference to the Christian teaching that 'Joy shall be in heaven over one sinner that repenteth more than over ninety and nine just persons, which need no repentance',[34] and that Jesus came 'not to call the righteous, but sinners to repentance'.[35] Who those sinners are for Mozart will become apparent in the following chapter.

XVIII

Die Zauberflöte

A fantastic hotch-potch of the sublime and the ridiculous, the spiritual and the popular, quasi-religious ritual and street comedy, formally *Die Zauberflöte* reflects the abandonment in much of Mozart's late music of the integrated complexity of classicism in favour of a sometimes almost childlike simplicity of expression, and (as in the Requiem), a juxtaposition of musical languages, with little apparent desire to achieve formal integration or homogeneity. Charles Rosen noted Mozart's renunciation of harmonic colour in *Die Zauberflöte*,[1] and whereas in *Idomeneo*, (an aria-based opera) twelve out of the fourteen arias employ sonata form, Mozart virtually dispensed with sonata form in *Die Zauberflöte*. If we consider *Le nozze di Figaro* to have represented the high point of Mozart's classical synthesis, an artistic expression of the last, supreme moment of social optimism within the Viennese Enlightenment, it is significant that after 1786 he wrote only two further works in the genre that best conveyed the classical ideal of integration: the piano concerto.

Theodor Adorno once described Beethoven's late style as a disintegration of the heroic bourgeois synthesis of individual and objective reality that Beethoven had achieved in his middle-period music; a reflection of the social and political polarization in post-Napoleonic Europe. In his late string quartets Beethoven abandons classical dialectic (in particular, sonata form) to represent a fragmented, objectified landscape lit by, but no longer integrated with, the artist's own subjectivity. 'Beethoven does not bring about a harmonious synthesis of these extremes. Rather, he tears them apart,' says Adorno.[2] In Beethoven's late music the alienation of the individual from the real world is graphically conveyed in unrelated stylistic juxtapositions: baroque counterpoint alongside quasi-sonata forms, sublime serenity alongside rustic dances. Something similar seems to have happened in Mozart's late music, the effect not of intimations of mortality (as is so often sentimentally implied) but of the bleak social and political climate of his last years.

Così fan tutte, written to the distant sounds of walls tumbling in Paris, reflects the disillusion of Austrians in the late 1780s with the endless promises of material solutions to the social and political disturbances of the era. *Die Zauberflöte* conveys the longing of those who had become

distrustful of the public and political realm, to cultivate even more studiously the individual, inner spiritual sphere of humanity so neglected in
Enlightenment discourse. A few years later Hegel, in the footsteps of
Schiller, was to assert that the characteristic of true classical art was that
it knew no disjunction between the real and the ideal. But when the
material divests itself of the spiritual, as Enlightenment materialism had
so effectively done (and as is demonstrated in *Così fan tutte*), the spiritual
is forced to withdraw back to heaven (as in *Don Giovanni*) or to become
internalized:

For in the epoch of Romantic art, the Spirit knows that it cannot find its truth
by immersing itself in the flesh of reality; on the contrary, it assures itself of its
truth by retracing its steps from the external back into its own internality, leaving
the outer world as an inadequate form of existence . . . The true content of
Romantic art is absolute inwardness.[3]

By Hegel's definition, *Die Zauberflöte* is a truly Romantic work; a journey
into spiritual introspection.

RETREAT FROM THE PUBLIC REALM

The last years of Joseph II's reign had been characterized by a widespread
retreat from political engagement, and from the virulent social argument
and discussion so typical of the first half of the decade. In part this was
the direct result of Joseph's clampdown on public debate; by 1790, when
Joseph had reintroduced complete censorship of the press, the relaxed
and uninhibited freedom of discussion of the salons and coffee-houses
of Vienna is reported by Johann Pezzl in *Skizze von Wien* to have been
replaced by sullen, tight-lipped resentment.[4] In the later 1780s political
and satirical themes had virtually vanished from the poetry published in
the Viennese *Musenalmanach*, and the social satires and parodies of the
first half of the 1780s had given way to the more escapist magical and fairy
dramas in Marinelli's Leopoldstadt theatre and Schikaneder's Theater auf
der Wieden. Ten years previously, Pezzl claims in the *Skizze* in 1789,
the theatre in Vienna had been an altar at which people had worshipped,
a new religion which had been imported from Hamburg (the home of
Lessing's original national theatre dedicated to the moral improvement
of society); now people recognize theatre for what it should be – entertainment.[5]

The greatness of *Die Zauberflöte* lies in the fact that its esoteric inwardness is presented in a form of entertainment that is popular and universal,
and that it reaches out with its spiritual message to all who are willing
not merely to see, but to hear (the distinction made by Mozart himself).[6]

Die Zauberflöte is a quintessentially Viennese work: magical, street-wise, spectacular and farcical. In the folk theatre of the Viennese suburbs (attended by all classes of society), Mozart at last found the indigenous German art, rooted in community and tradition, which he had always sought, and which enabled him finally to write the German opera that had always eluded him (*Die Zauberflöte* was Mozart's greatest work, Beethoven asserted, because it was the only work in which he showed himself as 'a German Master').[7] But the traditional Viennese theatre had never lost touch with the sphere of the divine, and thus Mozart was able to give form to his spiritual wisdom in a way that was easily grasped and understood. For this reason the symbolism of *Die Zauberflöte* reaches more widely and engages its audience more directly than do the complex personal allegories of William Blake, Mozart's exact contemporary and spiritual twin.

Die Zauberflöte is the greatest work of art to emerge from the retreat from public engagement in Viennese art. But paradoxically, within this most Viennese work Mozart reflected the wider concerns of German culture, with which he had also always longed to identify himself. And the preoccupations of *Die Zauberflöte* can best be understood in relation to this broader movement in German culture at the end of the eighteenth century, articulated by philosophers and writers such as Kant, Goethe and Schiller, whose works represent both a culmination and a transcendence of Enlightenment thought. Significantly, *Die Zauberflöte* was highly regarded by Goethe, who held Schikaneder's talent in high esteem and compared the opera to his own *Faust* in its combination of spectacle for the masses and a more profound message for the spiritually aware.[8] Like Schikaneder, Goethe undertook an (unfinished) sequel to *Die Zauberflöte*.[9] Because of the opera's relevance to the intellectual movements of its age, we need to understand the general climate in which it was written, in particular, the response in Germany to the French Revolution.

THE FRENCH REVOLUTION

The French Revolution was initially greeted with ecstatic expressions of support by the majority of German *Aufklärer*, who saw in the programme of its early stages the practical fulfilment of so many of the ideals of the Enlightenment. Kant, already in his mid-sixties, was moved to quote Simeon's words upon being presented with the infant Christ. 'Lord now lettest thou thy servant depart in peace'.[10] But as events deteriorated into chaos and bloodshed the euphoria wore off, to be replaced by dismay, and eventually disgust as the news of the execution of the king and the subsequent Terror travelled across Europe. Even by 1790 it had become evident to the politically aware what the outcome of the Revolution must be. In London Edmund Burke's *Reflections on the Revolution in France*, the most thorough attack on the principles of the Revolution, and most prescient analysis of its likely course and horrific conclusion, appeared as early as November 1790, as the final performances of *Così fan tutte* were taking place, and well before the events which later branded themselves upon the consciousness of Europe as the stigmata of Revolution – the September Massacres of 1792, the execution of Louis XVI or the Jacobin Terror. One of the bibles of modern conservatism, Burke's *Reflections*, which used the Revolution in France as an excuse to launch a vehement counter-attack upon the Enlightenment itself, was already being read in Germany by 1791 (in which year Adam Weishaupt's former lieutenant, Adolph von Knigge, published a critical review of the book).

Both Goethe and Schiller responded strongly to the French Revolution. Goethe produced a series of minor and ill-regarded works expressing his horror of the kinds of political enthusiasm that led to irrational mob rule and social chaos, and of ideological programmes that resulted in totalitarian social engineering. Schiller produced a more considered response in his famous *Letters on the Aesthetic Education of Man*, in which he insisted that attempts to alter society through purely rational means, and to objectify in the state a moral and political maturity not yet attained by its citizens, must inevitably lead to political oppression. Only when men and women have attained individual maturity will they be ready for the political demands of a revolutionary society.

The German experience of enlightened despotism in Prussia and Austria had already prepared many German writers and artists to consider the world of politics with a mistrust confirmed rather than prompted by the French Revolution. Schiller's wariness of political engagement is evident well before the French Revolution: 'We must evade them or meet them, we must undermine them or be vanquished by them,'[11] he had written of politicians, and in *Don Carlos* and *Fiesco* he explored the idea that all political undertakings, in particular those carried out by rational idealists like the Marquis of Posa (the liberal hero of *Don Carlos*), have the potential to corrupt even those with the best intentions, and may lead to despotism. The Revolution itself brought no change in the basic principles of Schiller's humanitarian idealism, simply to his perception of how his vision of society might be fulfilled.

Goethe, who in later years frequently found himself branded as a reactionary conservative in comparison to Schiller, always repudiated this wounding imputation. 'It is true', he told his amanuensis Eckermann in 1824, 'that I could not help disliking the French Revolution ... But at the same time I was no friend of arbitrary tyrannical rule, and I was absolutely convinced that it is never the people who are to blame for any great revolution, but the government.'[12] Goethe's organic conception of society made it impossible for him to accept attempts to tinker with the natural rhythms of development and change, let alone uproot the social plant. He was also notably dismissive of utilitarianism, dubbing its chief spokesman Jeremy Bentham as 'an ultra-radical idiot'.[13] But as with Schiller, Goethe's alternative conception of a society made up of mature and rounded individuals was formed well before the Revolution; the first (unfinished) version of *Wilhelm Meister*, the work in which he developed and expanded Wieland's typically German concept of *Bildung*, was written in the 1770s.

The unhealthy tendency of intellectuals and artists to withdraw from engagement in public affairs in Germany has often been noted. *Staatsgeheimraat* (permanent under-secretary) Goethe, diligently inspecting mines in Weimar, proves rather than disproves the rule. For it was notorious that those German intellectuals or writers unable to find jobs as teachers were often forced to accept bureaucratic employment that precluded active political (as opposed to administrative) engagement in public life. Mme de Staël was shocked to discover that Wieland, Schiller and Goethe rarely read newspapers. As Thomas Mann, one of the last upholders of this strain of German culture[14] wrote in his *Confessions of an Unpolitical Man*:

I believe it to be the plain and unshakeable truth that the German concept of freedom will always be of an intellectual-spiritual nature . . . To ask [the German] to transfer his allegiances from inwardness to the objective, to politics, to what the peoples of Europe call *freedom*, would seem to him to demand that he do violence to his own nature.[15]

The avoidance of political engagement, already evident in German culture in the mid-eighteenth century, merely manifested itself more forcefully as the French Revolution turned from heroic drama into a tragedy of blasted aspirations. In an essay written in 1793 in response to the rise of Robespierre, Wieland's comments were typical: 'If things are to get any better for humanity, reform must occur not through governmental and constitutional reform, but by individuals themselves.'[16] The metaphysical idealism that flowered in Germany in the 1780s and 1790s can also be seen as a response to the perceived shortcomings of political programmes and actions. (Significantly, Georg Forster, one of the few Germans of the age willing to engage in direct revolutionary action – in the Mainz Revolution – was notably hostile to Kant's idealism.)[17] Fichte, who carried the subjectivist implications of Kantian metaphysics to its most extreme conclusions, wrote in 1795 'My system is the first system of liberty. As the French nation liberated men from external chains, my system liberates them from the chains of the Thing-in-itself [the Kantian *Ding-als-sich*], or of external influence, and sets him forth in his first principle as a self-sufficient being.'[18]

> Enter the holy temple of the spirit,
> If thou would'st flee from life's discordant throng:
> For freedom dwells but in the realm of visions,
> And beauty lives but in the poet's song.[19]

is Schiller's stirring advice.

Fichte's metaphysical idealism was not simply the response of a disillusioned reactionary. He remained a fervent believer in the political ideals of the French Revolution, considering them to represent the triumph of the ideal in the real world. But for many, the retreat into individualist idealism was accompanied by a supine acceptance of political oppression, on the grounds that inner freedom was the truest condition of man's autonomy (the logic of Kant's oft-criticized submission to the increasingly reactionary Prussian state in the 1790s). This inner-directed idealism provides a clue to *Die Zauberflöte*, and shows how easily the language of metaphysical idealism could slide imperceptibly into the poetry of inner spiritual development and transformation, and from thence into the realms of the mysticism and supernaturalism typical of early Romanticism. The Faustian pursuit of knowledge becomes the quest for spiritual wisdom; rational *Aufklärung* is superseded by the inner illumination of *Erleuchtung*.

THE *BILDUNGSOPER*

The German word for inner development is *Bildung*, and the most characteristic German form of the novel is the *Bildungsroman*. The *Bildungsroman* follows the typical pattern of the eighteenth-century novel of the education of a young hero or heroine who undergoes a series of adventures in which he or she is exposed to a number of what would today be called 'learning experiences' – events and accidents which prepare the inexperienced young hero or heroine for society. But in the *Bildungsroman*, as opposed to novels like Marivaux's *Marianne*, Fielding's *Tom Jones* or Fanny Burney's *Evelina*, greater emphasis is placed upon the internal development of the hero. In the early Enlightenment novel of education such as Terrasson's *Sethos*, upon which *Die Zauberflöte* draws very substantially for details of its plot, external events offer the hero discrete units of understanding, which one by one eradicate ignorance and superstition. Sethos is, like

Tamino, a young prince who undergoes a series of educative trials in the pyramids of Egypt, an initiation designed to strengthen his powers of reason and his knowledge, and to make him fit to rule. According to the soundly rationalist Terrasson, 'An initiate is a new man, in whom the love of virtue and his duty has taken the place of all those passions which were previously the motives of all his actions.'[20]

The initiatory theme survives as a central image in the eighteenth-century *Bildungsroman*.[21] The novel usually cited as the first *Bildungsroman* is Wieland's *Geschichte des Agathon* of 1766–7. It is the story of the education of a young Greek (his name indicates his innate, Rousseauvian goodness) who, through a series of encounters, attains eventual wisdom and contentment by learning to overcome the need for the rule of religion and the state, thence to become (the Enlightenment's highest aspiration) 'wie ein Gott über dem Chaos' ('like a God above Chaos').[22] In one scene of the novel Agathon undergoes initiation in the famous Mysteries of Eleusis, and his adventures end when he finds contentment in a mystical Pythagorean community.

With *Werther*, *Agathon* was one of the most widely read German novels of the period, and it made a huge impact on Adam Weishaupt, the founder of the Illuminati, who frequently cited it as one of the most important influences upon his own conception of the meaning of masonic initiation. But initiatory works abound in late eighteenth-century German culture. Closer to home (for Mozart) were Alxinger's two chivalric epics *Doolin von Maynz* and *Bliomberis*. The latter, which appeared in the same year as *Die Zauberflöte*, tells the story of an Arthurian knight who discovers a secret brotherhood in Africa. Borrowing some tricks from the ubiquitous *Sethos*, Bliomberis undergoes the elemental trials also undertaken by Tamino and finally gains entrance to a Temple of the Sun. A few years previously Goethe had written an unfinished poem, *Die Geheimnisse* (published in the Viennese edition of his works in 1789), about a Parsifal-like knight who applies for admission to a mysterious brotherhood. At its conclusion he hears the sound of a 'mysterious' flute that fills the heart with joy, and sees three boys wearing girdles of intertwining roses (Mozart's and Schikaneder's Three Boys descend in a chariot bedecked with roses).

The greatest of German *Bildungsromane* is Goethe's *Wilhelm Meister*.[23] It is ostensibly a contemporary and realistic novel. Wilhelm is a young bourgeois, the son of a prosperous merchant, who spurns his comfortable background for the lure of the theatre and leaves home to pursue his dream. As the story progresses, however, events and characters become increasingly mysterious. Wilhelm finds himself at the centre of a whole complex of relationships between apparently disparate people which, it transpires, is directed by a shadowy secret society – the Society of the Tower. By the end of the novel it has become apparent that the supposedly random occurrences in Wilhelm's life, which he thought to be 'proceeding freely and in secret' have all been, as Wilhelm himself recognizes, 'observed, even guided', as part of a careful programme of spiritual education.[24]

Wilhelm Meister contains one scene in which Wilhelm undergoes what is undoubtedly a masonic initiation, replete with strange ritual liturgies and symbols of death to frighten the initiate. But Wilhelm is later given to understand that the initiation rituals themselves are simply 'juggleries and hocus-pocus' to mystify and satisfy the childish curiosity of those whose chief concern is not the 'formation of the character' (*Bildung*).[25] The real initiation is the education that Wilhelm has undergone throughout the course of the novel, which has brought him to an inner maturity that enables him to enter the community prepared for him.

THE MYTHS AND SYMBOLS OF INITIATION

The common sources that fuelled these eighteenth-century literary depictions of initiation, and also the actual rituals of freemasonry themselves, stretch back to the initiation myths and rituals of the earliest dawn of mankind, many of which still survive in present-day primitive cultures. Understanding of these overcomes one of the main problems that *Die Zauberflöte* has always presented to critics: that of its plot.

According to many commentators, the story of *Die Zauberflöte* changes course half-way through the opera. At the beginning we are introduced to a mourning mother whose daughter has been snatched from her by an evil demon, and a hero whose mission is to rescue the daughter. One third of the way through the story the situation is apparently reversed: the Queen is revealed to be wicked; the abductor Sarastro is a wise and noble priest; and instead of rescuing the princess, the hero joins her and is initiated into the mysteries of the priestly order. Unwearyingly it has been argued that Mozart and Schikaneder must have changed the story of the opera half way through its writing.[26]

But the transformation of the Queen of Night implies no change of course when seen in relation to the archetypal initiatory story patterns upon which the opera ultimately draws. This becomes clear if we borrow from Joseph Campbell his analysis of the universal structure of the myths and rituals of initiation from all over the world. The structure can be broken down into two main sections, which tally with the two apparently disparate parts of *Die Zauberflöte*. The first is described as 'The Call to

Adventure', and has five distinct episodes: (i) The Hero is Lost – in a dark forest or a wild place; (ii) The Hero Refuses the Call; (iii) Supernatural Aid is Offered – a guide, talismans, etc.; (iv) Crossing of the Threshold – the hero meets the Custodian and Guardian of the threshold. The Guardian tests whether the hero is ready for the challenges within; (v) The Belly of the Whale – or entry into the underworld.[27]

So far it is clear that Act I of *Die Zauberflöte* follows the ancient narrative incident for incident. Tamino, a foreign prince, is lost in a wild and rocky place, where he encounters, and almost succumbs to, a serpent. Having been rescued from peril, he is called by the Queen of Night and presented with his mission. Although Tamino accepts the challenge, his newly acquired alter-ego Papageno refuses, and has to be offered the magic bells as a talisman (later restored to him by the supernatural guides of the archetypal story, the Three Boys). Reaching the gates of Sarastro's kingdom, Tamino is confronted by the Guardian of the Threshold, the Speaker, who questions and tests Tamino. At the end of the act, the Prince, blindfolded, is allowed admission to the symbolic underworld of the Temple.

The second section involves the initiation proper. To quote Joseph Campbell again:

Beyond the threshold, then, the hero journeys through a world of unfamiliar yet strangely intimate forces, some of which severely threaten him (tests) some of which give magical aid (helpers). When he arrives at the nadir of the mythological round, he undergoes a supreme ordeal and gains his reward. The triumph may be represented as the hero's sexual union with the goddess-mother of the world (sacred marriage), his recognition by the father-creator (father atonement), or his own divinization (apotheosis).[28]

All three occur in *Die Zauberflöte*. (Campbell, incidentally, makes no mention of *Die Zauberflöte* anywhere in his largely anthropological study.)

Initiation exists in primitive societies to mark the moment when the young individual is expected to adopt and internalize the customs and laws of the society into which he or she is born, and to abandon the regressive, amoral and pre-social bonds of childhood and nature.[29] To free oneself from the regressive bonds of nature is, as Jung recognized, to attain individuation – autonomy and distinctness from the inchoate mass and from the archetypal figurations of dream and fantasy that otherwise control and dominate one's life. The most consistent image for that process is the ability to free oneself from the ties of the mother, which, Joseph Campbell tells us, are usually represented in both an alluring maternal and an horrific form.[30] Thus Jung noted that in the individual's struggle to free himself from the regressive mother complex, a dragon or serpent was a recurrent 'symbolic image for the "devouring" aspect of the attachment to his mother',[31] a symbol that recurs in many cultures – from aboriginal circumcision rites to the dream of one of Jung's patients in which, at the moment that he was being freed of the bonds of his mother complex, a serpent bit his genitals.[32] In *Die Zauberflöte*, Tamino's flight from the serpent represents the first step in his attempt to escape his regressive instincts, which are also embodied in their maternal form by the persuasive motherly appeal of the Queen of Night, who is associated with darkness and with the primordial aspects of nature and of the lure of the mother.

When Tamino reaches the gates of the Temple of Sarastro, its portals and columns indicate to him that this is the seat of 'Skill, Industry and Art'. Tamino has arrived, therefore, at the threshold of civilization, the place where man triumphs over nature, raising himself from submission to her laws to create society and culture. But before he can embrace these, he must first confront the father-figure who represents the negative image that the initiate has of the mature world of human society. In the archetypal initiation myths, the father-figure is always presented initially as an ogre. According to Campbell,

The ogre aspect of the father is a reflex of the victim's own ego – derived from the sensational nursery scene that has been left behind, but projected before; and the fixating idolatory of that pedagogical nonthing is itself the fault that keeps one steeped in a sense of sin, sealing the potentially adult spirit from a better balanced, more realistic view of the father, and therewith of the world.[33]

This is the image of Sarastro with which Tamino sets out on his journey, having been told by the Three Ladies that Pamina has been kidnapped from her mother by a 'böser Dämon' – an evil demon, whom he accordingly condemns at the portals of the temple as 'inhuman, a tyrant'.

It is this image of the father-figure which he has to expunge if he is to attain individuation and autonomous acceptance of social culture. As the hero enters society he gains a new, positive image of the father, who is commonly represented, we are told by Campbell, as 'the iniating priest through whom the young being passes on into the larger world'[34] – Sarastro, as he is eventually revealed to Tamino. And just as the hero comes to terms with the father-figure not by rejection but by re-representation, he must also come to terms with the feminine forces of nature which, in their regressive form, he has necessarily escaped; he has, in Jungian terminology to 'rescue the anima figure from the devouring aspect of the mother image'.[35] This aspect of the anima figure is clearly represented by the captive Pamina, with whom Tamino attains eventual higher reunification.

On one level, therefore, *Die Zauberflöte* can be interpreted as a story of the process by which the individual gains integration into society and achieves individuation – a complementary process that lies at the centre of the later Enlightenment's preoccupations. As such, it presents a mythic answer to the *impasses* of the bourgeois opposition of the individual and society, and to the dangerous, individualist regressiveness represented by all forms of popular Rousseauism. It reminds us that the individual and society do not stand in isolated and hostile distinctness, but that the individual only attains individuation through social existence, recalling, as Goethe writes in *Wilhelm Meister*, 'the measure by which, and up to which, our inner nature has been shaped by culture'.[36] Mozart and Schikaneder, like Goethe, recognized in the mythic stories of initiation a symbol for this process.

In rediscovering these symbols, the later German Enlightenment revived a strain of social and psychological wisdom that had been to all intents and purposes lost during the eighteenth century. As M. H. Abrams has written, 'The several decades beginning with the 1790s constituted a genuine epoch in intellectual and cultural history; not, however, by absolute innovation but by a return to a mode of hereditary wisdom which was redefined, expanded, and applied to the emerging world of continuous political, industrial and social revolution and disorder.'[37] Where the earlier, rationalist Enlightenment had dismissed mythical thought as a stage of infantile reasoning in human history, later Enlightenment thinkers came to recognize (as in Herder's reinterpretation of the Bible as poetical rather than historical truth) that mythical and archetypal stories contained eternal, spiritual wisdoms about human existence.

The raw material of this symbolism had, however, never been lost. For the structural patterns and the imagery of initiation had survived in numerous forms long after the rituals themselves had ceased to be central to Western cultures. Thus, as Mircea Eliade pointed out, initiatory themes are clearly preserved in fairy stories, which had survived in many forms in eighteenth-century literature, often catering for the eighteenth century's rococo taste for the fantastical and exotic.[38] The fairy-tale element in *Die Zauberflöte* came specifically from the widely read fairy stories collected (and in some cases artfully invented) by Wieland, and from the popular magical theatre of the Viennese suburbs. But initiation rituals were also enshrined in freemasonry, which had (as far as we know) inherited them from the apprenticeship rites of the medieval guilds, rites that had then been deliberately overlaid with much esoteric symbolism, preserved and keenly studied in older texts of the magical and occult.

THE *FELIX CULPA*

The initiation journey undertaken by Tamino as an individual parallels a second journey: the spiritual journey of the human race itself. Herder in his *Ideen* referred to the *Bildungsgeschichte* – the history of the human race as a history of its *Bildung*. As so often, it was Rousseau's history of humankind that set the scene. Kant, Herder and Schiller, like many later commentators, noted that the biblical myth of the expulsion from the Garden of Eden recounts this very story. Eden – designated as the realm of *Instinkt*,[39] by Schiller – is the place where Man once lived in primal unity with nature. But by tasting of the tree of knowledge Man lost his innocence, and thus, *felix culpa*, took the first step towards freedom from the merely sensual and instinctual by assuming the spiritual autonomy and dignity of ethical choice (Man's highest form of freedom, according to Rousseau and Kant). 'Ye shall be as Gods',[40] the serpent had promised Eve in tempting her to taste of the fruit of the Tree of Knowledge of Good and Evil, a foreshadowing of the divine aspirations of the later Enlightenment, thrice enjoined in *Die Zauberflöte* itself.[41]

But humankind longs for the greater wholeness lost when it sundered itself from nature to take control of its destiny and gain spiritual freedom. 'While we were still only children of nature we were happy, we were perfect: we have become free and we have lost both advantages. Hence a twofold and very unequal longing for nature: the longing for happiness and the longing for the perfection that prevails there,' writes Schiller in *Über naive und sentimentalische Dichtung*. 'The moment we begin to feel the oppression of culture, we experience the painful longing to go back home, and hear, far off in the alien country of art, the moving voice of the mother,' he continues,[42] warning against the siren voices that delude us into belief that we can be drawn back to lost nature. 'The name of my mother rings sweetly to me!', sings Pamina longingly to Sarastro when he announces his intentions to unite her with Tamino; 'It is she! It is she!' Her regressive longings are curtailed by Sarastro with necessary firmness. Lest we forget the necessity of the original expulsion, we are reminded by Kant of the angel with the flaming sword who bars man's path back to Eden: 'irresistibly compelling reason', which 'does not allow him to return into that condition of crudity and simplicity out of which it has dragged him'.[43]

Having gained its freedom and autonomy, Schiller tells us, humankind must nevertheless regain some higher restoration of its lost unity with nature, to redeem the disjunctions between need and desire, necessity and freedom in a time when, in the words of Schelling, 'there will no longer be any difference between the world of thought and the world of reality'.[44] (The agonizing sense of reason's separation from nature had led Rousseau to deplore the 'tyranny of reflection'.)[45] To attain this Schiller insists that man must overcome the fragmentation of his faculties which has taken place in modern society (and will increasingly take place in a technical, industrial society) by rediscovering and reconstructing his own original unity of being.[46] Through materialism the modern age has simply re-subjected itself to nature, and for a second time 'must emancipate itself from the blind forces of Nature'. But this will only be done by a 'return to her simplicity, truth and fullness' that bears in mind the highest ideals of nature, and preserves the spirituality of man.[47]

THE THREE TEMPLES

This process is charted in *Die Zauberflöte*. Arriving at the threshold of his quest, Tamino is confronted by three Temples: The Temple of Wisdom, the Temple of Nature and the Temple of Reason. Seeking to enter in turn the temples of Reason and Nature, Tamino is repulsed by strange voices from within which sternly command him to go back. Why, we must wonder, is Tamino repulsed from the Temples of Nature and Reason, the twin deities of the Enlightenment, consistently symbolized in Enlightenment thought by the tutelary deities of Sarastro's kingdom (to which Tamino now seeks entry), the gods Isis and Osiris?[48] The answer is that Tamino cannot attain progressive wisdom through either nature or reason on their own. In Schiller's history, the shallow reason of Enlightenment culture is not adequate to the task of educating Man. And knowledge of the inner truth of nature cannot be attained through scientific reason alone (as Born and his disciples had believed). Nature 'scorns an inadequate student', explained Goethe; 'mere empirical intelligence cannot reach her'.[49] Kant reminds us that graven on the Temple of Isis ('Mother Nature') is the inscription, 'No mortal has raised the veil from my face.'[50]

But neither can Man attain knowledge of nature by returning to the pre-lapsarian, pre-conscious stages of development, or by seeking illicit access to the hidden secrets of nature. Tamino at the three temples is therefore like Goethe's Faust who, wearied in his efforts to attain knowledge through rational, instrumental enquiry (the Temple of Reason) rejects science and philosophy in hope of gaining direct access to the Life Spirit itself. Turning to magic, he summons the Spirit of Earth, the force by which the spirit of the Deity is clothed in the life of nature (the Temple of Nature). But Faust is repulsed by the Earth Spirit: 'The mighty Spirit spurned my weak despair/ And Nature closed to me her sacred doors,'[51] and left to embark upon his journey of self discovery. Similarly, in *his* quest for knowledge, Tamino is turned away from the Temples of Reason and Nature, and is received instead at the Temple of Wisdom (entering perhaps through what Blake called the 'doors of perception'),[52] the point of access to the higher reintegration of reason with nature which human- kind seeks.

Men, Schiller writes in the *Aesthetic Education*, 'must fall away from Nature by the abuse of Reason before they can return to her by the use of Reason.'[53] Hence Isis and Osiris preside over the temple as symbols of nature and reason reunited. The final tests that Tamino and Pamina have to undertake are the tests of fire and water, believed by the Egyptians (according to Born) to have been the primary elements in the creation of the universe.[54] Tamino has already undergone and passed the tests of reason. He was forced to withstand the temptations of the Three Ladies, and, like Orpheus (who failed) to resist Pamina and her pleas for acknow- ledgement of her love. (As Tamino withstands his cruel test of reason, Papageno – natural man – significantly longs to be 'back in my straw hut or in the forest'.) Now Tamino must undergo the elemental test of nature; having first fallen away from nature through reason, he must now, fortified by reason, regain nature.

'Erkühne dich, weise zu sein,' enjoins Schiller[55] – 'Dare to be wise'; the later Enlightenment's retort to Kant's 'Sapere aude' ('Dare to know'), in *Was ist Aufklärung?* And Tamino accordingly re-enacts the quest for harmonious wholeness through wisdom. It is no longer an outer journey of education for the good citizen, but an inner journey towards a spiritual goal. Novalis's unfinished novel *Die Lehrlinge zu Sais* ('The Apprentices at Sais', 1798–9), one of many *Zauberflöte*-like Egyptian initiatory stories of the 1790s, is set in the Temple of Isis at Sais. Under the guidance of a Sarastro-like old master, one of the initiates in search of wisdom finally succeeds in reaching the statue of the goddess Isis. 'He lifted the veil of the goddess at Sais. But what did he see? He saw – marvel of marvels – himself.'[56] Nature is not outside Man; Man is a part of nature, and her spiritual secrets therefore lie within himself. 'So long as you look at outer things simply as a reasoning being, you must deny the existence of God,' said Rudolf Steiner in explaining the ancient mysteries; 'for God is hidden from the senses . . . God lies spellbound in the world and you need His own power to find Him. You must awaken that power in yourself.'[57] 'The mysterious way leads inwards,' wrote Novalis.[58]

THE SEARCH FOR DIVINITY

Die Zauberflöte celebrates the spirituality of humankind, and its search for spiritual fulfilment within life. Much of its symbolism is drawn from the Gnostic theory of the immanence of the divine spark of eternal light in matter. 'Is God then in matter?' asks the Gnostic pupil of Hermes Trismegistus, the mythical Egyptian sage to whom were attributed the greatest powers of esoteric wisdom in antiquity. Trismegistus explains, in terms of apparent paradox, that 'the intellect is drawn from the very substance of God; and so some men are Gods, and their humanity is near to divinity'.[59]

Gnosticism as a form of religious belief flourished in the Mediterranean basin during the early centuries of Christianity, and was based on a fusion of hellenistic and Eastern cultures, elements of neo-Platonism (the mystical interpretation of Plato which flourished in the third century), dualism and Eastern mysticism that we now know to have been present in early Christianity itself. Foremost among the principles of Gnosticism is that Man is a spiritual being whose origins derive from a heavenly sphere, and who is trapped in the world of matter from which his soul seeks to escape back to the spiritual realm of goodness and light, where he can regain the unity he once enjoyed with the Primal Being. The first stage in that quest is the attainment of knowledge, or Gnosis, which enables us to recognize the divine particle of light within us, and to strive for fulfilment of our higher spiritual nature. Among the common symbols of Gnostic and mystic–neo-Platonic belief are those of life itself as spiritual death; of the journey through life as a series of trials, in which Man seeks to rid himself his enslavement to matter; and of mankind's search for spiritual unity, in which the conflicting elements in its nature must be reconciled to attain wholeness. (The original meaning of individual, we should remember, is 'indivisible'.)

Gnosticism placed great emphasis upon internal truth, and upon personal rather than collective redemption; an apt system of belief for late eighteenth-century Germany. The symbols of Gnosticism are plainly evident in the *Die Zauberflöte*. Mired in the sensual world of matter at the outset of the story, Tamino begins his spiritual journey when he enters the portals of wisdom (gnosis) and, passing through the dark bowels of the earth, begins to slough off his gross material body to attain the light and perfection of the divinity inherent in his humanity. His upward journey is counterposed by the sedentary course of Papageno through the opera.

Papageno is a *Naturmensch*, as he describes himself, but not in the sense of Rousseau's noble savage – quite the opposite. Asked by Tamino (who is not quite sure whether the birdman he encounters is actually human)[60] how he lives, Papageno replies, 'Through eating and drinking'. As material man, satisfying no more than his basic animal needs, Papageno is a harmless Don Giovanni, a comic lover of the earthly pleasures of food and drink and women, happily splashing around in the swamps of his sensual desires.[61] 'I am not interested in Wisdom' he claims, honestly; 'I am a natural man, quite satisfied with sleep [the condition of Gnostic ignorance], food and drink; and if it were possible to catch a pretty wife . . .' When asked how he keeps himself, he replies, 'durch tausch' – through exchange; he is therefore also *homo oeconomicus*, capitalist man, whose instant response on learning that there are people living outside his own region is that it offers possibilities for 'Spekulation'. For his lack of spiritual enlightenment Papageno is told that he deserves 'to spend the rest of your life in the darkest clefts of the earth . . . You will never know the heavenly joys of the initiated.' He is undeterred. Given the choice of earthly renunciation or having to promise his hand to a hideous old crone, he chooses the latter.

SPIRITUAL MARRIAGE

Tamino, on the other hand, chooses the spiritual path, symbolized by spiritual marriage. Kierkegaard notoriously complained of *Die Zauberflöte* that since marriage was the ultimate expression of the sphere of the ethical, it was unsuitable as a subject for the sensual art of which Mozart was master. For this reason, he believed (as did Schopenhauer, who was equally blind to the opera's spiritual messages, and subjected it to a curiously *biedermeier* interpretation)[62] that *Die Zauberflöte*, as an allegory of marriage, was inferior to Mozart's erotic comedies.[63] In *Die Zauberflöte* marriage is no longer the complex classical ideal of social integration of *Le nozze di Figaro*; it is a symbolic union, a consummation of the desired reunion of all the wrongly separated elements of life: matter and spirit, masculine and feminine, God and the world, Christ and his Church. Even Monostatos – he who stands alone – knows the longing for reunion: man with woman, black with white. 'To live for ever without a wife would be truly hellfire.' Hell is separation and exclusion, but reunion cannot be gained – as he attempts – through rape.

In the duet 'Bei Männern', sung by Papageno and Pamina after Papageno has rescued Pamina from the lascivious advances of Monostatos (the embodiment of Pamina's pre-social sexual desires), the new spiritual ideal of marriage is gently celebrated. This simple hymn to the power of love, so childishly naïve, and yet in its innocence resembling the wide-eyed wisdom of a child, should – we might think – belong to Tamino and

Pamina. But although it is a dramatically inapposite moment to introduce a homily to love and marriage (Papageno and Pamina ought to be fleeing for their lives), Schikaneder and Mozart clearly wished that it should occur at a moment at which it could sung by a couple who are not romantically involved, to make it clear that this is a statement of a spiritual, and not a romantic (far less an erotic), ideal of love.

The duet starts with a simple apostrophizing of love by Pamina and Papageno in turn. But in Pamina's first line, 'In men who know the feeling of love a good heart cannot be lacking', the love that is celebrated is not Eros, to whom Belmonte or the Countess sang, the god who sustains harmony in the world through erotic attraction, but rather, a love more like a Platonic force in the *Symposium* which leads man to the perfection of truth and beauty that is God. In the final section of the duet, this sweetly ill-matched pair sing together of the 'higher purpose' of love – its transcendent purpose – which is to lead to the spiritual union of man and woman, nature and spirit. Mozart's humble ditty appended to a letter to his father just after his own marriage to Constanze, *Mann und Weib ist ein leib*[64] is now elevated to spiritual heights: 'Mann und Weib and Weib und Mann / Reichen an die Gottheit an', Pamina's vocal line twice soaring to transport the simple melody to its higher level of aspiration. Through spiritual union will man and woman transcend their earthly ties and 'attain divinity'. Significantly, Mozart made a small alteration in Schikaneder's text when he set it to music; originally, Schikaneder had written 'Reichen an die *Götter* an'. Mozart's alteration implies not simply that men and women will aspire to reach the gods, but that they will attain divinity itself.[65]

The spiritual symbolism of marriage is confirmed in the following scene, in which, having knocked at the Temple of Wisdom, Tamino is greeted by the guardian of the gate, the Speaker, with whom he engages in a series of questions and answers which replicate the masonic catechism of admission to the lodge. The melodic and harmonic climax (and the conclusion of the scene) comes when Tamino is finally told by the Speaker, in a phrase of compassionate beauty that continues to echo through the following scene, that the truth he seeks will be revealed to him 'as soon as friendship's hand leads you into the shrine, for everlasting union [*Band*]'. The term *Band* is ambiguous; it may literally mean band, to refer to the brotherhood of the temple.[66] But it can also refer to the eternal bond or union of marriage. The fulfilment of Tamino's quest, which began when he fell in love with the portrait of Pamina (again a symbol of a non-erotic, ideal love, or even simply a transcendent spiritual ideal that lifts him out of the quagmire of his material senses) depends upon union with Pamina. Denied entry to the Temple at this moment by the Speaker, Tamino is subsequently accepted for initiation only when he finally meets Pamina and is presented as an applicant with her.

Rousseau saw marriage as an ideal union of the complementary principles of reason and feeling, an image taken up by Kant, who suggested that 'In matrimonial life the united pair should, as it were, constitute a single moral person, which is animated and governed by the understanding of the man and the feeling of the wife'.[67] But in spiritual terms this union of complementary opposites becomes, as Jung pointed out, the search for wholeness; a restoration of the androgynous unity that was believed to have prevailed in the cosmos before the Fall. (We recall Blake's description of Man's 'fall into Division and his Resurrection to Unity'.)[68] 'It is by means of Unity that each one shall find himself again,' one Gnostic text tells us; 'By means of a Gnose, he shall purify himself of diversity with a view to Unity, by devouring the matter within himself like a flame, Obscurity by Light and Death by Life.'[69] A second marital symbol, also common to Gnosticism, is of material Man's reunification with the spirit; of Man's discovery of his own spiritual being, and of what one theologian once called 'the union of ineffable godhead with humanity'.[70]

THE IDEALIZED WOMAN

In the mystical view of marriage, the role of the woman – Pamina in *Die Zauberflöte* – takes on a new spiritual dimension that must be properly understood if we are not to end up talking nonsense about Mozart's advocacy of female equality or masonic membership for women. Pamina is indeed Tamino's guide and, having accompanied him through the trials of fire and water, is received with him in the Temple of the Sun. But the symbolism precludes any crass social interpretation, for the spiritual idealization of Pamina here is a clear fulfilment of the eighteenth century's moral idealization of women. As we have seen (pp. 111–115), the adoration of women as bearers of moral virtue is repressive rather than liberating, and consigns women to restricted spheres of activity, burdening them with responsibility for both the guilt and redemption of society.[71] Women, wrote one remarkably percipient eighteenth-century (male) feminist, 'are oppressed and adored'.[72]

If, as many commentators have insisted, women provide the moral centre of gravity in so many of Mozart's operas, it must not therefore be taken as evidence of feminist sensibility. Indeed, it was precisely this adoration of the supposed feminine virtues which roused the greatest of eighteenth-century feminists, Mary Wollstonecraft, to argue that if women were to attain true autonomy and maturity they must, on the contrary, be expected to exercise exactly the same moral virtues as men. Women should be 'considered not only moral but rational creatures',[73] she demanded, and should refuse to accept the passive moral roles thrust upon them by male society.

The repressive adoration of women is invariably accompanied by a dualistic attitude, hinted at in Lovelace's fatal obsession with testing whether Clarissa ('most light') is angel or woman,[74] or Alfonso's question whether Fiordiligi and Dorabella are 'women or goddesses?', a dualism that perpetuates the age-old images of woman as either saint or sinner, Virgin or Magdalen, on the pedestal or in the gutter. This explains the problem over which so many commentators have laboured in *Die Zauber-flöte*. On the one hand we are offered the portrayal of Pamina, who is not only allowed to undergo initiation as an equal to Tamino, but who even leads him through the final tests of fire and water. On the other, we are confronted with the crass anti-feminism of the portrayal of the Queen and her Three Ladies, and by the typical masonic injunctions against women, issued by the Two Priests in Act II. There is no contradiction. *Die Zauberflöte* simply gives structural form to the Enlightenment's consistently dichotomous attitude to women: in the public sphere (as represented by the Queen and her Ladies in the opera) they are feared and denigrated, whilst in the private, domestic, moral and spiritual sphere they are idolized.

As so often, this dualism was given its most influential expression by Rousseau. Sophie, female victim of his educational programme for women to complement that of Emile, 'loves virtue . . . because it is a woman's glory and because a virtuous woman is little lower than an angel . . . because she sees nothing but poverty, neglect, unhappiness, shame, and disgrace in the life of a bad woman.'[75] Rousseau's belief, fuelled by his own manifest sexual fear of women, was that women were possessed of huge and malign power in society by virtue of the sexual and emotional hold that they had over men. In the public forum women were dangerous; they were too close to nature for society to allow them to partake of citizenship, and should be confined to the home.

In Act II of *Die Zauberflöte* the Queen tells Pamina how, before his death, Pamina's father had entrusted the emblem of the sun to the care of the priests of Isis, telling the Queen, 'Sarastro will be the manly guardian . . . These matters are not accessible to your woman's spirit. Your duty is to submit yourself, and also your daughter completely to the guidance of the Wise Men.' Sarastro warns Pamina as she tells him of her longing for her mother, 'A man must guide [leiten] your heart. For without that, every woman tends to overstep her sphere of influence.' In van Swieten's and Haydn's *Creation* Adam offers to guide Eve through life ('Ich leite dich'), and she in turn promises obedience and submission to his will. Eve guided by Adam attains bliss; Eve left to her own devices will bring damnation upon mankind. The highest aim to which a woman can aspire is to serve and love men; woman, according to Rousseau, is specially created for Man's delight,[76] and in this he is at one with the Church fathers ('for man is the beginning and end of every woman,' writes Aquinas, citing Augustine; 'as God is the beginning and end of every creature'.)[77] In the duet 'Bei Männern' Pamina, a princess, meekly listens while the dolt Papageno asserts that 'sharing their [men's] sweet desires is then the first duty of womanhood'. One of Schikaneder's verses which Mozart omitted from the final text is that sung to Papagena by the Three Boys:

> Komm her, du holdes, liebes Weibchen!
> Dem Mann sollst du dein Herzchen weihn!
> Er wird dich lieben, süsses Weibchen,
> Dein Vater, Freund, und Bruder seyn!
> Sey dieses Mannes Eigenthum!

[Come here, you gracious, lovely woman!/ To man should you consecrate your heart!/ He will love you, sweetest woman,/ Will be your father, friend and brother!/ Be the property of this man!]

Was this too much even for Mozart to stomach? Or did musical considerations dictate the excision?[78] Sarastro himself makes it clear that Pamino's role in the opera is to serve Tamino's spiritual enlightenment: 'The gods have dedicated Pamina, the gentle maiden, to the youth'.

Rousseau's views on women were widely held, in particular in Germany. Goethe's anti-feminism is notorious. 'If she wants to read, surely she can choose a cookbook,'[79] was his comment on the question of female education. Although he abandoned the earlier Enlightenment's simplistic equation of sexual and moral virtue, the stereotypes remain. Gretchen in *Faust* is both sinner and saint – the fallen woman who at the end of the story redeems Faust; a successful Donna Elvira. Goethe's other female characters are generally passive bearers of moral integrity in societies that are morally confused and socially disturbed: his Iphigenia, like Pamina herself, is prepared to die for her gospel of truth amidst the savage Taureans. In *Die Wahlverwandschaften* Ottolie brings moral equilibrium to a restless society by an act of selfless renunciation; like Clarissa, she dies of no observable outward symptoms. Goethe himself, through his platonic relationship with Charlotte von Stein in the 1780s, became obsessed with the notion of self-improvement through ideal relationships.

Goethe's Rousseauvian dualism is to be found just as clearly in Schiller, many of whose poems combine lofty humanitarian sentiments with the cheapest anti-feminist jibes. The most famous of all Schiller's poems, the *Ode to Joy*, is clearly addressed to the male reader, and exhorts the man 'blessed with a good wife' to be joyful.[80] Alxinger and Blumauer are also drearily predictable when they come to write about women, with knowing nudges and winks about the untrustworthiness and fickleness of women set alongside encomiums to their domestic virtues and their tender nurturing of men from birth to grave.[81] Blumauer's poem *Lied der Freiheit* warns against the numerous snares which tempt men from freedom. These include princely honours, the lure of gold, political power, and ... women.

> Wer unter eines Mädchens hand
> Sich also ein Sklave schmiegt,
> Und von der Liebe festgebannt
> In schnöden Fesseln liegt.
> Weh dem! der ist ein armer Wicht
> Er kennt die goldne Freyheit nicht.

[Woe to him who nestles as a slave under a maiden's hand, and lies fast bound in the vile fetters of love. He is a poor devil who knows not golden freedom.][82]

The verse is as commonplace as the sentiment. But Mozart was so taken with this poem that he set this particular stanza as a song – K.506.

It would have been difficult for Mozart not to have been influenced by Enlightenment attitudes to women. Like Rousseau and Goethe, he married a woman who, for all her admirable qualities, was renowned for her lack of intellectual or cultural sophistication, a sure indication of a difficulty in reconciling an idealized vision of womanhood with the reality of a woman as a sexual and domestic partner. Instead, Mozart entered into idealized troubadour-love relationships with his young (but slightly older than he) female patrons such as the Countess Thun and Baroness von Waldstätten. 'Dearest, best and loveliest of all, gilt, silvered and sugared, most valued and honoured gracious Lady Baroness!'[83] he addresses Baroness Waldstätten in a playful but unmistakable courtly love-letter. Revealingly, a couple of months later he wrote to his father warning him against having any further dealings with the Baroness and advising against the Salzburg musician Ignaz Finck taking up a position as tutor with the Baroness, 'as she wants to have someone for herself and not for her children ... Further, I should like you to realize that the words which I used, *herself – for herself,* imply a good deal.'[84] Surely the Baroness (who was separated from her husband, and was known for her flightiness) must have shocked the adoring but proper young composer by making a pass at him, thus shattering his angelic idealization of her?

Much of the anti-feminist poetry of Alxinger and Blumauer was specifically masonic. The masonic hostility to women is perhaps the most revealing indication of the Enlightenment's real attitude to the sex, for here was a society, dedicated to the propagation of truth and morality, which excluded women (along with madmen and children) as being unworthy to participate. The ostensible grounds for the exclusion were grossly trivial – that women could not be relied upon not to gossip about the craft's secrets, and that they seduced men from the path of rectitude. (The insatiable curiosity of women about freemasonry was a topic that provided the subject for a number of eighteenth-century comic dramas.)[85] The argument is unapologetically presented in the dismissive duet sung by the Two Priests in Act II of *Die Zauberflöte*, in which they warn Tamino and Papageno against the wiles of women. Guardians of Mozart's feminist conscience suggest that he set this particular duet in a deliberately perfunctory way to indicate his disapproval of the text. A far more effective way of indicating his disapproval would have been to have refused to have set the text at all – he left out some of the other more naïve sections of Schikaneder's libretto. In fact, the message of this brief duet is all too clearly confirmed when it is immediately followed by a scene in which the Three Ladies appear and attempt to practise precisely the deceits and wiles upon Tamino and Papageno about which they have just been warned, thus proving the soundness of the lesson administered by the Two Priests.

As a dramatist Mozart was incapable of engaging with a character in an opera without compassion and understanding. There is even something touchingly sad about the thwarted desires of Osmin and Monostatos. But we should not mistake Mozart's boundless empathy with the feminine characters in his operas for a feminist sensibility quite out of tune with his culture and age. The tendency to anti-feminist dualism in his portrayal of female characters is clear. The redemptive virtues of Ilia in *Idomeneo* are pitilessly contrasted with the dangerously uncontrolled and self-destructive passions of Elettra. In *Die Entführung* Blonde displays steadfastness as resolute as Konstanze's in defending her virtue against Osmin, but even as she does so she is giving Osmin lessons in the art of seduction, and employing the ingratiating and insinuating tones that echo an earlier, equally cynical, maidservant – Serpetta in *La finta giardiniera* – and can be heard from Despina in *Così fan tutte*. Bearing out the Rousseauvian male's worst fears, Blonde cheerfully warns Osmin that, whatever men may think, it is not women who are the slaves of men, but men who are enslaved by women. There is an unmistakable note of shrillness in Marcellina's catalogue of the indignities suffered by womankind in her Act IV aria in *Figaro*, in contrast to Susanna's more resourceful efforts to redress sexual injustices.

Pamina, on the other hand, the ideal of womanhood, is the spiritual partner of Tamino, his guide and muse. Simone de Beauvoir noted the many different manifestations of this idealized role:

Woman is Soul and Idea, but she is also a mediatrix between them: she is the divine Grace leading the Christian towards God, she is Beatrice guiding Dante in the beyond, Laura summoning Petrarch to the lofty summits of poetry. In all the doctrines that unify Nature and Spirit she appears as Harmony, Reason, Truth. The gnostic sects made wisdom a woman, Sophia, crediting her with the redemption of the world and even its creation.[86]

The image, of course, is of particular importance to the Romantics. In Hölderlin's classical novel *Hyperion* (1797), Diotima the hero's beloved, 'Beauty itself', assumes the Pamina role and shows Hyperion the way to 'the new kingdom of the new divinity',[87] and in Novalis's *Märchen* the hero Hyazinth leaves his mistress Rosenblute in order to seek Isis. When he finds her and lifts her veil, Isis is revealed to be none other, this time, than Rosenblute herself.

THE GNOSTIC TRADITION

The multi-layered symbolism of *Die Zauberflöte* reveals that Mozart and Schikaneder were clearly conversant with Gnostic traditions. The very opening of the opera recalls the Gnostic *Hymn of the Pearl* in which a Prince from the east (as Tamino is described in the text) arrives in Egypt to seek wisdom, and as a preliminary is forced to fight with a serpent.

Jung, who like Freud combined his medical activities with a wide-ranging literary erudition, recognized that in those aspects dedicated to the development of the human psyche there was much in Gnosticism which adumbrated his own understanding of the development and needs of the inner human personality. Knowing the works of Goethe well, and recognizing the Gnostic elements in so much of Goethe's work, Jung asked himself how so much obviously Gnostic symbolism could have survived into the eighteenth century. He found an answer when he chanced upon an old book of Alchemy, the study of which led him to realize that Alchemy had not simply been a form of primitive chemistry,[88] nor even merely the trade of hucksters claiming to possess the philosopher's stone which could turn base metals to gold (although there *were* many enough alchemists dedicated to turning muck into brass.) It was an elaborate spiritual system which drew upon ancient Gnostic, Cabbalistic and Hermetic esotericism, and in which the pursuit of the progressive purification of metals to attain gold was understood as a symbol of Man's quest for spiritual purification ('transform yourselves into living philosophical stones' was the injunction of one sixteenth-century alchemist).[89] To the alchemist the divine light was within all matter: 'It burns and is not seen, for it shines in a dark place. Every naturall Body is a kind of Black Lanthorn, it carries the Candle within it, but the light appears not, it is Ecklips'ed with the Grosseness of the matter,'[90] wrote Thomas Vaughan, brother of the poet Henry. The chemical *conjiuncto* of elements, the 'Chemical Wedding' as it was described in a text-book of seventeenth-century Rosicrucianism, was seen as a symbol of the union of the opposing elements in Man's soul.

Alchemy had provided one of the missing links between the traditions of Gnosticism and the late eighteenth century. Earlier Renaissance neo-Platonists such as Ficino and Pico della Mirandola had rediscovered and reinterpreted the texts of Cabbalism (the tradition of Jewish esoteric wisdom) and Hermeticism (the Gnostic wisdom of the sage Hermes Trismegistus, whom they believed to have lived in ancient Egypt before Plato and Moses – hence the establishment of the primacy of Egypt as the fount of esoteric wisdom; a far more important association for the authors of *Die Zauberflöte* than the earlier Enlightenment identification of Egypt as the seat of monotheism, science and rational morality). But it was in spiritual Alchemy, rather than in the more rarefied realms of renaissance neo-Platonism, that the symbolism of Gnosticism was most vividly kept alive.

From the detritus of a half-understood miscellany of magical symbolism later eighteenth-century German writers divined a spiritual programme. In Lessing's masonic dialogues *Ernst und Falk* the older and wiser interlocutor Falk restrains his younger, earnestly rational colleague's fulminations against the alchemical pursuits of mystical masons, making it clear that there is more to freemasonry than utilitarian social programmes and charitable deeds. We know that Goethe had immersed himself in alchemical tomes as a young man, and alchemical symbolism permeates his work.[91] *Faust* (in which Jung considered Alchemy to have reached its artistic and spiritual peak) contains a complete dictionary of alchemical references; but even the apparently realist novel *Die Wahlverwandschaften* derives its main premise from an alchemical theory, and is full of magical symbolic correspondences. Schiller's unfinished novel *Die Geisterseher* contains clear evidence that he too had studied the spiritual implications of Alchemy, traces of which recur in his *Aesthetic Education*. In England, Blake's extensive knowledge of Gnostic, alchemical, neo-Platonic and mystical writings is well established.

Among the mystics who influenced Blake most strongly was the mineralogist Emmanuel Swedenborg. It can be no coincidence that the greatest of the German Romantic mystical symbolists, Novalis, was also a mineralogist, for it seems clear that during the eighteenth century the apparently prosaic study of mineralogy and metallurgy entailed careful perusal of alchemical texts.[92] Both mineralogy and alchemy flourished in seventeenth- and eighteenth-century Vienna, a city famous (and later infamous) as a centre for alchemical studies far into the eighteenth century, and the most prominent mineralogist in late eighteenth-century Vienna was Ignaz von Born, who had an extensive knowledge of Alchemy as a quasi-scientific discipline. Born's study of Alchemy was most certainly not directed towards the occult, but precisely because scientists like Born had failed to penetrate the secrets of nature, others were ready to revisit Born's alchemical texts for different purposes.

THE ROSICRUCIAN ENLIGHTENMENT

Most significant of all as a source for the esoteric symbolism in *Die Zauberflöte* was the Rosicrucian freemasonry that Born and his colleagues at 'Zur wahren Eintracht' had so vehemently fought during the first half of the 1780s. Rosicrucianism had been founded in Regensburg in the 1750s[93] in a deliberately reactionary effort to counter the secular influence of Enlightened freemasonry and the prevalent materialism of the age. It soon attracted many who resented the egalitarian tendencies of the modern age: disappointed writers and artists convinced that society had failed to recognize their worth; impoverished aristocrats stripped of their recent feudal privileges; even rulers determined to restore the authority of hierarchy and faith. Frederick William II of Prussia, the reactionary nephew and heir of Frederick the Great (who succeeded his uncle in 1786) had been recruited to Rosicrucianism whilst Crown Prince, his shady recruiters Wöllner and Bischoffwerder subsequently becoming important ministers in his government.

Although historically unrelated to the esoteric Rosicrucian movements of the seventeenth century, eighteenth-century Rosicrucianism deliberately presented itself as the heir to the ancient occult wisdoms of the Hermeticists. But more specifically, Rosicrucianism set out to establish itself as an esoteric Christian freemasonry, and adopted many elements of Gnostic Christian and Jewish Cabbalistic esotericism. Much of the symbolism of Rosicrucianism was derived from the higher Scottish and Templar Grades of Revenge adopted by freemasonry when it reached the more status-conscious continent of Europe. The revenge in question, although sometimes linked to revenge for the Templar Grand Master Jean de Molnar, was primarily supposed to be for the murder of Hiram (also known as Adoniram in masonic lore, although they are two different characters in the biblical account), the master builder of Solomon's temple in Jerusalem, whose resurrection in masonic mythology was associated with the myths of the sun gods Osiris and Attis, and with Christ himself.

The apparent connection of Rosicrucianism with the revival of traditional Catholicism (of which Vienna was to become a centre in the early years of the nineteenth century) led many of the critics of Rosicrucianism like Nicolai to suggest that it was part of a larger Jesuit plot to regain influence throughout Europe. But in fact the aims of Rosicrucianism were ecumenical; its extremely covert agenda seems to have been to reunite the Christian religions under the banner of esoteric Christian freemasonry. This ideal was much in evidence at the end of the eighteenth century. One of its most famous literary expressions is Novalis's essay *Die Christenheit, oder Europa*. But in 1782 Joseph de Maistre, later to become the great voice of reactionary mystical Catholicism in post-Revolutionary Europe, proposed to the Wilhelmsbad Congress (convened in an attempt to sort out the arguments between all the different warring sects within German freemasonry) the formation of a secret masonic religion reuniting Christianity, and dedicated in its highest grades to the worship of the mystical NAME.[94] The mystical NAME, central to Cabbalism, reappears in the symbolism of *Die Zauberflöte* (see p. 307).

In Goethe's *Die Geheimnisse* (which also dates from 1782), the brotherhood to which the pilgrim Mark applies for admission is that of the world's twelve religions. The thirteenth member of the fraternity is called Humanus – *Anthropos* in the system of the great Christian Gnostic of the third century Valentinian; the original divine Man before the descent into matter; *Mensch* in Schiller's *Aesthetic Letters* and in the text of *Die Zauberflöte*. Humanus longs for release from all merely historical forms of religion, and finds this when the other faiths have found a common basis of understanding. Above the seat of Humanus in the *Parsifal*-like temple in which the mystic fraternity are enthroned is the mystic sign of the Rosicrucians: the cross adorned with a wreath of roses.[95]

Rosicrucianism had a strong following in Vienna. Count Dietrichstein, the Grand Master of all the lodges in the Habsburg territories and one of Mozart's most influential patrons, was well known as an active

Rosicrucian. Mozart's lodge 'Zur Wohltätigkeit' was, we have seen, a Catholic lodge. But when the Viennese lodges underwent their enforced amalgamations in 1786, twenty members of 'Zur Wohltätigkeit', including its Master Otto von Gemmingen and Mozart, cut off their close ties with their former sister lodge 'Zur wahren Eintracht' by uniting with another lodge, 'Zur gekrönte Hoffnung' (notorious for its Rosicrucian activities), to form a new lodge 'Zur neugekrönte Hoffnung'.[96] The reasons for the amalgamation are not hard to find. Despite its predominantly rational and practical religious predilections (increasingly questioned by the more spiritually minded), 'Zur Wohltätigkeit' had attracted a number of members also interested in the esoteric Christianity of Rosicrucianism. One of its most prominent and active members was Count Küfstein, Court Chancellor and amateur violinist who appears as a patron of Mozart on his 1784 subscription list. Küffstein was a keen Rosicrucian, and had formerly belonged to a lodge known to have been affiliated to another mystical Christian sect within German freemasonry known as the Chapter of Clermont.[97]

Gemmingen had been an ambassador in Regensburg, the centre of Rosicrucianism, before coming to Vienna, and provides us with further evidence for Mozart's own contact with esoteric pursuits. For Gemmingen was a member of an obscure masonic sect known as the Asiatic Brethren, founded in Berlin in 1780 by followers of the most prominent and respected Jewish *Aufklärer*, Moses Mendelssohn, and committed to reuniting Judaism and Christianity within freemasonry. In Vienna a group of Asiatic Brethren was established by Hans von Ecker und Eckhoffen, who had a particular interest in the Jewish mystical writings of the Cabbala.[98] The rituals of the Asiatic Brethren contained much that was drawn from the Cabbala, and the Brethren were condemned by Friedrich Münter as no better than the Rosicrucians.[99] An entry in the album of Mozart's fellow lodge-member Kronauer suggests that Mozart may himself have been an Asiatic Brother.[100]

A further member of Küffstein's former Chapter of Clermont lodge was Count Franz Joseph Thun, husband of Mozart's beloved Countess Wilhelmine Thun, and son of the dedicatee of Mozart's 'Linz' Symphony, Count Johann Joseph Thun, himself Grandmaster of the Bohemian Rosenkreuzer. Thun (described by Mozart as being 'peculiar')[101] was widely celebrated for his magical and alchemical studies; he was a well-known practising spiritual Mesmerist, and in 1787 a book recounting the Count's conversations with Gablidone, an emissary from the spirit world, was published, which contains a magnificent engraving as frontispiece depicting the Count amidst the symbols of his esoteric and magical crafts (see Plate 4.). (The lion lying in front of the mouth of a rocky cave is a common symbol for the higher grades of freemasonry.) One of the spirit Gablidone's prophecies is that the time is not far distant when a great revolution will banish the old religions from the earth and restore the true Kingdom of God.[102]

Count Thun had been a member of 'Zur wahren Eintracht' in the early 1780s, but after the masonic reform of 1785 he had, like Mozart, joined the Rosicrucian lodge 'Zur neugrekrönte Hoffnung'. A member of Mozart's former lodge 'Zur Wohltätigkeit' who is not recorded as a member of 'Zur neugekrönte Hoffnung' was Count Thun's son-in-law, Prince Karl Lichnowsky (later to be Beethoven's closest and most loyal patron). In 1789 Mozart travelled in the company of Lichnowsky to Berlin, where he was welcomed by the Rosicrucian monarch Frederick William II. The visit to Berlin has never been satisfactorily explained, and has always remained something of a mystery, since it was undertaken without professional engagements lined up, or prospects for an operatic commission in hand. 'The whole journey gives an improvised and perhaps even ill-considered impression,' writes one of Mozart's recent biographers.[103] The most likely explanation is that Lichnowsky and Mozart travelled to Berlin at Frederick William's invitation as Rosicrucian emissaries from Vienna.

Mozart himself gives a hint at Frederick William's particular interest in his visit in one of his letters to Constanze, written on the way to Berlin from Prague. 'Only a week ago Ramm left Prague to return home. He came from Berlin and said that the King had frequently and insistently enquired whether it was certain that I was coming to Berlin, as I had not yet appeared. He had said a second time: "I fear that he will not come at all".'[104] This was surely no ordinary musical trip.

It is very possible that the music-loving monarch (who had little else in common with his uncle) invited Mozart to Berlin to discuss Rosicrucian matters with him, and above all, the possibility of Mozart's writing an opera to promote the Rosicrucian cause. The king was perhaps not in a position to issue a commission to Mozart (although there is a hint in one of Mozart's letters from Berlin of mysterious financial dealings), and was able only to plant the seeds of the idea that eventually flowered in *Die Zauberflöte*. But shortly after Mozart's death Frederick William made a personal effort to give Constanze financial support by buying items from Mozart's estate, and four years later was to command that Constanze be given a benefit performance of *La clemenza di Tito*. Furthermore, in March 1792, only three months after Mozart's death, the king attempted to get *Die Zauberflöte* performed in Berlin. He sent the score to the director of the National Theatre for examination, and received the reply that the work would be incomprehensible to an audience 'ignorant of certain mysteries, and incapable of seeing through the dark and heavy veil of allegory'.[105] Unwilling to accept the verdict, the king betrayed his preternatural interest in the Rosicrucian allegory he may have inspired when he again pressed for it to be performed in May, with no success.

A ROSICRUCIAN ALLEGORY

Die Zauberflöte is littered with Rosicrucian and esoteric Christian symbolism. The title engraving for the first libretto of the opera, printed by Mozart's lodge brother Ignaz Alberti in 1791, shows a Hermes column and an ibis – the sacred bird of Hermes or Mercury: the symbols of Hermeticism. The print depicts a temple, and in the foreground, beside the tools of the operative masons' craft, can be seen the head and shoulders of a dead man: presumably the murdered temple builder Hiram/Adoniram, the Rosicrucian symbol for Christ. (Mozart himself is three times referred to as Adoniram in the masonic funeral oration presented at his lodge after his death.) From the arch of the temple itself hangs a chain with a five pointed star – the emblem of Rosicrucianism.

Throughout the opera too can be found an elaborate numerology that confirms the opera's relation to the higher degrees of mystical masonry, and in particular to Cabbalism, which was profoundly concerned with the mystic symbolism of numbers. At the end of the opera, Pamina and Tamino are acclaimed with the words 'Strength has overcome/and crowns as reward/Beauty and Wisdom/with its eternal diadem!' Beauty, Strength and Wisdom are the attributes of the highest degree of the higher Rituals of the Scottish Rites of Freemasonry, upon which Rosicrucians built their own system. Within the higher degrees, the thirtieth is the degree of Revenge (it is in Scene 30 that the Queen and her followers are banished to eternal night). The eighteenth degree is the degree of the *Sovereign Rose-Croix* itself, and the magic symbolism of the number eighteen recurs throughout the opera. For example, Sarastro first appears in Act I, scene 18; at the beginning of the second act, there are eighteen priests and eighteen chairs; Papagena announces that she is eighteen years old.[106]

The elaborate symbolism of the opera is a sure indication that *Die Zauberflöte* carries within it a Rosicrucian programme.[107] Schikaneder himself, although not a member of a masonic lodge in Vienna, had been involved in freemasonry while he was living and working in the Rosicrucian city of Regensburg (which Mozart visited on his way to Frankfurt in 1790). Although in Vienna he excelled in popular theatre, even his popular works often contained spiritual messages. *Die Luftballon* of 1786 uses the topical image of an ascent in a hot-air balloon as a symbol of escape from material problems to attain 'harmony of the soul'.[108] The work Schikaneder wrote immediately before *Die Zauberflöte* was another story drawn from Wieland's *Dschinnistan* collection, but its title, *Das Stein der Weisen*, is alchemical (as is the title of his sequel to *Die Zauberflöte*, *Das Labyrinth*).

The coded secrets of *Die Zauberflöte* are almost certainly those of esoteric Christianity, in which the sun worship which characterizes the opera must be understood as a symbol of the universal worship of Christ, manifested as both Osiris (the god of Sun and Reason) in the opera and Hiram/Adoniram in masonic symbolism. Interestingly, Thomas Paine believed that Christianity was 'a parody on the Sun and the twelve signs of the Zodiac, copied from the ancient religions of the eastern world',[109] and the French scholar Charles Dupuis also suggested in 1795 that Christ was a symbol for universal sun-worship.[110] Authority for the theories of esoteric Christianity could have been drawn from highly respectable sources, including works like Campanella's *Città del Sole* (a seventeenth-century Egyptian setting for the truths of universal Christianity), but also in the purposefully anti-mystical *Journal für Freymaurer*, which contains a learned article on esoteric Christianity and Gnosticism by Michaeler suggesting that early Christians had engaged in 'disciplini aracani'.[111]

In the esoteric, Gnostic Christian tradition in general, Christ is the redeemer who was sent to free humanity from its enslavement to matter; the bringer of spiritual grace who is sacrificed by God through his descent into matter bearing the divine spark which leads humanity out of its darkness. Material evil could not be eradicated on earth without the redeeming grace of Christ. Reminding us of Tamino's struggle with the serpent at the beginning of *Die Zauberflöte*, Blake explains the role of the Gnostic Christ in his *Everlasting Gospel*:

> And thus with wrath he did subdue
> The Serpent Bulk of Nature's dross,
> Till he had nailed it on the Cross.[112]

But *Die Zauberflöte* is also an allegory of a very specific tradition of Gnostic Christianity, the dualistic tradition in which Christ's grace redeems humanity not only from material subjection, but from the principle of evil in the universe – a principle which has, we should remember, no place in traditional Christianity, in which evil is attributed solely to man's earthly sinfulness. In recalling this particular strain of Gnosticism, *Die Zauberflöte* reveals itself very clearly as a post-Enlightenment opera.

THE RETURN OF EVIL

In March 1791, as Mozart was working on *Die Zauberflöte*, Pope Pius VI issued a papal brief in response to the events of the French Revolution in which, to counter the sacrilegious divinization of man in France, he reaffirmed the Catholic dogma of original sin. In relation to Catholic dogma, the Pope was asserting nothing new; but his intervention nonetheless marks a crucial moment in the European reaction against the Enlightenment, a reaction partly – but only partly – hastened by the French Revolution itself. For during the 1790s a succession of those who had brought the Enlightenment to its spiritual fulfilment in the 1780s – Kant, Goethe, Blake and Mozart – turned away from its progressive optimism and its belief in the possibility of social and ethical perfection, and began to reassert a belief in the reality of evil in the universe.

As we have seen (p. 64), the denial of original sin was one of the most fundamental tenets of Enlightenment faith, for it was upon this that the possibility of Man's self-improvement – moral, intellectual, social – was based. But by abolishing sin, Man had not eradicated human evil from the world. 'True, it is almost turned to a fairy tale,' says Goethe's Mephistopheles of the belief in his old incarnation, Satan, 'And yet mankind has failed to benefit – The Evil one is banned: evils prevail.'[113]

The *philosophes*, in particular the early Rousseauist communists Morelly and Mably, had attributed what Man dubs evil to the malign effects of property, power and ignorance. Laclos, a good Rousseauist, attributed the hideous malevolence of his anti-hero and anti-heroine in *Les liaisons dangereuses* to the corruption of society, thus specifically denying the existence of metaphysical evil or sin.[114] But in his late essay of 1793 entitled *Religion within the Limits of Reason Alone*, Kant argued that wickedness was not simply faulty behaviour (a falling away from good, as traditional Christianity had taught) or the result of ignorance or social decadence. Evil, like good, is an absolute condition, and those who act wickedly do so out of evil volition. The realms of good and evil, of light and darkness, Kant tells us, must be understood to be 'separated from each other by an immeasurable gulf'.[115]

Kant's extraordinary late change of heart regarding evil (condemned by Goethe as a retreat into unwarranted metaphysics) reflects a European-wide change of consciousness around the year 1790. It is especially apparent in works of art. So certain had been most eighteenth-century artists of the unreality of evil that they relished the representation of apparent evil for the pleasure of showing how easily it could be overcome. Hence the popularity of the Gothic horror novel. But Coleridge, at work in the 1790s on a never-completed epic poem called *The Origins of Evil*, objected strongly to the complacent rationalizations of the doyenne of the genre, Mrs Radcliffe.[116] And in Matthew Lewis's *The Monk* (1796), perhaps the masterpiece of the genre, every one of Mrs Radcliffe's careful rationalizations is deliberately flouted. The novel is full of gruesome and manifestly real evil, and flaunts a real-life demon. In a very different anti-Gothic novel of the 1790s, Jane Austen's *Northanger Abbey* (1798), its naïve heroine is disabused of her morbid fantasies (stimulated by reading too many Gothic novels) only to discover that real, if less glamorous, evils lurk within ordinary human behaviour. General Tilney, exonerated of the lurid crime in Catherine's imagination of murdering his wife, proves himself to be a far more realistic monster: a tyrannical father and ruthlessly unmannerly host who cruelly ejects his young guest when it no longer suits him to entertain her.

This shift in the Gothic novel of the 1790s can be directly charted in the work of one artist. Goya, the supporter of the Spanish Enlightenment, underwent a severe crisis during the French Revolution, and his paintings and etchings thenceforth became darker and more bitter. The great series of etchings called the *Caprichos* are the work of a rationalist bewildered and confused by the irrationality of the world around him. At the spectacle of such ignorance, superstition, sloth, deception and gullibility Goya found it increasingly difficult to regard the 'impossible monsters' bred by the sleep of reason as beyond possibility. In the late series of haunting images that Goya painted on the walls of his house, one becomes persuaded that the phantoms and demons of his imaginary world are as real as the human misery of the real world.

For many former Enlightenment thinkers the only tolerable explanation for the failure of so many Enlightenment projects was the presence of metaphysical evil, a force at work in the world to counter and foil the efforts of reason, light and progress. Paradoxically, restoration of belief in evil was, for some, the necessary adjunct to any belief in progress at all. If the forces of progress had failed, it was because they had underestimated the active agency of evil in the cosmos; education and exhortation to virtue would not be enough. Those who sought progress would just have to redouble their efforts and combat evil at its sources – which were beyond the reach of social reform or political action. These attitudes emerge in the Enlightenment's changing use of its favourite metaphor of light and darkness.

THE METAPHOR OF LIGHT AND DARKNESS

In their use of the symbolism of light and darkness the seventeenth-century rationalists borrowed the Christian metaphor of 'the light of faith' and turned it to their own ends. Reason was the beacon or candle used to dispel the darkness, and light was a tool, a means to an end, rather than the end itself. Meanwhile, Newton had denied the ontological existence of darkness in his *Opticks*, where he argued that darkness was simply absence of light. The idea that darkness was evil and was something to be feared, Locke argued, was not innate; it was developed in the human being through suggestion and experience.[117] In van Swieten's and Haydn's *The Creation*, darkness as a force is banished once and for ever by God's light. Van Swieten specifically asked that the words 'And there was light', sung by the chorus with an explosion of C-major joy on the word 'light', should be sung only once; the struggle is not infinitely repeatable.[118] From henceforth any moments of shadow which fall over humankind occur only when God himself turns his face away. Pezzl dismissed the biblical account of the creation altogether, objecting that it gave a metaphysical priority to darkness which Enlightened Man could not accept.[119].

By 1801, when *The Creation* was written, such innocent faith had been long out of fashion. Goethe, who obstinately considered his revision of Newton's *Opticks* to be his most important work, argued that darkness had its own independent existence that could not be banished by light. Darkness continues to exist within light, evidence of the indwelling (and Goethe believed necessary) principle of negation in life.[120] In the 1790s darkness and light often represented absolute principles, the real states of metaphysical good and evil. And as such we must interpret their symbolic use in *Die Zauberflöte*. In Mozart's earlier operas the symbol of night and darkness had provided a cover for deception and confusion. Sometimes it even prompted honesty and revelation; but it carried no moral or metaphysical implication (just as it was difficult to characterize Don Giovanni as morally 'evil'). But when in *Die Zauberflöte* Tamino, at the profoundest point of his ignorance and despair, having been repulsed in his quest for enlightenment by the Speaker, sings 'O endless night, when will you vanish?/ When will my eyes find the light?' his words are set in the key of A minor, the key furthest removed from the opera's central masonic key of E flat major. Night and darkness are the conditions of absolute distance and exclusion from revelation and wisdom.

THE DUALISTIC COSMOS

Night and darkness in *Die Zauberflöte* must therefore be overcome; evil must be banished from the cosmos – an infinitely repeated process which has to take place in each individual as he or she follows the path to spiritual wisdom. A long way from Goethe's wise acceptance of the dialectical reality of evil in nature, the metaphysics of *Die Zauberflöte* partake of a particular strain of dualistic Gnosticism which perceives evil as an absolute principle at work to destroy the cosmos.

Three major versions of the Gnostic system may be discerned, which traverse a course from optimism to pessimism. In the optimistic (and Goethean, pantheist) version, every particle of matter contains a spark of divine light; 'the earth lives, moves, with a divine life, the stars are living divine animals, the sun burns with a divine power, there is no part of Nature which is not good, for all are part of God', one such Gnostic text tells us.[121] The salvation of human beings occurs when they recognize that divine spark in themselves and in creation. Pessimistic Gnosticism has been ascribed to the third century Persian prophet Mani, founder of the religion of Manichaeism (itself based upon the more ancient Persian Zoroastrian system). In this system all matter is considered to be irredeemably evil, and the only course for Man as a spiritual being lost in the quagmire of material evil lies in asceticism, denial and renunciation (or sometimes, in total, abandoned acceptance of the earthly and sensual).

All this was recounted with some scholarly knowledge in an anonymous article in Born's *Journal für Freymaurer*, 'Über die Magie der alten Perser und die Mithraischen Geheimnisse',[122] which tells of the light of wisdom believed to have arisen in the Orient before the Greeks. Discussing the two commonly accepted forms of Zoroastrianism, the author notes that the optimistic form of Zoroastrianism was adopted by the Cabbalists, Gnostics and neo-Platonists, in their belief that 'A time will come in which [the divine spark] released through the work of fire [as in Tamino and Pamina's trial, but also in the grace of the alchemical Christ], will regain its original freedom, and be united with the general cosmos'. The second, pessimistic form, the Manichaean belief that matter is entirely evil, the author dismisses as being not properly Zoroastrian. Instead, in true Zoroastrianism the presence of evil in the universe is attributed to Abrimen (or, more usually, Ahriman) the evil demi-urge who created and holds in his thrall the material universe, and who is locked in perpetual conflict with Orzmund, the cosmic principle of light: 'Good and Evil, Light and Obscurity, are in constant battle until the end of finite time.'[123] As Joseph Campbell has written of the Zoroastrian theogony, Ahriman was understood as 'the active power of darkness – not the mere absence of light, but a sucking void that drew things down into chaos, insatiable as the bottomless pit, and warring continually against the principle of light'.[124] In the masonic article referred to above the writer discusses the common variants of the name of the prophet Zoroaster – including names such as 'Zerrtoschtro' from which the name of Sarastro is clearly derived.[125]

303

The presence of Zoroaster as Sarastro in *Die Zauberflöte* tells us that the struggle between the Queen of Night and the Priests of the Temple of the Sun must be read as a metaphysical struggle between the primal forces of evil and good. This is not as obvious as it might seem. Not only, as we have seen, was the reality of evil not a common Enlightenment belief, but as Jung constantly reminded his readers, the archetypes of the human psyche and of world myth are properly morally ambivalent: they can be put to use for both good and ill. The regressive mother archetype represented by the Queen of Night is not in itself evil, yet the Queen of Night must undoubtedly be seen as a symbol of evil in the opera. After her first appearance as grieving mother she is revealed to be a force of the greatest malignancy against whom all the powers of reason and light have to be directed. 'I know everything,' Sarastro tells Pamina, making the Queen's cosmic ambitions clear. 'I know that she is roaming in the underground vaults of the Temple and plots revenge against me and mankind.'

After the Queen has attempted to incite Pamina to murder Sarastro, Pamina pleads with Sarastro to spare her mother punishment. Sarastro's response (prefaced with a gently ironic 'You shall see how I revenge myself on your mother') is his noble aria 'In diesen heil'gen Hallen', Mozart's last and most consoling vision of mankind reconciled in mutual love and forgiveness: 'In these sacred halls we know no revenge . . . for we forgive our enemies.' The opera at this moment promises, therefore, to follow the central Mozartian progression from vengeance to forgiveness; from the 'hellish vengeance' against Sarastro which 'boils in the heart' of the Queen of Night, expressed in a classic vengeance aria in D minor (the key of Elettra's aria in *Idomeneo*, and the duet between Anna and Ottavio in *Don Giovanni*), to the reconciliation of love and forgiveness – the core of Mozart's vision of Christian Enlightenment.

But the opera does not end with forgiveness, whatever Sarastro may preach. It ends with the Queen and her followers being consigned to eternal night in a Last Judgement scene to match the description of the downfall of the rebel angels in *The Creation*, or the images of Hell conjured by Mozart in the Requiem. There is only one possible explanation: ultimately, there can be no reconciliation with evil.

In the dialogue with the Speaker Tamino is told, conventionally enough according to masonic principles, that he is debarred from entering the Temple of Wisdom because he is driven by death and vengeance. But in the opening scene of Act II it is revealed that Tamino's success in the trials of initiation will strengthen the secret order, and will reward virtue and punish the vices [*Laster*] represented by the Queen. The prerogative to punish evil overrides the renunciation of vengeance. What right have we as mortals, Dostoievsky asked, to undertake to forgive the crimes of others? Even if the sin has been committed against ourselves, it remains outside our power to forgive crimes. According to Dostoievsky, forgiveness is a moral outrage; it is itself a violation of the categories of good and evil.[126] For Sarastro not to punish Monostatos for attempting to rape Pamina would be to offend justice. Good and evil must remain implacably opposed, locked in everlasting struggle. Hence all allegories of the fight between good and evil, whether they be *Die Zauberflöte*, *Star Wars* or *Superman*, give rise to sequels. Cosmic evil will never be conclusively expunged from the universe until the end of recorded time; it always survives to fight another day.

The reinstatement of the principle of evil in late Enlightenment thought implies a retreat from worldly solutions to human and social problems – an acceptance of the ineluctable nature of evil in the universe that demands new strategies of confrontation. 'Wise men will apply their remedies to vices, not to names,' writes Burke, the champion of the 1790s New Right, in 1791; 'to the causes of evil, which are permanent, not to the occasional organs by which they act, and the transitory modes in which they appear.'[127] For Blake the struggle with the permanent causes of evil is a spiritual rather than a material battle, and cannot be undertaken through merely earthly morality. 'Many Persons, such as Paine and Voltaire, with some of the ancient Greeks, say *we will not converse concerning Good and Evil; we will live in Paradise and Liberty.* You may do so in Spirit, but not in the Mortal Body as you pretend, till after the Last Judgement.'[128]

By 1791 the experience of Mozart and his contemporaries in Austria had made him well aware, like Blake, of the inadequacy of material social reform and of the shallowness of the Enlightenment's secularized ethical systems, religious or otherwise. In a telling letter to Constanze of July 1791 Mozart writes with heavy irony (lost when, as usual, quoted out of context) of virtues which he would once have held supreme. Encouraging Constanze to repay a debt (part of a private and impenetrable joke) with a few boxes on the ear, he continues, 'For I maintain that kindness cures everything, that magnanimous and forbearing conduct has often reconciled the bitterest enemies.'[129] When Tamino's qualifications for undergoing the trials of initiation are considered by the priests it is announced that he is 'virtuous and beneficent'. But these admirable social virtues, once the highest ideals of the Enlightenment, are now merely the preconditions for the spiritual journey Tamino must make.

In the Quintet in the first scene of *Die Zauberflöte*, Tamino and Papageno are given the magic flute and bells by the Three Ladies, companions to the Queen of Night, and are told of the Three Boys who will guide them on their way. How the Queen came to have possession of the flute, whose beneficent powers are so agreeably advertised by the Ladies, is explained later by Pamina; it was cut from the roots of an oak tree by Pamina's father, the original guardian of the emblem of the sun, which is now in Sarastro's care (to ensure that it did not fall under the malign power of the Queen). The Three Boys are, as Northrop Frye explains, the natural spirits of romance tales 'who elude the moral antithesis of heroism and villainy ... as servants or friends of the hero, they impart the mysterious rapport with nature that so often marks the central figure of romance'.[130] But more problematic is that the Ladies, before bestowing the gifts, issue a moral homily to truth, of which it is impossible not to approve. Papageno has been punished by the Ladies, for lying to Tamino in claiming that he had killed the serpent, by having his mouth sealed with a padlock. Having freed Papageno, the Ladies join with him and Tamino in singing, 'If all liars were to receive such a padlock over their mouths! Then instead of hate, calumny, and black rancour, love and brotherhood would reign.'

How can we reconcile the fact that this admirable sentiment issues from the mouths of three characters who later in the opera are revealed to be themselves incomparably deceitful and untrustworthy? Must we resort to the old story of the change of plan half way through the opera? Not if we recognize that the sentiment is inadequate, if not downright wrong. If every liar received a padlock on his mouth, hate and rancour would most certainly not change to love and brotherhood, as the pious nursery-rhyme claims. The imposition of padlocks (censored newspapers, secret police surveillance, abolition of public meetings) does nothing to guard against the chaos (itself identified as the root of moral evil in many cosmological systems; one of the mottoes of the higher thirty-third masonic Grade is 'ordo ab chaos') that threatened Mozart's society. Only when a moral virtue such as truth comes from within the individual – as it suddenly, ecstatically comes to the fleeing Pamina when she is confronted by Sarastro and passionately vows to tell rather than conceal the truth – does it carry any power to confront and vanquish evil. (Pamina's line that she must tell 'the truth, even if it were a crime' is somewhat baffling. How can it be a crime to tell the truth? One explanation is to interpret the line to mean 'even if the deed about which she must be truthful [her escape] were a crime'. But in his essay 'On Telling a Lie for Benevolent Motives' Kant explains how the other meaning is not self-contradictory: telling a lie is always, categorically, wrong – even

if the truth involves telling a potential murderer where his victim is –
since we can never be fully cognisant of all of the possible outcomes of
our deeds.)[131]

THE ROSICRUCIAN REDEMPTION

By 1791 Rosicrucian Christians such as Mozart seem to have come to
believe that redemption was both a cosmic event embracing all time and
history, and, as the Alchemists taught, that it involved each individual's
active and lonely struggle with the evil principle in the universe, aided by
God's grace manifested in Christ. The association of Hiram/Adoniram
with Christ establishes the centrality of the mystical Christian symbolism
of Rosicrucianism. Christ was recognized as the bringer of grace for all
humankind, but only those who were initiated into the mystery were
able to recognize his grace. In the widespread, Swedenborg-influenced
Swedish Zinnendorf sect of Gnostic Christian freemasonry (with which
the Viennese lodge 'Zur gekrönte Hoffnung' was associated) Christ was
recognized as the supreme Master who would lead Humanity to the 'Unio
Mystica' with God, who is light.[132] The Rosicrucians adopted the mystic
principle of the Alchemists that the Word made flesh in Christ was a sign
of the immanence of the spiritual in the material creation, an immanence
exemplified in the mystical correspondence between Christ's redeeming
power to restore man to spiritual cleanliness and the purification of base
metals to gold.[133] The hushed and infinitely mysterious motet *Ave Verum
Corpus*, which also dates from 1791, was written for the festival of Corpus
Christi, a festival which seems to have been of particular importance to
Mozart.[134] In Gnostic Christianity, the moment of God's descent into
matter as the body of Christ is also the moment in which humanity
becomes God.

Drawing from Cabbalistic beliefs in the magical power of numbers and
the Hebrew letters (which were believed to constitute the name of God),
esoteric Christianity also immersed itself in the symbolism of the Name
– the secret name of Christ contained in the magic pentagram in which
the letter 'S' (symbolizing fire and light) was added to the tetragram
'JHVH', the symbol of the sacred name of God in the era of law, before
the era of grace brought by Christ. As Rudolf Steiner explained in his
analysis of the Rosicrucian symbolism of Goethe's *Die Geheimnisse*,
'Before the Christ-principle, the Sun of Righteousness, could appear on
earth, the Jahve-principle had to send down on the earth the light of
righteousness, toned down in the Law, to prepare the way'.[135] In *Die
Zauberflöte* references to the mystical name of Christ appear in the scene
with the Two Black-Armoured Men who guard the entrance to the Trials

of Fire and Water. The text they sing is taken almost directly from Terrasson's *Sethos*. But the original text of the Lutheran chorale to which Mozart sets the *Sethos* words, 'Ach, Gott in Himmel', contains references to 'The Word . . . revealed on the Cross'[136] (the text of the *Ave Verum Corpus* is also about the death of the true body of Christ 'on the cross for mankind'.) In the printed libretto for the opera we are told that the Armoureed Men read to Tamino from 'transparent writing graven on a pyramid'; at the words 'fire, water, air and earth', it is suggested[137] the 'JHVH' tetragram would have appeared. (The inclusion of a Protestant chorale also hints further at the opera's ecumenical aspirations.)

In esoteric Christianity the era of grace brought by Christ (the Son of Man – Anthropos – as well as the Son of God, a designation that suggests he comes from within humanity itself, rather than from beyond) offers the possibility of spiritual gnosis, or wisdom, the first step in the fight to repulse the evil influences of the world and regain spirituality. Redemption was not an historical event that had vicariously absolved humanity (as in conventional Christianity) but rather, the event that gave creation – and each individual within creation – the power of self-liberation: the power to overcome evil, and to bring order to the primal chaos through which evil manifests itself. It is not Sarastro, nor Isis and Osiris, who banish the Queen and her hordes from the Temple of the Sun; it is the trimphant passage of Tamino and Pamina themselves, through their spiritual trials and their ultimate attainment of divinity, which allows them to ascend to the realm of light – the Gnostic *pleroma*, or fullness.

As so often in Gnostic allegory, the individual journey of Tamino and Pamina mirrors the universal. In one of the Manichaean systems there are four stages of cosmic redemption, in which four ambassadors are sent to earth by the primal principle of Light to rescue the world. First: Man himself; second: Spirit; third: the 'leading wise man' and, at his side, Sophia 'the maiden of light'; fourth: the bringers of grace, including Christ and Mani himself. If we read Tamino as spiritual Man (as opposed to Papageno, who is Man before the advent of spirit), his encounter with Sarastro and Pamina represents the third stage of redemption.[138] The final stage, achieved with the arrival of the era of grace at the end of time, abolishes evil, allowing humankind to be reunited with God.[139] The Ode for Mozart's own funeral oration concludes with the lines:

> Now in thy grave sleep softly
> The sleep that death doth bring,
> 'Til Adoniram call thee
> Nine times to join our ring.

Where reunited solely
Through God's eternal word,
We hear the thrice-sung Holy:
Jehovah is our Lord.[140]

THE ARISTOCRATIC REVIVAL

As Mozart was setting Schikaneder's text for *Die Zauberflöte* to music he made numerous small changes as he went along, one of which is particularly telling. In the final lines which the chorus sing at the end of Act I Schikaneder had written: 'If virtue and righteousness pave the Great Path with renown ['*den grossen Pfad mit Ruhm bestreut*'], then the earth will be a heavenly kingdom and mortals will be like the gods.' Mozart changed the words 'den grossen Pfad' (a masonic formula) to 'der Grossen Pfad'. The sense of the change implies that it is the virtue and righteousness only of the *Great* that will now achieve divinity. It is an alteration which leads us to the heart of the later Enlightenment's quest for spiritual truth.

The widespread aristocratic revival – political, social and cultural – of the later eighteenth century was, to some extent, the logical conclusion to all the Enlightenment stood for. For although in its early stages many of the Enlightenment's arrows had been directed at the feudal nobility, usually in alliance with absolutism, by the end of the century the encroachments of absolutist power, and the increasingly threatening egalitarianism of the age, had forced the later Enlightenment to measure its own exclusiveness more carefully. Against the unholy alliance of despot and democrat, the later Enlightenment often found itself joining forces with the beleaguered aristocracy.

Here, more than anywhere, is the line that demarcates progressive thought in the eighteenth century from its development in the nineteenth century. For all Enlightenment utterances, irrespective of topic, were addressed to (and exclusively concerned the interests of) an educated and cultivated élite. Beyond the walls of its gilded enclave the Enlightenment could see only the brutish multitude: the mob, the *canaille*, or their German equivalent, the *Pöbel* (the word used by Mozart himself to describe the unruly *friseurs* at the imperial ball in 1782). The Enlightenment was quite unable to address the wider problems of the majority of society, let alone of incipient industrialization, and beyond the expression of a few vaguely humanitarian sentiments, did whatever it could to exclude the swinish masses from its view.

The masses embodied everything the Enlightenment feared most: ignorance, superstition, anarchy and chaos. Throughout the century it is impossible to find a dissenting voice. The masses smoulder and seethe below the surface of Enlightenment optimism, like some monstrous Id, always reminding the *philosophes* of the fragility of reason and the transitoriness of progress. 'The people will always be composed of brutes between man and beast,'[141] claims Voltaire; 'The general mass of the species is made neither to follow, nor to know, the march of the human spirit,' Diderot tells us in the *Encyclopédie*;[142] 'The people consists of idiots,' writes Kant;[143] 'Among the lower and more numerous classes we are confronted with crude, lawless instincts, unleashed with the loosening of the bonds of civil order, and hastening with ungovernable fury to their animal satisfactions,'[144] warns Schiller in the *Aesthetic Education*.

The prevalence of this attitude explains the almost total absence of arguments for political democracy in Enlightenment discourse. To the Enlightenment democracy implied simply government by the mob, and that, Montesquieu argued, was next best thing to the Enlightenment's greatest fear, anarchy.[145] Furthermore, as Montesquieu acutely noted, the people have fondness for tyrants, and the historical record showed that the passage from democracy to anarchy invariably ended in tyranny. Gibbon accordingly identified the first step in the downfall of the Roman Empire as the misguided extension of citizenship to all Romans. 'There is no greater enemy to liberty than the people,'[146] wrote Turgot, the French *philosophe* who became, for a brief period, Louis XVI's reforming Chief Minister.

The lower orders are kept well out of sight in Enlightenment art and discourse. When they do appear, it is only as peasants, either decorative, to remind the jaded sensibilities of an over-civilized society of the restorative pleasures of the natural life, or Rousseauist – ideally moral and honest. The one artist of the Enlightenment who did deliberately set out to represent the people was Goya, and his picture was not a pretty one. Those Marxist historians and art-historians who argue that Goya's paintings indicate modern history's first stirrings of compassion and political faith in the working man have failed to recognize the limits of what it was possible for Enlightened Man to think, or to look carefully enough at the drawings, paintings or etchings themselves. On the walls of the Academia San Fernando in Madrid the truth leaps at one with startling clarity. For here Goya's lumpen *pueblo*, potato-headed, leering and stamping Nibelungen, seem horribly to mock Goya's more humane portraits of his Enlightened friends, colleagues and patrons who, wraithlike and haunted, are all too aware of the fragility of their projects and of their faith in progress.

So it is nonsense to look for egalitarian or democratic sentiments in Enlightened discourse, let alone to describe *Die Zauberflöte* as a 'proletarian' opera.[147] I believe H. C. Robbins Landon is mistaken when he imagines the simplicity of Mozart's late style to be evidence of a popular *Volkstümmlichkeit*, a sign of Mozart's belief in the old adage '*vox populi, vox dei*'.[148] '*Vox populi, vox Dei*, is nonsense,' says the Catholic writer Johann Rautenstrauch in a masonic pamphlet of 1786. 'The voice of the people is the voice of fools.'[149] 'It is said *vox populi vox dei*,' wrote Beethoven, one of the last survivors of the Enlightenment. 'I never believed it.'[150] The famous lines in *Die Zauberflöte* in which one of the priests of the Temple, upon questioning Tamino's eligibility as an applicant to the order on the grounds that he is a prince, receives the reply from Sarastro, 'Noch mehr, er ist Mensch', is not evidence of democratic sentiment. 'Mensch' refers to the gnostic 'anthropos': Goethe's *humanus*, or Blake's Albion; Man as spiritual being. In Schiller's *Aesthetic Education Menschheit* is the attribute that entitles Man to be considered a being endowed with the capacity to aspire to the *Gottheit*.[151]

Although endowed with earthly status, Tamino is also a *Mensch*, capable of striving for the highest spiritual ideals of humanity. Furthermore, Tamino's status as a prince is not simply the stuff of fairy stories. In *Sethos* Terrasson argued that high birth is preferable for those who are to be entrusted with power since it precludes ambition,[152] and Tamino deliberately introduces himself to Papageno with the words that he is 'royal' (*fürstlich*). In *Die Zauberflöte*, Tamino's status is a token of the late Enlightenment's insistence that it is 'the great', spiritual princes like Tamino rather than *Naturmenschen* like Papageno, for whom aspiration to divinity is reserved.

The aristocratic counter-revolution in late eighteenth-century Europe was not simply political. It was a manifestation of the late Enlightenment's broader belief, reflected in *Die Zauberflöte*, that the survival of civilization and its values depended upon the preservation of the more permanent spiritual values of true aristocratic culture and society. The emergence of this new understanding of the function of the aristocracy is marked by a shift from the notion of a nobility, founded upon hereditary power and status, to the modern concept of aristocracy – rule by the élite (named after the supposed political principles of Aristotle). Hence Rousseau's often unnoticed belief that the best form of government would be some form of elective aristocracy,[153] not of birth, but of education and culture: a spiritual aristocracy that would counter the materialistic and egalitarian tendencies of the age.

One response to the encroachments upon the real power of the aristocracy was therefore to enhance the special appurtenances of aristocratic culture. In Germany in the later eighteenth century, the aristocracy was encouraged to look back with pride to the imagined romance of the feudal era, and to an age when knightly chivalry had preserved honour and civilization amidst robbery, rapine and anarchy. Alxinger's Arthurian *Bliomberis*, and *Doolin von Maynz*, set in the times of the Emperor Charlemagne, convey his own romantic aristocratic ideology, and the poems of Aloys Blumauer are full of nostalgic references to 'that old, golden knightly age'.[154] Popular German novels of the 1790s (known as *Ritterromane*) convey a marked idealization of feudalism and of the Christian, medieval Empire, more holy than Roman. On his tomb in the Augustinerkirche in Vienna Leopold II is depicted by Vienna's most distinguished neo-classical sculptor Franz Anton Zauner[155] not as a Roman Emperor (as is his brother Joseph in the equestrian statue on the square outside, also by Zauner), but in the chivalric armour of a medieval knight.

In his essay 'Versuch einer Geschichte der alten Ritterschaft, in Bezug auf die Freimaurerey' Blumauer attempted a systematic proof of the connection between Templars and freemasonry, by depicting the Templars as medieval proto-masons bringing peace, justice and morality to an age of *Faustrecht* ('law of the fist').[156] Alxinger's neo-aristocraticism was also intimately tied up with his masonic interests; in a number of his masonic poems he talks of the 'uninitiated' (the *Eingeweihte*) as the despised *Pöbel* or 'mob'.[157] Such sentiments were to become widespread in the development of freemasonry and its accumulation of tokens of aristocratic status during the course of the eighteenth century. Aristocratic English freemasons divested themselves of their swords on entering a lodge; bourgeois freemasons were invested with one in Germany. It was not long before lodges dedicated to different sections of society emerged. In Bordeaux class differences were perpetuated in lodges reserved specifically for aristocrats and magistrates, and others for the lesser bourgeoisie. In 1785 the provincial master of the Bordeaux lodges rejected an application for the foundation of a new lodge on the grounds that the majority of its applicants were workers whose presence would lower the dignity of the *Art Royale*, and risk abuse of the privilege of equality.[158] Although less rigid, the same distinctions are evident in Vienna, where the lodge 'Zur gekrönte Hoffnung', dominated by Rosicrucians, was well known as the preserve of the greater aristocracy.

The inherent exclusiveness of freemasonry provided a refuge for the later Enlightenment's increasing élitism, and its cultural and spiritual concept of aristocracy is evident in the attitude of an artist like Goethe. Bourgeois himself, Goethe characterized the aristocratic culture of Germany, imported wholesale from France, as shallow and frivolous. Yet at the same time Goethe appeared to believe that only in an aristocratic society, rooted in leisure and financial security, in traditions of duty and service (traditions that hark back to a vision of a feudal past later to be adopted by the Romantics) could true culture flourish. In Germany such personal cultivation was beyond the reach of the bourgeoisie. 'The bourgeois may not ask "What art thou?" He can only ask "What hast thou?",' claims Wilhelm Meister.[159] Leaving home to pursue his dream of art in the theatre, Wilhelm is helped to his vision of aristocratic cultivation by the quasi-masonic Society of the Tower, a spiritual élite dedicated to personal cultivation. When Goethe talks of 'the triumph of nobility over baseness',[160] he is talking of just such a spiritual nobility, founded upon *Bildung*, 'the new bond that tied well educated nobles and commoners together and established them as a proud and self-reliant aristocratic fraternity, transcending the boundaries of birth, status, profession, rank and wealth'.[161] 'Culture', says Johann Pezzl in the *Skizze von Wien*, 'brings with it necessary inequality of classes.'[162]

This notion of spiritual aristocracy became increasingly prevalent in late eighteenth-century German culture. It was of particular importance to the bourgeois artist who had cut himself loose from the artist's traditional moorings and wished to assert his independence and dignity in the crowded anonymity of the marketplace. Subjected to the crude mechanisms of market exchange, which were to become the only measure of his value, the bourgeois artist placed increasing emphasis upon his spiritual exclusivity. The earlier leaders of the Enlightenment had talked of a Republic of Letters; those of the generation of the 1790s envisaged instead an intellectual and artistic aristocracy.

THE PATENT OF GENIUS

The inheritance to which the artist could appeal in presenting his patents of nobility was that of genius, and by the end of the eighteenth century the artist was laying claim to the highest aristocratic pretensions. Edward Gibbon in his autobiography suggests that it would not be wrong 'to pronounce the descendant of a king less truly noble than the offspring of a man of genius'.[163] Oliver Goldsmith was able to complain that at a social gathering a mere lord had taken 'no more notice of me than if I had been an ordinary man', and Dr Johnson supported him with the sentiment that 'a noble man ought to have made up to such a man as Goldsmith'.[164] It was in the eighteenth century that artists started to enter the pantheons erected to the new secular divinities of the age. Poets' Corner in Westminster Abbey came into being during the eighteenth – not, as many people imagine, the nineteenth – century.

The concept of artistic genius, developed in mid-eighteenth-century aesthetics, celebrated the creative power in the artist that lifted him from his role as a passive mirror of reality, or a skilled manipulator of classical rules, to the status (which he or she still precariously enjoys) of inspired soothsayer and prophet in society. The notion of genius (derived from the classical idea of the personal genius that was supposed to guide every person's life) became especially important as a means of escape from the materialist trap. La Mettrie, Helvétius and Diderot all extolled the imagination in particular as the essential spark that prevented men from becoming otherwise identical machines, and Burke talks of the mind possessing 'a creative power of its own'.[165] In Kant's *Critique of Judgement*, artistic imagination is a noumenal freedom similar to that of ethical choice, and artistic genius a power that is thereby able to determine its own rules. (For Blake in *Jerusalem*, the imagination is Jesus himself, the redemptive power in Man.)[166]

In his *Dictionnaire de musique* of 1768, under the entry *Genius*, Rousseau made an early claim for the musician to be accorded new status. 'The musician of genius encompasses the entire universe within his art. He paints his pictures in sound; he makes the very silence speak.'[167] And the musician's claims to genius grew as eighteenth-century aesthetics shifted its focus from the imitative features of artistic activity to the expressive, and thence to the imaginative, ideal and spiritual aspects of creation.

Beethoven, we are told, was the first great musician to have claimed possession of the new Romantic genius of the composer. Certainly Beethoven is the typical self-conscious artist/genius, lost in his own world of inner vision and his belief that his music was an expression of the spiritual ideal, and that life itself was a mere 'sacrament of art'.[168] Accordingly, like so many of those brought up on the ideals of the Enlightenment, he believed in the necessity of a society organized on aristocratic principles. The political radicalism learnt in his youth never left him, but a letter of the 1820s, drafted but not sent, tells us of his ambivalence: 'between ourselves, although we are convinced Republicans [a dangerous thing to say in Vienna after 1815] yet there is something to be said for oligarchic aristocracy'.[169] Beethoven also believed firmly in his own human superiority, writing disconsolately in his conversation book in 1820 that 'the middle class burgher ought to be excluded from the society of higher men, and here I am fallen among them'.[170] Curiously, this tormented man was not content with the unique aristocracy of his genius. He sought the outer indications of nobility, came to believe that he was of noble birth, and fought to have his supposedly aristocratic origins publicly acknowledged, eventually engaging in humiliating litigation. Schindler reports that when in late 1818 court proceedings proved that Beethoven was not noble, it 'drove Beethoven beside himself; for he considered it the grossest insult that he ever received'.[171]

I believe that by the end of the 1780s Mozart himself had come to espouse a comparable aristocratic assessment of his own genius, an assessment that marked a profound transformation of his outlook on the world as an artist. In breaking away from his father and his princely employer in 1781 Mozart had laid claim to enjoy no more than the freedom, autonomy and dignity offered by proper financial rewards for his talents. Mozart had a just estimation of those talents, coupled with an expectation that the music-loving *amateurs* of late eighteenth-century Vienna and Europe would recognize his value in financial terms, unlike the princely patrons and lofty prelates who had hitherto spurned him in favour of mediocrities. Mozart's notion of his worth at that stage of his life was therefore an essentially bourgeois one. The letters written at the time of his humiliation by Colloredo and his steward Count Arco demonstrate that he had a finely tuned understanding of the universal relationship between self-respect and the desire for retribution and revenge upon those who lower our self-esteem in the eyes of ourselves or others. But he intended to take the historical, bourgeois form of revenge; not the quick satisfaction of the duel (aristocrats never liked fighting duels with the bourgeoisie), but the longer lasting historical triumph of wealth and repute.

Mozart's brave assertion of freedom and independence failed, for reasons many of which were beyond his control. Unlike London or Paris, Vienna simply did not have a sufficiently developed bourgeois infrastructure to sustain a freelance composer like Mozart. Music publishing was still in its infancy, with terms that did little to favour the composer, and wholly inadequate copyright laws unable to meet the demands of a new, marketable concept of individual genius. The economic boom of the early Josephine decade was succeeded by severe recession, prompted by Joseph's vainglorious war with Turkey. By 1789 Mozart's normally abundant output had shrunk to pitiful proportions. Constantly unwell, and increasingly in financial difficulties, the normally prolific Mozart was experiencing enormous difficulties in completing a whole series of major compositions. Unable to support himself any longer with the subscription concerts he had so successfully mounted at the beginning of the decade, (recession had driven audiences away), he even found himself unable to finish the string quartets for which he had received a commission from Frederick William II of Prussia.

It is against the background of failing energies and a floundering career that Mozart's later masonic activities must be considered. Material failure often prompts artists to spurn material values, and to assert alternative, more lasting and worthy values. In particular, such failure is likely to prompt an emphasis upon the spiritual exclusiveness of the artist.

Mozart had been brought up by his father to believe in the superiority of his genius from an early age; the sign from God to refute the materialists and atheists (the 'Voltaireans').[172] But in later life he had other opportunities to affirm the spiritual importance of his art. In 1789, for instance, on his way to Berlin, Mozart paid a visit to Christian Körner, the brother-in-law of Doris Stock, for whom Mozart sat for the famous silverpoint portrait now in Leipzig. Körner was a close friend of Schiller, his musical mentor and the first aesthetician to make a consistent effort to apply the idealism of Kant and Schiller to music, and to proclaim the spiritual superiority of music over the other arts.[173] Mozart could have had no more important point of contact with the spiritual idealism of his northern German contemporaries. (Lichnowsky, with whom he travelled, was, incidentally, one of the first Kantians in Vienna.)[174]

The possibility that Mozart had come to espouse an increasingly spiritual view of his art explains many of the activities of the later years of his life. After 1786, despite the fact that most of his intellectual colleagues within freemasonry had left the movement, Mozart stayed on, one of an ever dwindling and increasingly beleaguered number. For most of his colleagues, freemasonry had lost its *raison d'être*, and by the 1790s the climate of suspicion bred by the French Revolution had gained the secretive activities of the freemasons some disrepute; the police chief Count Pergen warned Leopold II that the French Revolution itself had been fomented by the freemasons – a conspiracy theory that was to make some running throughout Europe. Yet despite this hostility, Mozart remained loyal to the movement, to the extent of writing a masonic opera long after the effective demise of the movement as a significant social and intellectual force in Vienna. What made him stay? Undoubtedly, in addition to the esoteric Christian programme of Rosicrucianism, Mozart was attracted by the spiritual exclusivity of the movement. This gave an artist like Mozart, apparently spurned by the exoteric world, access to a corpus of exclusive spiritual wisdom enjoyed by an intellectual aristocracy that sustained his own estimation of the value of his unique genius.

Within Rosicrucian freemasonry Mozart was able to immerse himself in symbolic codes and systems that confirmed the secret, mystical significance of his music. One of the books in Mozart's library hints at his own exploration of musical mysticism. *Die Metaphysic in Connecion mit der Chemie* (an obviously alchemical title), published in 1777, shows how naturally the metaphysical idealism of Kant would lead to the 'magischer idealismus' of Novalis and the Romantics.

Its author, Friedrich Christoph Oetinger, Gnostic Christian and admirer of the seventeenth-century mystic Jacob Böhm, makes an initial distinction between metaphysical and natural sciences: 'Metaphysics are a science of supernatural things; Chemistry of material.' Oetinger frequently cites Kant, reinterpreting Kant's intellectual metaphysics of the unknowable as proof of his own metaphysics of the supernatural and divine. But since the metaphysical can only be reached through the physical (as Goethe also teaches), it is 'through Chemistry that man arrives at the idea of the holier text'. Electricity, for instance, is explained by Oetinger as the presence of the elemental fire in earthly bodies. The 'signatures of nature', he suggests, are the true theology of nature, the emblematic evidence of the presence of spiritual truths within nature. Of particular importance to Oetinger, and presumably to Mozart too, was the mystical significance of musical numerology, a neo-Platonic interpretation of music as the link between the earthly and the spiritual. This gave the composer himself the powers of sympathetic magic possessed by the famous Hermetic Magi of the past.[175] Through music, Oetinger claims, humanity is able to transcend its earthly bounds to gain direct union with the absolute.[176]

'In natural magic there is nothing more efficacious than the Hymns of Orpheus, if there be applied to them suitable music, and the disposition of soul, and other circumstances known to the wise,'[177] wrote Pico della Mirandola, the great Renaissance neo-Platonist and Hermeticist. His mentor Marsilio Ficino used to sing these Orphic songs, accompanying himself on the lyre, to tune into the cosmic Pythagorean harmonies emitted by the spheres, and to draw down to earth the benign influences of the planetary constellations – in particular, that of the sun.

Die Zauberflöte, of course, is an Orphic story; a parable of the magic powers of art, and especially of music, to redeem humankind from its subjection to earthly nature, and ultimately to reunite humanity with the cosmos and restore harmony and bliss. Tamino, with his magic flute, has the power to rouse, and at the same time to tame, wild beasts. But as in the symbol of the boy who tames a wild lion with the gentle melody of his flute at the end of Goethe's *Novelle*,[178] the power of the flute is a symbol not of the subjugation of nature by art, but of mankind's escape from its subjugation to a baser nature, and its reconciliation with a higher concept of nature through art. The magic flute is carved from an ancient oak, and at the moment of its creation was baptized by the elements; its powers are a gift from nature herself. With his flute Tamino is able to summon Pamina, his ideal, and Pamina in turn restores the flute to him before they undergo the final trials. Armed with his flute, Tamino, like Orpheus, enters the underworld and there invokes his art to conquer death itself, to hold at bay the flux of earthly transience and material decay. Through the mysterious power of the flute Tamino and Pamina are able to penetrate the raging elements and emerge unscathed and purified.

Novalis pictured a magical past when he looked back to the prowess of another mythical musician, Arion, in his novel *Heinrich von Ofterdingen* and imagined an era when art and nature were one, before the Fall:

In olden times the whole of nature must have been more alive and conscious than it is today . . . There were bards then who were able to apply the strange sounds of their marvellous instruments in such a way as to awaken the secret life of the forests, the spirits hidden in tree trunks . . . they tamed terrible beasts and induced savage men to become civilized and orderly.[179]

It was the role of art, Kant had believed, to restore that unity, not to be achieved 'until fulfilled art again becomes nature, which is the ultimate goal of the moral destiny of the human race'.[180] That 'eternal and original unity' of Man and nature had been sundered, Schelling argued, by the processes of thought and language.[181] But in music the lost unity of sign and meaning is restored, since in music the gulf between subject and object is abolished. 'The highest, purest reach of the contemplative act is that which has learned to leave language behind it', writes George Steiner. 'It is only by breaking through the walls of language that visionary observance can enter the world of total and immediate understanding.'[182] Rilke addresses Orpheus himself:

> Gesang, wie du ihn lehrst, ist nicht Begehr,
> nicht Werbung um ein endlich noch Erreichtes;
> Gesan ist Dasein. Fur den Gott ein Leichtes.

[Song as you teach it, is not desire, not suing for something yet in the end attained; song is existence.[183] Easy for the god.]

Orpheus was a worshipper of Apollo, and the apollonian powers of music are celebrated in Tamino's magic flute; the powers of form, harmony and grace by which humanity remakes nature in the shape of its ideal. Papageno, on the other hand, is bestowed with the dionysiac power of music, a power that celebrates the joys of ecstatic, physical expression in art – in particular, in dance. For Nietzsche, apollonian art was the shining art of human dreams, whereas the dionysiac restored humanity more directly to its original unity with nature. Papageno, spiritually unregenerate man, is still endowed with the gift of art to console (like Tamino, he plays his magic bells at his moment of greatest despair); to summon his partner to him (the Three Boys, emissaries of the spirit world, remind him of his bells as he laments his separation from Papagena; to their magic sounds she at last comes to him); and with the power of music over nature. Tamino's flute conquers by pacifying the beasts and elements; its power is strange and archaic. Papageno's bells, on the other hand, conquer by their summons to dance. The slaves who hold Pamina captive are enchanted by Papageno's bells to dance away to a tune of such pristine, heartlifting innocence that for a moment the burdens of care and anxiety miraculously fall away.

Mysticism, wrote Lucien Goldmann, 'if it is pantheistic in tendency, leads to the absorption of the individual in the cosmos; if it is theocentric, to his total identification with God. It can thus be expressed only in lyricism or in songs of praise.'[184] 'The holiness of sacred music, the jocund humour of folk-tunes, are the pivots round which all true music revolves ... Worship or dance,' wrote Goethe.[185] Like Beethoven's late music, *Die Zauberflöte* celebrates these pivots. Tamino, told by the mysterious voices within the temple that Pamina is still alive, knows of only one way to convey his thanksgiving to the Almighty; to raise his flute and play. Papageno, roused from despair by the Three Boys, takes his bells and strikes up a joyous dance.

Epilogue

All Human Forms identified, even Tree, Earth & Stone: all
Human Forms identified, living, going forth & returning wearied
Into the Planetary lives of Years, Months, Days & Hours; reposing,
And then Awaking into his Bosom in the Life of Immortality.[1]

Mozart's vision of humanity redeemed through art, forgiven, and reconciled with nature and the absolute, was a vision that also reunited his
art and his faith. The Rosicrucians believed that there was a time when
Adam in paradise had possessed supreme wisdom from God about nature
and all created things, and that fallen humanity is forever reminded by
the angels (who are so omnipresent in the Cabbala, and who are perhaps
recalled by the Three Boys in *Die Zauberflöte*) of its lost wisdom.[2] The
Rosicrucians 'wanted to turn the course of society and of nature towards
the original state of paradise', explained Ernst Bloch; their task was 'above
all of leading the fallen world over to Christ'.[3] Perhaps it would be truer
to say that for Mozart it is Christ himself – identified with the redeeming
power of the artistic imagination by Blake,[4] so often the secret librettist
of Mozart's own spiritual world – who leads the fallen world back to
God.

It would be as wrong to imagine Mozart in the last months of his life
lost in an esoteric spirit world, (like some ancient necromancer from
Goethe's *Faust*) as to return to the old picture of the frenzied composer
tormented by his intimations of approaching death. In his last year, and
in particular in the creation of *Die Zauberflöte*, he seems to have gained
some tranquillity from the assurance of *belonging* he had always sought;
to have reconciled the many conflicting elements in his own life, and to
have found a release from the restless search for the external objects of
self-identification that had so often failed him. This spiritual peace led
him to a more just estimation of the value of honest, earthly things:
success in German opera, an artistic form he had now made entirely his
own; recognition among his peers (Antonio Salieri was full of warm praise
for *Die Zauberflöte*, which he attended as Mozart's guest); the renewed
pleasures of his work and of his family.

Most telling, Mozart wished to present his spiritual message to the world, and had no desire to guard its secrets jealously within an occult fraternity. Like Goethe, he considered his art to possess both an outer and an inner, esoteric significance. But those inner truths were accessible to all with ears to hear: those who were willing to relinquish their enslavement to the purely material and to recognize the importance of cultivating inner spirituality. That he fervently desired that people *should* recognize spiritual values, and that he wrote *Die Zauberflöte* with the purpose of enabling them to do so (and not as a secret work for initiates only) is clear from some of his letters. He attended performances of the opera whenever possible, sitting in the audience and often observing the audience's reactions closely. It was silent appreciation rather than rowdy applause which particularly pleased him. In a letter of 8 October 1791 Mozart reported to Constanze his intention to take her mother to see *Die Zauberflöte*. Frau Weber had been given a copy of the libretto to read beforehand (indicating how important he considered the text – he was particularly pleased that Salieri liked the libretto), but Mozart suspected that 'in her case what will probably happen is that she will *see* the opera but not *hear* it': a clear hint at a distinction in Mozart's mind between the outer story and its inner truths, ultimately conveyed by the music.[5]

Mozart's letter goes on to describe the behaviour of another, unnamed member of the audience at a performance of the opera whose response had particularly annoyed him. He had

applauded everything most heartily. But he, the know-all, showed himself to be such a thorough *Bavarian* that I could not remain or I should have had to call him an ass. Unfortunately I was there just when the second Act began, that is, at the solemn scene [in which the priests consider Tamino's candidature; interestingly, the scene is largely in spoken dialogue]. He laughed at everything. At first I was patient enough to draw his attention to a few passages. But he laughed at everything. Well, I could stand it no longer. I called him a Papageno and cleared out.

Let us leave Mozart with his own last letter, written to Constanze at Baden two months before his death, a vignette of his routines in the last months of his life sketched with the clarity of a silverpoint drawing. Mozart has been worried about his small son Karl's schooling (the boy chatters too much, and does nothing at the school but run around in the garden all day long, as he has unwisely admitted to his father) and he has already made arrangements for Karl to be transferred from his present boarding school to the Piarists' school in the Leopoldstadt. He drives out to the suburb of Perchtoldsdorf to collect his son and take him for a day out from school. To the boy's delight – as Mozart reports – he is taken to a performance of *Die Zauberflöte*, in the company of Salieri, Catarina Cavalieri (the first Konstanze in *Die Entführung*) and Karl's grandmother. After the performance Mozart drives Salieri and Cavalieri home, sups with his sister-in-law Josefa Hofer, Karl's aunt, and then takes the child home to bed, where both sleep soundly. The next day he and Karl will drive out to Baden to join Constanze, when Mozart clearly looks forward to seeing his wife again.[6]

Although Mozart was absorbed at this time in the composition of the clarinet concerto and the Requiem, there is no hint here of feverish travail and battles against ill-health. Instead there is an ordinary, practical serenity which suggests that Mozart had at last found peace of mind.

Notes

Where a modern edition or translation of an earlier text exists, this is the edition cited below and in the Bibliography.

PREFACE

1. J. W. von Goethe, *Conversations and Encounters* (1960), p. 62.

2. W. Ruf, *Die Rezeption von Mozarts 'Le nozze di Figaro'* (1977), p. 2.

INTRODUCTION: ENLIGHTENMENT AND THE EIGHTEENTH CENTURY

1. A. Pope, *Poetical Works* (1978), *The Dunciad*, Bk IV, 629–56.
2. Goethe, *Gedenkenausgabe* (1949), vol. IX, *Maximen und Reflexionen*.
3. Quoted in P. Gay, *The Enlightenment, an Interpretation* (1969), vol. II, p. 24.
4. Voltaire, *Lettres philosophiques* (1972), p. 41.
5. Quoted in C. Behrens, *The Ancien Régime* (1989), p. 94.
6. Voltaire, *Dictionnaire philosophique* (1972), p. 285.
7. J. Pezzl, *Faustin, oder das philosophische Jahrhundert* (1785), p. 332.

I THE EDUCATION OF A BOURGEOIS ARTIST

1. See E. Winter, *Baroque Absolutismus und Aufklärung in der Donaumonarchie* (1971).
2. L. Muratori, *The Science of Rational Devotion*, p. 45. The translation, published in Ireland in 1789, shows how widespread was Muratori's influence.
3. E. Anderson (ed) *The Letters of Mozart and his Family* (1985), 25.9.82 (hereafter cited as *Letters*).
4. Ibid., 26.5.70.
5. O. E. Deutsch, *Mozart: A Documentary Biography* (1990), p. 28.
6. Quoted in *Zaubertöne–Mozart in Wien* (1990), p. 38.
7. Ibid., p. 38.
8. *Letters* 7.5.83.
9. Ibid., 20.12.77.
10. Ibid. See the poem attached to the letter.
11. Ibid., 18.12.77.
12. Ibid., 13.9.82; Baroness von Waldstätten also lent Wolfgang some of her 'good books' (see Ibid., 2.10.82).
13. H. Hatfield, *Aesthetic Paganism in German Literature* (1964) p. 40.
14. *Letters*, 23.2.78.
15. *Zaubertöne*, p. 33.
16. J-J. Rousseau, *Confessions* (1953), Bk 9.
17. A. Cazes, *Grimm et les encyclopédistes* (1933), p. 45.
18. Ibid.
19. *Letters*, 28.5.64.
20. Ibid., 18.4.65.
21. T. Hobbes, *Leviathan*, (1968), p. 15.
22. *Letters*, 23.2.78.
23. Ibid., 16.6.81.
24. Ibid., 10.4.82.

25. Ibid., 9.5.81.
26. Ibid., 19.5.81.
27. Ibid., 9.5.81.
28. These small-town oligarchic families were infamous: 'Their members often displayed a pride and exclusiveness calculated to make any but the most arrogant aristocrat blush.' (Klaus Epstein, *The Genesis of German Conservatism* (1966), p. 62.)
29. *Letters*, 16.10.77.
30. Ibid., 25.2.78.
31. Ibid., 7.8.78.
32. Ibid., 11.9.78.
33. Ibid., 6.5.81.
34. H. Maschler, *Tobias Philipp Freiherr von Gebler* (1935), p. 66.

II LA FINTA GIARDINIERA

1. C. Rosen, *The Classical Style*, (1971), p. 189.
2. *NMA, La finta giardiniera.*
3. C. Osborne, *The Complete Operas of Mozart* (1978), p. 94.
4. Quoted in W. H. Bruford, *Germany in the Eighteenth Century* (1965), p. 227.
5. Abbé Terrasson, *Sethos* (1731), Preface, p. iii.
6. *Letters* 7.8.78.
7. C. Goldoni, *Pamela* (trans. 1756), Preface.
8. 'What a spectacle is that of a charming creature in the throes of grief! How her looks show off to their best advantage' (A. Brookner, *Greuze* (1972), p. 26).
9. D. Hume, *A Treatise of Human Nature* (1969), p. 507.
10. Quoted in N. Hampson, *The Enlightenment* (1968), p. 28.
11. In M. Novak, *Defoe and the Nature of Man* (1963), p. 93.
12. Goethe, *The Sorrows of Young Werther* (1962), p. 83.
13. L. Mozart, *A Treatise on the Fundamental Principles of Violin Playing* (1948), p. 25.
14. Hume, *Moral and Political Philosophy* (1975), p. 175.
15. Ibid., p. 176.
16. Quoted in R. F. Brissenden, *Virtue in Distress* (1974), p. 47.
17. Rousseau, *A Discourse on Inequality* (1984), p. 101.
18. Hume, *A Treatise of Human Nature*, p. 370.
19. Ibid., p. 620.
20. T. H. White, *The Age of Scandal* (1986), p. 626.
21. R. Welleck, *A History of Modern Criticism* (1955), vol. I, p. 172.
22. Brookner, op. cit., p. 35.
23. Ibid., p. 21.
24. Brissenden, op. cit., p. 4.
25. *Letters*, 26.6.81.
26. 'All the rest of my life and of my misfortunes followed inevitably as a result of that moment's madness,' he later lamented (*Rousseau, Confessions*, p. 328).
27. 'Society is, so to speak, a divinity to the philosophe; the only divinity he will worship.' (Quoted in D. Beales, *History, Society and the Churches* (1985), p. 172.)
28. Brissenden, op. cit., p. 27.
29. D. Diderot, *Le fils naturel*, trans. as *Dorval: or the Test of Virtue* (1767), iv, 3.
30. Quoted in T. Tanner, *Jane Austen* (1986), p. 28.
31. Ibid., p. 26.
32. Rousseau, *The Social Contract and Discourses* (1973), p. 6.
33. Rousseau, *Confessions*, p. 362.
34. Rousseau, *La nouvelle Héloïse* (1967).
35. G. Pestelli, *The Age of Mozart and Beethoven* (1984), p. 48.
36. The device of the third section of the overture running into the opening number of the opera was not uncommon in *opera buffa*; Mozart uses it again in his overture for the unfinished opera *Lo sposo deluso*; but its polemical use in the context of *La finta giardiniera* is obvious.

37. Rousseau, *Lettre à d'Alembert* (1960), p. 79.
38. H. Fielding, *Tom Jones* (1987), p. 300.
39. Lord Chesterfield, *Letters to His Son* (1929), p. 103.
40. J. Boswell, *Life of Johnson*, vol I. (1934–6), p. 266.
41. *Letters*, 16.2.78.
42. *Zaubertöne – Mozart in Wien*, p. 30.
43. *Letters*, 25.7.81.
44. 'Close your heart to the world' (Ibid., 23.2.78); 'please behave like an Englishman' (Ibid. (1970), 9.2.78).
45. J. Starobinski, *Jean-Jacques Rousseau* (1957), p. 4. Jane Austen's young heroines also frequently display the bafflement of innocence at the disjunction of words and deeds in society.
46. Rousseau, *The Social Contract and Discourses*, p. 6.

47. J. Austen, *Sense and Sensibility* (1906), p. 67.
48. Rousseau, *Lettre à d'Alembert*, p. 59.
49. E. Burke, *Reflections on the Revolution in France* (1986), p. 284.
50. Rousseau, *A Discourse on Inequality*, p. 153.
51. Rousseau, *Emile* (1974), p. 217.
52. Ibid., p. 8.
53. Goethe, *The Sorrows of Young Werther*, p. 63.
54. Austen, op. cit. p. 78.
55. S. Richardson, *Clarissa*, vol. III (1986), p. 179.
56. Austen, *Mansfield Park* (1970), p. 80.
57. C. L. Montesquieu, *Persian Letters* (1986), Letter 80.
58. *Letters*, 13.7.81.
59. A. Blumauer, *Gedichte* (1787).

III OPERA AND THE ENLIGHTENMENT

1. Quoted in M. McKeon, *The Origins of the English Novel* (1988), p. 14.
2. C. F. von Blanckenburg, *Versuch über den Roman*.
3. Quoted in T. Eagleton, *The Function of Criticism*, p. 11.
4. Burke, *Reflections on the Revolution in France*, p. 176.
5. C. Flaischlen, *Otto Heinrich von Gemmingen* (1890), p. 70.
6. It often appears under the title *The Theatre as a Moral Institution*.
7. F. Schiller, *Sämtliche Werke*, vol. 5 (1962), pp. 818–31.
8. Ibid.
9. S. Johnson, *Lives of the English Poets*, vol. II (1967), p. 106.
10. J. C. Gottsched, *Versuch einer critischen Dichtkunst* (1751), p. 739.
11. R. Steele and J. Addison, *Selections from The Tatler and The Spectator* (1982), p. 75.
12. Gottsched. op. cit., p. 742.
13. J. Racine, *Oeuvres complètes* (1962), *Phèdre*.
14. A. R. Oliver, *The Encyclopédistes as Critics of Music* (1947), p. 6.

15. Ibid.
16. J. Locke, *Some Thoughts Concerning Education* (1964), p. 162.
17. R. Saisselin, *The Rule of Reason* (1970), p. 139.
18. E. J. Wasserman, *Aspects of the Eighteenth Century* (1965), p. 181.
19. Quoted in P. Kivy, *The Corded Shell* (1980), p. 42.
20. C. Burney, *Memoirs of the Life and Writings of the Abate Metastasio*, vol. III, (1796), p. 19.
21. See *Mozart Jahrbuch* 1978/9, pp. 55–61.
22. Quoted in W. Bruford, *Theatre, Drama and Audience in Goethe's Germany* (1950), p. 44.
23. Grimm, in *Correspondance littéraire*, vol. III (1813), March 1764.
24. G. E. Lessing, *Werke* vol. IV (1973) p. 596.
25. Oliver, op. cit., p. 66.
26. Ibid., p. 104.
27. Ibid.
28. Rousseau, *Dictionnaire de musique* (1768).
29. Wassermann, *Aspects of the Eighteenth*

Century, p. 191. It is not coincidental that Rousseau's emphasis upon melody conveniently provides justification for his own compositional deficiencies.

30. *Mozart. A Documentary Biography*, Deutsch, p. 185.

31. Leo Balet, *Die Verbürgerlichung der Deutschen Kunst, Literatur und Musik im 18. Jahrhundert* (1936), p. 306.

32. E. Wangermann, *Aufklärung und Staatsbürgerliche Erziehung* (1978), p. 67.

33. J. Winckelmann, *Gedenken über die Nachahmung der griechischen Werken* op. cit. (1755).

34. Quoted in Gluck, *The Collected Correspondence and Papers*, ed. H. and E. H. Mueller von Asow (1962), pp. 22, 24.

35. Lessing, *Laokoon* (1970), p. 7.

36. Lessing, *Werke*, vol. IV, p. 597.

37. Quoted in J. R. Vrooman, *Voltaire's Theatre* (1970).

38. Gluck, op. cit., pp. 22, 24.

39. Ibid., p. 177.

40. Quoted in F. Blume, *Classic and Romantic Music* (1972), p. 21.

41. H. Honour, *Neo-Classicism* (1983), p. 141.

42. R. L. Herbert, *David, Voltaire, Brutus and the French Revolution* (1972), p. 113.

43. Emilia Galotti was described by Lessing as 'a bourgeois Virginia'.

44. J. Sonnenfels, *Gesammelte Schriften*, vol. VI *Der Mann ohne Vorurtheil* (1783).

45. According to Leopold Mozart, true friendship was 'one of the greatest wonders of this world' (*Letters*, 4.12.77); 'The wealthy do not know what friendship means, especially those who are born to riches', wrote Mozart. (Ibid., 7.8.78).

46. Lessing, *Werke*, vol. IV, p. 595.

47. Diderot, *Le fils naturel*.

48. Goldoni, *Memoirs*, vol. I (1926), p. 264.

49. *Letters*, 7.5.83.

50. M. Hunter, 'Pamela – The Offspring of Richardson's Heroine in Eighteenth-Century Opera', *Mosaic*, XVIII (1985).

51. Quoted in B. Brophy, *Mozart the Dramatist* (1988), p. 217.

IV THE GERMAN ARTIST

1. *Letters*, 3.7.78.
2. Ibid., 1.5.78.
3. Ibid., 2.10.77.
4. Goethe, *Conversations and Encounters*, p. 158.
5. E. F. Ritter, 'Johann Baptiste von Alxinger and the Austrian Enlightenment', *European University Papers*, series I, vol. 34 (1970).
6. Ibid., p. 5.
7. F. Blume, *Classic and Romantic Music*, p. 28.
8. G. P. Gooch, *Germany and the French Revolution* (1920), p. 21.
9. Goethe, *Literarischer Sansculottismus, Gedenkenausgabe*, vol. XIV, p. 181.
10. H. C. Robbins Landon, *Haydn* (1980), vol. III, p. 237.

11. *Letters*, 7.2.78.
12. Ibid., 11.2.78.
13. Ibid., 16.2.78.
14. Ibid., 23.2.78.
15. Ibid., 16.3.78.
16. Ibid., 2.10.77.
17. Ibid., 1.11.77.
18. S. S. Taylor, *The Theatre of the French and German Enlightenment* (1979).
19. Bruford, *Theatre, Drama and Audience in Goethe's Germany*, p. 268.
20. A. von Klein, *Günther von Schwarzburg: Ein Singspiel* (1777), Preface.
21. *Letters*, 12.11.78.
22. Ibid., 18.12.78.
23. Ibid., 14.11.77.

V *ZAIDE*

1. *Letters*, 29.1.78; 4.2.78.
2. Ibid., 18.4.81.
3. The theme of Gluck's opera *La rencontre imprévue* will be recognized in the title.
4. Published in *NMA, Zaide* (Appendix).
5. *Letters*, 7.8.78.
6. Ibid. 12.11.78.
7. Ibid. 24.11.78.

VII *IDOMENEO*

1. Grimm, in *Correspondance littéraire*, vol. III (March 1764).
2. P. France, *Diderot*, (1983) p. 98.
3. M. G. Flaherty, 'Opera and incipient Romantic Aesthetics', in H. E. Pagliardo (ed.), *Studies in Eighteenth-Century Culture*, (1972), vol. II, pp. 205–18.
4. Deutsch, *Mozart. A Documentary Biography*, p. 155.
5. D. Heartz, '*Idomeneo* and the Tradition of Sacrifice Drama' (1989).
6. Quoted in G. Steiner, *The Death of Tragedy* (1961), p. 36.
7. C. Burney, *Metastasio* (1796), vol III, pp. 376–82.
8. F. Nietzsche, *The Birth of Tragedy* (1956) p. 71.
9. Euripides, *Iphigenia in Tauris*, trans. F. Melian Stanwell (1929).
10. Euripides, *Helen* (1959).
11. 'Nos prêtres ne sont pas ce qu'un vain peuple pense; / Notre crédulité fait tout leur science' [Our priests are not what people vainly think; our credulity gives them their science] (*Oedipe*, IV, 1).
12. Euripides, *Helen*, ll. 753–4.
13. Euripides, *Iphigenia in Tauris*. ll. 570–75.
14. I. Kant, *The Philosophy of Kant*, ed. C. J. Friedrich, (1977), p. 132.
15. Ibid., p. 138.
16. Voltaire, *Dictionnaire philosophique, Prêtre*, p. 346.
17. E. Nixon, *Voltaire and the Calas Case* (1961), p. 132.
18. Schiller, *Sämtliche Werke* (1962), vol. II, *Don Carlos*, V: 10.
19. Voltaire, op. cit., *Juste*, p. 273.
20. Montesquieu, *Persian Letters*, (1973), p. 83.
21. 'Pascal, êtes-vous fou?' exclaimed Voltaire, in response to the man he dubbed 'the sublime misanthrope', quoted in E. Cassirer, *The Philosophy of the Enlightenment* (1979), p. 145.
22. Pope, *Poetical Works, Essay on Man*, IV, 35–6.
23. Ibid., I, 289–94.
24. *Letters*, 3.7.78.
25. Ibid., 9.7.78.
26. Ibid., 3.7.78.
27. Ibid., 4.12.77.
28. 'What are the gods of Homer, Aeschylus and Sophocles?' asked Diderot. 'They are the vices of men, or their virtues, and the great phenomena of nature personified; that is true theogony' (*Entretiens sur le fils naturel*).
29. From the text of Mozart's masonic cantata, K.619.
30. The favourite tragic flaw – the cause of the otherwise virtuous Oedipus's downfall.
31. A. Lemierre, *Oeuvres* (1810), Idomenée, IV, 2.
32. Voltaire, *Romans et contes* (1972), p. 520.
33. F. Tönnies, *Community and Society* (1957).
34. H. S. Maine, *Ancient Law* (1931), p. 141.
35. Hobbes, *Leviathan*, p. 201. See also Locke, *An Essay Concerning Human Understanding* (1961).
36. Diderot, in *Encyclopédie*, vol. XVI, *Serment*.
37. Hobbes, op. cit., p. 197.
38. Diderot, in op. cit., vol. IV, *Contrat*.
39. In A. Behn, *Oroonoko* (1986), p. 152.

40. See G. Clive, *The Romantic Enlightenment* (1960), p. 151.
41. H. E. Strakosch, *State Absolutism and the Rule of Law* (1967), p. 155.
42. Hobbes, op. cit., p. 197.
43. 'Der missversteht die Himmlischen, der sie/Blutgierig wahnt: er dichtet ihnen nur/Die eignen grausamen Begierden an' (*Iphigenie auf Tauris*, I, 4; from the verse version of 1787).
44. Gay, *The Enlightenment*, vol. II (1969), p. 187.
45. J. Milton, *Samson Agonistes*, l. 410.
46. A-F. Prévost, *Histoire du chevalier des Grieux et de Manon Lescaut* (1967).
47. Pope, op. cit., IV, 1.
48. N. Hampson, *The First European Revolution* (1969), p. 21.
49. Quoted in Cassirer, op. cit., p. 135.
50. Muratori, *The Science of Rational Devotion* (trans. 1789).
51. J. Eybel, *Was ist ein Pfarrer?* (1782), p. 56.
52. O. von Gemmingen, *Der Weltmann* (1782), p. 250.
53. Gay, op cit., vol. I, p. 194.
54. Ibid. p. 193.
55. The 'Zoroastrian Riddles and Proverbs' were written and distributed at the Viennese Carnival of 1786 by Mozart. See Maynard Solomon, 'Mozart's Zoroastrian Riddles', *American Imago*, vol. XLII.
56. L. Crocker, *Nature and Culture* (1963), p. 164.
57. A. Danchet, *Idomenée* (1714), II: 4.
58. Voltaire, *Nanine* (1749), Preface.
59. Diderot, *La religieuse*, trans. as *The Nun* (1974).
60. N. Bryson, *Word and Image* (1986), p. 84.
61. C. M. Wieland, *Werke*, vol. I (1964), *Agathon*.
62. Hume, *A Treatis of Human Nature*, p. 538.
63. Quoted in W. Allanbrook, *Rhythmic Gesture in Mozart* (1983), p. 2.
64. Pope, op. cit., III, 10.
65. Jonathan Swift, naturally, reversed the accepted characterizations of the goddesses whilst retaining their traditional enmity: 'VENUS, a beautiful and good-natured Lady, was the Goddess of Love; Juno, a terrible Shrew, the Goddess of Marriage; and they were always mortal enemies.' Quoted in J. Hagstrum, *Sex and Sensibility* (1980), p. 148.
66. As the young Manon Roland, wife of the French Revolutionary Girondin Jean-Marie Roland, delightedly discovered (quoted in Claude Petitfrère, *Le scandale du 'Mariage de Figaro'* (1989), p. 88).
67. L. Stone, *The Family, Sex and Marriage in England, 1500–1800* (1977), p. 31.
68. Ibid., p. 30; the Church eventually became so keen on its newfound duties that it decided to supervise the act of consummation too. The priest, as Philippe Ariès put it, 'wormed his way into the ceremony, to bless the bed with incense and holy water'. (P. Ariès and A. Bejin, *Western Sexuality* (1985), p. 140–57).
69. Montesquieu, *L'esprit de lois* (1952), XXVI, 14.
70. The Act was to bring about the famous elopements to Gretna Green, just over the Scottish border where English law did not prevail.
71. *L'amour conjugal*, we may recall, is also the subtitle of Bouilly's play *Leonore*, the basis for the libretto of Beethoven's *Fidelio*, which derives some of its resonances from the Alcestes story.
72. *Letters*, 3.7.78.
73. Ibid., 15.12.81.
74. Ibid.
75. Ibid.
76. Ibid., 5.2.78.
77. As Hobbes had described the law of nature against vengeance, which commanded that 'men look not at the greatness of evil past, but the greatness of the good to follow'. (Hobbes, op. cit., p. 210.)
78. Montesquieu, *Persian Letters*, p. 191.
79. Lessing, *Ernst und Falk, Werke*, vol. VIII, pp. 452–88.

80. Quoted in T. Eagleton, *The Ideology of the Aesthetic* (1990), p. 58.
81. C. Burney, *Metastasio*, vol. II, p. 324.
82. N. W. Wraxall, *Memoirs 1799* (1806), p. 252.
83. P. Nettl, *Forgotten Musicians* (1951), p. 190.
84. Ellinor G. Barber. *The Bourgeoisie in Eighteenth-Century France* (1955), p. 84.
85. Rousseau, *The Social Contract and Discourses*, p. 166.
86. Voltaire, *Dictionnaire Philosophique*, p. 285.
87. 'The Holy Family', was how Marx would scornfully designate it. (*The Holy Family*, 1844).
88. Steele and Addison, *Selections from the Tatler and the Spectator*, p. 259.
89. R. van Dülmen, *Der Geheimbund der Illuminaten* (1975), p. 179.
90. R. Niklaus, *A Literary History of France* (1970) p. 298.
91. M. Jay, *Adorno* (1984), p. 92.
92. D. Defoe, *Robinson Crusoe* (1965), p. 35.
93. *Letters*, 13.7.78.
94. V. and M. Novello, *A Mozart Pilgrimage* (1955), p. 115.

VII VIENNA AND THE ENLIGHTENMENT

1. Deutsch, *Mozart. A Documentary Biography*, pp. 587–92.
2. G. Gugitz, *Johann Pezzl* (1906).
3. J. Pezzl, *Faustin* (1785), p. 12.
4. Ibid., p. 299.
5. *Letters*, 4.4.81.
6. See H. Wagner, 'Das Josephinische Wien und Mozart' (1979).
7. D. Beales, 'Christians and Philosophes', in *History, Society and the Churches* (1985), p. 185.
8. L. Bodi, *Tauwetter in Wien* (1977), p. 45.
9. Gay, *The Enlightenment*, vol. II, p. 425.
10. P. P. Bernard, *Jesuits and Jacobins* (1971), p. 53.
11. Beales, op. cit., p. 180.
12. E. Crankshaw, *Maria Theresa* (1969), p. 301.
13. Quoted in E. N. Williams, *The Ancien Régime in Europe* (1984), p. 475.
14. Beales, *Joseph II* (1987), p. 101.
15. Cameralism was the political theory of absolutism which taught the primacy of the economic interests of the state.
16. Beales, *Christians and Philosophes*, p. 187.
17. H. C. Robbins Landon, *Haydn: The Early Years* (1980), p. 324.
18. Sonnenfels, *Gesammelte Schriften*, vol. I, (1783), p. 104.
19. W. Ruf, *Die Rezeption von Mozarts 'Le nozze di Figaro* (1977), p. 38.
20. Hobbes, *Leviathan*.
21. Locke, *An Essay Concerning Human Understanding*, Bk II, Ch. 28, paras 6–10.
22. Rousseau, *The Social Contract and Discourses*, p. 206.
23. Burke, *Reflections on the Revolution in France*, p. 212.
24. Steele and Addison, *Selections from the Tatler and the Spectator*, p. 199.
25. Bernard, op. cit., p. 141.
26. Hampson, *The Enlightenment* (1968), p. 69.
27. 'I never espoused any party with violence', claimed Addison, the neutral spectator (Steele and Addison op. cit., p. 199).
28. F. Heartz, *The Development of the German Public Mind* (1962), p. 89.
29. Sonnenfels, op. cit., vol. I, p. 101.
30. Quoted in Eagleton, *The Ideology of the Aesthetic*, p. 43.
31. Quoted in Bodi, op. cit., p. 41.
32. Sonnenfels, op. cit., vol. IV, p. 9.
33. Ibid., vol. II, p. 342.
34. Bodi, op. cit., p. 166.
35. Quoted in Bodi, op. cit., p. 167.
36. Ibid., p. 82.
37. Gugitz, *Das Wiener Kaffeehaus* (1940), p. 71.

38. Ibid., p. 9.
39. Ibid., p. 10.
40. C. O'Brien, 'Ideas of Religious Toleration at the Time of Joseph II', *Transactions of the American Philosophical Society*, (1969), p. 60.
41. E. F. Ritter, *Johann Baptiste von Alxinger* (1970), p. 13.
42. Sonnenfels, op. cit. vol. III, p. 119.
43. R. A. Kann, *A Study in Austrian Intellectual History from Late Baroque to Romanticism* (1960), p. 205.

44. Strakosch, *State Absolutism and the Rule of Law*, p. 142.
45. R. P. von Thurn, *Joseph II als Theaterdirektor* (1920), p. 33.
46. Has Nancy Storace, Mozart's first Susanna, left the company because of her marriage, he asks in one letter, or because she has a better engagement elsewhere? (Ibid., p. 50).
47. Bodi, op. cit., p. 94.
48. Ritter, op. cit., p. 24.
49. Beales, *Joseph II*, p. 253.
50. Thurn, op. cit., p. 1.
51. Bodi, op. cit., p. 119.
52. Beales, op. cit., p. 132.

VIII MOZART'S ARRIVAL IN VIENNA

1. *Letters*, 24.3.81. In his short essay *The Family Romance* Freud suggested that all children go through a phase in which, discovering that their parents are less than perfect, they set up for themselves exalted substitutes – usually kings or queens, or in Freud's examples the Emperor, in dreams and fairy stories – whom they then pretend are their real parents. It is very probable that Mozart may literally have undergone Freud's process of transference in his later than usual rebellion against his father (which was clearly combined with the Freudian trauma of recognizing his superiority to his father as a musician).
2. *Letters*, 12.9.81.
3. E. M. Link, *The Emancipation of the Austrian Peasant, 1740–1798* (1949), p. 132.
4. Deutsch, *Mozart. A Documentary Biography*, p. 539.

5. Robbins Landon, *The Mozart Compendium* (1990), p. 128.
6. *Letters*, 12.5.81.
7. Pezzl, *Skizze von Wien*, p. 86.
8. Quoted in E. N. Williams, *The Ancien Régime in Europe*, p. 229.
9. Pezzl, op. cit., p. 89.
10. Forster, natural scientist, Mozart's exact contemporary, had sailed on Captain Cook's second voyage to the South Seas, and was to be one of the leaders of the ill-fated Mainz Revolution in 1791.
11. K. Harpprecht, *Georg Forster* (1990), p. 302.
12. *Letters*, 22.12.81.
13. Deutsch, op. cit., pp. 573–82. A. Einstein, *Mozart* (1971), p. 159.
14. *Letters*, 10.4.82.
15. Ibid., 11.4.81.
16. Ibid., 18.4.81.

IX DIE ENTFÜHRUNG AUS DEM SERAIL

1. *Letters*, 26.9.81.
2. Ibid., 16.6.81.
3. Ibid., 1.7.81.
4. E. Said, *Orientalism* (1985).
5. J. B. von Alxinger, *Sämtliche Gedichte* (1788), vol. I, p. 125.
6. *Letters*, 19.10.82.

7. W. D. Wilson, *Humanität und Kreuzungsideologie* (1984), p. 7.
8. Quoted in Hampson, *The Enlightenment*, p. 148.
9. Ibid., p. 126.
10. Sonnenfels, *Gesammelte Schriften*, vol. III, pp. 366–75.

12. S. Lukes, *Individualism* (1973), p. 81.
13. H. Brunschwig, *Enlightenment and Romanticism in Eighteenth-century Prussia* (1974), p. 26.
14. Strakosch, *State Absolutism and the Rule of Law*, p. 105.
15. Hobbes, *Leviathan*, p. 125.
16. Harpprecht, *Georg Forster*, p. 406.
17. Crocker, *Nature and Culture*, p. 65.
18. Ibid., p. 34.
19. Montesquieu, *Persian Letters*, Letter 161.
20. M. Mitteraurer and R. Sieder, *The European Family* (1982), p. 76.
21. Mozart himself clearly felt that the vocal artifice of Italian *fioritura* was inimical to true expressiveness; of the aria 'Trennung war mein banges los' he wrote 'I have tried to express her feelings as far as an Italian bravura aria will allow it' (*Letters*, 26.9.81).
22. The existence of such a story in the age of Crusades is surprising, until one recalls that it gained its widest popularity during the thirteenth century, when Christendom was attempting to make a rapprochement with Islam after the repeated failure of a whole series of Crusades. See R. W. Southern, *Western Views of Islam in the Middle Ages* (1962).
23. T. Heywood, *The Fair Maid of the West* (1631), Part II, V, Scene 1.
24. *Shorter Oxford Dictionary*: 'Constancy'.
25. T. Paine, 'Letter to the Abbé Raynal', in *The Thomas Paine Reader* (1987), p. 162.
26. Rousseau, *Letter à d'Alembert*, p. 82.
27. S. Richardson, *Selected Letters*, ed. J. Carroll (1964).
28. Goethe, *Torquato Tasso*, II: 6.
29. Rousseau, *Emile*, p. 354.
30. Quoted in R. P. Utter and G. B. Needham, *Pamela's Daughters* (1937), p. 32.
31. Hume, *A Treatise of Human Nature*, p. 624.
32. Quoted in Utter and Needham, op. cit.
33. Richardson, *Selected Letters*, p. 142.
34. Gemmingen, *Der Weltmann*, p. 107.
35. An observation made by N. John in 'Monostatos: Pamina's Incubus', *Opern und Opernfiguren* (1989).
36. Richardson, *Clarissa*, vol. III, p. 338. The moral imperative of seduction seeped into real life too. In 1773 a male correspondent in an agony-aunt column (they existed in the eighteenth-century; the world's first agony aunt may have been Defoe) wrote that, in testing his betrothed he had 'succeeded in seducing his loved one, but now is tortured by the fact that he cannot marry her' (Utter and Needham, op. cit., p. 289).
37. I. Watt, *The Rise of the Novel* (1957), p. 197.
38. P. Aubin, *The Strange Adventures of the Count de Vinevil* (1721), Preface.
39. Quoted in R. Donnington, *Wagner's Ring and its Symbols* (1974), p. 265.
40. Deutsch, *Mozart. A Documentary Biography*, p. 209.
41. W. R. Chetwood, *The Generous Freemason* (1731).

X FREEMASONRY AND THE CATHOLIC ENLIGHTENMENT

1. *Journal für Freymaurer* (1784), vol. I, pp. 135–92.
2. Bodi, *Tauwetter in Wien*, p. 77.
3. Winter, *Baroque Absolutismus und Aufklärung in der Donaumonarchie*, p. 191.
4. Paine, 'Common Sense', in *The Thomas Paine Reader*, p. 66.
5. Voltaire estimated that Christianity had created in all 9,718,800 victims (Gay, *Voltaire's Politics* (1959), p. 252).
6. Quoted in Bruford, *Theatre, Drama and Audience in Goethe's Germany*, p. 119.
7. Quoted in P. Hazard, *The European Mind* (1964), p. 328.
8. Quoted in C. Blum, *Diderot: the Virtue of a Philosopher* (1974), p. 6.

9. Hume, *A Treatise of Human Nature*, p. 507.
10. A. Smith, *The Theory of Moral Sentiments* (1759).
11. J. L. Talmon, *The Origins of Totalitarian Democracy* (1986), p. 21.
12. Blum, op. cit., p. 67.
13. Lessing, *Ernst und Falk* in *Werke* (1979), vol. VIII, pp. 252–88.
14. Quoted in D. Knoop and G. P. Jones, *The Genesis of Freemasonry* (1947), p. 180.
15. Quoted in M. C. Jacob, *The Radical Enlightenment* (1981), p. 296.
16. Kant, *Religion Within the Limits of Reason Alone* (1960), pp. 89, 86.
17. Lessing, op. cit., vol. VIII, pp. 252–288.
18. Quoted in Gooch, *Germany and the French Revolution*, p. 31.
19. See Jacob, op. cit.
20. cf. Forster, in V. Braunbehrens, *Mozart in Wien* (1986), p. 254.
21. Braunbehrens, op. cit., p. 255.
22. *Physikalischen Arbeiten* (1783).
23. Braunbehrens, op. cit., p. 255.
24. E. Rosenstrauch-Königsberg, *Freimaurer, Illuminat, Weltburger* (1984), p. 74.
25. Braunbehrens, op. cit., p. 255.
26. Rosenstrauch-Königsberg, op. cit., p. 78.
27. R. Keil, *Wiener Freunder* (1883), p. 21.
28. Quoted in E. Zellwecker, *Das Urbild des Sarastros* (1953), p. 76.
29. *Journal für Freymaurer*, vol. I, p. 11.
30. Ibid., p. 10.
31. Ibid., p. 5.
32. Alxinger, *Sämtliche Gedichte* (1788), vol. II, appendix p. 6.
33. Paine, op. cit. p. 251.
34. Braunbehrens, op. cit., p. 171.
35. Professor of Aesthetics at Vienna University, the first Kantian in Vienna, and author of Haydn's anthem *Gott erhalt Franz der Kaiser*.
36. Dubious, since it is Karoline Pichler's later, ungracious memories of Mozart we have to thank for the portrait of Mozart in Peter Schaffer's play *Amadeus*.
37. The masonic song *Lied zur Gesellenreise*, K.468; and Blumauer's *Lied der Freiheit*, K.506, respectively.
38. Deutsch, *Mozart*, p. 287.
39. Ibid., p. 291.
40. Ibid., pp. 243–58.
41. The evidence hangs upon the disputed datings of the masonic song *O heiliges Band*, K.148, whose text celebrates the St John Lodge in Salzburg.
42. 'The best two are "Zur wahren Eintracht", of which the master is Born. The m[asonic] Journal which comes from this you can see at Brother Moldenhauer ... Gemmingen, the author of the *Hausvater* is similarly M[aster] of the Lodge "Zur Wohltätigkeit". These are the two best' (quoted in Rosenstrauch-Königsberg, op. cit., pp. 72–3).
43. T. G. Blanning in R. Porter and M. Teich (eds), *The Enlightenment in National Context* (1981), p. 118.
44. F. Nicolai, *Beschreibung einer Reiser durch Deutschland und die Schweitz im Jahre 1781* (1783–4), Bk II, Ch. 12.
45. G. R. Cragg, *The Church and the Age of Reason* (1960), p. 219.
46. A. von Arneth, *Maria Theresia und Joseph II* (1867–8), vol. III, p. 468.
47. Cragg, op. cit., p. 219.
48. Bernard, *Jesuits and Jacobins* (1971), p. 86.
49. O. Sashegyi, *Zensur und Geistesfreiheit unter Joseph II* (1958), p. 21.
50. Cragg, op. cit., p. 98.
51. Wangermann, *Aufklärung und Staatsbürgerliche Erziehung* (1978), p. 50.
52. Quoted in Sashegyi, op. cit., p. 39.
53. Cragg, op. cit., p. 220.
54. One of his least enlightened deeds was to order the flogging of a sect of Bohemian Deists who had refused to recant.
55. O'Brien, 'Ideas of Religious Toleration at the Time of Joseph II', p. 57.

56. Gemmingen, *Der Weltmann*, vol. IV, p. 111.
57. O'Brien, op cit., p. 57.
58. Ibid., p. 56.
59. M. Brandl, *Marx Anton Wittola* (1974), p. 33.
60. Ibid., p. 129.
61. Also the meaning of the name of Pezzl's Pater Boniface in *Faustin*.
62. Gemmingen, op. cit., vol. III, p. 45.
63. H. Reinalter, *Joseph II und die Freimaurer* (Graz and Vienna, 1987), p. 61. Michaeler's conflation of freemasonry and Muratorian Christianity was not new. The Salzburg circle in which Muratorian ideas first flourished in the 1740s had suffered from imputations that they were in fact freemasons – the result of a confusion with the Italian name for masons: 'Muratori'.

64. Deutsch, op. cit., p. 451.
65. *Letters* 11/12.2.78.
66. Wolfgang.
67. *Letters*, 13.6.81.
68. Deutsch, op. cit., p. 289.
69. Quoted in P. Nettl, *Mozart and Masonry*, p. 23.
70. E. Gibbon, *Memoirs of my Life* (1984), p. 64.
71. J. Kirkby, *Automathes* (1745).
72. 'I have not come to destroy men but to make them happy,' is Wittola's typical rereading of St Luke's 'I have not come to destroy men's lives but to save them'. (Luke 9:56) Wittola's reading is in his *Schreiben eines österreichischen Pfarrers über die Toleranz* (1781).
73. *Letters*, 13.11.77.
74. Ibid., 4.1.83.

XI THE RETURN TO ITALIAN OPERA

1. *Letters*, 17.8.82.
2. Ibid., 10.4.82.
3. Numerous writers during the Josephine period were indeed employed in the burgeoning Austrian bureacracy, giving rise to the description of Josephine literature as *Beamteliteratur* – civil service literature.
4. Bodi, *Tauwetter in Wien*, p. 129.
5. Sonnenfels, *Gesammelte Schriften*, vol. III, p. 113.
6. Gemmingen, *Der Weltmann*, vol. V, p. 188.
7. Nicolai, *Beschreibung einer Reise durch Deutschland und die Schweiz*, Bk II, Ch. 12, p. 878.
8. Robbins Landon, *Haydn at Eszterháza* (1978), p. 31.
9. Philip Hafner's play *Megära, die förchterliche Hexe* ('Megara, the fearsome Witch') was all the rage in the 1760s; it contains many elements of the popular Viennese stage which were to reappear in *Die Zauberflöte*: the apostrophizing of a beloved's portrait; a mock suicide scene; and the spectacular entry of the witch Megara herself.
10. *Letters*, 30.1.68.
11. Gemmingen, op. cit., p. 22.
12. Ibid., p. 236.
13. *Realzeitung*, 21.2.86.
14. Bernard, *Jesuits and Jacobins*, p. 86.
15. Keil, *Wiener Freunder*, p. 86.
16. Ironically, as early as 1765 Sonnenfels himself had come to blows with the great publisher Trattner by complaining that Trattner was flooding Vienna with northern-German literature and inhibiting the development of native Austrian writers.
17. Rupert Feuchtmuller, *Kunst in Österreich*, vol. II (1973), p. 135.
18. Joseph II was a great admirer of the St Michael group; but his Censorship Commission firmly banned the representation of anything obviously religious from the Viennese stage as being indecorous.

19. H. Maschler, *Tobias Philipp Freiherr von Gebler* (1933), p. 66.
20. Mann, *The Operas of Mozart*, p. 295.
21. *Letters*, 1.11.77.
22. For a lively discussion of this Quartet, see W. Mann, *The Operas of Mozart* (1977), pp. 312–4.
23. Goethe, *Italian Journey* (1986), p. 420.

24. *Letters*, 5.2.83.
25. Ibid., 21.12.82.
26. Ibid., 5.22.83.
27. Quoted in R. Goldberg, *Sex and Enlightenment* (1984), p. 95.
28. Lorenzo Da Ponte, *Memoirs* (1929) p. 152.

XII LE NOZZE DI FIGARO

1. Dante, quoted in the introduction to *The Divine Comedy: Inferno* (1985), p. 42.
2. Vanbrugh, *The Provok'd Wife*, V:4.
3. Humankind cannot enjoy both the simple contentment of the animal condition, and at the same time hope for something better, as Schiller tells in his poem *Resignation* (*Sämtliche Werke*, vol. I).
4. Goethe, Faust, Pt I (1949), Faust's Study.
5. Schiller, *Über naive und sentimentalische Dichtung* (*Sämtliche Werke*, vol V, p. 717).
6. Rousseau, *Emile*, p. 44.
7. Goethe, *Gedenkenausgabe*, vol. I *Metamorphosen der Tiere*.
8. Schiller, op. cit., vol. V, p. 760.
9. Rousseau, *La nouvelle Héloïse*, Pt IV, Letter 11.
10. De Sade, *Philosophy in the Boudoir*, (1966), p. 324.
11. *Letters*, 26.5.84.
12. In seventeenth-century Holland, more than a hundred years before the Viennese *Stubenmädchenbroschuren*, there had also been a strong literary and visual tradition representing servants as subversive spirits in the household, their presence 'a kind of Trojan horse of worldliness effecting an illicit entry into the moral citadel of the burgher household' as Simon Schama puts it (Schama, *The Embarrassment of Riches* (1987), p. 460).
13. J. McManners, *Death and the Enlightenment* (1981), p. 374.
14. Maine, *Ancient Law*, p. 140.

15. Link, *The Emancipation of the Austrian Peasant, 1740–1798* (1949), p. 111.
16. Rousseau, *Social Contract and Discourses*, p. 169.
17. Eagleton, *The Ideology of the Aesthetic*, p. 282.
18. Only in Romantic operas do valets lead revolutions: viz. Giordano's *Andrea Chénier*, which presents, as it were, the revolutionary outcome that will *not* happen in *Figaro*.
19. Lessing, *Emilia Galotti* (1969), V:7.
20. Quoted in Balet, *Die Verbürgerlichung der Deutschen Kunst und Musik im 18. Jahrhundert*, p. 127.
21. Rousseau, *Social Contract and Discourses*, p. 139.
22. Quoted in Hampson, *The Enlightenment*, p. 215.
23. Schiller, *Die Räuber*, V, 2.
24. Montesquieu, *L'esprit des lois*, Bk II, 4.
25. Pezzl, *Skizze von Wien*, p. 245.
26. Schama, *Citizens*, (1989), p. 117.
27. Robbins Landon, *The Mozart Compendium*, p. 65.
28. Sonnenfels, *Gesammelte Schriften*, vol. VIII, pp. 182–205.
29. Gemmingen, *Der Weltmann*, pp. 2, 49–57.
30. A brief recounting of the plot of Voltaire's play quickly indicates the similarities. The farmer Mathurin wants to marry the steward's daughter Acante, but his former beloved Colette is pursuing him for the marital promises previously made to her, and is holding out (like Marcellina) against money that he owes her. Mathurin is anxious that his wedding to Acante be held as soon as possible

to prevent the local seigneur, the Marquis, from claiming his *droit de seigneur*, the *jus primae noctis* which is supposed to give him access to every girl on the estate when she gets married. The outcome of the play, however, is very different from that of Figaro. The Marquis falls in love with Acante, who is then abducted by a wicked aristocratic relative of the Marquis. Acante turns out, naturally, to be herself noble and marries the good Marquis, who had possessed far too much honour to abuse his largely symbolic right. Mathurin has to abide by the promises he originally made, and returns to Colette.

31. Quoted in John Wood's Introduction to Beaumarchais, *The Barber of Seville/The Marriage of Figaro* (1964).

32. Sashegyi, *Zensur und Geistesfreiheit unter Joseph II* (1958), p. 57.

33. Comparable attitudes were to be conveyed by van Swieten's Censorship Commission in expressing its anxiety at the increased number of public reading rooms in Vienna, in which 'careless maids and immature youths' might read books for no more than a few pennies (Sashegyi, op. cit., p. 25).

34. Da Ponte, *Memoirs*, p. 131.

35. Tanner, *Adultery in the Novel* (1986), p. 15.

36. Rousseau, *Emile*, p. 8.

37. Rousseau, *Social Contract and Discourses*, p. 178.

38. Rousseau, *La nouvelle Héloïse*, Pt I, Letter 11.

39. Ibid., Pt I, Letter 31.

40. 'a natura, al dover lor dritti io rendo': the line is Da Ponte's rather than Beaumarchais's.

41. Montesquieu, *Persian Letters*, Letter 116.

42. A. Macfarlane, *Marriage and Love in England 1300–1840* (1986), p. 151.

43. Ibid., p. 176.

44. In Vanbrugh's *The Provok'd Wife* of 1697, Lady Brute daringly applies Locke's breakable political contract

theory to marriage: 'The argument's good between the King and the people, why not between the husband and the wife?' Vanbrugh, *The Provok'd Wife*, I, 1.

45. Strakosch, *State Absolutism and the Rule of Law*, p. 157.

46. Divorce was also legalized in the French Revolution. But as in the conservative reaction following Joseph II, it was outlawed again by Napoleon. Authoritarian societies (such as Stalinist Russia, which penalized divorce, reversing the libertarian attitudes of the early Bolsheviks) have always been mistrustful of soluble vows.

47. F. Engels, *The Origin of the Family*, p. 142.

48. Macfarlane, op. cit., p. 134.

49. Hogarth planned, but never completed, a second sequence of paintings, *The Happy Marriage*, as a companion to *Marriage-à-la-Mode*. Like Tolstoy, he obviously found happy marriages less interesting than unhappy ones.

50. Quoted in K. M. Rogers, *Feminism in Eighteenth-century England* (1982), p. 11.

51. *Shamela* was Fielding's unkind parody of *Pamela*, in which he suggests that Pamela/Shamela is really a scheming adventuress, rather than an innocent victim.

52. Johnson, *The History of Rasselas* (1968), Ch. 22.

53. J. L. Flandrin, *Families in Former Times* (1976), p. 133.

54. Beaumarchais, *Eugénie* (1768), p. xxxi.

55. *Letters*, 7.2.78.

56. Ibid., 4.11.87.

57. Ibid., 15.12.81.

58. Ibid., 8.4.89.

59. Ibid. 16.5.89.

60. Ibid. 5.7.91.

61. Ibid. 7.7.91.

62. For further discussion of the injustice done to Constanze by posterity, see Robbins Landon, *Mozart's Last Year*, pp. 182–99.

63. One sixteenth-century theologian had decreed that 'Those who prevent their men and women servants from marrying when it is opportune for them to do so, and who see that otherwise they will be in danger of fornicating and forming some guilty liaison, commit a sin,' (Flandrin, op. cit., p. 142).

64. M. Mitteraurer and R. Sieder, *The European Family* (1982), pp. 122–6.

65. Take, for example, Mary Wollstonecraft's unsisterly portrait of the aristocratic wife Eliza, in the novel *Mary*, who is 'indolent', a reader of 'sentimental novels', who 'accompanied the lovers to the lonely arbors, and would walk with them by the clear light of the moon. She wondered why her husband did not stay at home. She was jealous – why did he not love her, sit by her side, squeeze her hand, and look unutterable things?' Wollstonecraft, *Mary* and *The Wrongs of Woman* (1976), p. 3.

66. Montesquieu, op. cit., Letter 55.

67. For a detailed analysis of this aria, see Mann, *The Operas of Mozart*, pp. 431–3.

68. Quoted in Ernst Bloch, *The Principle of Hope*, (1986), p. 211.

69. Engels, op. cit., p. 136.

70. Rousseau, *Emile*, p. 354.

71. Rousseau, *Lettre à d'Alembert*, p. 128.

72. Ariès and Bejin, *Western Sexuality*, pp. 140–152.

73. Link, op. cit., pp. 50–60.

74. Quoted in Strakosch, op. cit., p. 148, Joseph's subjects took violent exception, for instance, to his (on paper) eminently sensible proposals in 1785 to restrict the wasteful cost of funerals, and in the same year the first rumblings of discontent at Joseph's religious reforms occurred in Belgium; people, it seemed, *wanted* the old ceremonials and superstitious customs.

75. Quoted in *Zaubertöne – Mozart in Wien*, p. 460.

76. Burke, *Reflections on the Revolution in France*, p. 183.

77. Ibid., p. 194.

78. Goethe, *Conversations and Encounters* (1960), p. 138.

79. Hampson, op. cit., p. 240.

80. Bauer, op. cit., p. 30.

81. In Moritz von Schwind's drawings for the wedding procession in *Le nozze de Figaro*, made in 1825, the opera appears to be set in Wagner's Nuremberg rather than Beaumarchais's Spain; highly appropriate, since *Die Meistersinger* is German art's greatest celebration of the need for change to take place within the framework of communal cohesion and historical wisdom.

82. Goethe, *Italian Journey*, p. 24.

83. 'You have faith and hope; I congratulate you for that, they will procure you eternal life,' claims Voltaire. 'Your theological virtues are heavenly gifts, your cardinal virtues are excellent qualities which help to guide you, but they are not virtues in respect of your fellow man. The prudent man seeks his own good, the virtuous man does good to others', (Voltaire, *Dictionnaire philosophique, Vertu*).

84. 'On these two commandments [to love God and one's neighbour] depend all the law and the prophets' (Matthew 22:37).

85. Cassirer, *The Philosophy of the Enlightenment*, p. 166.

86. Hampson, op. cit., p. 99.

87. Kant, *Religion with the Limits of Reason Alone* (1960), p. 113.

88. W. Blake, *Complete Writings* (1966), p. 757.

89. L. Feuerbach, *The Essence of Christianity* (1853), p. 240.

90. Blake, op. cit., p. 753.

91. Hobbes, *Leviathan*, p. 163.

92. Ibid., p. 173.

93. Quoted in Bruford, *Theatre, Drama and Audience in Goethe's Germany*, p. 111. Crusoe calls his disobedience to his father his 'original sin'; Tom

Jones is booted out of Paradise Hall for concupiscence, and eventually reunited with his long-lost father; Clarissa disobediently leaves her paternal home by the garden gate, and returns to die and be received, finally blessed, in heaven.

94. This distinction is evident, the other way round, in the incident in which Louis XV, thinking that he was dying after having been stabbed in an assassination attempt, forgave his would-be assassin Damiens – a fact that did not prevent Louis from having Damiens horribly tortured and executed.

95. 'To have received from one, to whom we think ourselves equall, greater benefits than there is hope to Requite . . . puts a man into the estate of a desperate debtor; . . . and obligation is thraldome . . . which is to one's equall hatefull. But to have received benefits from one, whom we acknowledge far superior, enclines to love' (Hobbes, op. cit., p. 163).

96. B. Spinoza, *Improvement of Understanding* (1901), p. 3.

97. P. Tillich, *Dynamics of Faith* (1959), p. 100.

98. Corinthians 5:18–19.

99. Stendhal, *Vie de Mozart* (1990), p. 89.

XIII THE MEANING OF CLASSICISM

1. G. H. Lewes, *The Life of Goethe* (1864).

2. Goethe, *Conversations and Encounters*, p. 194.

3. *Letters*, 28.12.82.

4. Goethe, op. cit., p. 141.

5. Kant, *The Philosophy of Kant*.

6. Goethe, *Gedenkenausgabe*, vol. II *Natur und Kunst*.

7. Hampson, *The Enlightenment*, p. 201.

8. E. Goethe, *Wilhelm Meister*, vol. II (1925), p. 79.

9. Quoted in Blume, *Classic and Romantic Music*, p. 9.

10. Ibid., p. 10.

11. *Letters*, 20.11.77.

12. Ibid., 26.10.81.

13. In the Trio 'Marsch, marsch, marsch' at the end of Act I of *Die Entführung* we note that Mozart still employs strict academic counterpoint as a joke.

14. Bach's fugues, Goethe once said, were like the pure, unmaterialized form which had existed in God's heart before the creation (see E. Bloch, *Essays on the Philosophy of Music* (1974), p. 223).

15. Fugal forms seem to have played a comparable role in Haydn's musical development: witness the fugal finales of several of his Opus 20 string quartets.

16. Gluck, *The Collected Correspondence and Papers*, p. 99.

17. Da Ponte, *Memoirs*, p. 129.

18. Quoted in G. Schmidgall, *Literature as Opera* (1977), p. 77.

19. Quoted in Rosen, *The Classical Style*, p. 177.

20. Sonata form also creates a dynamic rather than a passive relationship with the listener, reflecting the Lockean definition of personal identity as an identity of consciousness through duration in time, achieved through the workings of the memory, without which we can have no sense of our own continuity and personal history. With its play of arousal of expectation and delay of fulfilment, its use of symmetrical forms, and its dependence upon a purposeful prospect of fulfilment, classical sonata-form relies far more heavily upon the active contribution of the listener and his or her memory than baroque music (which commands more passive attention), and in doing so confirms his or her independent existence. It also conveys the later eighteenth-century's increasing consciousness of history as an unfolding process

immanent in reality, in which every
present moment contains within it
both past and future.

21. Quoted in Cassirer, *Rousseau, Kant and Goethe* (1945), p. 91.
22. Quoted in J. Todd, *Sensibility* (1986), p. 25.
23. Quoted in Eagleton, *The Ideology of the Aesthetic* (1990), p. 41.
24. J. Rushton, *Classical Music* (1986), p. 124.
25. Schiller, *On the Aesthetic Education of Man*, Letter 4, para. 3.
26. Ibid., Letter 20, para. 3.
27. Ibid., Letter 11, para. 9.
28. Ibid., Letter 27, para. 12.
29. Schiller, *Sämtliche Werke*, vol. I, pp. 237–8.
30. I am indebted to Wye Allanbrook's masterly analysis of Mozart's use of dance-forms in his operas, *Rhythmic Gesture in Mozart* (1983), for this discussion.
31. Da Ponte, op. cit., p. 129.
32. Montesquieu, *Persian Letters*, Letter 46.
33. See Sashegyi, *Zensur und Geistesfreiheit unter Joseph II* (1958), p. 13.
34. Quoted in Beales, 'Christians and Philosophes', in *History, Society and the Churches*, p. 172.
35. J. Sacks, BBC Reith Lectures, 1990 (*The Listener*, 15.11.1990).
36. B. Pascal, *Pensées* (1966), no. 201.
37. T. Mann, *Doktor Faustus* (1968), p. 89.
38. Burke, *A Philosophical Enquiry into the Origin of our Ideas of the Sublime and Beautiful* (1958), Bk II, 1–22.
39. Ibid., II, 17–20.
40. Burke, *Reflections on the Revolution in France*, p. 283.
41. Wieland, *Sympathien* (1795), p. 97.
42. The great theological virtues have never left us. We need only consider Beethoven's Leonora, who embodies each of St Paul's trinity of Christian virtues: Faith (her very name, Fidelio, and her marital fidelity), Hope (the subject of her great aria 'Komm Hoffnung'), and Love (the wellspring of her heroism, eventually transmuted into universal love as she swears to rescue the unknown prisoner 'whoever you are'). In *Fidelio* Leonora's faith, hope and love have become transcendent ideals with the power to liberate humanity from material imprisonment. *Fidelio* is as much a metaphysical as a political drama.
43. Goethe, *Gedenkenausgabe*, vol. VI, *Iphigenia*, IV:5.
44. Ibid., vol. I.
45. Ibid., vol. IX, *Maximen und Reflexionen*.
46. Blake, *Complete Writings*, p. 750.
47. Diderot, in *Encyclopédie*, vol. XI, *Opera*.
48. Heiseler, *Schiller*, p. 108.
49. Quoted in P. Le Huray and J. Day, *Music and Aesthetics in the Eighteenth and Early Nineteenth Centuries* (1981), p. 236.
50. Deutsch, *Mozart. A Documentary Biography*, p. 450.
51. M. Tippett, *Moving into Aquarius* (1984), pp. 67–85.
52. Schiller, *Sämtliche Werke*, vol. II, pp. 815–824.
53. Goethe, *Gedenkenausgabe*, vol. XX, Goethe–Schiller correspondence, 29.12.97.
54. Bruford, *Theatre, Drama and Audience in Goethe's Germany*, (1950) p. 304.
55. Quoted in Le Huray and Day, op. cit., p. 489.
56. Quoted in J. Starobinski, *Les Emblèmes de la raison* (1973), p. 163.
57. Blake, op. cit., p. 97.
58. Goethe, *Gedenkenausgabe*, vol. IX, 'Maximen und Reflexionen'.
59. Schiller, *Sämtliche Werke*, vol. V, p. 722.

XIV THE COLLAPSE OF JOSEPHINISM

1. Rosenstrauch-Königsberg, *Freimaurer, Illuminat, Weltburger*, p. 75.
2. Reinalter, *Aufgeklärter Absolutismus* (1980), p. 199.
3. Bodi, *Tauwetter in Wien*, p. 151.

4. Quoted in A. Fitzlyon, *Lorenzo Da Ponte* (1982), p. 83.
5. Pezzl, *Skizze von Wien*, vol. III, p. 351.
6. Wangermann, *From Joseph II to the Jacobin Trials* (1969), p. 36.
7. Sashegyi, *Zenzur und Geistesfreiheit unter Joseph II.*
8. Wangermann, *The Austrian Achievement* (1973), p. 162.
9. Daughter of Mozart's patron Hofrat Greiner, and a devout Catholic writing in a period when Vienna had become the centre of the Romantic Catholic revival.
10. She cites Holbach's notorious *Système de la nature* and Laclos's *Les liaisons dangereuses* as two books that were introduced into the Greiner household.
11. K. Pichler, *Denkwürdigen aus meinem Leben* (1844), p. 118.
12. Quoted in M. C. Jacob, *The Radical Enlightenment* (1981), p. 124.
13. Quoted in A. J. Ayer, *Thomas Paine* (1989), p. 152.
14. Quoted in R. F. Brissenden, *Virtue in Distress* (1974), p. 16.
15. R. van Dulman, *Der Geheimband der Illuminaten* (1975), p. 105.
16. *Realzeitung*, p. 142. Weishaupt had also condemned masonic esotericism, and what he dubbed 'Thorheiten' [idiocies] (H. Grassl, *Aufbruch zur Romantik* (1968), p. 210).
17. Born had been a Jesuit, and many others of his circle were educated by the Jesuits.
18. Rosenstrauch-Königsberg, op. cit., p. 74.
19. Reinalter, *Joseph II und die Freimaurer*, pp. 107, 135.
20. *Letters*, 4.2.78.
21. Ibid.
22. Ibid., 22.2.78.
23. Deutsch, *Mozart. A Documentary Biography*, p. 296.
24. Holbach, in M. Cranston, *Philosophers and Pamphleteers* (1986), p. 125.
25. M. Mendelssohn, *Phaedon; or the Death of Socrates* (1789), pp. 95, 129.
26. *Letters*, 5.12.81.
27. *Journal für Freymaurer*, vol. I, pp. 144–5.
28. Ibid.
29. Rosenstrauch-Königsberg, op. cit., p. 75.
30. Reinalter, op. cit., p. 21.
31. P. A. Autexier, *Mozart et Liszt Sub Rosa* (1984).
32. *Zerfliesset heut', geliebte Brüder*, K.483.

XV   DON GIOVANNI

1. D. J. Enright, *The Alluring Problem* (1988), p. 45.
2. Quoted in John McManners, *Death and the Enlightenment* (1981), p. 178.
3. Gemmingen, *Der Weltmann*, p. 250.
4. J. Kerman, *Opera as Drama* (1956), p. 123.
5. B. Brophy, *Mozart the Dramatist* (1988), pp. 242–65.
6. I. Singer, *Mozart and Beethoven* (1977).
7. *Letters*, 4.4.87.
8. Goldoni, *Memoirs* (1926), p. 189.
9. H. Maschler, *Tobias Philipp Freiherr von Gebler* (1935), p. 66.
10. Fielding, *Tom Jones* (1987), Bk XII, Ch. 12.
11. Quoted in E. J. Dent, *Mozart's Operas* (1947), p. 129.
12. Byron, *The Poetical Works* (1912), *Don Juan*, Stanza 1.
13. Scene VI, quoted in S. Kunze, *Don Giovanni von Mozart* (1972).
14. Da Ponte, *Memoirs*, Introduction, p. 5.
15. Deutsch, *Mozart. A Documentary Biography*, p. 392.
16. P. C. de Laclos, *Les liaisons dangereuses* (1979), pp. 38, 39.
17. S. Kierkegaard, *Either/Or* (1959), p. 107.
18. cf. the two piano quartets; the pair of string quintets K. 515 and 516; the piano concertos in D minor and C major, K.466 and 467, and in A major and C minor, K.488 and 491,

entered in Mozart's catalogue together in March 1786.

19. *Letters*, 5.12.81.
20. M. Foucault, *The Order of Things* (1970).
21. G. Vico, *The New Science of Giambattista Vico* (1968), para. 982.
22. Burke, *A Philosophical Enquiry into the Origin of our Ideas of the Sublime and Beautiful* (1958), p. 42.
23. Rousseau, *Confessions*, p. 410.
24. The fetishistic ribbon which Cherubino steals from Susanna as a token of the Countess is to be found in Rousseau's *Confessions*, in *Werther*, in Goethe's poem *Der Bandel*, and in Mozart's domestic part-song (in Viennese dialect) *Liebes Mandel, wo ist's Bandel?*, K.441.
25. Masturbation, as Rousseau noted, is a vice that allows those with a lively imagination 'to dispose, so to speak, of the whole female sex at their will' (*Confessions*, p. 109).
26. Montesquieu, *Persian Letters*, Letter 30.
27. T. Bestermann, *The Age of Enlightenment* (1967), p. 48
28. In the most Pirandellian of Marivaux's plays, *Les acteurs de bonne foi*, the characters take part in a play in which they discover that they are acting themselves, and find themselves making unexpected revelations to each other.
29. Quoted in Utter and Needham, *Pamela's Daughters*, p. 26.
30. In the brilliantly provocative and insightful version of the opera by the Mexican Compania Divas, Giovanni is played by every member of the (largely female) cast in turn, a striking representation of his anonymity.
31. Rousseau, *La nouvelle Héloïse*, Part III, Letter 11.
32. The unstable vulnerability of the betrothed maiden is clearly recognized in many popular mythologies, which believe that if she dies in her transitional state she becomes a Lamia, a vampiric living deadwoman.
33. Montesquieu, *Persian Letters*, Letter 48.
34. A. Clark, *Women's Silence, Men's Violence* (1987), pp. 46–58.
35. Quoted in R. Sennett, *The Fall of the Public Man* (1974), p. 103.
36. Quoted in M. Byrd, *London Transform'd* (1978), p. 91.
37. Quoted in Brissenden, *Virtue in Distress*, p. 27.
38. Quoted in Cranston, *Philosophers and Pamphleteers*, p. 127.
39. Quoted in Blum, *Diderot: the Virtue of a Philosopher*, p. 6.
40. De Sade, *Juliette*, quoted in Crocker, *Nature and Culture*, p. 402.
41. 'Man is the cheapest commodity on the market, and among all our important rights of property, the rights of the individual have always been considered last.' (Rousseau, *Emile*, p. 211).
42. The problem of the legitimacy of the 'natural' was to strike the eighteenth-century explorers of the South Seas most forcefully when they discovered that the delightful practices of sexual freedom of the islanders were sometimes accompanied by the less appealing customs of human sacrifice and cannibalism.
43. Laclos, op. cit., p. 264.
44. Kierkegaard, *Either/Or*, Bk I, p. 91.
45. Montesquieu, op. cit., Letter 48.
46. Rousseau, *Emile*, p. 249.
47. Quoted in H. Reiss, *Goethe's Novels* (1969), p. 205.
48. Kant, *Religion Within the Limits* (1960).
49. Haller's own studies into the involuntary stimulation of muscles had prompted La Mettrie to dedicate his *L'homme machine* to him.
50. Quoted in K. Epstein, *The Genesis of German Conservatism* (1966), p. 68.
51. Ibid.
52. Locke, *An Essay Concerning Human Understanding*, p. 174.
53. Ibid. p. 23.

54. Voltaire, *Philosophical Dictionary*, p. 54.

55. Ibid.

56. Sonnenfels, *Gesammelte Schriften*, vol. 3, p. 255.

57. Ibid.

58. Quoted in H. C. Payne, *The Philosophes and the People*, p. 64.

59. Rousseau, *Social Contract and Discourses*, p. 273.

60. Rousseau, *Emile*, p. 247.

61. Rousseau, *Social Contract and Discourses*, p. 274.

62. Ibid., p. 276.

63. Voltaire, *Dictionnaire philosophique*, p. 186.

64. F. E. Manuel, *The 18th Century Confronts the Gods* (1959), p. 67.

65. Voltaire, op. cit., p. 249.

66. Quoted in L. Strauss, *Natural Right and History* (1953), p. 208.

67. Rousseau, *Social Contract and Discourses*, p. 7.

68. With more historical foundation, it is evident that much of the platonic system is derived from the Orphic mystery religions current in Plato's day.

69. The *Encylopédie* makes clear that initiatory *esoteric* religions in ancient Egypt and Greece were no more than the wisdom of the legislators, scholars and scientists of the community; Ignaz von Born's Egyptian mages in the *Journal für Freymaurer* are also scientists and lawyers.

70. Quoted in Allanbrook, *Rhythmic Gesture in Mozart*, p. 215.

71. Pascal, *Pensées*, no. 418.

72. Wangermann, *The Austrian Achievement*, p. 124.

73. *Realzeitung*, 21.2.86.

74. Wangermann, *From Joseph II to the Jacobin Trials*, p. 16.

75. Gugitz, *Johann Pezzl*, p. 172.

76. The great opening chord stretches from the top to the bottom of the stave, but leaves the bass resonating menacingly after the chord has ended, as if to tell us that the divine law rings through creation even after God's immediate revelation has withdrawn. The unsettling suspensions and scales which follow convey the mysteriousness of God's grace, which keeps its own counsel guarded from mere human pretensions to justice and morality ('How unsearchable His judgements' says St Paul; Romans, 11:3).

77. The hesitant opening, heavy with foreboding, becomes reassuringly authoritative with the chorus's first 'Requiem', rising to a hopeful climax on 'et lux perpetua'; the solo soprano's gentler 'Te decet' is accompanied by a compassionate descending violin phrase that subsequently combines with and softens the stern opening 'Requiem' motif. The terrifying 'Dies Irae' is followed by the 'Tuba Mirum' in which the trumpet that summons to Judgement (in fact a trombone, since Luther's last trumpet was a *posaune*) then gently weaves its solace around the repentant sinner. The solo quartet's promise of bliss at the words 'Cum vix Justus' is succeeded by the 'Rex Tremendae', depicting the implacable majesty of God, before whom the supplicant yearningly pleads, 'Salva me fons pietatis' ('Save me, O fount of mercy'). Grace itself seems to descend from its very fount in the following movement, the 'Recordare', in endless overlapping phrases, like wavelets whose source is as vast as the ocean. Again the brutal reminder that sinners are confounded ('Confutatis', the tenors and basses from the depths) to be redeemed by the distant female voices as if from heaven itself. Running through it all is the longing for peace and the promise of ultimate forgiveness.

78. Kierkegaard, op. cit.

79. Montesquieu, op. cit., Letter 57.

80. A. Camus, *The Rebel* (1982), p. 21.

81. Ibid., p. 219.

82. Hampson, *The Enlightenment*, p. 200.

83. Deutsch, op. cit., p. 452.

84. Quoted in W. James, *The Varieties of Religious Experience* (1985), p. 37.

XVI *COSÌ FAN TUTTE*

1. N. Frye, *Anatomy of Criticism* (1990).
2. Ibid., p. 178.
3. Ibid., p. 185.
4. Ibid., p. 202.
5. Da Ponte, *Memoirs*, p. 159.
6. O'Brien, *Ideas of Religious Toleration at the Time of Joseph II*, p. 32.
7. Wangermann, *The Austrian Achievement*, p. 158.
8. Wangermann, *From Joseph II to the Jacobin Trials*, p. 45.
9. Quoted in *Zaubertöne – Mozart in Wien*, p. 60.
10. Wangermann, op cit., p. 73.
11. Quoted in L. Goldmann, *Immanuel Kant* (1971), p. 130.
12. Quoted in Gay, *The Enlightenment*, vol. II, p. 169.
13. Hume, like Montesquieu, was of course aware that human beings can behave with bewildering variety in different cultures or climates; but this was all the more reason for penetrating beneath the variations.
14. Hume, *A Treatise of Human Nature*, p. 42.
15. Quoted in Ibid., Introduction, p. 9.
16. Quoted in J. Cruickshank, *French Literature and its Background* (1968–70), p. 25.
17. In L. Bredwold, *The Natural History of Sensibility* (1962), p. 34.
18. Hume, op. cit.
19. It will surprise no one to discover that this essence turns out to be wholly affirmative of the status quo; women attempt to seize control only to reveal their constitutional incapacity to do so; servants gladly return to their former position.
20. Rosen, *The Classical Style*, p. 314.
21. V. Goluben, *Marivauxs Lustspiele in Deutschen Übersetzungen des 18. Jahrhunderts* (1904).
22. J. Stone, in Robbins Landon, *The Mozart Compendium*, p. 240.
23. A private joke is usually suggested for the Ferrarese provenance; Da Ponte's mistress Adriana Ferrarese del Bene

sang the role of Fiordiligi in the first performances.
24. Link, *The Emancipation of the Austrian Peasant*, p. 75.
25. Rousseau, *Emile*, p. 255.
26. Locke, *Some Thoughts Concerning Education*, p. 53.
27. Rousseau, op. cit., p. 10.
28. Ibid., p. 29.
29. Ibid., p. 34.
30. Ibid.
31. I. O. Wade, *The Philosophe in French Drama of the Eighteenth Century* (1926).
33. For Mozart it is invariably the woodwind in the orchestra that convey sensuality and poetic feeling, while the strings largely supply the formal structure for musical argument.
34. Rousseau, op. cit. p. 53.
35. Ibid., p. 29.
36. Goethe, *Wilhelm Meister*, Bk 8, Ch. 5.
37. Rousseau, op cit., p. 34.
38. 'She had an excellent heart, ' her disposition was affectionate, and her feelings were strong; but she knew how to govern them' (Austen, *Sense and Sensibility*, p. 4).
39. Ibid.
40. *Letters*, 9.7.78.
41. The problem of how life arises from matter was discussed at length in Ebbert's *Naturlehre*, a book on natural history, owned by Mozart.
42. R. Darnton, *Mesmerism and the End of the Enlightenment in France* (1986), p. 114.
43. Marat was a keen political mesmerist before he found more dangerous outlets for his messianic visions in the French Revolution.
44. Stone, *The Family, Sex and Marriage in England, 1500–1800*, pp. 332–3.
45. *Realzeitung*, 14.3.86, pp. 162–7.
46. Laclos, *Les liaisons dangereuses*, p. 184.
47. Quoted in M. Horkheimer and T. Adorno, *The Dialectic of Enlightenment* (1973), p. 101.
48. Brissenden, *Virtue in Distress*, p. 27.

49. M. Wollstonecraft, *Mary* and *The Wrongs of Woman* (1767), p. 40.

50. 'Virtue' as reputation was soon recognized as a valuable marketable commodity. 'To be sure ma'm', cries Fielding's Mrs Honour to her mistress, recalling the success of Pamela, 'one's virtue is a dear thing, especially to us poor servants; for it is a livelihood' (*Tom Jones*, p. 322). This was not only the case for servants: the dowry paid to Mozart's sister Nannerl by her elderly husband was made 'in praemium virginitatis' – as the price for virginity (Hildesheimer, *Mozart*, p. 198).

51. F. Burney, *Evelina*, vol. I, p. 164.

52. Wollstonecraft, *Vindication of the Rights of Woman* (1975), p. 241.

53. Rousseau, *Emile*, p. 328.

54. Rousseau, *Confessions*, p. 190.

55. Crocker, *An Age of Crisis* (1959), p. 218.

56. Mary Wollstonecraft, writing to her faithless lover Gilbert Imlay, knew rationally that this was not necessarily the cast. 'I consider fidelity and constancy as two distinct things', she bravely affirmed; but she continued with the disclaimer that most of us find impossible to avoid: 'yet the former is necessary to give life to the other'. (Quoted in C. Tomalin, *The Life and Death of Mary Woolstonecraft* (1985), p. 196.)

57. Quoted in Cranston, *Philosophers and Pamphleteers*, p. 126.

58. Quoted in Hampson, *The Enlightenment*, p. 94.

59. 'Whether one has killed one's father or has abstained from doing so is not really the decisive thing,' said Freud about the Oedipus complex: 'One is bound to feel guilty in either case.' (Freud, *Civilization and its Discontents* (1939), p. 121.)

60. Rousseau, *Emile*, p. 251.

61. Crocker, op. cit., p. 238

62. Rousseau, *La nouvelle Héloïse*, Bk I, Letter 32.

63. Quoted in Pagliardo (ed.), *Studies in Eighteenth-Century Culture*, vol. III (1973), p. 275.

64. Eagleton, *The Ideology of the Aesthetic*, p. 282.

65. Nietzsche, *The Genealogy of Morals* (1956), p. 191.

66. Quoted in P. France, *Diderot* (1983), p. 41.

67. Diderot, *The Nun*, p. 102.

68. Quoted in J. Lough, *The Encyclopédie* (1971), p. 191.

69. Goethe, *Die Wahlverwandschaften* (1986), p. 106. *Die Wahlverwand-schaften* is surely the original magical-realist novel.

70. Goethe, *Gedankenausgabe*, vol. II, *Das Tagebuch*.

71. Rousseau, *Reveries of the Solitary Walker* (1979), pp. 50, 60.

72. Rousseau, *Emile*, p. 249.

73. Ibid., p. 254.

74. Goethe, *Gedenkenausgabe*, vol. VI, *Iphigenie* I, 3.

75. Rousseau, *Emile*, p. 249.

76. Nietzsche, op. cit.

77. Rousseau, *A Discourse on Inequality*, p. 136.

XVII LA CLEMENZA DI TITO

1. Contract published in Robbins Landon, *1791, Mozart's Last Year*, p. 88.

2. D. F. Tovey, *Essays in Musical Analysis* vol. VI (1940), p. 28.

3. In his thematic catalogue.

4. Quoted in G. Gruber, *Mozart and die Nachwelt* (1985), p. 61.

5. Ibid., p. 105.

6. C. Burney, *Memoirs of Metastasio*, p. 12.

7. 'Politics is magic. He who knows how to summon the forces from the deep, him will they follow' (quoted in C. E. Schorske, *Fin-de-siècle Vienna* (1961), p. 172).

8. Pezzl, *Faustin*, p. 348.

9. G. Des Marez, *Guide Illustrée de Bruxelles* (1979), p. 271.

10. Rousseau suggested that a republic was any state 'governed by laws' (*Social Contract and Discourses*, p. 192); Paine that it was government by 'election and representation' (*The Thomas Paine Reader*, p. 256); Kant that it was a state in which legislature and executive were separated.

11. Burney, op. cit., p. 317.

12. Ibid., vol. II, p. 324.

13. Ibid., vol. III, p. 34.

14. *The Merchant of Venice*, II, 1, ll. 188–95.

15. 'One law for the Lion and Ox is oppression', as Blake insists (quoted in Honour, *Romanticism* (1986), p. 289).

16. R. Rosenblum, *Transformations in Late Eighteenth-century Art* (1967), p. 190.

17. Seneca, *Minor Dialogues* (1889), pp. 417–21.

18. V. G. Kiernan, *The Duel in European History* (1989), p. 76.

19. 'I show [pity] most of all when I show justice/For then I pity those I do not know,/Which a dismiss'd offence would after gall' (Shakespeare, *Measure for Measure*, II, 2, ll. 100–102).

20. Quoted in I. Nagel, *Autonomie und Gnade* (1985), p. 107.

21. Harpprecht, *Georg Forster*, p. 447.

22. A. Wandruszka, *Leopold II*, vol. II (1965), p. 217.

23. In Beethoven's *Fidelio* the sovereign as the representative of absolute justice has become so godlike in his own right that he has retreated to more distant heights, and merely sends an emissary to administer his judgement.

24. The extensive role of the Third Estate in France and of the Commons in England had almost no equivalent in the Habsburg domains.

25. Quoted in Braunbehrens, *Mozart in Wien*, p. 238.

26. Link, *The Emancipation of the Austrian Peasant*, p. 135.

27. Rosenberg, *Bureaucracy, Aristocracy and Autocracy*, p. 190.

28. Bodi, *Tauwetter in Wien*, p. 251. Another aristrocratic proponent of the *thèse nobiliaire* was Alxinger, with whom Mozart was to work on a revision of *Acis and Galatea* in 1788.

29. A view seemingly supported by his widespread use of secret police powers to restore authority, to which Da Ponte fell victim as an undesirable in 1790.

30. L. Hoffmann, *Babel* (1790).

31. Quoted in Link, op. cit., p. 148.

32. The work he saw was Salieri's *Axur, re d'Ormus*, an adaptation by Da Ponte of Beaumarchais's model libretto *Tarare*, affirming the principles of responsible monarchy.

33. *Letters*, 3.10.90.

34. Luke, 15:7.

35. Matthew, 8:13.

XVIII *DIE ZAUBERFLÖTE*

1. Rosen, *The Classical Style*, p. 254.

2. Quoted in May, *Adorno* (London, 1984), p. 144.

3. G. W. F. Hegel, *Sämtliche Werke* (Stuttgart, 1928), Pt II, 3: *Vorlesungen über die Aesthetik*.

4. Pezzl, *Skizze von Wien*, p. 245.

5. Ibid., p. 245.

6. *Letters*, 8–9.10.91.

7. Beethoven, *Letters, Journals and Conversations* (1956), p. 109.

8. Quoted in Bruford, *Theatre, Drama and Audience in Goethe's Germany*, p. 304.

9. Goethe's sequel is a characteristic attempt by the great realist to relate the opera's spiritual truths back to the real world. Sarastro leaves the temple to become The Wanderer (mysteriously referred to in Schikaneder's text). Within the temple, he says, mankind learns to know itself and its innermost being, and to hear the voices of the gods;

but the truths of nature and of everyday humanity can only be known through the pilgrim's journey in the wide world (*Gedenkenausgabe*, vol. VI, p. 1103).

10. Quoted in Balet, *Die Verbürgerlichung der Deutschen Kunst, Literatur und Musik im 18. Jahrhundert*, p. 104.

11. Quoted in R. Kosellek, *Critique and Crisis* (1988), p. 103.

12. Goethe, *Conversations and Encounters*, p. 127.

13. Ibid., p. 275.

14. And eventually, with the rise of Nazism, which he recognized as its logical outcome, its most vehement critic in *Doktor Faustus*.

15. Quoted in Bruford, *The German Tradition of Self-Cultivation* (1975), p. vii.

16. Quoted in Balet, op. cit., p. 129.

17. Harpprecht, *Georg Forster*, p. 402.

18. Quoted in K. Epstein, *The Genesis of German Conservatism* (1966), p.449.

19. Schiller, *Der Antritt des neuen Jahrhunderts, Sämtliche Werke*, vol. I.

20. Terrasson, *Sethos*, p. 190.

21. Indeed, it has even been suggested that the very form of the novel itself as evolved in Hellenistic times is initiatory; every classical novel being a mystery text, a re-enactment of the story of the separation, loss and eventual reuniting of Isis and Osiris. Hegel recognized the modern German novel of his day as a bourgeois version of the medieval knightly quest romance.

22. Quoted in H. Grassl, *Aufbruch zur Romantik* (1968), p. 193.

23. It was written in two parts, over many years, as *Wilhelm Meisters Lehjahre* (1777–95) and *Wilhelm Meisters Wanderjahre* (1821–9).

24. Goethe, *Wilhelm Meister*, vol. II, p. 70.

25. Ibid., p. 106.

26. The usual explanation being given that Schikaneder's rival Marinelli at the Leopoldstadt Theatre had got in first with a magic opera based upon a very similar story to that of *Die Zauberflöte*,

also from Wieland's collection of fairy-tales, *Dschinnistan*. Brigid Brophy, recognizing affinities with the Demeter and Persephone story, and knowing of the conflation of Demeter with Isis in the classical Mysteries, suggested that the Queen of Night was intended to represent the goddess Isis herself, but that to have done so would have given the secret symbolism of freemasonry away. Unfortunately, she confused classical and eighteenth-century symbolism (Brophy, *Mozart the Dramatist*, pp. 131–202).

27. J. Campbell, *The Hero with a Thousand Faces* (1988), pp. 491–97.

28. Ibid., p. 246.

29. They also serve, as Jung reminded, to confront the initiate with the reality of death and to help him overcome his fear of death so that he can live without being paralysed by that fear, an important element in the Enlightenment's own programme.

30. Campbell, *The Masks of God* (1959).

31. Jung, *Man and his Symbols* (1983), p. 117.

32. Jung, *Symbols of Transformation* (London, 1956), para. 585.

33. Campbell, *The Hero with a Thousand Faces*, p. 130.

34. Ibid., p. 19.

35. Jung, *Man and his Symbols*, p. 117.

36. Goethe, op. cit., vol. II, p. 79.

37. Abrams, *Natural Supernaturalism* (1971), p. 146.

38. M. Eliade, *Birth and Rebirth* (1958).

39. Schiller *Sämtliche Werke*, vol. IV, p. 768.

40. Genesis 3:5.

41. Haydn and van Swieten betray the naïvety of their vision, still rooted in an earlier stage of Enlightenment thought, when they retell the story of the Garden of Eden – the garden of the earlier Enlightenment's delusory idyll of nature – in *The Creation*. The story ends before the Fall, with Uriel singing to a blissful Adam and Eve, 'O happy pair, and happy for evermore,

if vain delusions do not lead you astray, to desire more than you have, and to know more than you should.' In *The Seasons* Haydn and van Swieten also present a vision of humanity innocently living in pre-lapsarian harmony with nature. Significantly, Schiller thoroughly disliked Haydn's oratorios, considering them to have enslaved music to the imitation of material reality.

42. Schiller, op. cit., vol. IV, pp. 708–9.

43. Kant, *Conjectural History of the Origin of Man* quoted in Abrams, op. cit., p. 205.

44. Abrams, op. cit., p. 31.

45. Quoted in G. Lloyd, *The Man of Reason* (1984), p. 70.

46. Schiller, *On the Aesthetic Education of Man*, Letter 6, paras 3 and 8.

47. Ibid., Letter 7, para. 3.

48. Thus in his often-cited but rarely read article on the *Mysteries of the Egyptians*, Born asserted that the ultimate purpose of both freemasonry and the Egyptian priests of earlier times was to attain understanding of nature. 'Knowledge of Nature is the aim of our undertakings. This patron, seamstress and nurse of all creation we honour under the image of Isis' (*Journal für Freymaurer*, p. 22). According to Plutarch, it was Osiris who introduced civilization, cultivation, laws and religion to Egypt, and Alexandre Lenoir's exhaustive 1812 study of the Egyptian roots of freemasonry clearly identifies Isis and Osiris as representing nature and reason (J. Baltrusaitis, *La quête d'Isis* (1967), p. 63).

49. 'Nature will stand no nonsense. She scorns an inadequate student; only to one who is adequate and true and pure will she yield her secrets . . . Mere empirical intelligence (*Verstand*) cannot reach her; Man must be capable of rising to the highest level of metaphysical reason (*Vernunft*) if he is to achieve contact with the divinity which manifests itself in

primary phenomena, which dwells behind them and from which they proceed' (Goethe, *Conversations and Encounters*, p. 188).

50. Kant, *The Critique of Judgement* (1952), p. 179.

51. Goethe, *Faust*, Pt. I: *In Faust's Study*.

52. Blake, *Complete Writings*, p. 154.

53. Schiller, op. cit., Letter 6, para. 1.

54. The two armed men talk of the four elements (their text lifted directly from *Sethos*); for explanation of the discrepancy, see J. Chailly, *The Magic Flute*, pp. 142–7.

55. Schiller, op. cit., Letter 8, para. 6.

56. Quoted in R. Cardinal, *German Romantics in Context* (1975), p. 35.

57. R. Steiner, *Christianity as Mystical Fact* (1972), p. 31.

58. Quoted in Honour, *Romanticism*, p. 316.

59. F. Yates, *Giordano Bruno and the Hermetic Tradition* (1982), p. 34.

60. Birds are an old symbol of the instinctual in man, cf. Aristophanes *The Birds*, translated by Goethe as *Papagey* (R. H. Spaethling, 'Folklore and Enlightenment . . .' in *Eighteenth-Century Studies*, vol. IX (1975)).

61. Like Don Giovanni, his terms of appreciation are enumerative; the breeding of children, all of whom will be identical replicas of their parents, like animals, is anticipated as an accumulative contest between papa-papa-papa-genos and papa-papa-papa-genas.

62. Schopenhauer, 'Aphorismen zur Lebenswelt', in *Counsels and Maxims* (1890). The *biedermeier* interpretation of *Die Zauberflöte* survives in Wagner's *Die Meistersinger*; that opera, and not *Parsifal* as Peter Conrad maintains, is the real nineteenth-century heir of *Die Zauberflöte*. Wagner's Nuremberg is a closed community from which a questing hero seeks at first to rescue a heroine, and then to gain admission, saving the community. Sach's renunciation of his

love for Eva is like Sarastro relinquishing Pamina (Act I, Finale).

63. Kierkegaard, *Either/Or*, pp. 78, 82.

64. *Letters*, 24.8.82.

65. P. Branscombe, '*Die Zauberflöte*: some textual and interpretive problems', *Proceedings of the RMA*, 92, 1965–6.

66. As in Mozart's song *O heiliges Band*, K. 174.

67. Quoted in Lloyd, op. cit., p. 76.

68. Blake, op. cit., p. 264.

69. H. Jonas, *The Gnostic Religion* (1958), p. 25.

70. Quoted in G. Bataille, *Eroticism* (1987), p. 223.

71. Wagner conveyed his understanding of this dual role in the character of Kundry in *Parsifal*.

72. William Alexander, in C. H. Flynn, *Samuel Richardson* (1982), p. 82.

73. Wollstonecraft, *A Vindication of the Rights of Woman*, p. 124.

74. Richardson, *Clarissa*, vol. III, p. 338.

75. Rousseau, *Emile*, p. 257.

76. Ibid., p. 322.

77. Quoted in Lloyd, op. cit., p. 35.

78. Branscombe, op. cit.

79. Quoted in Bruford, *Culture and Society in Classical Weimar* (1962), p. 334.

80. At the end of Beethoven's *Fidelio* Leonora's heroism is put firmly in its place when it is extolled as good wifeliness: 'He who has such a wife is lucky.'

81. Alxinger, *Sämtliche Gedichte, Schwesternlied*.

82. Blumauer, *Sämtliche Werke*, vol. IV (1819), p. 35.

83. *Letters*, 2.10.82. Pezzl also describes the Viennese salon hostesses as 'Musarions', after Wieland's ideal feminine guide in the poem of that name (Pezzl, *Skizze von Wien*, p. 89).

84. Ibid., 8.1.83.

85. For example, Goldoni's *Le donne curiose* and the Viennese play *Die Freymaurer* (anon) of 1784.

86. S. de Beauvoir, *The Second Sex* (1988), p. 211.

87. Abrams, op. cit., p. 239. I am aware that Hölderlin is not properly classified as a Romantic, but like Goethe and Schiller his classicism is suffused with Romantic images.

88. As represented in Joseph Wright of Derby's painting *The Alchymist* of 1771, in which the alchemist in pursuit of the philosopher's stone stumbles upon phosphorous.

89. Jung, *Psychology and Alchemy* (1989), p. 148.

90. Quoted in K. Raine, *Blake and Tradition* (1969), p. 223.

91. Goethe, *Dichtung und Wahrheit* (1971), Bk VIII.

92. Another mineralogist, fodder for those who adhere to the Baʳonian theory that he, rather than Schikaneder, wrote the text of *Die Zauberflöte*, was Karl Ludwig Gieseke, First Slave in the first performances of the opera, and later Professor of Mineralogy at Dublin University.

93. Epstein (op. cit., p. 55) gives the date 1775; but this is contradicted in all other sources.

94. René le Forestier, *La franc-maçonnerie templière et occultiste* (1970), pp. 614–19.

95. Goethe, *Die Geheimnisse*.

96. Autexier, op. cit.

97. Forestier, op. cit., pp. 221–42.

98. Reinalter, *Freimaurer und Geheimbunde* (1983), p. 240.

99. Ibid.

100. See *Zaubertöne–Mozart in Wien*, p. 444.

101. *Letters*, 24.3.81.

102. Lavater (pseud.), *Lavaters Protokoll über den Spiritus Familiaris Gablidone* (1787), p. 9.

103. Braunbehrens, *Mozart in Wien*, p. 347.

104. *Letters*, 10.4.89.

105. Deutsch, *Mozart. A Documentary Biography*, p. 444.

106. In the engraving of Count Thun is planted a reference to Psalm 18; his spirit messenger Gablidone announces that the great Revolution will take place in 1800.

107. It is likely that Mozart, having

received inspiration for a Rosicrucian work from Frederick William, bided his time until circumstances were right. The accession of Leopold II may have provided the amenable political climate. Unlike his brother, Leopold was sympathetic to the activities of secret societies, and there is evidence that Leopold was himself involved in Rosicrucianism, giving rise to a brief Rosicrucian revival in Vienna during his short reign (K. Frick, *Die Erleuchteten* (1973), pp. 351–2).

108. When the first manned balloons descended to earth in the early 1780s the startled peasants in whose fields they landed took their occupants to be gods descended to earth. But when a few years later a print was issued to celebrate a balloon flight in Lyons, a poem was appended to it which ran:

An infinite space separated us from the skies;
But, thanks to the Montgolfiers, whom genius inspires,
The eagle of Jupiter has lost his empire,
And the feeble mortal can approach the Gods.
[Darnton, *Mesmerism*, p. 20]

109. Quoted in Ayer, *Thomas Paine*, p. 175.

110. F. E. Manuel, *The Eighteenth Century Confronts the Gods* (1959), p. 260.

111. *Journal für Freymaurer*, vol. II, p. 47. One study of the common symbolism of all religions, published in France in the same year as *Die Zauberflöte* by a member of the French mystical branch of masonry known as Illuminism (not to be mistaken for the German Illuminati), suggested that Isis herself was the representation of the highest deity, from whose very name the name of Jesus was derived. (Baltrusaitis, op. cit., p. 89.)

112. Blake, *Complete Writings*, p. 749.

113. Goethe, *Faust*, Pt I; *Witch's kitchen*.

114. L. Versini, *Laclos et la tradition* (1968), p. 625.

115. Kant, *Religion within the Limits*, p. 53.

116. Quoted in D. F. Varma, *The Gothic Flame* (1957), p. 105.

117. S. L. Gillman, 'Das-ist-der-Teufel-sich-er-lich', in *Austriaca* (1975).

118. M. Stern, 'Haydns Schöpfung', in *Haydn Studien* (1966).

119. Pezzl, *Marokkanische Briefe* (1784), p. 57.

120. Goethe notably praised Shakespeare for being willing to acknowledge the existence of evil in the universe (S. S. B. Taylor, *The Theatre of the French and German Enlightenment* (1979), p. 75.

121. Quoted in Yates, op. cit., p. 22.

122. *Journal für Freymaurer*, vol. III.

123. Ibid., p. 51.

124. Campbell, *The Masks of God*, p. 780.

125. *Journal für Freymaurer*, vol. III, p. 10.

126. Dostoievsky, *The Brothers Karamazov*, Book V, Ch. 4.

127. Burke, *Reflections*, p. 248.

128. Quoted in Raine, p. 168.

129. *Letters*, 9.7.91.

130. Frye, *Anatomy of Criticism*, p. 196.

131. MacIntyre, *A Short History of Ethics* (1966), p. 195.

132. Frick, op. cit., p. 272.

133. The neo-Platonist Christian Philo used to address the divine Logos directly as 'The Son of God' (R. Steiner, *Christianity as Mystical Fact* (1972), p. 57).

134. He took part in a Corpus Christi procession in June 1791 (Deutsch, op. cit., p. 397).

135. R. Steiner, in *Goethe, The Mysteries, with a Lecture by Rudolf Steiner* (1987), p. 4.

136. J. Dalchow et al, *Mozarts Tod* (1971).

137. See Robbins Landon, *1791, Mozart's Last Year*, p. 129.

138. Sarastro and the priests of the temple are specifically described as the 'Wise Men' in Schikaneder's text.

139. Bloch, *The Principle of Hope* (1986), p. 1246.

140. Deutsch, op. cit., p. 450.

141. Payne, *The Philosophes and the People*, p. 29.
142. Gay, *The Enlightenment*, vol. II, p. 519.
143. Ibid. Herder, who more than anyone was responsible for inventing the very Germanic concept of the people as the *Volk*, ensured that a clear (and ultimately dangerous) distinction was made between the *Volk* and the *Pöbel*.
144. Schiller, *On the Aesthetic Education of Man*, Letter 5, para. 4.
145. Montesquieu, *L'esprit des lois*, Bk III, 3.
146. Quoted in Payne, op. cit., p. 166.
147. Brophy, *Mozart the Dramatist*, p. 231.
148. Robbins Landon, op. cit., p. 54.
149. Quoted in Reinalter, *Joseph II und Die Freimaurer*, p. 74.
150. Beethoven, *Letters, Journals and Conversations*, p. 73.
151. Schiller, op. cit., Letter 11, para. 9.
152. Terrasson, *Sethos*, p. 9.
153. Rousseau, *Social Contract and Discourses*.
154. Blumauer, *Sämtliche Werke*, vol. III, p. 26.
155. A former member of 'Zur wahren Eintracht', and creator of an allegorical sculpture in honour of Ignaz von Born.
156. Blumauer, op. cit. (1884), p. 208.
157. 'Entfleuch von hier unheiliger Pöbel,/Entweihe diesen Tempel nicht;' ('Be banished from here unholy people,/Desecrate not this temple' (Alxinger, *Sämtliche Gedichte*, vol. I, p. 281.
158. D. Mornet, *Les origines intellectuals de la révolution française* (Paris, 1933), p. 357.
159. Goethe, *Wilhelm Meister*, vol. I, p. 250.
160. Goethe, *Conversations and Encounters*, p. 127.
161. Rosenberg, *Bureaucracy, Aristocracy and Autocracy*, p. 186.
162. Pezzl, *Skizze von Wien*, p. 128.
163. Gibbon, *Memoirs of my Life*, p. 42.
164. White, *The Age of Scandal*, p. 6.
165. Burke, op. cit., p. 203.
166. Blake, op. cit., p. 624.
167. Quoted in Le Huray and Day, *Music and Aesthetics*, p. 109.
168. Beethoven, op. cit., p. 135.
169. M. Solomon, 'Beethoven and the Enlightenment', in *Telos*, 19. Beethoven's comment was not contradictory as it may seem; most eighteenth-century republics – for example, Geneva, Venice – had been oligarchies.
170. Ibid.
171. Ibid.
172. *Letters*, 3.7.68.
173. Le Huray and Day, op. cit.
174. R. Bauer, *La réalité, royaume de Dieu*.
175. The master grades of the Rosicrucians were known as the grades of the Magi.
176. F. C. Oetinger, *Die Metaphysic in Connecion mit der Chemie* (1770).
177. Yates, op. cit., p. 79.
178. Goethe, *Gedankenausgabe*, vol. IX, *Novelle*.
179. Quoted in J. Godwin, *Harmonies of Heaven and Earth* (1987), p. 15.
180. Quoted in Abrams, op. cit., p. 206.
181. Ibid.
182. G. Steiner, *Language and Silence* (1985), p. 30.
183. R. M. Rilke, *Sonnets to Orpheus* (1974), III.
184. L. Goldmann, *The Hidden God* (1964), p. 148.
185. Quoted in S. Langer, *Philosophy in a New Key* (1942).

XX EPILOGUE

1. Blake, *Jerusalem*, in *Complete Writings*, p. 747.
2. Forestier, *La franc-maçonnerie templière et occultiste*, pp. 535–60.
3. Bloch, *The Principle of Hope*, p. 63.
4. 'Abstract Philosophy warring in enmity against Imagination/Which is the

Divine Body of the Lord Jesus, blessed
for ever.' Blake, op. cit., p. 654.

5. *Letters*, 8–9.10.91.
6. Ibid. 14.10.91.

Bibliography

Abafi, Lajos, *Geschichte der Freimaurerei in Oesterreich-Ungarn*, 5 vols (Budapest, 1890–99).

Abrams, Meyer Howard, *Natural Supernaturalism. Tradition and Revolution in Romantic Literature* (Oxford, 1971); *The Mirror and the Lamp. Romantic Theory and the Critical Tradition* (Oxford, 1953).

Adel, Kurt, *Paul Weidmann* (Vienna, 1966).

Allanbrook, Wye Jamieson, *Rhythmic Gesture in Mozart. Le Nozze di Figaro and Don Giovanni* (Chicago, 1983).

Alxinger, Johann Baptiste von, Alxingers, *Sämtliche Gedichte* (Klagenfurth and Laibach, 1788); *Bliomberis* (Leipzig, 1791).

Arblaster, Anthony, *The Rise and Decline of Western Liberalism* (Oxford, 1987).

Ariès, Philippe and Bejin, André, *Western Sexuality* (Oxford, 1985)

Arneth, A. von, *Maria Theresia und Joseph II* (Vienna, 1867–8).

Aubin, Penelope, *The Strange Adventures of the Count of Vinevil* (London, 1721).

Austen, Jane, *Mansfield Park* (1814; repr. Oxford, 1970); *Northanger Abbey* (1811; repr. Oxford, 1971); *Sense and Sensibility* (1811; repr. Everyman, London, 1906).

Autexier, Philippe A., *Mozart et Liszt Sub Rosa* (Poitiers, 1984).

Ayer, Alfred J., *Thomas Paine* (London, 1989).

Bachelard, Gaston, *The Psychoanalysis of Fire* (London, 1987).

Balet, Leo, *Die Verbürgelichung der Deutschen Kunst, Literatur und Musik im 18. Jahrhundert* (Strassburg, 1936).

Baltrusaitis, Jurgis, *La quête d'Isis. Introduction à la Egyptomanie* (Paris, 1967).

Barber, Elinor G., *The Bourgeoisie in Eighteenth-Century France* (Princeton, 1955).

Barth, Karl, *Wolfgang Amadeus Mozart* (Basel, 1956).

Bataille, Georges, *Eroticism* (London, 1987); *Literature and Evil* (London, 1990).

Batley, Edward, *A Preface to the Magic Flute* (London, 1969).

Baudet, Henri, *Some Thoughts on European Images of Non-European Man* (Yale, 1965).

Bauer, Roger, *La réalité, royaume de Dieu* (Munich, 1965).

Bauer, Wilhelm, and Deutsch, Otto Erich, *Mozart. Briefe und Aufzeichnungen*, 7 vols (Kassel, 1962–75).

Beales, Derek, *Joseph II* (Cambridge, 1987); (ed.), *History, Society and the Churches* (Cambridge, 1985) Essays in honour of Owen Chadwick.

Beaumarchais, Pierre August Caron de, *The Barber of Seville/The Marriage of Figaro* (trans., Harmondsworth, 1964); *Théâtre* (Paris, 1965).

Beauvoir, Simone de, *The Second Sex* (London, 1988).

Beethoven, Ludwig van, *Letters, Journals and Conversations* (London, 1956).

Behn, Aphra, *Oroonoko and other Stories* (London, 1986).

Behrens, Catherine, *The Ancien Régime* (London, 1989).

Benjamin, Walter, *Illuminations* (London, 1970).

Berman, Marshall, *The Politics of Authenticity. Radical Individualism and the Emergence of Modern Society* (London, 1971).

Bernard, Paul P., *Jesuits and Jacobins. Enlightenment and Enlightened Despotism in Austria* (Illinois, 1971).

351

Bestermann, Theodore [studies presented to], *The Age of Enlightenment* (Edinburgh and London, 1967).

Blake, William, *Complete Writings* (Oxford, 1966).

Bloch, Ernst, *Essays on the Philosophy of Music* (Cambridge, 1974); *The Principle of Hope* (Oxford, 1986).

Blum, Carol, *Diderot: the Virtue of a Philosopher* (New York, 1974).

Blume, Friedrich, *Classic and Romantic Music* (London, 1972).

Blumauer, Aloys, *Sämtliche Werke* (Königsberg, 1819; Vienna, 1884); *Gedichte* (Vienna, 1787).

Boccaccio, Giovanni, *The Decameron* (trans. John Payne; Cleveland, 1947).

Bodi, Leslie, *Tauwetter in Wien. Zur prosa der österreichischen Aufklärung* (Frankfurt, 1977).

Born, Gunthard, *Mozarts Musiksprache* (Munich, 1985).

Boswell, James, *The Life of Johnson* (Oxford, 1934–64).

Brandl, Manfred, *Marx Anton Wittola* (Steyr, 1974).

Branscombe, Peter, '*Die Zauberflöte*: some textual and interpretive problems', in *Proceedings of the Royal Musical Association*, no. 92 (1965–6).

Braunbehrens, Volkmar, *Mozart in Wien* (Munich, 1986).

Bredvold, Louis, *The Natural History of Sensibility* (Detroit, 1962).

Brett, Raymond, *The Third Earl of Shaftesbury* (London, 1951).

Brissenden, Robert, *Virtue in Distress. Studies in the Novel of Sentiment from Richardson to Sade* (London, 1974).

Brookner, Anita, *Greuze* (London, 1972).

Brophy, Brigid, *Mozart the Dramatist* (London, 1988).

Bruford, Walter, *Culture and Society in Classical Weimar* (Cambridge, 1962); *The German Tradition of Self-Cultivation* (Cambridge, 1975); *Germany in the Eighteenth Century. The social background of literary revival* (Cambridge, 1965); *Theatre, Drama and Audience in Goethe's Germany* (London, 1950).

Brumfitt, John, *The French Enlightenment* (London, 1972).

Brunschwig, Henri, *Enlightenment and Romanticism in Eighteenth-century Prussia* (Chicago, 1974).

Bryson, Norman, *Word and Image. French Painting of the Ancien Régime* (Cambridge, 1986).

Burke, Edmund, *A Philosophical Enquiry into the Origin of our Ideas of the Sublime and Beautiful* (1757; repr. London, 1958); *Reflections on the Revolution in France* (1790; repr., Harmondsworth, 1968).

Burney, Charles, *Memoirs of the Life and Writings of the Abate Metastasio* (London, 1796).

Burney, Fanny, *Evelina* (1788; repr. Oxford, 1968).

Byrd, Max, *London Transform'd* (London, 1978).

Byron, *The Poetical Works* (Oxford, 1912).

Campbell, Joseph, *The Hero with a Thousand Faces* (London, 1988); *The Masks of God: Primitive Mythology* (New York, 1959).

Camus, Albert, *The Rebel* (Harmondsworth, 1962).

Cardinal, Roger, *German Romantics in Context* (London, 1975).

Carpanetto, Dino, and Ricuperati, Giuseppe, *Italy in the Age of Reason, 1685–1789* (London, 1987).

Casanova, Giacomo, *Memoirs* (New York and London, 1958–60).

Cassirer, Ernst, *The Philosophy of the Enlightenment* (Princeton, 1979); *Rousseau, Kant, and Goethe* (Princeton, 1945).

Cazes, André, *Grimm et les encyclopédistes* (Paris, 1933).

Chadwick, Owen, *The Popes and European Revolution* (Oxford, 1981).

Chailly, Jacques, *The Magic Flute. Masonic Opera* (London, 1972).

Chesterfield, Philip Dormer Stanhope, Earl of, *Letters to his Son* (1774; repr. Everyman, London, 1929).

Chetwood, William, *The Generous Freemason* (London, 1731).

Clark, Anna, *Women's Silence, Men's Violence: Sexual Assault in England* (London, 1987).

Clive Geoffrey, *The Romantic Enlightenment* (New York, 1960).

Corneille, Pierre, *The Cid/Cinna/The Theatrical Illusion* (trans. John Cairncross, Harmondsworth, 1975).

Cottrell, Alan P., *Goethe's View of Evil* (Edinburgh, 1982).

Cragg, Gerald, *The Church and the Age of Reason. 1648–1789* (Harmondsworth, 1960).

Crankshaw, Edward, *Maria Theresa* (London, 1969).

Cranston, Maurice, *Philosophers and Pamphleteers* (Oxford, 1986).

Crocker, Lester, *An Age of Crisis. Man and the World in Eighteenth-Century Thought* (Johns Hopkins, 1959); *Nature and Culture. Ethical Thought in the French Enlightenment* (Johns Hopkins, 1963).

Cruickshank, John, *French Literature and its Background* (Oxford, 1968–70).

Dalchow, Johannes; Duda, Gunther; Kerner, Dieter, *Mozarts Tod. 1791–1971* (Pahl, 1971).

Danchet, Antoine, *Idomenée* (Paris, 1714).

Da Ponte, Lorenzo, *Memoirs* (London, 1929).

Darnton, Robert, *Mesmerism and the End of the Enlightenment in France* (Harvard, 1986).

Defoe, Daniel, *Robinson Crusoe* (1719; repr., Harmondsworth, 1965).

Dent, Edward J., *Mozart's Operas* (Oxford, 1947).

Des Marez, G., *Guide illustrée de Bruxelles* (Brussels, 1979).

Deutsch, Otto Erich, *Mozart und die Wiener Logen* (Vienna, 1932); *Mozart. A Documentary Biography* (London, 1990).

Diderot, Denis, *Oeuvres de théâtre* (Amsterdam, 1772); *Les bijoux indiscrets, or the Indiscreet Toys* (London, 1749); *Le fils naturel*, trans. as *Dorval; or the Test of Virtue* (London, 1767); *Jacques the Fatalist* (Harmondsworth, 1986); *Le Neveu de Rameau*, in *Selected Writings* (New York and London, 1963); *La religieuse* (trans. as *The Nun*, Harmondsworth, 1974). (*See also Encyclopédie.*)

Dodds, Eric, *The Greeks and the Irrational* (Berkeley and London, 1951).

Donakowski, Conrad L., *A Muse for the Masses. Ritual and Music in the Age of Democratic Revolution. 1770–1870* (Chicago, 1972).

Donnington, Robert, *Wagner's Ring and its Symbols* (London, 1974).

Dulmen, Richard van, *Der Geheimband der Illuminaten* (Stuttgart, 1975).

Eagleton, Terry, *The Ideology of the Aesthetic* (Oxford, 1990).

Ebbert, Johann Jacob, *Ebberts Naturlehre* (Troppau, 1784).

Einstein, Alfred, *Mozart* (London, 1971).

Eliade, Mircea, *Birth and Rebirth. The Religious Meanings of Initiation in Human Culture* (New York, 1958); *The Sacred and the Profane. The Nature of Religion* (New York and London, 1959).

Elshtain, Jean (ed.), *The Family in Political Thought* (Brighton, 1982).

Encyclopédie de Diderot (and Jean de Rond d'Alembert), 17 vols. (Paris, 1751–65).

Engels, Friedrich, *The Origin of the Family* (London, 1972).

Enright, Dennis, *The Alluring Problem. An Essay on Irony* (Oxford, 1988).

Epinay, Mme la Ligne d', *Les pseudo mémoires* (Paris, 1951).

Epstein, Klause, *The Genesis of German Conservatism* (Princeton, 1966).

Euripides, *Helen*, in *The Complete Greek Tragedies, Euripides II* (Chicago, 1959); *Iphigenia in Aulis* (trans. F. Melian Stanwell, London, 1929); *Iphigenia in Tauris* (trans. Gilbert Murray, London, 1910).

Eybel, Joseph, *Was ist ein Pfarrer?* (Vienna, 1782).

Fäy, Bernard, *Le franc-maçonnerie et la revolution intellectuelle du XVIIIᵉ siècle* (Paris, 1961).

Feuchtmuller, Rupert, *Kunst in Österreich*, vol. II (Vienna, 1973).

Feuerbach, Ludwig, *The Essence of Christianity* (London, 1853).

Fielding, Henry, *Joseph Andrews* and *Shamela* (1742/1741; repr. Oxford, 1971); *Tom Jones* (1749; repr., Harmondsworth, 1987).

Fitzlyon, April, *Lorenzo Da Ponte* (London and New York, 1982).

Flaischlen, Cäsar, *Otto Heinrich von Gemmingen* (Stuttgart, 1890).

Flandrin, Jean Louis, *Families in Former Times. Kinship, Household and Sexuality* (Cambridge, 1976).

Flynn, Carol Houlihan, *Samuel Richardson. A Man of Letters* (Princeton, 1982).

Ford, Boris, *The New Pelican Guide to English Literature. From Dryden to Johnson* (Penguin, Harmondsworth, 1982).

Forestier, René le, *La franc-maçonnerie templière et occultiste* (Paris, 1970).

Foucault, Michel, *The Order of Things* (New York, 1970).

France, Peter, *Diderot* (Oxford, 1983).

Freud, Sigmund, *Civilisation and its Discontents* (London, 1930).

Frick, Karl, *Die Erleuchteten* (Graz, 1973); *Licht und Finsternis* (Graz, 1975).

Friedrichsmeyer, Sara, *The Androgyne in early German Romanticism* (Bern, 1983).

Fromm, Erich, *You Shall be as Gods* (London, 1967).

Frye, Northrop, *Anatomy of Criticism* (Harmondsworth, 1990).

Fubini, Mario, *La cultura illuministica in Italia* (Turin, 1957).

Gay, Peter, *The Enlightenment*: vol. I, *The Rise of Modern Paganism* (London, 1967); vol. II, *The Science of Freedom* (London, 1969); *The Party of Humanity* (London, 1964); *Voltaire's Politics. The Poet as Realist* (Princeton, 1959).

Geiringer, Karl, [A Tribute to], *Studies in Eighteenth-century Music* (London, 1970).

Gemmingen, Otto von, *Der Weltmann* (Vienna, 1782).

Gibb, Hamilton, and Bowen, Harold, *Islamic Society and the West* (Oxford, 1950).

Gibbon, Edward, *Memoirs of my Life* (Harmondsworth, 1984).

Gillman, Sander L., 'Das-ist-der-Teufel-sich-er-lich', in *Austriaca, Festschrift für Heinz Pollitzer* (Tübingen, 1975).

Gluck, Christoph Willibald, *The Collected Correspondence and Papers*, H. and E. H. Mueller von Asow (eds) (London, 1962).

Godwin, Joscelyn, *Harmonies of Heaven and Earth* (London, 1987); *Music, Mysticism and Magic* (London, 1986); *Mystery Religions and the Ancient World* (London, 1986).

Goethe, Johann W. von, *Gedenkenausgabe der Werke, Briefe und Gespräche*, 16 vols (Zurich, 1949); *Conversations and Encounters* (London, 1960); *Dichtung und Wahrheit* (1833; trans. London, 1971); *Faust* (I), *Faust* (II) (1808/1832; trans. Harmondsworth, 1949/1959); *Italian Journey* (trans. Harmondsworth, 1970); *The Mysteries* (with a lecture by Rudolf Steiner; New York, 1987); *Die Leiden des jungen Werther* (1774; trans. as *The Sorrows of Young Werther* (New York, 1962); *Die Wahlverwandschaften* (1809; trans. as *Elective Affinities*, Harmondsworth, 1986); *Wilhelm Meisters Lehrjahre* (1796); *Wilhelm Meisters Wanderjahre oder Die Entsagenden* (1821–9; both trans. by T. Carlyle as *Wilhelm Meister*, Everyman, London, 1925).

Goldberg, Rita, *Sex and Enlightenment. Women in Richardson and Diderot* (Cambridge, 1984).

Goldmann, Lucien, *The Hidden God* (London, 1964); *Immanuel Kant* (London, 1971); *The Philosophy of the Enlightenment* (London, 1973).

Goldoni, Carlo, *La buona figliuola: Dramma giocoso in tre atti di Polisseno Fegejo. P. A.* (Italy, 1762); *Memoirs* (London, 1926); *Pamela* (trans. London, 1756).

Goluben, Victor, *Marivauxs Lustspiele in Deutschen Übersetzungen des 18. Jahrhunderts* (Heidelberg, 1904).

Gooch, George, *Germany and the French Revolution* (London, 1902).

Goodwin, Albert (ed.), *The European Nobility in the Eighteenth Century* (London, 1953).

Gottsched, Johann Christoph, *Versuch einer critischen Dichtkunst* (Leipzig, 1751).

Gould's History of Freemasonry (London, 1931).

Grassl, Hans, *Aufbruch zur Romantik* (Munich, 1968).

Grimm, F. M. (ed.), *Correspondance littéraire* (Paris, 1813).

Gruber, Gernot, *Mozart und die Nachwelt* (Salzburg and Vienna, 1985).

Gugitz, Gustav, *Johann Pezzl. Zu seinem 150 Geburtstag* (Vienna, 1906); *Das Wiener Kaffeehaus* (Vienna, 1940).

Habermas, Jurgen, *Strukturwandel der Öffentlichkeit* (Neuwied, 1962).

Hagstrum, Jean A., *Sex and Sensibility. Ideal and Erotic Love from Milton to Mozart* (Chicago and London, 1980).

Hammer, Carl, *Goethe and Rousseau* (Kentucky, 1973).

Hampson, Norman, *The Enlightenment* (Harmondsworth, 1968); *The First European Revolution* (London, 1969); *A Social History of the French Revolution* (London and Toronto, 1963).

Harpprecht, Klaus, *Georg Forster, oder Die Liebe zur Welt* (Hamburg, 1990).

Hatfield, Henry, *Aesthetic Paganism in German Literature* (Harvard, 1964).

Hazard, Paul, *The European Mind* (London, 1964); *European Thought in the Eighteenth Century* (London, 1954).

Heartz, Daniel, 'Idomeneo and the Tradition of Sacrifice Drama' in Glyndebourne Festival Opera Programme (1985).

Heartz, Frederick, *The Development of the German Public Mind* (London, 1962).

Hegel, Georg Wilhelm Friedrich, *Sämtliche Werke* (Stuttgart, 1928).

Heiseler, Bernt von, *Schiller* (London, 1962).

Heitner, Robert R., *German Tragedy in the Age of Enlightenment* (California, 1963).

Heller, Erich, *The Artist's Journey into the Interior* (London, 1965).

Herbert, Robert L., *David, Voltaire, Brutus and the French Revolution* (London, 1972).

Heywood, Thomas, *The Fair Maid of the West* (London, 1631).

Hildesheimer, Wolfgang, *Mozart* (London, 1982).

Hobbes, Thomas, *Leviathan* (1651; repr. Harmondsworth, 1968).

Hoffmann, Leopold, *Babel* (Vienna, 1790).

Holton, Robert, *The Transition from Feudalism to Capitalism* (London, 1985).

Honour, Hugh, *Neo-Classicism* (Harmondsworth, 1983); *Romanticism* (Harmondsworth, 1986).

Horkheimer, Max and Adorno, Theodore, *The Dialectic of Enlightenment* (London, 1973).

Hume, David, *Moral and Political Philosophy* (New York, 1975); *A Treatise of Human Nature* (1739; repr. Harmondsworth, 1969).

Hunt, John Dixon, *The Figure in the Landscape. Poetry, Painting and Gardening in the Eighteenth Century* (Johns Hopkins, 1976); Hunt, and Willis, Peter, *The Genius of the Place. The English Landscape Garden 1620–1820* (Massachusetts, 1988).

Hunter, Mary, 'The Fusion and Juxtaposition of Genres in Opera Buffa, 1770–1800', *Music and Letters*, vol. 67 (Oct 1986); '*Pamela* – The Offspring of Richardson's Heroine in Eighteenth-century Opera', *Mosaic*, vol. XVIII (1985).

Huray, Peter Le, and Day, James, *Music and Aesthetics in the Eighteenth and Early Nineteenth Centuries* (Cambridge, 1981).

Jacob, Margaret C., *The Radical Enlightenment. Pantheists, Freemasons and Republicans* (London, 1981).

James, William, *The Varieties of Religious Experience* (Harmondsworth, 1985).

Jay, Martin, *Adorno* (London, 1984).

John, Nicholas, 'Monostatos: Pamina's Incubus', in *Opern und Opernfiguren. Festschrift für Joachim Herz* (Salzburg, 1989).

355

Johnson, Samuel, *Lives of the English Poets* (1781; repr. New York, 1967); *The History of Rasselas* (1759; repr. Oxford, 1968).

Jonas, Hans, *The Gnostic Religion* (Boston, 1958).

Journal für Freymaurer (Vienna, 1784).

Julian of Norwich, *Revelations of Divine Love* (Harmondsworth, 1966).

Jung, Carl Gustav, *Man and his Symbols* (London, 1983); *Psychology and Alchemy* (London, 1989); *Symbols of Transformation*, in *Collected Works*, vol. V (London, 1956).

Kann, Robert A., *A Study of Austrian Intellectual History from Late Baroque to Romanticism* (London, 1960).

Kant, Immanuel, *The Philosophy of Kant* (Carl. J. Friedrich (ed.), New York, 1977); *Kritique der Urteilskraft* (1790, trans. as *The Critique of Judgement*, Oxford, 1952); *Die Religion innerhalb der Grenzen der blossen Vernunft* (1793; trans. as *Religion Within the Limits of Reason Alone*, New York, 1960).

Keil, Robert, *Wiener Freunder. 1784–1808* (Vienna, 1883).

Kerman, Joseph, *Opera as Drama* (New York, 1956).

Kierkegaard, Søren, *Either/Or* (Princeton, 1959).

Kiernan, Victor, *The Duel in European History* (Oxford, 1989).

Kirkby, John, *Automathes. The Capacity and Extent of the Human Understanding* (London, 1745).

Kivy, Peter, *The Corded Shell* (Princeton, 1980).

Klein, Anton von, *Günther von Schwarzburg* (Mannheim, 1777).

Knoop, Douglas and Jones, Gwilym, *The Genesis of Freemasonry* (Manchester, 1947)

Koch, Richard, *Br. Mozart. Freimaurer und Illuminaten* (Munich, 1911).

Komorzynski, Egon, *Emanuel Schikaneder. Ein beitrag zur Geschichte des Deutschen Theaters* (Vienna, 1951).

Koselleck, Reinhart, *Critique and Crisis. Enlightenment and the Parthenogenesis of Modern Society* (Oxford, 1988).

Kunze, Stefan, *Don Giovanni von Mozart* (Munich, 1972).

Laclos, Pierre Choderlos de, *Les liaisons dangereuses* (1782; trans. Harmondsworth, 1961).

La Mettrie, Julien Offray de, *L'homme machine* (repr. Paris, 1966).

Langer, Susanne, *Philosophy in a New Key* (Harvard, 1942).

Lavater (pseud.), *Lavaters Protokoll über den Spiritus Familiaris Gablidone* (Frankfurt and Leipzig, 1787).

Lebrun, Richard Allen, *Throne and Altar. The Political Thought of Joseph de Maistre* (Ottawa, 1965).

Lemierre, Antoine, *Oeuvres* (Paris, 1810).

Lessing, Gotthold Ephraim, *Werke* (Darmstadt, 1979); *Emilia Galotti* (1772; trans, London, 1969); *Laokoon* (1766; trans. London, 1970).

Lessnoff, Michael, *Social Contract* (London, 1986).

Lewes, George, *The Life of Goethe* (London, 1864).

Lewis, Matthew, *The Monk* (Oxford, 1987).

Link, Edith Murr, *The Emancipation of the Austrian Peasant. 1740–1798* (Columbia, 1949).

Lloyd, Genevieve, *The Man of Reason. 'Male' and 'Female' in Western Philosophy* (London, 1984).

Locke, John, *An Essay Concerning Human Understanding* (1690; repr., Everyman, London, 1961); *Some Thoughts Concerning Education* (1693; repr. Virginia, 1964); *Two Treatises of Government* (1690; repr., Everyman, London, 1975).

Longyear, Robert, *Schiller and Music* (Chapel Hill, 1966).

Lough, John, *The Encyclopédie* (London, 1971).

Lukács, Georg, *Goethe and his Age* (London, 1979).

Lukes, Steven, *Individualism* (Oxford, 1973).

Macfarlane, Alan, *Marriage and Love in England, 1300–1840* (Oxford, 1986).

MacIntyre, Alasdair, *After Virtue. A Study in Moral Theory* (London, 1985); *A Short History of Ethics* (New York, 1966).

McKay, Derek, *Prince Eugene of Savoy* (London, 1977).

McKeon, Michael, *The Origins of the English Novel* (Johns Hopkins, 1988).

McManners, John, *Death and the Enlightenment* (Oxford, 1981).

Maine, Henry Sumner, *Ancient Law* (Oxford, 1931).

Malins, Edward, *English Landscaping and Literature* (Oxford, 1966).

Mann, Thomas, *Doktor Faustus* (Harmondsworth, 1968).

Mann, William, *The Operas of Mozart* (London, 1977).

Manuel, Frank E., *The Eighteenth Century Confronts the Gods* (Harvard, 1959); with Manuel, Faith, *Utopian Thought in the Western World* (Oxford, 1979).

Marivaux, *Théâtre complet* (Paris, 1964); *Le Paysan parvenu*, trans. as *Up from the Country* (Harmondsworth, 1980).

Maschler, Helene, *Tobias Philipp Freiherr von Gebler* (Munich, 1935).

Mason, Haydn, *Voltaire* (London, 1975).

Mendelssohn, Moses, *Phädon, oder über die Unsterblichkeit der Seele* (1767; trans. as *Phaedon; or the Death of Socrates*, (London, 1789).

Metastasio, Pietro, *Teatro* (Turin, 1962).

Michel, Regis, *David, l'art et le politique* (Paris, 1988).

Mitchell, Donald and Robbins Landon, Howard Chandler, *The Mozart Companion* (London, 1986).

Mitford, Nancy, *Madame de Pompadour* (London, 1955).

Mitteraurer, Michael and Sieder, Reinhard, *The European Family* (Oxford, 1982).

Molière, *Don Juan* (1665; repr. in *The Miser and Other Plays*, Harmondsworth, 1962).

Montesquieu, Charles-Louis de Secondat, *L'esprit des lois* (1748; repr. Chicago, 1952); *Les lettres persanes* (1721; trans. as *Persian Letters*, Harmondsworth, 1973).

Mornet, Daniel, *Les origines intellectuelles de la Révolution française. 1715–1787* (Paris, 1933).

Mozart, Leopold, *A Treatise on the Fundamental Principles of Violin Playing* (Oxford, 1948).

Mozart, W., *Briefe und Aufzeichnungen* (Kassel, 1962–75).

Mozart, *The Letters of Mozart and his Family*, 3rd edn trans. Emily Anderson (London, 1985).

Muratori, Ludovico, *The Science of Rational Devotion* (trans. Dublin, 1789).

Murphy, Jeffrie G., and Hampton, Jean, *Forgiveness and Mercy* (Cambridge, 1990).

Musto, Renato and Napolitano, Ernesto, *Una favola per la ragione. Mite e storia nel 'Flauto magico' di Mozart* (Milan, 1982).

Nagel, Ivan, *Autonomie und Gnade. Über Mozarts Opern* (Munich, 1985).

Nelson, T. G., *Comedy. The Theory of Comedy in Literature, Drama and Cinema* (Oxford, 1990).

Nettl, Paul, *Forgotten Musicians* (New York, 1951); *Mozart and Masonry* (New York, 1957).

Neue Mozart Ausgabe (NMA) (Kassel, 1955–).

Nicolai, Friedrich, *Beschreibung einer Reiser durch Deutschland und die Schweitz im Jahre 1781* (Berlin, 1783–4).

Nietzsche, Friedrich, *The Birth of Tragedy/The Genealogy of Morals* (New York, 1956).

Niklaus, Robert, *A Literary History of France. The Eighteenth Century* (London and New York, 1970).

Nixon, Edna, *Voltaire and the Calas Case* (London, 1961).

Novak, Maximilian, *Defoe and the Nature of Man* (Oxford, 1963).

Novello, Vincent and Mary, *A Mozart Pilgrimage: Being the Travel Diaries of Vincent and Mary Novello in the Year 1829* (Rosemary Hughes (ed.), London, 1955).

O'Brien, Charles, 'Ideas of Religious Toleration at the Time of Joseph II', *Transactions of the American Philosophical Society*, New Series: vol. LIX (1969).

Oetinger, Friedrich Christoph, *Die Metaphysic in Connecion mit der Chemie* (1777).

Okin, Susan Moller, *Women in Western Political Thought* (Princeton, 1979).

Oliver, Alfred Richard, *The Encyclopédistes as Critics of Music* (New York, 1947).

Osborne, Charles, *The Complete Operas of Mozart* (London, 1978).

Oxford Companion to German Literature, (Oxford, 1986).

Padover, Saul, *The Revolutionary Emperor. Joseph II of Austria* (London, 1967).

Pagliardo, Harold E. (ed.), *Studies in Eighteenth-Century Culture*, vol. II (Cleveland and London, 1972); vol. III (1973).

Paine, Thomas, *The Thomas Paine Reader* (Harmondsworth, 1987).

Palmer, R. R., *The Age of Democratic Revolution* (Princeton, 1959); *Catholics and Unbelievers* (Princeton, 1939).

Pascal, Blaise, *Pensées* (Harmondsworth, 1966).

Pascal, Roy, *The German 'Sturm und Drang'* (Manchester, 1953).

Payne, Harry C., *The Philosophes and the People* (Yale, 1976).

Pestelli, Giorgio, *The Age of Mozart and Beethoven* (Cambridge, 1984).

Petitfrère, Claude, *Le scandale du 'Mariage de Figaro'* (Paris, 1989).

Pezzl, Johann, *Marokkamsche Briefe* (Vienna, 1784); *Faustin, oder das philosophische Jahrhundert* (Vienna, 1785); *Skizze von Wien* (Vienna and Leipzig, 1789).

Pichler, Karoline, *Denkwürdigen aus meinem Leben* (Vienna, 1844).

Pope, Alexander, *Poetical Works* (Oxford, 1978).

Porter, Roy, and Teich, Mikulas (eds), *The Enlightenment in National Context* (Cambridge, 1981).

Preibisch, Walter, *Quellenstudien zur Mozarts 'Die Entführung aus dem Serail'* (Sammelbände der Internationalen Musik-Gesellschaft, 1908–9).

Prévost, Antoine-François, *Histoire du chevalier des Grieux et de Manon Lescaut* (Paris, 1967).

Pushkin, Alexander, *Mozart and Salieri* (trans. Antony Wood, London, 1987).

Racine, Jean, *Oeuvres complètes* (Paris, 1962).

Raine, Kathleen, *Blake and Tradition* (London, 1969).

Realzeitung oder Beitrage und Anzeigen von Geleherten und Kunstachen (Vienna, 1783–6).

Reed, Terence, *The Classical Centre. Goethe and Weimar, 1775–1832* (London, 1980).

Reinalter, Helmut, *Aufgeklärte Absolutismus* (Graz, 1980); *Freimaurer und Geheimbunde in 18. Jahrhundert in Mitteleuropa* (Frankfurt, 1983); *Joseph II und die Freimaurer* (Graz and Vienna, 1987); (ed.), *Joseph von Sonnenfels* (Vienna, 1988).

Reiss, Hans, *Goethe's Novels* (London, 1969).

Rendall, Jane, *The Origins of Modern Feminism* (London, 1985).

Richardson, Samuel, *Clarissa Harlowe* (1747–8; repr. Everyman, London, 1932); *Pamela* (1740; repr. Everyman, London, 1986); *Selected Letters*, ed. John Carroll (Oxford, 1964).

Richter, Josef, *Briefe aus dem Himmel* (Berlin and Vienna, 1786).

Ricoeur, Paul, *The Symbolism of Evil* (Boston, 1967).

Rilke, Rainer Maria, *Sonnets to Orpheus* (trans. Herter Norton, New York, 1942).

Ritter, Erwin Frank, 'Johann Baptiste von Alxinger and the Austrian Enlightenment', *European University Papers*, Series I, vol. XXXIV (Berne, 1970).

Robbins Landon, Howard Chandler, *Haydn. Chronicle and Works* (5 vols) (London, 1976–1980); *The Mozart Compendium* (London, 1990); *1791. Mozart's Last Year* (London, 1988).

Roberts, John, *The Mythology of the Secret Society* (London, 1972).

Rogers, Margaret, *Feminism in Eighteenth-Century England* (Brighton, 1982).

Romance of Floire and Blanchefleur, The (anon., trans. Merton Hubert, North Carolina, 1966).

Rommel, Otto, *Die Alt-Wiener Volkskömodie* (Vienna, 1952).

Rosen, Charles, *The Classical Style* (London, 1974).

Rosenberg, Alfons, *Don Giovanni, Mozarts Oper und Don Juans Gestalt* (Munich, 1968).

Rosenberg, Hans, *Bureaucracy, Aristocracy and Autocracy. 1660–1815* (Harvard, 1958).

Rosenblum, Robert, *Transformations in Late Eighteenth-Century Art* (Princeton, 1967).

Rosenstrauch-Köningsberg, Edith, *Aloys Blumauer. Leben und Werken. Ein geistesgeschichtliche Studie* (Diss., Vienna, 1970). *Freimaurer, Illuminat, Weltburger. Friedrich Munters Reisen und Briefe in ihren europaischen Bezügen* (Berlin, 1984).

Rousseau, Jean-Jacques, *Confessions* (1781; trans. Harmondsworth, 1953); *Dictionnaire de musique* (Paris, 1768); *Discours sur les sciences et les arts* (1750; in *The Social Contract and Discourses*, Everyman, London, 1973); *Discours sur l'origine et les fondemens de l'inégalité parmi les hommes* (1755; trans. as *A Discourse on Inequality*, Harmondsworth, 1984); *Du contrat social* (1762; in *The Social Contract and Discourses*, Everyman, London, 1973); *Emile* (1762; trans. Everyman, London, 1974); *Julie, ou La nouvelle Héloïse* (1761; Paris, 1967); *Lettre à d'Alembert* (1758; trans. as *Politics and the Arts*, Illinois, 1960); *Rêveries du promeneur solitaire* (1777; trans. as *Reveries of the Solitary Walker*, Harmondsworth, 1979).

Rudolph, Kurt, *Gnosis – The Nature and History of an Ancient Religion* (Edinburgh, 1983).

Ruf, Wolfgang, *Die Rezeption von Mozarts 'Le nozze di Figaro'* (Wiesbaden, 1977).

Rushton, Julian, *Classical Music* (London, 1986).

Sade, Marquis de, *Philosophy in the Boudoir* (New York, 1966).

Said, Edward, *Orientalism* (Penguin, Harmondsworth, 1985).

Saisselin, Rémy G., *The Rule of Reason and the Ruses of the Heart* (Ohio, 1970).

Sashegyi, Oskar, *Zensur und Geistesfreiheit unter Joseph II* (Budapest, 1958).

Schama, Simon, *Citizens* (New York, 1989); *The Embarrassment of Riches* (New York, 1987).

Schiller, Friedrich, *Sämtliche Werke* (Munich, 1962); *Über die ästhetische Erziehung des Menschen in einer Reihe von Briefe* (1795; trans. as *Letters on the Aesthetic Education of Man* (Oxford, 1967); *Die Räuber* (1781; trans. as *The Robbers* and *Wallenstein*, Harmondsworth, 1979).

Schmidgall, Gary, *Literature as Opera* (Oxford, 1977).

Schneider, Ferdinand Josef, *Die Freimaurerei und ihr Einfluss auf die geistliche Kulture in Deutschland am Ende des XVIII Jahrhunderts* (Prague, 1909).

Schneider, Heinrich, *The Quest for the Mysteries. The Masonic Background for Literature in Eighteenth-Century Germany* (New York, 1947).

Schopenhauer, Arthur, *Counsels and Maxims* (London, 1890); *Essays and Aphorisms* (Harmondsworth, 1970).

Schorske, Carl E., *Fin-de-siècle Vienna* (Cambridge, 1961).

Schwartz, Joel, *The Sexual Politics of Jean Jacques Rousseau* (Chicago, 1984).

Seneca, *Minor Dialogues* (London, 1889).

Sengle, Friedrich, *Wieland* (Stuttgart, 1949).

Sennett, Richard, *The Fall of the Public Man* (Cambridge, 1974).

Shorter, Edward, *The Making of the Modern Family* (London, 1976).

Singer, Irving, *Mozart and Beethoven. The Concept of Love in their Operas* (Johns Hopkins, 1977).

Solomon, Maynard, 'Beethoven and the Enlightenment', *Telos*, 19 (Washington, 1974); 'Mozart's Zoroastrian Riddles', *American Imago*, vol. 42 (winter 1985).

Sonnenfels, Joseph von, *Gesammelte Schriften* (Vienna, 1783).

Southern, Richard, *Western Views of Islam in the Middle Ages* (Harvard, 1962).

Spaethling, Robert H., 'Folklore and Enlightenment in the Libretto of Mozarts Magic Flute', *Eighteenth Century Studies*, vol. 9 (1975).

Spinoza, Benedict de, *Improvement of Understanding* (Washington, 1901).

Starobinski, Jean, *Les emblèmes de la raison* (Paris and Milan, 1973); *Jean-Jacques Rousseau. La transparence et l'obstacle* (Paris, 1957).

Steele, Richard, and Addison, Joseph, *Selections from the Tatler and the Spectator* (Harmondsworth, 1982).

Steiner, George, *The Death of Tragedy* (London, 1961); *Language and Silence* (London, 1985).

Steiner, Rudolf, *Christianity as Mystical Fact* (London, 1972).

Stendhal (Beyle, Henri), *Vie de Mozart* (1814; France, 1990).

Stern, Martin, 'Haydns Schöpfung – Geist und Herkunft des van Swietenisch Librettos', *Haydn Studien*, Heft 3, Band I (Köln, 1966).

Stone, Lawrence, *The Family, Sex and Marriage in England 1500–1800* (London, 1977).

Strakosch, Henry E., *State Absolutism and the Rule of Law* (Sydney, 1967).

Strauss, Leo, *Natural Right and History* (Chicago, 1953).

Swift, Jonathan, *Gulliver's Travels and Selected Writings* (London, 1934).

Talmon, Jacob, *The Origins of Totalitarian Democracy* (London, 1986).

Tanner, Tony, *Adultery in the Novel* (Johns Hopkins, 1986); *Jane Austen* (London, 1986).

Taylor, Samuel, *The Theatre of the French and German Enlightenment* (Edinburgh and London, 1979).

Terrasson, Jean Abbé, *Sethos; histoire ou vie tirée des monumens anecdotes de l'ancienne Egypt* (Paris, 1731; trans. Mr Lediard, London, 1732).

Texte, Joseph, *Jean-Jacques Rousseau and the Cosmopolitan Spirit in Literature* (London, 1899).

Thurn, Rudolf Payer von, *Joseph II als Theaterdirektor* (Vienna and Leipzig, 1920).

Tillich, Paul, *Dynamics of Faith* (London, 1959); *Theology of Culture* (Oxford, 1959).

Timm, Hermann, *Die Heilige Revolution* (Frankfurt, 1978).

Tippett, Michael, *Moving into Aquarius* (London, 1984).

Todd, Janet, *Sensibility. An Introduction* (London, 1986); *Women's Friendship in Literature* (New York, 1980).

Tomalin, Claire, *The Life and Death of Mary Wollstonecraft* (Harmondsworth, 1985).

Tönnies, Ferdinand, *Community and Society* (Michigan, 1957).

Tovey, Donald Francis, *Essays in Musical Analysis*, 6 vols (Oxford, 1940).

Trenker, Sophie, *The Greek Novella in the Classical Period* (Cambridge, 1958).

Trilling, Lionel, *Sincerity and Authenticity* (Oxford, 1972).

Tuck, Richard, *Natural Right Theories. Their Origin and Development* (Cambridge, 1979).

Utter, Robert Palfrey and Needham, Gwendolin Bridges, *Pamela's Daughters* (London, 1937).

Varma, Devendra, *The Gothic Flame* (London, 1957).

Venturi, Franco, *Utopia, Reform and Enlightenment* (Cambridge, 1971).

Versini, Laurent, *Laclos et la tradition* (Paris, 1968).

Vico, Giambattista, *The New Science of Giambattista Vico* (Cornell, 1968).

Voltaire (François-Marie Arouet de), *Dictionnaire philosophique* (1764; trans. as *Philosophical Dictionary*, Harmondsworth, 1972); *Le droit de seigneur* (Paris, 1763); *Lettres philosophiques* (1733; trans. as *Letters on England*, Harmondsworth, 1980); *Nanine* (Paris, 1749); *Oedipe* (The Hague, 1719); *Romans et contes* (Paris, 1972); *Zaïre* (Paris, 1733).

Vrooman, Jack, *Voltaire's Theatre* (Geneva, 1970).

Wade, Ira. O., *The Philosophe in French Drama of the Eighteenth Century* (Princeton and Paris, 1926).

Wagner, Hans, 'Das Josephinische Wien und Mozart', *Mozart Jahrbuch 1978/9* (Kassel, 1979).

Wandruszka, Adam, *Leopold II*, vol. II, 1780–1792 (Vienna and Munich, 1965).

Wangermann, Ernst, *Aufklärung und Staatsbürgerliche Erziehung, Gottfried van Swieten*

(Vienna, 1978); *From Joseph II to the Jacobin Trials* (Oxford, 1969); *The Austrian Achievement. 1700–1800* (London, 1973).

Wasserman, Earl R., *Aspects of the Eighteenth Century* (Johns Hopkins, 1965).

Watt, Ian, *The Rise of the Novel* (London, 1957).

Weaver, William and Chiusid, Martin, *A Verdi Companion* (London, 1980).

Weidmann, Paul, *Johann Faust. Ein allegorisches Drama* (Prague, 1775).

Welleck, René, *A History of Modern Criticism* (London, 1955).

Westermarck, Edward, *The History of Human Marriage* (London, 1921).

White, T. H., *The Age of Scandal* (Oxford, 1986).

Wieland, Christoph Martin, *Complete Works* (Munich, 1964–68); *Sympathien*, trans. as *The Sympathies of the Soul* (London, 1795).

Wind, Edgar, *Pagan Mysteries of the Renaissance* (London, 1958).

Williams, Ernest, *The Ancien Régime in Europe* (London, 1984).

Williams, Gwynn A., *Goya and the Impossible Revolution* (Harmondsworth, 1984).

Wilson, W. Daniel, *Humanität und Kreuzungsideologie um 1780* (New York, 1984).

Winckelmann, Johann, *Gedenken über die Nachahmung der griechischen Werken* (Friedrichstadt, 1755).

Winter, Eduard, *Baroque Absolutismus und Aufklärung in der Donaumonarchie* (Vienna, 1971); *Der Josephinismus. Die Geschichte des Österreichischen Reformkatholizismus. 1740–1848* (Berlin, 1962).

Wittola, Marc Anton, *Schreiben eines österreichischen Pfarrers über die Toleranz* (Vienna, 1781).

Wollstonecraft, Mary, *Mary* (1788; in *Mary* and *The Wrongs of Woman*, Oxford, 1976); *Vindication of the Rights of Woman* (1792; repr. Harmondsworth, 1975).

Wood, Allen W., *Kant's Moral Religion* (Cornell, 1970).

Wraxall, N. William, *Memoirs of the Courts of Berlin, Dresden, Warsaw and Vienna, in the Years 1777, 1778 and 1779* (London, 1806).

Yates, Frances, *Giordano Bruno and the Hermetic Tradition* (London, 1982); *The Rosicrucian Enlightenment* (London, 1972).

Zaubertöne – Mozart in Wien (Exhibition Catalogue, Vienna 1990).

Zellwecker, Edwin, *Das Urbild des Sarastros. Ignaz von Born* (Vienna, 1953).

Index

362

JUN 2 4 1993